CULTURES IN COLLISION AND CONVERSATION

Essays in the Intellectual History of the Jews

JUDAISM AND JEWISH LIFE

ACADEMIC
STUDIES
PRESS

CULTURES IN COLLISION AND CONVERSATION:

Essays in the Intellectual History of the Jews

DAVID BERGER

Boston
2011

Library of Congress Cataloging-in-Publication Data

Berger, David, 1943-
  Cultures in collision and conversation : essays in the intellectual history of the Jews / David Berger.
      p. cm. -- (Judaism and Jewish life)
  Includes bibliographical references and index.
  ISBN 978-1-936235-24-7 (hardback)
  1. Judaism--Relations. 2. Intercultural communication--Religious aspects--Judaism. 3. Judaism--
History. 4. Jews--History. 5. Jews--Intellectual life. 6. Messianic era (Judaism) I. Title. II. Title: Essays
in the intellectual history of the Jews.
  BM534.B47 2011
  296.3'9--dc22

                            2010054451

Book design by Ivan Grave

On the cover:
Mishneh Torah. Spain, 14th century (a fragment).
Reproduced with permission of the National Library of Israel.

Published by Academic Studies Press in 2011
28 Montfern Avenue
Brighton, MA 02135, USA
press@academicstudiespress.com
www.academicstudiespress.com

For Pearl

CONTENTS

Contents

Yearning for Redemption

Epilogue

INTRODUCTION

The cultures that collide and converse in this book range temporally from antiquity to the present and geographically from Israel to Europe to the United States. As Jews embarked on a physical trajectory that they defined as exile, they simultaneously set forth on a rich and complex intellectual voyage that required them to confront the worldviews of their neighbors along with internal differences of doctrine and philosophical orientation that were themselves often born—at least in part—out of engagement with the external environment. Thus, the culture of a small and sometimes insular people took on an almost global character.

The first section of this volume addresses Jewish approaches to the proper parameters of interaction with the values, beliefs, and intellectual life of the larger society. The longest of the essays is an almost book-length endeavor to provide an analytical overview of the range of positions on this question in all the centers of Jewish life from the dawn of the Middle Ages to the eve of the Enlightenment. In its most intense form, the struggle over this issue erupted in a fierce controversy centered on the works of Maimonides. Despite the passions engendered by these debates, the orientations of the major protagonists were often far from one-dimensional, and two of the essays in this section attempt to capture the nuanced position of Nahmanides, one of the central figures of the Jewish Middle Ages, and to assess the impact of the philosophical milieu on one of his seminal doctrines. If the stance of an individual thinker can defy easy classification, characterizing entire subcommunities is all the more challenging. In the larger study, I set forth the evolving scholarly position that no longer sees medieval Ashkenazic Jewry as isolated from its environment, but the essay on Ashkenazic modes of thought cautions against allowing the pendulum to swing too far.

With the rise of the Jewish Enlightenment or haskalah, resistance to significant acculturation came to be restricted to the segment of Jewry labeled "Orthodox"—perhaps even to the smaller subdivision assigned the particularly problematic label "ultra-Orthodox." With some hesitation, I have incorporated a youthful essay published in a student journal assessing the complex position on haskalah and secular learning of a rabbi and biblical commentator of considerable influence who clearly belongs in the company of uncompromising traditionalists but was nonetheless sufficiently cognizant of contemporary intellectual currents that some adherents of the Enlightenment saw him as a model whom the traditionalist community should strive to emulate. While the classical Maimonidean controversy has long faded into the distant past, Maimonides himself remains acutely relevant to any discussion of Judaism's embrace of "external" culture; in an essay based on an address to a non-academic audience, I attempt to limn and assess the multiple images of his persona proffered by contemporary Jews often seeking themselves in the great medieval legist and philosopher.

Academic Jewish Studies are a quintessentially modern development with an ambivalent relationship to movements of acculturation in the medieval and modern past. If I am not entirely comfortable in describing this field in its fullness as my ideological home, it is surely my professional home. The first section of the book begins and ends with ideologically charged essays with deeply personal elements addressing the challenges and significance of an enterprise that thoughtful Jews ignore at their intellectual and even spiritual peril.

The second, briefest section deals with the interpretation of the Bible, but it decidedly reflects the theme of cultural interaction. The understanding of the wisdom of Solomon among medieval commentators varied in intriguing ways that mirror the philosophical—or non-philosophical— orientation of the exegetes in question, and in the case of Isaac Abravanel may even reveal traces of his experience in the royal courts of Portugal and Spain. As to the charged question of the morality of biblical heroes, I argue that Jewish perceptions were profoundly affected by the nature of external challenges in both medieval and modern times.

And then there is the End of Days. While the beliefs and movements analyzed in this section are almost bewildering in their thematic and chronological variety, they all reflect the impact or at least relevance of ideas and forces in the larger society: Rome as the paradigmatic enemy of Israel in late antiquity; the effect of medieval rationalism on portraits of the messianic scenario; the plausibility or implausibility of ascribing differences in messianic activism to rationalism and non-rationalism; the degree to which the modern redemptive movement called Zionism could color academic analysis of the distant past; and the factors—both sociological and religious—that have enabled a contemporary messianic movement espousing doctrines once excluded from authentic Judaism to achieve legitimation in the bosom of the Orthodox community.

The introduction to a collection of this sort would normally incorporate ruminations about the personal factors that triggered the author's interest in the field as well as the evolution of his or her work over a period of decades. In this case, however, I am excused from this task because I have already fulfilled it. A companion volume published by Academic Studies Press last year (*Persecution, Polemic, and Dialogue: Essays in Jewish-Christian Relations*) begins with an introduction that— at least in part— engages precisely these questions. More important, the opening chapter of this book provides considerable detail about the unfolding of my scholarly work and its connection to my deepest commitments. Finally, the epilogue about my father reveals the wellsprings of my eventual career in a way that a routine introduction could never convey. At this point, I will only add that the atmosphere and ideology that suffuse Yeshiva University, where I was educated and currently teach, place many of the issues addressed in this book at the center of their universe of discourse, and I cannot fail to underscore the effect of this unique institution on my approach to scholarship, to religion, and to life.

This volume, like the earlier one, is not an exhaustive collection of what I have written about its theme. First of all, several articles in the volume on Jewish-Christian relations qualify as discussions of the intellectual history of the Jews, and they are naturally not included here. Many short pieces are not of a sufficiently scholarly nature even though they touch upon relevant themes.[1] A case could have been made

---

[1] "Missing Milton Himmelfarb," *Commentary* 123:4 (April, 2007): 54-58; "Introducing Michael Wyschogrod," *Modern Theology* 22 (2006): 673-675; "On Marriageability, Jewish

for the inclusion of three review essays and several fairly substantive reviews, but I decided to leave out material that does not stand on its own.[2] One full-fledged article whose genesis is described in the opening chapter does not appear here despite its decidedly scholarly content and direct relevance to the issues addressed in the first section of the book because it is predominantly religious rather than academic in character and motivation.[3]

For the same reason, I hesitated before deciding to include the article about Lubavitch messianism. During the last fifteen years, I have devoted much time and energy with what can generously be described as mixed results to a religiously motivated effort to deny religious authority within Orthodoxy to believers in the Messiahship of the Lubavitcher Rebbe. Religious polemic of this sort does not belong in this volume. However, the article that I incorporated proffers a relatively irenic, primarily sociological analysis of the reasons for a phenomenon that at first glance appears difficult to understand. Including it in this volume provides the reader with a window into an important dimension

Identity, and the Unity of American Jewry," in *Conflict or Cooperation? Papers on Jewish Unity* (New York, 1989), pp. 69-77; "Response" in J. Gutmann et al., *What Can Jewish History Learn From Jewish Art?* (New York, 1989), pp. 29-38 (a scholarly piece, but one that cannot really stand without the article to which it responds).
The following symposia: "What Do American Jews Believe?" *Commentary* (August, 1996): 19-21; "Reflections on the State of Religious Zionism," *Jewish Action* 60:1 (Fall, 1999), pp. 12-15; "Reflections on the Six-Day War After a Quarter-Century," *Tradition* 26:4 (1992): 7-10; "Divided and Distinguished Worlds," *Tradition* 26:2 (1992): 6-10 (criticism and response, *Tradition* 27:2 [1993]: 91-94); "The State of Orthodoxy," *Tradition* 20:1 (1982): 9-12.

2   The full review essays are "The Study of the Early Ashkenazic Rabbinate" (in Hebrew) [a review of Avraham Grossman, *Hakhmei Ashkenaz ha-Rishonim*], *Tarbiz* 53 (1984): 479-487; "Modern Orthodoxy in the United States: A Review Essay" [of Samuel C. Heilman and Steven M. Cohen, *Cosmopolitans and Parochials: Modern Orthodox Jews in America*], *Modern Judaism* 11 (1991): 261-272; "Must a Jew Believe Anything? [by Menachem Kellner]: A Review Essay," *Tradition* 33:4 (1999): 81-89. (I note for the record that Kellner's response to my review in the afterword to the second edition of his book leaves me thoroughly unpersuaded.) I did publish one review essay in the earlier volume, but that was because it contains an argument for the general reliability of Nahmanides' version of the Barcelona disputation that should in my view have a significant, even decisive, impact on this long-debated scholarly crux. I am of course not holding my breath in the expectation that this will actually happen.

3   "On Freedom of Inquiry in the Rambam—and Today" (with Lawrence Kaplan), *The Torah U-Madda Journal* 2 (1990): 37-50. I would have of course needed Prof. Kaplan's permission to reprint the article in this volume, but I believe that he would have allowed me to do so.

of my recent work without, I hope, undue violation of the bounds of appropriate scholarly detachment.

I have thus far been careful not to repeat material that appeared in the introduction to the earlier volume, but there is no point in avoiding repetition when I need to express sentiments that I have already formulated to the best of my ability. Here then are the final paragraphs of that introduction with the joyful addition of a single word announcing Shira's arrival into the world and the family:

I am grateful to Simcha Fishbane for inviting me to publish this collection of essays and to Meira Mintz, whose preparation of the index served as a salutary reminder of the thoughtfulness and creativity demanded by a task that casual observers often misperceive as routine and mechanical. Menachem Butler was good enough to produce pdf files of the original articles that served as the basis for the production of the volume. I can only hope that the final product is not entirely unworthy of their efforts as well as those of the efficient, helpful leadership and staff of Academic Studies Press among whom I must single out Kira Nemirovsky for her diligent and meticulous care in overseeing the production of the final version.

I am also grateful to the original publishers of these essays for granting permission to reprint them in this volume.

Finally, when publishing a book that represents work done over the course of a lifetime, an author's expression of gratitude to wife and family embraces far more than the period needed to write a single volume. Without Pearl, whose human qualities and intellectual and practical talents beggar description, whatever I might have achieved would have been set in a life largely bereft of meaning. And then there are Miriam and Elie—and Shai, Aryeh and Sarah; Yitzhak and Ditza—and Racheli, Sara, Tehilla, Baruch Meir, Breindy, Tova, and Batsheva; Gedalyah and Miriam—and Shoshana, Racheli, Sheindl, Baruch Meir, and Shira. Each of these names evokes emotions for which I am immeasurably grateful and which I cannot even begin to express.

THE CULTURAL ENVIRONMENT: CHALLENGE AND RESPONSE

IDENTITY, IDEOLOGY AND FAITH:

Some Personal Reflections on the Social, Cultural and Spiritual Value of the Academic Study of Judaism

From: *Study and Knowledge in Jewish Thought*, ed. by Howard Kreisel (Beer Sheva, 2006), pp. 11-29. *Delivered as the English keynote address at a conference at Ben Gurion University of the Negev in Beer Sheva. (The Hebrew keynote was presented by Eliezer Schweid.) The topic and essential title ("Personal Reflections on the Social, Cultural and Spiritual Value of the Academic Study of Judaism") were chosen by the organizers of the conference.*

Academic Jewish Studies are a pivotal anchor of Jewish identity. It hardly needs to be said that most identifying Jews are not practitioners of Jewish studies, while many, if not most, are not active consumers either. But even in a democratic age, the sort of identity that we mean when we speak of Jewishness is molded in large measure by the minority who seriously engage the traditions and texts of an ancient and challenging culture.

It is commonly stated that Judaism is an unusual and perhaps unique amalgam of peoplehood and religion and, as I once wrote in a different context, one advantage of commonplaces is that they are usually true. While secular Jews might want to replace the religious component with culture or civilization, it remains clear, or it should, that reading novels with Jewish themes, playing klezmer music, and even living in the land of Israel and speaking Hebrew do not in themselves confer a sense of Jewishness that provides sufficient continuity with the historic Jewish people. Moreover, the national component of Jewish identity is rooted not only in the reality and centrality of a millennial tradition focused on religion, but also in the very fact that Jews lived without a land for so many generations and had no choice but to define themselves through extraordinarily powerful cultural-religious norms. To shed those norms entirely or to understand them as altogether secondary is to denude Jewishness of the meaning that it has accumulated over all those generations. It follows, then, that even the most basic affirmation of Jewish identity requires some interaction with the historic culture of the Jewish people in its classical forms, though these forms might be transmuted to accord with the sensibilities of contemporary secular Jews.

That the connectedness to the Jewish cultural past has been severely attenuated or lost among massive sectors of Diaspora Jewry hardly needs to be said, but it is only slightly more necessary to note that the same is largely true of the Jews of Israel. After an unbalanced religious soldier sprayed gunfire in a church in Jaffa, he was asked why he had done this. According to the *Jerusalem Post*, he "said it was a shame that he had to explain in court his motive for the shooting, which, he said, was self explanatory and written in the Torah. His motive, he said, was to destroy all idols, and anything which represented 'foreign labor' and did not relate to Judaism."[1] Thus, *avodah zarah*, literally "foreign worship," one of the foundational conceptions in Judaism, evoked no resonance whatever for an Israeli journalist, who thoroughly misunderstood the soldier's intent. Moving to somewhat more esoteric knowledge, a Hebrew reference to the classic work of R. Saadya Gaon made use of the standard abbreviation for the author's name, so that the citation read "Rasag, *Emunot ve-De'ot*." A scholar who studies medieval Jewish philosophy informs me that an Israeli translator understood the abbreviation as a number and rendered the reference into English as "263 Beliefs and Opinions."

These anecdotes can be multiplied and, in the face of the depressing reality that they illustrate, questions of more than a straightforward educational sort arise. We must, of course, ask about what pedagogical reforms are needed to convey knowledge of Jewish culture and history, a question that lies outside the parameters of my assignment and of my competence. But we must also ask how the content of that history and that culture is to be preserved, recovered, and understood. The elementary reply is that one consults with experts and, in the modern world, expertise generally rests with people who have been trained, and

---

[1]   "Soldier who shot up church sent for psychiatric evaluation. Suspect says he was destroying idols," *Jerusalem Post*, May 25, 1995, p. 12.

who often remain, in an academic environment. Thus, academic experts in Jewish studies should, it would appear, serve as the highest authorities in determining the parameters of Jewish identity, the content of Jewish culture, perhaps even the policies of the Jewish State.

This last sentence followed ineluctably, or so it seemed, from a chain of premises and reasoning so simple that affirming them appeared superfluous to the point of embarrassment. Yet the real embarrassment is the sentence itself, which cannot but elicit smiles, or worse, at the self-importance of what the late Governor George Wallace of Alabama described as pointy-headed intellectuals. Popular attitudes toward the role of academics, whose disciplines cannot easily be separated from their persons, are in fact marked by deep ambivalence. People consult experts, but they embrace those whose views accord with their own, and often, sometimes with good reason, direct withering contempt toward those whose positions they reject.

We would do well, then, to approach the question before us with due humility. Academics often disagree regarding the most fundamental realities at the heart of their scholarly discourse. The questions of objective meaning, of the interaction between the observer and the evidence, of the elusiveness of truth, have become so pervasive that many important scholars have essentially thrown in the towel, despairing of achieving certain knowledge and embracing a multivalent reality dependant upon the perspective of the observer. In extreme form, ideology determines reactions to the point where respected figures inform us that in light of the distortions in all autobiographies, Rigoberta Menchu's wholesale fabrications and Edward Said's repeated misrepresentations of his childhood are of no moment, that they are examples of the seamless web entangling subjective and external reality.

This approach aside, even unchallenged scholarly conclusions can be applied in very different ways in the arena of public policy, culture, or the life of the spirit. There are lessons to be learned from history, but they are filtered through values that are themselves rarely generated by academic investigation. Thus, the Holocaust has been seen as evidence that Jews must distrust, even despise, Gentiles, relying only on their own strength and resolve, and at the same time as evidence that Jews must treat others all the more sensitively in light of the unspeakable suffering caused by mindless bigotry. These differing conclusions are based on the examination of an unassailable historical reality recognized by both parties; it is other values that determine how that reality will be used.

Moreover, the broad range of the term "study of Judaism" complicates our discussion further, including as it does every discipline in the humanities and social sciences, every chronological period, every methodological approach. The social, cultural, and spiritual value of investigating the evolution of *halakhah* is not the same as that of studying the development of the Yiddish theater, though the latter is certainly understood by many Jews as a manifestation of Judaism; midrashic approaches to women and the nature of Israeli treatment of Arabs in 1948 both raise moral questions, but they can hardly be addressed within the same framework.

This consideration, too, does not exhaust the complexities of our inquiry, since the value of the academic study of Judaism demands assessment in contrast to alternatives that differ from one another profoundly. One is the abandonment of Jewish study, an option whose consequences we have already encountered. Another is the pursuit of such study in a traditional mode. Thus, animated debates swirl in the Modern Orthodox, or *dati-leumi*, community about studying Talmud with a critical approach that points to layers of composition and development. A distinguished rabbi who advocates a traditional approach once reported a remark regarding this matter in the name of Jacob Katz. The Talmud asserts that for every forbidden food, God has provided a kosher alternative with a similar taste ("*Kol mai de-asar lan rahamana shara lan ke-vateh*"). Katz, after emerging from a lecture by an Orthodox scholar that was suffused with the critical approach to Talmudic study, remarked, "*Kol mai de-asar lan rahamana shara lan ke-vateh. Asar lan biqqoret ha-Miqra: shara lan biqqoret ha-Talmud.*" ("Whatever God has forbidden to us, he has permitted to us something similar to it. He has forbidden to us biblical criticism; he has permitted to us talmudic criticism.")

A final alternative is attachment to Judaism and its past neither through a critical study of the tradition nor through an intense examination of its texts in the manner of the yeshivot, but through instinct and memory. This last word looms especially large in contemporary discourse as the alternative to history; it is understood roughly as the construction of a past filtered through the accumulated experience of a people, its rituals, its beliefs, and its psychic needs, with little or no attention to the findings of critical historians.

In his seminal *Zakhor*, Yosef Hayim Yerushalmi concluded with a pessimistic peroration about the near irrelevance of academic history to Jewish life even in a modern age in which tradition has lost much of its force.[2] But Yerushalmi's lament, for all its rhetorical power and large element of truth, underestimates the degree to which historical study in an academic mode, working in tense but symbiotic concert with mythopoeic memory, has influenced and even transformed the ideology of Jews in the course of the last century. Jewish nationalism rested on nostalgic memories, transmuted messianic longings, and driving social realities, but it drew upon historical scholarship to a degree that should not be dismissed. I have never forgotten a striking formulation that I heard long ago from Arnold Band, whose field is not Jewish history but Hebrew literature. The Hebrew translation of Graetz's *History*, he said, was the most influential novel in the annals of the Zionist movement. One can, of course, argue that this is the case precisely because that monumental study is suffused by ideology, but for all its manifold and evident biases, it is surely a work of critical scholarship. If Graetz's blatant ideological *Tendenz* excludes him from the ranks of genuine, even great, historians, no less is true of Gibbon.

As the Zionist movement unfolded, it defined itself through a selective, creative reading of history. Some of this was no doubt dubious, but precisely because Zionism saw itself as a secular movement, and most of its leaders were in fact skeptical of beliefs held on faith, it relied on academic historians to validate its claims. David Myers, himself a student of Yerushalmi, has written much about the interaction between Zionism and historiography,[3] and a coterie of scholars have examined the interplay between academic history and nationalist myth in the Zionist understanding of the Maccabees, Massada, Bar Kokhba, and Tel Hai.[4] The nationalist moment is most blatant in the works of Joseph Klausner, so blatant that some uncharitable observers would deny him the status of academic historian at all.[5] However that may be, the

[2]   Y. H. Yerushalmi, *Zakhor: Jewish History and Jewish Memory* (Seattle, 1982), pp. 94-103.
[3]   D. N. Myers, *Reinventing the Jewish Past: European Jewish Intellectuals and the Zionist Return to History* (New York and Oxford, 1995).
[4]   See, for example, Y. Zerubavel, *Recovered Roots: Collective Memory and the Making of Israeli National Tradition* (Chicago and London, 1994).
[5]   See my "Maccabees, Zealots, and Josephus: The Impact of Zionism on Joseph Klausner's *History of the Second Temple*," in the *Louis H. Feldman Jubilee Volume.* [Reprinted in this volume.]

role of the academic enterprise in the evolution of Zionist ideology is beyond question.

In recent years, the historians' debate about the behavior of Israelis in 1948 provides a contemporary window into the interplay between the pursuit of academic history and the ideological needs of a nation, or of its critics. As in the case of cold-war revisionism in the United States and the German controversy about the uniqueness of the Holocaust and its relationship to the Gulag, one does not have to be a professional historian to grasp the critical importance of the academy to the deepest interests and most fundamental self-image of a society. While one might argue that debates about the historical behavior of Jews are not the study of Judaism, the line in instances like this is indistinct to the point of irrelevance.

The relationship between academic study and the establishment of a Jewish state is not a one-way street. If the former affects perceptions of the latter, the latter can affect the practice of the former. The establishment of the state has allegedly provided some Israeli historians with a sense of freedom to examine what they see as problematic Jewish behavior with less concern for consequences than that of Diaspora scholars. Thus, we periodically hear that unapologetic history, such as Yisrael Yuval's famous and controversial article arguing for a connection between the killing of crusade-era Jewish children by their parents and the birth of the ritual murder accusation, could only have been written in the Jewish State.[6] Whether this is true remains uncertain, and whether the era of possible consequences has ended is regrettably even less certain, but the perception itself testifies to the complexity and significance of the interaction, in a new sense, between town and gown.

The value of the academic study of Judaism is not limited to the national dimension. Since I was asked to provide personal reflections, let me turn now to another arena reflecting my deepest personal commitments and concerns: the intersection between the academic study of Judaism and the living religion itself. I did not go to graduate school in Jewish history because of an interest in history per se. I studied the economic history of the Jews *ke-illu kefa'anni shed* — as if the metaphorical demon was compelling me. The diplomatic moves of court Jews, the battles of Judah Maccabee, the vagaries of Jewish legal standing in the innumerable principalities of the Holy Roman Empire interested

---

6   See Y. Yuval, "Ha-Naqam ve-ha-Qelalah, ha-Dam ve-ha-'Alilah," *Zion* 58 (1992): 33-90.

me little if at all. Learning about them was an unfortunate price that needed to be paid to gain the necessary credential, although I have since learned to tolerate such study and sometimes even to experience more or less fleeting moments of mild interest. What I wanted to understand was my religion — its texts, its thinkers, its responses to challenge from within and without, and the parameters of its openness and resistance to change, although fascination with the relationship between Judaism and Christianity awakened an abiding interest in the interaction between the bearers of those faiths that extended beyond the realm of religion alone and into the often bloody streets of medieval Europe.

My own trajectory and motivations are surely not unique or even unusual. It is no accident that the greatest interest in the study of Judaism within the Israeli academy comes from the religious sector. One might assume that secular Israelis would want to pursue the academic study of their people and its culture no less than the religious; outside the area of Hebrew literature and some of the social sciences, however, this does not appear to be the case.

What, then, is the impact of academic Jewish studies on Judaism today? In the non-Orthodox religious movements on the contemporary Jewish landscape, the academic study of Judaism carries more weight and authority than in any other setting. I vividly recall a remark by Gerson Cohen at a public event held in the Jewish Theological Seminary when he was its chancellor. Jewish historiography in an academic mode, he said, is Torah as we understand it. Similarly, in response to initiatives within the Reform movement that advocated a turn toward traditionalism in a number of controversial respects, Robert Seltzer and Lance Sussman vigorously affirmed that a critical analysis of historical development stands at the core of Reform Judaism.[7] Here again, we need to correct

---

[7] "Just as our predecessors reconsidered their Judaism as a result of political emancipation, Reform Judaism should continue to acknowledge the implications of historical scholarship and the comparative study of religion, which have transformed our understanding of the nature of religion as such. Doing so is not measuring Judaism by an external and alien standard; it is a matter of courageous truthfulness in facing up to the intellectual breakthroughs of the modern world that have occurred since the Enlightenment. Modern historical consciousness requires that one always consider the setting and context of every classical work and phase of Judaism from the emergence of ancient Israel to the present." (R. M. Seltzer and L. J. Sussman, "What are the Basic Principles of Reform Judaism?" in: J. S. Lewis ed., *Thinking Ahead: Toward the Next Generation of Judaism: Essays in Honor of Oskar Brecher* (Binghamton, New York, 2001),

Yosef Hayim Yerushalmi's poignant assertion that history, as distinct from memory, has little resonance in Judaism even today. At least for the intellectual leadership of Conservative and Reform Judaism, history takes center stage.

The social, even spiritual impact of this orientation became especially striking when the Conservative movement needed to decide whether or not to ordain women. Here was a decision of monumental religious significance, one that would presumably limn the contours of the movement for generations to come. Conservative Judaism's rabbinic arm has a Halakhah Committee presumably empowered to decide matters of Jewish law. Yet, despite a largely successful effort to inject an ad hoc, non-academic body at a preliminary stage, this issue was ultimately to be decided by a vote of the faculty of the Jewish Theological Seminary, a faculty chosen almost exclusively by academic criteria and containing individuals whose adherence to the Conservative movement was dubious at best. Thus, a far-reaching decision determining the trajectory and ideology of a religious movement was to be made by academics. Now, I do not deceive myself into thinking that Conservative Judaism would not now be ordaining women had the Seminary faculty voted against this step several decades ago. Larger forces would surely have reversed such a decision by now. Nonetheless, this process is illustrative of the authority that academic training can confer in a movement that places it near the center of its values.

The impact of the academic study of history on a core religious experience of Judaism exploded into public controversy a few years ago when a prominent Conservative rabbi in the United States, speaking and writing around the time of Passover, publicly questioned the historicity of the exodus. His assertion surely reflected the views of a majority of academicians in the field, but Conservative rabbis, even those who may have agreed with the substance of his position, felt acutely uncomfortable in the wake of such an open declaration. Generally speaking, the Conservative rabbinate is religiously more traditional than its flock — we recall Marshall Sklare's famous *bon mot* in an earlier time that the

p. 10). "Historical Consciousness has been a primary force in shaping Reform Judaism since the emergence of *Wissenschaft des Judentums*." (L. J. Sussman and R. M. Seltzer, "A Crisis of Confidence in the Reform Rabbinate?" *Issues and Dilemmas in Israeli and American Jewish Identities. Occasional Papers in Jewish History and Thought*, No. 18 [New York, 2002], p. 28).

movement has an Orthodox seminary, a Conservative rabbinate, and a Reform laity — but in this case many rabbis (though certainly not all) were *more* skeptical of tradition than a constituency unfamiliar with the iconoclasm of contemporary archaeologists. The struggle to navigate the tensions spawned by the interaction of academic history with religious faith, with a critically important ritual of great social significance, with a biblical story of the highest visibility that is evoked in innumerable ceremonial contexts, and with a resistant laity provided a case study of the complexity of such interaction in a movement deeply concerned with both history and memory.

In the community of Orthodox Jews that is my primary home, the role of academic Jewish Studies is uniquely problematic. In certain circles, the entire academic enterprise is prohibited or suspect, and in no realm more so than Jewish Studies, where spiritual dangers lurk in every nook and cranny. Even in circles that permit and even value higher academic learning, including Jewish learning, it is not professors but rabbis who, if I may quote the most problematic Jew of all, sit on the seat of Moses. Yet, it is precisely in such a community that the social, cultural, and spiritual dynamics of the interaction with academic Jewish studies are most intriguing and perhaps most fruitful.

In a recent talk at Yeshiva University, I observed that the most arcane fields of academic Jewish studies can pulse with life in the eyes of a committed Jew. *Inter alia*, I had in mind the distinguished Semitic linguist specializing in the history of Hebrew who told me that his field was "relevant" only at Yeshiva. Yeshiva University was, he said, a place where he was besieged with practical questions motivated by religious concerns, where the problem of whether a particular *sheva* was *naʿ* or *nah* could actually matter, could even, for a Torah reader about to begin his assignment, constitute an emergency. But, with all the genuine respect, and even awe, that I feel for the knowledge and insight of my linguist friend, his expertise is not my primary area of concern, nor do I suppose that it is yours.

Several of the most sensitive questions in contemporary Jewish life, questions about which the position of Orthodox Jewry matters well beyond the inner confines of the group itself, intersect with the academic study of Judaism and its history. These include attitudes toward secular learning, rabbinic authority, halakhic change, and more. While some of the ensuing discussion reflects an inner-Orthodox discourse, the briefest reflection will remind us how different Israeli society would look if haredi Jews affirmed the permissibility of higher secular education, or if the authority of a few rabbis in matters of politics and government policy were not seen as absolutely determinative by large segments of the religious community.

From a non-Orthodox perspective, the question of the permissibility and value of pursuing secular learning appears bizarre, yet within the Orthodox community the stance affirming the desirability of that pursuit is almost beleaguered. It is certainly possible, even without recourse to an academic approach to classical sources, for a traditional rabbi to conclude that secular education is desirable; a combination of ideological propensities and a concentration on a limited array of sources is likely, however, at least in the current environment, to inspire a position hostile to such pursuits. An academic approach, which looks at a broader spectrum of texts, will often point in a different direction.

To illustrate, a rabbi at Yeshiva University wrote an article more than a decade ago arguing that a Maimonidean ruling in the section of the *Mishneh Torah* dealing with idolatry forbids the study of any area of knowledge that contains the potential of raising doubts regarding fundamentals of the faith. Of course, the rabbi was well aware that Maimonides was also the author of the *Guide of the Perplexed*, but he dismissed this point with a generic argument about a special exception that governed this work. In a response that I co-authored with Lawrence Kaplan, we incorporated the *content* of the *Guide*, not merely the fact of its existence, into a broader analysis of the issue, and noted a letter of Maimonides in which he exhorted others to study the works of philosophers whose heretical tendencies could not be denied.[8]

I must note immediately that the somewhat smug tone of these remarks requires qualification. If certain traditionalists approach the relevant texts with propensities to find a restrictive position, Orthodox academics approach them with the desire to confirm their own prior inclinations. Since the basic ethos of the academy requires openness to unwanted conclusions, such academics cannot be certain that these inclinations will always be confirmed. A case in point struck me quite

---

8   See Y. Parnes, "Torah u-Madda and Freedom of Inquiry," *The Torah u-Madda Journal* 1 (1989): 68-71; L. Kaplan and D. Berger, "On Freedom of Inquiry in the Rambam — and Today," *The Torah u-Madda Journal* 2 (1990): 37-50.

some time ago, when I was intrigued by the convergence of two analyses of Mendelssohn, one by Yehezkel Kaufmann in *Golah ve-Nekhar* and the other by a contemporary traditionalist rabbi.

The Jewish Observer, the journal of Agudath Israel of America, had published an article about Mendelssohn that was, at first glance, surprisingly positive. This positive assessment, however, was designed to serve an ideological purpose central to the Agudah: the affirmation of the supreme importance of relying on religious authority. How is it, the author asked, that this essentially good Jew spawned a movement of rebellion against the Torah? The answer, he argued, is that for all his adherence to the Torah, Mendelssohn did not submit to the judgment of the great rabbis of his day.[9]

Despite this "kosher" objective, the article's favorable assessment of Mendelssohn aroused a storm of protest in a community where the purported founder of the Haskalah is seen as a quintessential villain. The journal consequently published a brief piece by the Novominsker Rebbe, Rabbi Yaakov Perlow, then the youngest member of the *Moezet Gedolei ha-Torah*, who argued that Mendelssohn's world view was, in fact, a radical one.

> Admittedly, [Mendelssohn] was an observant Jew, but culturally he was a thoroughbred German. He may have technically discharged his obligations to Jewish law; this, however, was but a circumscribed aspect of his being. His social and intellectual impact lay elsewhere — in the Enlightenment ... and in the cultural assimilation that he and his friends and family embraced with such fervor.[10]

I doubt that Rabbi Perlow has read *Golah ve-Nekhar*, but his argument was almost precisely that of Kaufmann, who made it at greater length and no less vigorously.

> Mendelssohn observed all the commandments in practice and...was thus loyal in a dogmatic sense to the tradition of Judaism. And yet, in Mendelssohn's views, life, and work, there exists a profound "transformation of values" ... The old ideal of Judaism — a culture which is all religion, all "Torah" — is no longer the ideal of Mendelssohn ... His cultural ideal is far

---

9 See A. Shafran, "The Enigma of Moses Mendelssohn," *The Jewish Observer* 19:9 (December, 1986): 12-18.

10 *The Jewish Observer* 19:10 (January, 1987): 13.

broader ... In this cultural conception, "the Torah" could be assigned only a modest place.[11]

Even if Rabbi Perlow did read *Golah ve-Nekhar*, the point about convergence remains the same. In sum, an academic orientation, which attempts to read the sources in all their variety and in their historical context, can yield conclusions congenial to traditionalists as well as modernists, though the very variety of its findings affords choices often precluded by practitioners of a prescriptive and more narrowly focused approach.

Elsewhere, addressing essentially the same issue, the Novominsker made an observation far more problematic for a historian. "The attempts that were made in past Jewish history, in medieval Spain and in nineteenth-century Germany, to accommodate Torah life with the culture of the times, were aimed at precisely that: accommodation, not sanctification. *Madda* and the pursuit of secular wisdom is never, in any Torah viewpoint, accorded the status of even a quasi-Torah obligation."[12] When reading this, I thought immediately of the title of an article by Herbert Davidson addressing precisely the thinkers of medieval Spain published twenty years before Rabbi Perlow's remark: "The Study of Philosophy as a Religious Obligation."[13] Several years later, when my own book-length essay on "Judaism and General Culture in Medieval and Early Modern Times" appeared,[14] I sent it to Rabbi Perlow, without any reference to his earlier remarks, and received a gracious response defending his overall position on other grounds. Here, academic study led to conclusions antithetical to assertions made out of a non-academic, traditionalist orientation, and this raises an issue that had a brief run several years ago as a *cause célèbre*: traditionalist attitudes toward the non-ideological study of history itself.

To my mind, this controversy highlighted the inextricable link between academic study and the most basic values affirmed by anyone who feels a connectedness to tradition. Rabbi Simon Schwab, the late

11   Y. Kaufmann, *Golah ve-Nekhar* (Tel Aviv, 1928), vol. 2, pp. 28-29.
12   *The Jewish Observer* 27:3 (April, 1994): 13.
13   See S. D. Goitein ed., *Religion in a Religious Age* (Cambridge, MA, 1974), pp. 53-68.
14   See G. J. Blidstein, D. Berger, S. Z. Leiman, and A. Lichtenstein, *Judaism's Encounter with Other Cultures: Rejection or Integration?*, J. J. Schacter ed. (Northvale, N.J. and Jerusalem, 1997), pp. 57-141.

rabbinic leader of the German community in New York, published an essay arguing that objective historical research may be appropriate in studying non-Jews, but it is inadmissible to publish findings ascribing flaws to rabbinic figures.[15] There may indeed have been such flaws, but writing about them will only undermine the image of such rabbis, who need to serve as models of proper behavior. Much can, and has, been written in response to this position, most notably a lengthy article by Rabbi Jacob J. Schacter,[16] but to me the most interesting point is an irony, almost a paradox, that reveals the critical significance of the historical enterprise.

All arguments in traditional Judaism regarding normative positions are, in an important sense, historical. We are not accustomed to think of them in such terms; on the contrary, non-academic rabbinic decisors are thought to argue, at least in their own self-perception, on the basis of texts perceived to be divorced from history. To an important degree, this is correct. But intellectual history is also history, and every rabbinic decisor who cites precedent is affirming something about the views of earlier authorities. Those views are captured in written works, but they are also reflected in actions and in oral observations preserved in the works or memories of others. When those who endorse Rabbi Schwab's position say that one should suppress the flaws of rabbis, and when they actively do so, they refer not only to peccadilloes that all would consider improper but to behaviors and positions that the rabbi in question may have considered correct but contemporary traditionalists consider wrong. Thus, one should not report that a particular rabbi said positive things about *maskilim*, or that he admired Rav Kook, or that he read secular books and newspapers. In other words, the observer, who affirms untrammeled respect for the rabbinic figure, substitutes his own judgment for that of the rabbi, and then appeals to that rabbi's sanitized image as a model for the posture of which he approves.

In his article, Rabbi Schacter made this point in the wake of a conversation with me, and noted my citation in this context of a passage by Yehezkel Kaufmann in an essay on a biblical theme. Bible critics, wrote Kaufmann, create and compose verses with their own hands, and proceed

---

15   Rabbi Simon Schwab, *Collected Writings* (Lakewood, 1988), p. 234.
16   J. J. Schacter, "Facing the Truths of History," *The Torah u-Madda Journal* 9 (1998-1999): 200-273.

to discover in them everything that they have inserted into them.[17] In our case, the objects of this tendentious intervention are people rather than texts, but the essential process is the same.[18] The very impulse to distort history is testimony to its centrality.

Rabbinic authority itself, especially in its contemporary formulation as *da'at Torah*, evokes controversy in which historical inquiry plays a particularly salient role. There are, of course, normative texts in play from the Talmud to Maimonides to Nahmanides to the *Sefer ha-Hinnukh* to *Mikhtav me-Eliyyahu* of Rabbi Eliyyahu Dessler. But the essential claim being made, at least in its strongest form, requires the assertion that absolute rabbinic authority in all areas of life was always recognized in normative Judaism. In principle, at least, this assertion can be tested. This is, of course, not the forum to perform that test, but I will say that my overall impression is that the evidence militates against the most extreme version of *da'at Torah* in vogue in certain haredi circles, but it also points in the direction of a greater degree of deference to rabbinic authority than some of the more liberal elements of Modern Orthodoxy are prepared to acknowledge.

A similar assessment seems appropriate with respect to the closely related issue of change in Jewish law. While the most traditionalist circles maintain that change is, and has always been, out of the question, non-Orthodox figures, and even some in the most liberal sectors of Orthodoxy, assert that rabbis have always succeeded in finding ways to permit what they feel must be permitted. Blu Greenberg's *bon*, or *mal*, *mot*, "Where there is a rabbinic will, there is a halakhic way," was provided with a telling Hebrew translation by my distinguished brother in-law David Shatz: "*Im tirzu, ein zo halakhah.*" This question has been subjected to scholarly scrutiny by Jacob Katz, Haym Soloveitchik, Yisrael Ta-Shma, and Daniel Sperber among others, and my sense, guided no doubt by my own predilections, is that social, humanitarian, and ideological factors — what I call competing religious values — have surely affected the willingness to rethink the plain meaning of texts, but in the final analysis the texts still matter. Here, again, the academic enterprise can impinge, for those who allow it, on the understanding of crucial areas of

17 Y. Kaufmann, *Mi-Kivshonah shel ha-Yezirah ha-Miqra'it* (Tel Aviv, 1966), p. 253.
18 See "Facing the Truths of History," p. 232, and the note there. (I am responsible for the fundamental point, though the acknowledgment in the note, which mentions my providing the citation from Kaufmann, can be construed in a more limited fashion.)

halakhah, but its application depends very much on the original values of the rabbinic consumer of scholarly research.

In the realm of concrete decision-making in specific instances, it is once again the case that the impact of academic scholarship does not always point in a liberal direction. In other words, the instincts and values usually held by academics are not necessarily upheld by the results of their scholarly inquiry, and if they are religiously committed, they must sometimes struggle with conclusions that they wish they had not reached. Thus, the decision that the members of the Ethiopian Beta Israel are Jewish was issued precisely by rabbis with the least connection with academic scholars. The latter, however much they may applaud the consequences of this decision, cannot honestly affirm that the origins of the Beta Israel are to be found in the tribe of Dan; here, liberally oriented scholars silently, and sometimes audibly, applaud the fact that traditionalist rabbis have completely ignored the findings of contemporary scholarship. Some academics do not hesitate to criticize and even mock such rabbis for their insularity and their affirmation of propositions inconsistent with scholarly findings, but on occasions like this the very same people are capable of deriding other rabbis for their intolerant refusal to *ignore* modern scholarship. One wonders, for example, what position will be taken by such academics with respect to the lawsuit filed by an Ethiopian cook who was fired from a Sephardi restaurant because what she cooks would not qualify as food cooked by a Jew (*bishul Yisrael*) by the standards of Sephardic *pesaq* even if a Jew were to kindle the oven.

In my own case, awareness of the relevance of the academic study of Judaism to the social, cultural and spiritual issues confronting contemporary Jewry emerged out of largely unanticipated developments. I am essentially a medievalist who wrote a dissertation consisting of a critical edition with introduction, translation, and analysis of an obscure thirteenth-century Hebrew polemic against Christianity. The number of people worldwide who had ever heard of the *Sefer Nizzahon Yashan* when I was in graduate school probably fell short of triple digits. My Master's thesis, on Nahmanides' attitude toward secular learning and his stance during the Maimonidean controversy, did deal with a central figure, but it hardly seemed like the harbinger of a career that would address urgent issues dividing contemporary Jews.

And yet, that Master's thesis reflected and honed interests that turned me into an advocate of the Modern Orthodox position favoring a broad curriculum, expressed not only in the aforementioned article defending the permissibility of reading heretical works but implicit in a book-length study of Jewish attitudes toward general culture in medieval and modern times to which I have also already alluded. While this was essentially a work of scholarship, it appeared in a book commissioned by Yeshiva University that ended with a frankly religious essay by Rabbi Aharon Lichtenstein. In current terminology, this was "engaged scholarship" whose larger objective was not disguised.

Perhaps more surprisingly, my work on medieval Jewish-Christian polemic as well as the history of what is usually called anti-Semitism propelled me into a series of contemporary controversies. The first was deeply medieval in character, although it concerned a new movement. The Jewish Community Relations Council of New York asked me to write a booklet with Michael Wyschogrod, a philosopher deeply interested in Christianity, to persuade Jews to resist the blandishments of Jews for Jesus. What emerged was one of the most polite Jewish polemics against Christianity ever composed, one which I know had its desired effect in at least a few instances, including the return to Judaism of a man who is now an important figure in Jews for Judaism, a major anti-missionary organization. In short, academic expertise was mobilized for spiritual self-defense.[19]

More broadly, I was gradually drawn into the growing and delicate arena of Jewish-Christian dialogue, where academic expertise in earlier encounters turns out to be critically important. Serious Christians do not want to hold discussions solely with dilettantes whose primary qualifications emerge out of their communal positions. Once involved, I found myself dealing not only with directly religious questions but with the role of the Church in historic anti-Semitism, the status of recent efforts to shed that past, and the very practical and highly contentious issue of the position of Christian groups regarding the State of Israel and its confrontation with terror.[20] Most recently, *qafaz alai rogzo shel* Mel

---

[19]   See *Jews and 'Jewish Christianity'*, (New York, 1978) [reprinted by Jews for Judaism, (Toronto 2002)].

[20]   "Jewish-Christian Relations: A Jewish Perspective," *Journal of Ecumenical Studies* 20 (1983): 5-32 [reprinted in: N. W. Cohen ed., *Essential Papers on Jewish-Christian Relations in the United States* (New York, 1990), pp. 328-361]; "Dominus Iesus and the Jews," *America* 185:7 (September 17, 2001):7-12 [reprinted in S. J. Pope and C.

Gibson — the controversy over Mel Gibson's film overtook me. Academic expertise in the New Testament, Christianity, Jewish-Christian polemic, anti-Semitism, and contemporary dialogue turned out to be a particularly relevant matrix of interests, and my effort to assess the debates over "The Passion" in the May 2004 issue of *Commentary* reflects but one of a multitude of requests and communal obligations thrust upon me by this unfortunate affair.

Finally, I turn to the strangest and most unexpected development of all. At a *sheva berakhot* celebration in Jerusalem, the father of the groom introduced me to an acquaintance as follows: "This is a person who specialized in Jewish-Christian polemics in the Middle Ages and suddenly discovered that most of the major Jewish arguments against Christianity now apply to Lubavitch hasidim." We have witnessed in the last decade a phenomenon that no Jew, academic or otherwise, could have imagined a generation ago. A belief in classic, posthumous messianism evoking the most obvious echoes of Christianity and Sabbatianism was born and has become entrenched in a movement seen by virtually all Jews as standing well within the confines of Orthodox Judaism. Its practitioners remain accepted not merely as Orthodox Jews but as qualified Orthodox rabbis in every respect. In this case, my academic interest in Jewish-Christian polemic and the related field of Jewish messianism interacted with my Orthodox beliefs to inspire an idiosyncratic campaign for the de-legitimization of those believers, a campaign that stands in tension with the openness and tolerance usually seen as the hallmark of the academic personality. "I have spent much of my professional life," I wrote, "with the martyrs of the crusade of 1096. It is not surprising that I react strongly when Orthodox Jewry effectively declares that on a point of fundamental importance our martyred ancestors were wrong and their Christian murderers were right."[21]

I cannot, of course, discuss the merits of the debate on this occasion,

C. Hefling eds., *Sic Et Non: Encountering Dominus Iesus* (New York, 2002)]; "*Dabru Emet*: Some Reservations about a Jewish Statement on Christians and Christianity," www.bc.edu/cjlearning; "The Holocaust, the State of Israel, and the Catholic Church: Reflections on Jewish–Catholic Relations at the Outset of the Twenty-First Century" (in Hebrew), *Hadoar* 82:2 (January, 2003): 51-55; "Revisiting 'Confrontation' After Forty Years: A Response to Rabbi Eugene Korn," www.bc.edu/cjlearning.

[21] *The Rebbe, the Messiah, and the Scandal of Orthodox Indifference* (London and Portland, Oregon 2001), p. 74. An updated Hebrew version, *Ha-Rebbe Melekh ha-Mashiah, Sha'aruriyyat ha-Adishut, ve-ha-Iyyum 'al Emunat Yisrael* (Jerusalem 2005), recently appeared.

but I will say that one of the most gratifying reactions to my book was that of Leon Wieseltier, who wrote that rarely has the academic study of Judaism so interacted with living Judaism. I must caution you that the book has also been described in print as *Mein Kampf* and its author as Osama bin Laden.[22] For our purposes, the point is not who is right and who is wrong, but the degree to which scholarly pursuits, and of the Middle Ages no less, can transform themselves into matters of burning relevance to the core of the Jewish religion.

For Jews living in Israel, this assertion is by no means surprising. A biblical scholar like Uriel Simon and an expert in medieval Jewish philosophy like Aviezer Ravitzky, not to speak of academically based philosophers like Yeshayahu Leibowitz and, *yibbadel le-hayyim tovim va-arukim*, Eliezer Schweid have long played important roles in the social, cultural, and spiritual discourse of the Jewish State. As we have seen, however superficially, this role is essential, but it is also complex and problematic. To construct the cultural and religious profile of a Jewish society in blithe disregard of the academy is an intellectual and spiritual failure of the first order; at the same time, the academic study of Judaism should, in most cases, serve as the handmaiden, rather than the mistress, of the deepest values that it helps to mold and inform.

---

[22] See Y. Dubrowski, "Chutzpah without a Limit" (in Yiddish), *Algemeiner Journal*, Jan. 18, 2002. The author proudly declares that he has not read the book; he has, however, heard about it, and this is "more than enough."

JUDAISM AND GENERAL CULTURE
IN MEDIEVAL AND EARLY MODERN TIMES

From: Gerald J. Blidstein, David Berger, Sid Z. Leiman, and Aharon Lichtenstein, *Judaism's Encounter with Other Cultures: Rejection or Integration?*, edited by Jacob J. Schacter (Jason Aronson: New York, 1997), pp. 57-141.

CONTENTS

PREFATORY NOTE

The attempt to provide an analytical overview of Jewish attitudes toward the pursuit of general culture in the millennium from the Geonic Middle East to the eve of the European Jewish Enlightenment is more than a daunting task: it flirts with the sin of hubris. The limitations of both space and the author required a narrowing and sharpening of the focus; consequently, this essay will concentrate on high culture, on disciplines which many medieval and early modern Jews regarded as central to their intellectual profile and which they often saw as crucial or problematic (and sometimes both) for the understanding of Judaism itself. Such disciplines usually included philosophy and the sciences, sometimes extended to poetry, and on at least one occasion embraced history as well. The net remains very widely cast, but it does not take all of culture as its province.

Not only does this approach limit the scope of the pursuits to be examined; it also excludes large segments of the medieval and early modern Jewish populace from consideration. Thus, I have not addressed the difficult and very important question of the cultural profile of women, who very rarely received the education needed for full participation in elite culture, nor have I dealt with the authors of popular literature or the bearers of folk beliefs.

Paradoxically, however, the narrower focus also has the effect of enlarging the scope of the analysis. The issue before us is not merely whether or not a particular individual or community affirmed the value of a broad curriculum. The profounder question is how the pursuit of philosophy and other disciplines affected the understanding of Judaism and its sacred texts. Few questions cut deeper in the intellectual history of medieval and early modern Jewry, and while our central focus must remain the affirmation or rejection of an inclusive cultural agenda, the critical implications of that choice will inevitably permeate every facet of the discussion.

THE DYNAMICS OF A DILEMMA

The medieval Jewish pursuit of philosophy and the sciences was marked by a creative tension strikingly illustrated in a revealing paradox. The justifications, even the genuine motivations, for this pursuit invoked considerations of piety that lie at the heart of Judaism, and yet Jews engaged in such study only in the presence of the external stimulus of a vibrant non-Jewish culture. Although major sectors of medieval Jewry believed that a divine imperative required the cultivation of learning in the broadest sense, an enterprise shared with humanity at large could not be perceived as quintessentially Jewish. Thus, even Jews profoundly committed to a comprehensive intellectual agenda confronted the unshakable instinct that it was the Torah that constituted Torah, while they simultaneously affirmed their conviction, often confidently, sometimes stridently, occasionally with acknowledged ambivalence, that Jewish learning can be enriched by wider pursuits and that in the final analysis these pursuits are themselves Torah. On the other side of the divide stood those who saw "external wisdom" as a diversion from Torah study at best and a road to heresy at worst, and yet the religious arguments that such wisdom is not at all external often made their mark even among advocates of the insular approach. The dynamic interplay of these forces across a broad spectrum of Jewish communities makes the conflict over the issue of general culture a central and intriguing leitmotif of Jewish history in medieval and early modern times.

THE ISLAMIC MIDDLE EAST AND THE GEONIM

The first cultural centers of the Jewish Middle Ages were those of Middle Eastern Jewry under Islam, and the Islamic experience was crucial in molding the Jewish response to the challenge of philosophical study. In the seventh century, nascent Islam erupted out of the Arabian peninsula into a world of highly developed cultures. Had this been the typical conquest of an advanced society by a relatively backward people, we might have expected the usual result of *victi victoribus leges dederunt*: as in the case of the barbarian conquerors of the Roman Empire or the ninth- and tenth-century invaders of Christian Europe, the vanquished would have ultimately imposed their cultural patterns, in however attenuated a form, upon the victors. The Islamic invasion, however, was fundamentally different. The Muslim armies fought in the name of an idea, and a supine adoption of advanced cultures would have robbed the conquest of its very meaning. At the same time, a blithe disregard of those cultures bordered on the impossible. Consequently, Islam, which was still in an inchoate state in the early stages of its contact with the Persian, Byzantine, and Jewish worlds, and whose founder had already absorbed a variety of influences, embarked upon a creative confrontation that helped to mold its distinctive religious culture.

The legacy of classical antiquity was transmitted to the Muslims by a Christian society that had grappled for centuries with the tensions between the values and doctrines of biblical revelation and those of Greek philosophy and culture. For the Fathers of the Church, there was no avoiding this difficult and stimulating challenge. As intellectuals living in the heart of Greco-Roman civilization, they were by definition immersed in its culture. The very tools with which patristic thinkers approached the understanding of their faith were forged in the crucible of the classical tradition, so that the men who molded and defined the central doctrines of Christianity were driven by that tradition even as they strove to transcend it. This was true even of those Fathers who maintained a theoretical attitude of unrelieved hostility toward the legacy of Athens, and it was surely the case for patristic figures who accepted and sometimes even encouraged the cultivation of philosophy and the literary arts provided that those pursuits knew their place.[1]

As Muslims began to struggle with this cultural challenge, a broad spectrum of opinion developed regarding the desirability of philosophical speculation. To suspicious conservatives, "reason" was a seductress; to traditionalist theologians, she was a dependable handmaiden, loyally demonstrating the validity of the faith; to the more radical philosophers, she was the mistress and queen whose critical scrutiny was the final determinant of all truth and falsehood.[2] Jews in the Islamic world confronted a similar

---

[1]   Despite—or precisely because of—its excessively enthusiastic description of patristic humanism, the rather old discussion in E. K. Rand, *Founders of the Middle Ages*, 2nd ed. (Cambridge, Mass., 1941), provides the most stimulating reminder of the importance of this issue to the Fathers of the Church.

[2]   For an account of the Muslim absorption of "the legacy of Greece, Alexandria, and the Orient," which began with the sciences and turned toward philosophy by the third quarter of the eighth century, see Majid Fakhry, *A History of Islamic Philosophy* (New York and London, 1983), pp. 1-36. Note especially p. xix, where Fakhry observes that "the most radical division caused by the introduction of Greek thought was between the progressive element, which sought earnestly to subject the data of revelation to the scrutiny of philosophical thought, and the conservative element, which disassociated itself altogether from philosophy on the ground that it was either impious or suspiciously foreign. This division continued to reappear throughout Islamic history as a kind of geological fault, sundering the whole of Islam."
In describing the manifestations of this rough division in a Jewish context, I have succumbed to the widespread convention of utilizing the admittedly imperfect term *rationalist* to describe one of these groups. As my good friend Professor Mark Steiner has pointed out, philosophers use this term in a far more precise, technical sense in an altogether different context. Intellectual historians, he argues, have not only misappropriated it but often use it in a way that casts implicit aspersions on traditionalists who are presumably resistant to reason. Let me indicate, then, that by rationalist I mean someone who values the philosophical works of non-Jews or of Jews influenced by them, who is relatively open to the prospect of modifying the straightforward understanding (and in rare cases rejecting the authority) of accepted Jewish texts and doctrines in light of such works, and who gravitates toward naturalistic rather than miraculous explanation. As the remainder of this essay will make abundantly clear, I do not regard this as a rigid, impermeable classification.

range of choices, but what was perhaps most important was that they faced those choices in partnership with the dominant society. In ancient times, the philosophical culture was part of a pagan world that stood in stark opposition to Jewish beliefs. Under such circumstances, committed Jews faced the alternatives of unqualified rejection of that civilization or a lonely struggle to come to grips with the issues that it raised. Although the philosophical culture of antiquity retained its dangers for medieval Jews under Islam, the culture with which they were in immediate contact confronted the legacy of the past in a fashion that joined Muslims and Jews in a common philosophic quest.

Needless to say, there were fundamental, substantive reasons for addressing these issues, but it is likely that the very commonality of the enterprise served as an additional attraction for Jews. Members of a subjected minority might well have embraced the opportunity to join the dominant society in an intellectual quest that was held in the highest esteem. This consideration operated with respect to many religiously neutral facets of culture from poetry to linguistics to the sciences. It was especially true of philosophy, which succeeded in attaining supreme religious significance while retaining its religious neutrality. Among the multiplicity of arguments that one hears from Jews opposed to philosophical study, the assertion that it involves the imitation of a specifically Muslim practice played no role precisely because the problems addressed were undeniably as central to Judaism as they were to Islam.

The existence of a religiously neutral or semi-neutral cultural sphere is critically important for Jewish participation in the larger culture. The virtual absence of such a sphere in Northern Europe before the high Middle Ages—and to a certain degree even then—ruled out extensive Ashkenazic involvement in the elite culture of Christendom and may well have been the critical factor in charting the divergent courses of Ashkenazim and Sephardim. The issue, of course, is not religious neutrality alone. During the formative period of Middle Eastern and Iberian Jewry, the surrounding civilization was dazzling, vibrant, endlessly stimulating. During the formative years of Ashkenazic Jewry, the Christian society of the North was primitive, culturally unproductive, and stimulated little more than the instinct for self-preservation.[3]

---

[3] Historians of the Carolingian Renaissance and other scholars who have rendered the

These central considerations were reinforced by a linguistic factor. In the Muslim orbit, the language of culture and the language of the street were sufficiently similar that access to one provided access to the other. By the end of the first millennium, Arabic had become the language of most Jews living under Islam, and mastery of the alphabet was sufficient to open the doors to an advanced literary culture. In Northern Europe this was not the case. Knowledge of German or even of early French did not provide access to Latin texts, and the study of such texts had to be preceded by a conscious decision to learn a new language.

The Jewish intellectual and mercantile class under Islam did not merely know the rudiments of the language. The letters of Jewish merchants that have survived in the Cairo Genizah are written in a good Arabic style, which must reflect familiarity with some Arabic literature.[4] The stylistic evidence is reinforced by the use of expressions from the Quran and *hadith*. In tenth-century Mosul, a group of Jewish merchants convened regularly to study the Bible from a philosophical perspective.[5] This level of knowledge underscores an additional, crucial point about the relationship between the cultural level of a dominant civilization and the degree to which Jews will be integrated into their environment. In a relatively backward society, any outsider can achieve economic success without attaining more than a superficial familiarity with alien modes of thought. In an advanced culture, maintaining ignorance while achieving success requires enormous dedication to both objectives; it may be possible, as some contemporary examples indicate, but it is extraordinarily difficult. The upper echelons of medieval Muslim society

term *Dark Ages* obsolete will no doubt take umbrage at this description, but even on a generous reading of the evidence, cultural activity took place within such narrow circles that I do not think apologies are necessary. For an overview and reassessment of the current status of research on early medieval Europe, see the discussion and extensive bibliography in Richard E. Sullivan, "The Carolingian Age: Reflections on its Place in the History of the Middle Ages," *Speculum* 64 (1989): 267-306.

For some observations on the importance of a neutral cultural sphere under Islam, see Joseph M. Davis, "R. Yom Tov Lipman Heller, Joseph b. Isaac Ha-Levi, and Rationalism in Ashkenazic Jewish Culture 1550-1650" (Harvard University dissertation, 1990), pp. 26-27. (Davis's dissertation, which I shall have occasion to cite again in the section on Ashkenazic Jewry, was submitted after this essay was substantially completed.)

4 See S. D. Goitein, *A Mediterranean Society* 2 (Berkeley, 1971), pp. 180-181. This is not to say that every Jewish merchant could read Arabic (cf. p. 179).

5 See Haggai ben Shammai, "Hug le-'Iyyun Pilosofi ba-Miqra be-Mosul ba-Me'ah ha-'Asirit," *Pe'amim* 41 (Autumn, 1989): 21-31.

valued cultural sophistication, and a Jew who wanted access to the movers and shakers of that society even for purely pragmatic reasons could not allow himself to remain unfamiliar with its language, its literature, and its thought. This is true not only for merchants; communal leaders who wanted to lobby for essential Jewish interests also required a sophisticated command of the surrounding culture, and the phenomenon of the acculturated Jewish courtier, which reached maturity in Spain, was born in this environment.

Familiarity with Arabic language and literature exercised a significant influence on the development of a new phase in the history of Hebrew poetry and prose. Here too the primary locus of this achievement was Muslim Spain, where Hebrew literature attained dazzling heights, but the beginnings were clearly rooted in the Geonic Middle East. Not surprisingly, the most significant figure in this development was R. Saadya Gaon, whose works often follow Arabic models and who explicitly expressed admiration for the accomplishments of the dominant culture, and there is reason to believe that the Gaon refined and embellished a new literary trend that had already begun in the Jewish communities in Egypt and Israel.[6]

Another pursuit which combined intellectual sophistication, prestige, integration into the larger society, and economic success was medicine. Medical education could be obtained privately and was part of any advanced curriculum, and so no significant impediment limited minority access to the field. Moreover, the service provided by a physician is so crucial that any tendency to discriminate will be brushed aside by the all-powerful will to live; it is no accident that those who wished to discourage the use of Jewish doctors in Christian Europe could do so only by instilling the fear of death by poison. It is consequently perfectly natural that both religious minorities in the Muslim world entered the medical profession to a degree that was entirely disproportionate to their numbers; by the thirteenth century, this phenomenon was sufficiently striking to impel a Muslim visitor to observe that most of the prominent Jews and Christians in Egypt were either government officials or physicians.[7]

---

6   See the eloquent remarks of Ezra Fleisher in his "Hirhurim bi-Devar Ofyah shel Shirat Yisrael bi-Sefarad," *Pe'amim* 2 (Summer, 1979): 15-20, and especially in his "Tarbut Yehudei Sefarad ve-Shiratam le-Or Mimze'ei ha-Genizah," *Pe'amim* 41 (Autumn, 1989): 5-20.

7   Goitein, *A Mediterranean Society* 2, pp. 242-243, 247-250. See also Goitein's "The Medical Profession in the Light of the Cairo Genizah Documents," *Hebrew Union College*

The flexible character of the educational system was not confined to medicine. The absence of governmental or communal control as the Islamic world was formulating its approach to the philosophical enterprise meant that no societal decision had to be made about proper curriculum, and diverse approaches could therefore coexist without formalized pressure for homogenization. In twelfth- and thirteenth-century Northern Europe, when medieval Christians first confronted the issue of philosophical study seriously, the situation was quite different. Ecclesiastical control of cathedral schools and the nascent universities created a more homogeneous position, which both legitimated and limited the philosophic quest. Thus, despite the persistence of diversity even in the Christian West, one can speak of a quasi-official, religiously domesticated philosophical approach, while Muslims and Jews faced an array of possibilities in which virtually no option was foreclosed.

It is hardly surprising, then, that the atmosphere of tenth-century Baghdad, which was the intellectual as well as political capital of the newly matured Muslim civilization, resonated with a bewildering variety of fiercely argued philosophical and religious doctrines. Two scholars attempting to convey a sense of the environment in which R. Saadya Gaon worked have reproduced a striking description which is well worth citing once again. A Muslim theologian who visited Baghdad explained why he stopped attending mass meetings for theological debate:

> At the first meeting there were present not only people of various [Islamic] sects, but also unbelievers, Magians, materialists, atheists, Jews and Christians, in short, unbelievers of all kinds. Each group had its own leader, whose task it was to defend its views, and every time one of the leaders entered the room, his followers rose to their feet and remained standing until he took his seat. In the meanwhile, the hall had become overcrowded with people. One of the unbelievers rose and said to the assembly: we are meeting here for a discussion. Its conditions are known to all. You, Muslims, are not allowed to argue from your books and prophetic traditions since we deny both. Everybody, therefore, has to limit himself to rational arguments. The whole assembly applauded these words. So you can imagine... that after these words I decided to withdraw. They proposed to me that I should attend another meeting in a different hall, but I found the same calamity there.[8]

Annual 34 (1963): 177-194.

8   Cited from *Journal Asiatique*, ser. 5, vol. 2 (1853): 93 by M. Ventura, *Rab Saadya Gaon* (Paris, 1934), pp. 63-64, and by Alexander Altmann in *Three Jewish Philosophers* (New

Both the vigor of the intellectual debate and the opposition to its excesses left their mark on contemporary Jewish texts. In R. Saadya's *Book of Beliefs and Opinions*, we find the first major philosopher of the Jewish Middle Ages arguing for the legitimacy of philosophical speculation against explicit criticism of the entire enterprise. Any attempt to assess the size and standing of the various parties to this dispute during the Geonic period faces serious obstacles. Saadya himself cited the argument that philosophical study bore the seeds of heresy and maintained that this position is proffered only by the uneducated.[9] Salo Baron has dismissed Saadya's assertion as "whistling in the dark."[10] Even if the Gaon's assessment does not result from wishful thinking alone, we cannot easily use it to determine the extent and character of the opposition since it may reflect Saadya's conviction that anyone making this argument is uneducated virtually by definition. At the same time, the passage is not historically useless. For all of Saadya's confidence, polemical aggressiveness, and exalted communal standing, I doubt that he could have written this sentence if recent Geonim or highly influential figures in the yeshivot had maintained a vehement, public stand against philosophical study. On the level of public policy in Saadya's Baghdad, philosophical speculation was either encouraged or treated with salutary neglect.

The introduction to *The Book of Beliefs and Opinions* vigorously sets forth some of the basic arguments for this pursuit:

> [The reader] who strives for certainty will gain in certitude, and doubt will be lifted from the doubter, and he that believes by sheer authority will come to believe out of insight and understanding. By the same token the gratuitous opponent will come to a halt, and the conceited adversary will feel ashamed.

The conviction that philosophical certainty is attainable and that reasoned faith is superior to faith based on tradition alone underlies

---

York and Philadelphia, 1960), part II, pp. 13-14. At the same time, the authorities did have a sort of inquisitorial mechanism for the enforcement of correct belief.

9 Saadia Gaon, *The Book of Beliefs and Opinions*, translated by Samuel Rosenblatt (New Haven, 1948), Introductory Treatise, p. 26.

10 *A Social and Religious History of the Jews* 8 (New York, 1958), p. 69. Baron (pp. 67-68) also cites a ninth-century Muslim who maintained that Jews were uninvolved in scientific pursuits because they considered "philosophical speculation to be unbelief."

this argument and reflects the views of the Muslim *mutakallimun* whose approach Saadya shared. Indeed, he anticipated the assertions of later Jewish thinkers by maintaining that the Bible itself requires such investigation. Isaiah, after all, proclaimed, "Do you not know? Do you not hear?... Have you not understood the foundations of the earth?" (40:21). And the Book of Job records the admonition, "Let us know among ourselves what is good" (34:4). Not only does Saadya take the term *know* as a reference to the understanding that results from philosophical speculation; he is so convinced of this that he regards these verses as decisive evidence that the talmudic rabbis could not possibly have intended to ban such speculation when they forbade investigation into "what is above and what is below, what is before and what is behind" (*M. Hagigah* 2:1).[11]

Saadya's confidence that reason can yield certainty is strikingly illustrated by his application to philosophy of a talmudic statement whose primary context was clearly that of Jewish law. The Rabbis inform us that legal questions used to be settled through an appeals process leading up to the high court in Jerusalem, but "ever since the number of disciples of Hillel and Shammai increased who did not attend scholars sufficiently, many disagreements have arisen in Israel"(*Tosefta Sanhedrin* 7:1). "This utterance of theirs," says Saadya, speaking of the benefits of philosophical speculation, "indicates to us that when pupils do complete their course of study, no controversy or discord arises among them."[12] It is difficult to argue against the sort of inquiry that is sure to lead to piety and truth.

Nonetheless, not everyone shared Saadya's certainty. The greatest of the Geonim other than Saadya was undoubtedly R. Hai, who flourished in the late tenth and early eleventh centuries. In some respects, his views on these issues paralleled those of Saadya. He permitted Jewish teachers to instruct children in mathematics and the art of writing Arabic, and in the same ruling he agreed to allow non-Jewish children to study in the synagogue (presumably with Jewish students) if there is no way to prevent this without jeopardizing peaceful neighborly relations. As Shlomo Dov Goitein has pointed out, it would appear to follow that considerable time might be devoted to subjects other than Torah.[13]

---

11   *Beliefs and Opinions*, pp. 9, 27.
12   *Beliefs and Opinions*, p. 13.
13   Goitein, *A Mediterranean Society* 2, p. 177. At the same time Goitein notes that genizah evidence does not indicate much formal study of arithmetic on the elementary level

A famous report informs us that R. Hai sent a student to consult the Christian *catholikos* for assistance in understanding a biblical verse, and while this does not bear directly on the question of general culture, it reflects habits of mind that might well lead to a willingness to explore beyond the boundaries of classical Jewish texts.[14]

At the same time, R. Hai had reservations about the results of philosophical study, and our assessment of his reservations depends to a critical extent on the authenticity of an important letter that he reportedly addressed to R. Samuel ibn Nagrela of Spain. The letter itself has come down to us in several versions. In the central passage that appears in all the sources, R. Hai admonishes R. Samuel to

> know that what improves the body and guides human behavior properly is the pursuit of the Mishnah and Talmud; this is what is good for Israel.... Anyone who removes his attention from these works and instead pursues those other studies will totally remove the yoke of Torah from himself. As a consequence of such behavior, a person can so confuse his mind that he will have no compunctions about abandoning Torah and prayer. If you should see that the people who engage in such study tell you that it is a paved highway through which one can attain the knowledge of God, pay no attention to them. Know that they are in fact lying to you, for you will not find fear of sin, humility, purity, and holiness except in those who study Torah, Mishnah, and Talmud.

A longer version of the letter preserved in the thirteenth-century *Sefer Me'irat 'Einayim* of R. Isaac of Acre places the issue in a concrete historical context. R. Hai forbids the study of *higgayon*, which undoubtedly means philosophy in this letter, and urges the constant study of Talmud in accordance with the practice of

> the beloved residents of Qairuwan and the lands of the Maghreb, may they be blessed in the eyes of Heaven. Would that you knew of the confusion, disputes, and undisciplined attitudes that entered the hearts of many

(pp. 177-178). For the text of R. Hai's responsum, see Simcha Asaf, *Meqorot le-Toledot ha-Hinnukh be-Yisra'el* 2 (Tel Aviv, 1930), pp. 4-5.

14   See Joseph ben Judah ibn Aqnin, *Hitgallut ha-Sodot ve-Hofa'at ha-Meorot: Perush Shir ha-Shirim*, ed. by A. S. Halkin (Jerusalem, 1964), p. 495.

      Whatever the provenance of the poem *Musar Haskel* attributed to R. Hai, it is worth noting the advice to teach one's son a craft and to study "wisdom," mathematics, and medicine. See Asaf, *Meqorot* 2, p. 8.

people who engaged in those studies in Baghdad in the days of 'Adud al-Dawla [977-983] and of the doubts and disagreements that were generated among them with respect to the foundations of the Torah to the point that they left the boundaries of Judaism.

He goes on to say that "there arose individuals in Baghdad [apparently somewhat later] who would have been better off as Gentiles"; indeed, they went so far that they aroused the anger of non-Jews who were presumably concerned about the spread of philosophical heresy that might contaminate Muslims as well. Because of the damage that this caused, R. Hai intervened to stop these miscreants in particular and Jewish intellectuals in general from engaging in such pursuits. The letter goes on to assert that even the Gaon R. Samuel b. Hofni, who had read such material, saw the damage that resulted and refrained from doing so any longer.

Since the days of Graetz, the authenticity of this document has been the subject of scholarly debate. In the most recent discussion, two new, conflicting considerations have been raised. On the one hand, the name of the ruler in Baghdad is reported with a level of accuracy that might not have been available to a late forger; on the other, the section preserved in *Me'irat 'Einayim* often uses the first person singular, while it was the practice of the Geonim, without exception, to write in the first person plural. If this letter in its entirety was written by R. Hai, it provides fascinating information about extreme rationalism among Jews in late tenth-century Baghdad and about a very strong Jewish counterreaction. My own inclination, however, is to treat the document with considerable skepticism. The unique appearance of the first person singular is surely a weighty consideration, and an expert in the history of medieval Islam assures me that 'Adud al-Dawla's name was not so obscure as to be unavailable to a thirteenth-century Iberian forger (not to speak of an earlier one) even in its precise form. The unconditional denunciation in the letter is considerably stronger than what we would expect from R. Hai's other writings: there were a number of other appropriate opportunities in the Gaon's voluminous correspondence for him to have expressed such views, and yet this passage remains unique; the assertion that R. Samuel ben Hofni, for whom speculative pursuits were clearly of central importance, would have abandoned them because of this incident is both implausible in the extreme and reminiscent of other rereadings of history of the sort that produced a document attesting to Maimonides' late embrace of kabbalah; and the specific reference to the abandonment of prayer, an issue which is unattested as far as I know in this early period, echoes similar charges in the literature of the Maimonidean controversy.

Whatever the authenticity of the original document, there is an illuminating aspect to the later textual history of this letter. One of the versions contains a brief addition clearly introduced by a reader who wanted to soften the antiphilosophical message of the Gaon. Where R. Hai criticized those who "pursue those other studies," our philosophically oriented copyist wrote "those other studies *alone*," and where R. Hai spoke about the purity and holiness of those who study Mishnah and Talmud, our copyist wrote that these qualities will be found only in those who study "Mishnah, Talmud, *and wisdom together, not wisdom alone*." These revisions, which were introduced by the interpolater into a letter of Nahmanides that quotes R. Hai, have been embraced to our own day by scholars who welcome an attenuation of the original message. In the event that the letter itself is inauthentic, there is a certain poetic justice in the undermining of its central point by yet another creative artist.[15]

---

[15]   R. Hai's letter is most conveniently available in *Ozar ha-Geonim to Hagigah*, pp. 65-66. The most recent discussion of the problem of authenticity, which cites earlier studies, is in Amos Goldreich's dissertation, *Sefer Me'irat 'Einayim le-Rav Yizhaq de-min Akko* (Jerusalem, 1981; Pirsumei ha-Makhon le-Limmudim Mitqaddemim, 1984), pp. 405-407. Goldreich notes Shraga Abramson's observation about the Geonim and the first person plural, which was made in a different context; see Abramson, *Rav Nissim Gaon* (Jerusalem, 1965), p. 307. When I raised the issue in a conversation with Prof. Abramson, he confirmed that there are no exceptions to this usage; since R. Hai became Gaon when Samuel ibn Nagrela was a small child, the possibility that the letter was written before the author assumed his position must, of course, be ruled out. (In a personal communication, Menahem Ben Sasson has suggested the possibility that a shift from plural to singular might have taken place in the course of translation from Arabic into Hebrew.) See too Zvi Groner in *'Alei Sefer* 13 (1986): 75, no. 1099. I am grateful to Ulrich Haarmann, my colleague at the Annenberg Research Institute when this essay was written, for his assessment of the degree of familiarity with 'Adud al-Dawla in the thirteenth century.

For an example of the fortunes of the pro-philosophy version of the letter, see the various printings of C. D. Chavel, *Kitvei Rabbenu Mosheh ben Nahman* (henceforth *Kitvei Ramban*), beginning with Jerusalem, 1963, 1, pp. 349-350. For the initial challenge to the letter's authenticity, see H. Graetz, "Ein pseudoepigraphisches Sendschreiben, angeblich von Hai Gaon an Samuel Nagid," *Monatsschrift für Geschichte und Wissenschaft des Judenthums* 11 (1862): 37-40. There is no concrete basis for Graetz's suspicions that the citation from R. Hai was inserted into Nahmanides' letter by a later copyist; consequently, if the letter is a forgery, we probably need to assume that it was produced

Whatever we make of the highly dubious report that R. Samuel ben Hofni stopped perusing philosophical books as a result of a particular incident, his study of such works is clearcut and their influence upon him was profound. He rejected a literal understanding of the raising of Samuel's spirit by the witch of Endor, and according to R. Hai he denied various miracles that the Talmud attributes to the ancient rabbis, arguing that such miracles are associated only with prophets and that the Talmudic reports are not "halakhah." The point here, if I understand the expression correctly, is not that the content of these passages classifies them as aggadic but rather that they are not normative in much the same way that a rejected legal position is not normative. Here, however, normative seems synonymous with "true," and the utilization of this category to reject the truth of a rabbinic narrative is striking, especially in the absence of any apparent effort at allegorization. Indeed, the most recent study of R. Samuel's thought argues that his position denying these talmudic miracles stemmed from a specifically Mu'tazilite position on the relationship between miracles and prophecy.[16]

Although various Geonim were favorably inclined toward the study of philosophy, it is clear that the curriculum of the advanced yeshivot was devoted to the study of Torah alone. I am unpersuaded by Goitein's suggestion that the reason for this was the feeling that only those whose

no later than the early months of the controversy of the 1230s and that it already deceived Nahmanides.

[16] See David Sklare, *The Religious and Legal Thought of Samuel ben Hofni Gaon: Texts and Studies in Cultural History* (Harvard University dissertation, 1992), p. 74. Sklare's dissertation, which appeared well after the completion of this study, presents a broad characterization of Jewish high culture in Geonic times from "extreme rationalism" to traditionalism; see chapter four, pp. 145-210. For attitudes toward *aggadah*, see pp. 64-75.

On the witch of Endor, see Radaq's discussion on I Samuel 28:25. For R. Hai's responsum, see *Ozar ha-Geonim* to *Hagigah*, p. 15. On R. Hai's own reservations about the authority of *aggadah*, see R. Abraham b. Isaac Av-Beit Din, *Sefer ha-Eshkol*, ed. by A. Auerbach (Halberstadt, 1868), 2, p. 47. There is some confusion about R. Samuel's views on the talking serpent in Genesis and the talking donkey in Numbers; see the discussion in Aaron Greenbaum, *Perush ha-Torah le-Rav Shmuel ben Hofni Gaon* (Jerusalem, 1979), pp. 40-41, n. 17. Whatever R. Samuel's position may have been, there were Geonic views that endorsed a nonliteral understanding of these accounts. For the expectation that R. Samuel would facilitate a student's pursuit of the sciences in addition to Mishnah and Talmud, see I. Goldziher, "Mélanges Judéo-Arabes, XXIII," *Revue des Études Juives* 50 (1905): 185, 187.

professional training would expose them to Greek science needed the protection afforded by the proper study of philosophy and theology. The private nature of philosophical instruction in the society at large made it perfectly natural for Jews to follow the same course; more important, the curriculum of these venerable institutions went back to pre-Islamic days, and any effort to introduce a curricular revolution into their hallowed halls would surely have elicited vigorous opposition. In any case, the absence of a philosophical curriculum in the academies has led to the recent suggestion that openness to Arabic culture by the later Geonim resulted precisely from the weakening of the yeshivot which freed someone like R. Samuel ben Hofni from the restraints of the traditional framework.[17]

We are even told in an early Geonic responsum that Bible was not taught in the academies. R. Natronai Gaon informs us that because of economic pressures which required students to work, the talmudic directive (*Kiddushin* 30a) that one-third of one's time be devoted to biblical study could no longer be observed, and the students relied upon another talmudic statement (*Sanhedrin* 24a) implying that Bible, Mishnah, and Midrash are all subsumed under Talmud. One wonders whether this was only a result of insufficient time. The all-consuming nature of talmudic study led to a very similar conclusion among Ashkenazic Jews; moreover, the fact that Judaism shared the Bible with Christianity and, to a degree, with Islam may have helped to generate an instinct that this was not a quintessentially Jewish pursuit. Only the Talmud was the special "mystery" of the Jewish people.[18]

The assertion that the Jews of Qairuwan studied Torah exclusively may well reflect their general orientation accurately. At the same time, we have evidence of some broader pursuits. Dunash ben Tamim of tenth-century Qairuwan wrote several astronomical works, one of which he composed to honor the local Muslim ruler, as well as a mathematical treatise and a commentary to *The Book of Creation* (*Sefer Yezirah*). Moreover, the famous question from Qairuwan about the composition

---

[17] So Sklare, *The Religious and Legal Thought of Samuel ben Hofni*, pp. 96-99, 139-140. As Sklare notes, R. Saadya himself was educated "outside the orbit of the Gaonic yeshivot." For Goitein's remark, see *A Mediterranean Society* 2, p. 210.

[18] For R. Natronai's observation, see Asaf, *Meqorot*, p. 4. Cf. Rabbenu Tam's remark in *Tosafot Qiddushin* 30a, *s.v. la zerikha leyomei*. On the oral law as the mystery of Israel, see *Pesiqta Rabbati* 5. On later reservations about biblical study, see below, n. 109.

of the Talmud that elicited a classic responsum by R. Sherira Gaon may have been inspired as much by an interest in history, which is also attested in other ways, as by Karaite pressures.[19] Needless to say, the sort of interest in history that expresses itself as a question about the Talmud is itself a manifestation of the study of Torah, but the definition of the boundaries between the sacred and the profane is precisely what is at issue in much of the medieval discussion of pursuits that transcend a narrow definition of Torah.

MUSLIM SPAIN AND MAIMONIDES

The cultural symbiosis between Judaism and Islamic civilization grew to maturity in the Middle East during the time of the Geonim, but its classic expression and most dazzling achievements emerged from Muslim Spain in the tenth, eleventh, and twelfth centuries. We have already seen that linguistic acculturation is a precondition for such a symbiosis, and familiarity with Arabic literature was one of the most important stimuli to the development of a distinctive Jewish literary voice. Moses ibn Ezra's treatise on Jewish poetry contains a striking passage which reveals a frank recognition of this process by medieval Jews themselves:

> When the Arabs conquered the Andalusian peninsula... our exiles living in that peninsula learned the various branches of wisdom in the course of time. After toil and effort they learned the Arabic language, became familiar with Arabic books, and plumbed the depths of their contents; thus, the Jews became thoroughly conversant with the branches of their wisdom and enjoyed the sweetness of their poetry. After that, God revealed the secrets of the Hebrew language and its grammar.[20]

The relationship between the study of Hebrew grammar, with all that it implies for the development of biblical exegesis, and the knowledge of a different Semitic language is self-evident. Medieval Jews had always known Hebrew and Aramaic, but the addition of Arabic, with its rich vocabulary and literature, enabled grammarians to understand the meaning of a host

---

[19]   See Menahem Ben Sasson, *Hevrah ve-Hanhagah bi-Qehillot Yisrael be-Afriqah ha-Zefonit bi-Yemei ha-Beinayim—Qairuwan, 800-1057* (Hebrew University dissertation, 1983), pp. 179, 185-186. R. Sherira's epistle is now available in N. D. Rabinowitch's English translation, *The Iggeres of Rav Sherira Gaon* (Jerusalem, 1988).

[20]   *Shirat Yisrael*, ed. by B. Z. Halper (Leipzig, 1924), p. 63, cited in Asaf, *Meqorot* 2, p. 23.

of difficult Hebrew words and to uncover the mysteries of the Semitic root. Unlocking the structure of the language provided a revolutionary tool for the indisputably religious enterprise of understanding the Bible. There can be no more eloquent testimony to the significance of this development than the extensive appeal to grammatical analysis by R. Abraham ibn Ezra, easily the greatest biblical exegete produced by the Jewry of Muslim Spain. It is consequently both remarkable and revealing that the greatest of medieval Jewish grammarians, Jonah ibn Janah, alludes to Talmudists who regard the study of language as "superfluous," "useless," "practically... heretical."[21]

The unavoidable connection between grammatical investigations and the study of non-Jewish works may well account for this attitude, which continued in certain circles through the Middle Ages and persists to our own day. It is difficult to think of any other consideration that could account for so extreme an assertion as the imputation of virtual heresy to grammarians. Considering the undeniable value of this pursuit for biblical study, opposition could be expressed only by Jews who attached little importance to the systematic study of the Bible itself and regarded the Talmud as the only proper subject of intense, regular, prolonged scrutiny. The denigration of biblical study, which we have already touched upon and which also persists in the same circles to this day, may well result not only from the fact that the Bible is shared with non-Jews but from the inevitable contact that it fosters with gentile scholarship and culture. A further consideration, which is not directly related to our theme, may have been the concern that biblical study undisciplined by the everpresent restraints of authoritative talmudic commentary could itself lead to heretical conclusions in matters of both theology and law.

Despite this evidence of opposition, the dominant culture of Andalusian Jewry embodied an avid pursuit not only of linguistic sophistication but of literary expression in the fullest sense. Ahad Ha-Am long ago coined the felicitous term *competitive imitation* (*hiqquy shel hitharut*) to describe the motivation and character of this culture,[22] and later scholars have elaborated the point with an accumulation of evidence of which Ahad

---

[21] *Sefer ha-Riqmah*, ed. by M. Wilensky (Berlin, 1929), p. v, cited in Asaf, *Meqorot*, 2, pp. 19-20.

[22] "Hiqquy ve-Hitbolelut," in *'Al Parashat Derakhim*, 2nd ed., 1 (Berlin, 1902), p. 175.

Ha-Am was only dimly aware. In the words of a recent study, "Golden Age Hebrew poetry... can be viewed as a literary discourse designed to mediate cultural ambiguity because it signifies both the acculturation to Arabic cultural norms *and* [emphasis in the original] the resistant national consciousness of the Jewish literati who invented it."[23]

Far more than ordinary intellectual competitiveness was at stake here. The beauty of Arabic was a crucial Muslim argument for the superiority of Islam. Since the Quran was the final, perfect revelation, it was also the supreme exemplar of aesthetic excellence, and its language must be the most exalted vehicle for the realization of literary perfection. When Jews compared the richness and flexibility of Arabic vocabulary to the poverty of medieval Hebrew, the Muslims' argument for the manifest superiority of their revelation undoubtedly hit home with special force. The quality of Arabic was evident not merely from a mechanical word count or even an analysis of the Quran; it shone from every piece of contemporary poetry and prose.

Consequently, Jews were faced with a dual challenge. First, they had to explain the undeniable deficiencies of the vocabulary of medieval Hebrew. For all its terrible consequences, the exile has its uses, and Andalusian Jews maintained that the untold riches of the Hebrew language had gradually been lost due to the travails of the dispersion. The numerous words that appear only rarely in the Bible and whose meaning we must struggle to decipher are but the tip of the iceberg; they testify to a language far more impressive than the one bequeathed to us by our immediate ancestors.

Moreover, and far more important, Jews were challenged to demonstrate that even the Hebrew at their disposal was at least as beautiful as Arabic and that Hebrew literature could achieve every bit as much as the literature of medieval Muslims. This created a religious motivation to reproduce the full range of genres and subjects in the Arabic literary repertoire, which meant that even the composition of poetry describing parties devoted to wine, women, men, and song could be enveloped by at least the penumbra of sanctity. There can be no question, of course, that even if the genre was born out of apologetic roots, it took on a life of its

---

23   Ross Brann, "Andalusian Hebrew Poetry and the Hebrew Bible: Cultural Nationalism or Cultural Ambiguity?" in *Approaches to Judaism in Medieval Times* 3, ed. by David R. Blumenthal (Atlanta, 1988), p. 103. See also Brann's book, *The Compunctious Poet: Cultural Ambiguity and Hebrew Poetry in Muslim Spain* (Baltimore, 1991).

own, and not every medieval wine song was preceded by a *le-shem yihud*; at the same time, every such poem was a conscious expression of Jewish pride, which in the Middle Ages had an indisputably religious coloration. Furthermore, the power and beauty of the religious poetry of the Jews of medieval Spain were surely made possible by the creative encounter with Arabic models. Some of the deepest and most moving expressions of medieval Jewish piety would have been impossible without the inspiration of the secular literature of a competing culture.

Jews could have accomplished their fundamental goal by establishing parity between Hebrew and Arabic, but such an achievement is psychologically insufficient and polemically tenuous. Consequently, we find the glorification of Hebrew over Arabic and the assertion, which we shall find in other contexts as well, that Arabic culture, including music, poetry, and rhetoric, was ultimately derived from the Jews.[24]

On a less exalted level, poetry also fulfilled a social function. Businessmen had poems written in their honor which served the pragmatic purpose of useful publicity as well as the psychological purpose of boosting the ego. The ability to write poetry was the mark of an accomplished gentleman, and this too encouraged the cultivation of the genre.[25] As I have already indicated in passing, the existence of the class of Jewish courtiers created a firm social base for a Jewish literary and philosophic culture. Jewish communities in Muslim Spain became dependent upon the representation afforded by courtiers, and that representation was impossible without a command of the surrounding culture. Since courtiers came to expect poetic flattery, their presence and patronage gave the poet both support and standing, although it hardly needs to be said that the relationship between patron and poet is never an unmixed blessing.

---

[24] The footnotes in Brann's article provide a recent bibliography of the substantial work on this theme. See especially A. S. Halkin, "The Medieval Jewish Attitude Toward Hebrew," *in Biblical and Other Studies*, ed. by Alexander Altmann (Cambridge, Mass., 1963), pp. 233-248, and Nehemiah Allony, "Teguvat R. Moshe ibn Ezra la-'Arabiyya' be-Sefer ha-Diyyunim ve-ha-Sihot (Shirat Yisrael)," *Tarbiz* 42 (1972/73): 97-113 (particularly the challenge from the beauty of the Quran on p. 101). Cf. also Norman Roth, "Jewish Reactions to the 'Arabiyya and the Renaissance of Hebrew in Spain," *Journal of Semitic Studies* 28 (1983): 63-84.
       Le-shem yihud describes a dedicatory prayer recited by later Jews before fulfilling a religious obligation. Despite the anachronism and the resort to Hebrew, I cannot think of a better way to make the point.

[25] See S. D. Goitein, *Jews and Arabs* (New York, 1955), p. 162.

Despite all this, disparagement of poetry and opposition to reliance on Arabic models were not unknown among the Jews of Muslim Spain. In some instances, however, even those who criticized what they perceived as an overemphasis on language and rhetoric did not reject the enterprise entirely, and there can be little doubt that the dominant social and intellectual class regarded literary skill as a fundamental component of a proper education. The ideal of *adab*, which roughly means general culture, was embraced by many Jews, and the praises of a great man would point to his mastery of the full range of medieval disciplines.[26]

Samuel ha-Nagid's description of God's kindness to him contains the central elements to be sought in the well rounded Jewish intellectual: "He endowed you [i.e., Samuel] with wisdom of His Scripture and His Law, which are classified first among the sciences. He instructed you in Greek knowledge and enlightened you in Arabic lore."[27] In this passage we find only the most general categories of learning, and the sole hierarchy of values places Torah above other pursuits. When the general sciences are broken down in greater detail, a more nuanced picture emerges in which philosophy takes pride of place while the remaining disciplines are necessary both for their own sake and for their usefulness in preparing the student for ever higher forms of study. As a result of this concept of "propaedeutic studies," virtually every field can bask in the reflected glory of the queen of the sciences.

"It is certainly necessary," writes Maimonides, "for whoever wishes to achieve human perfection to train himself at first in the art of logic, then in the mathematical sciences according to the proper order, then in the natural sciences, and after that in the divine science."[28] More complete lists include logic, mathematics, astronomy, physics, medicine, music, building, agriculture, and a variety of studies subsumed under

---

26 For references and discussion, see Bezalel Safran, "Bahya ibn Pakuda's Attitude toward the Courtier Class," in *Studies in Medieval Jewish History and Literature* [1], ed. by Isadore Twersky (Cambridge, Mass., 1979), pp. 154-196. For some tentative reservations about the thesis of Safran's article, see Amos Goldreich, "Ha-Meqorot ha-'Arviyyim ha-Efshariyyim shel ha-Havhanah bein 'Hovot ha-Evarim' ve-'Hovot ha-Levavot'," in *Mehqarim be-'Ivrit u-ba-'Aravit: Sefer Zikkaron le-Dov Eron*, ed. by Aharon Dotan (Tel Aviv, 1988), pp. 185, 199, nn. 22, 95.

27 Brann's translation (p. 108) from *Divan Shmuel ha-Nagid*, ed. by Dov Yarden, 1 (Jerusalem, 1966), p. 58.

28 *The Guide of the Perplexed*, translated by Shlomo Pines (Chicago and London, 1963), 1:34, p. 75.

metaphysics. So much significance was attributed to the propaedeutic studies that one of the polemicists during the Maimonidean controversy maintained that the only people who became heretics as a result of reading *The Guide of the Perplexed* were those who came to it without the proper preliminaries. This argument led him to a new application of a famous Maimonidean admonition. No one, said Maimonides, should approach the study of philosophy without first filling his stomach with the "bread and meat" of biblical and talmudic law. In our context, says Yosef b. Todros Halevi, that metaphor should be applied not to "the written and oral Torah" but to

> the other sciences like the sciences of measurement and physics and astronomy. These are known as the educational, pedagogic sciences... which lead the human intellect to approach the understanding of the divine science with a generous spirit, with passion and with affection, so that they can be compared to this world in its capacity as a gateway to the world to come.[29]

Not all philosophers assigned such weight to these preparatory studies. Thus, Abraham ibn Daud derided excessive preoccupation with medicine, with the "still more worthless.... art of grammar and rhetoric," and with "strange, hypothetical" mathematical puzzles, when the only valuable aspect of mathematics is the one that leads to a knowledge of astronomy. Endless concentration on the means would steal time better devoted to the end, which clearly remained the study of metaphysics.[30]

By far the most significant challenge to the prevailing ideal of the philosophers came in R. Judah Halevi's revolt against Andalusian Jewish culture, a revolt so far-reaching that it actually serves to underscore the centrality of philosophical inquiry for that culture. Halevi's

---

[29] *Qevuzat Mikhtavim be-'Inyenei ha-Mahaloqet 'al Devar Sefer ha-Moreh ve-ha-Madda'*, ed. by S. Z. H. Halberstam (Bamberg, 1875), p. 10. See *Mishneh Torah, Hil. Yesodei ha-Torah* 4:13. On the propaedeutic studies, see inter alia, Harry A. Wolfson, "The Classification of Sciences in Medieval Jewish Philosophy," *Hebrew Union College Jubilee Volume* (Cincinnati, 1925), pp. 263-315; A. S. Halkin, "Li-Demuto shel R. Yosef ben Yehudah ibn 'Aqnin," in *Sefer ha-Yovel li-kevod Zevi Wolfson*, ed. by Saul Lieberman (Jerusalem, 1965), 99-102; Halkin, "Yedaiah Bedershi's Apology," *Jewish Medieval and Renaissance Studies*, ed. by Alexander Altmann (Cambridge, Mass., 1967), p. 170; Halkin, "Ha-Herem 'al Limmud ha-Pilosophiah," *Peraqim* 1 (1967-68): 41; Baron, *History* 8, p. 143.

[30] *Sefer ha-Emunah ha-Ramah* (Frankfurt a. M., 1852), Part 2, Introduction, p. 45.

accomplishments as a poet and abilities as a thinker made him a sterling example of what Jewish *adab* strove to produce; when he revolted against the values of the Jewish elite, he challenged the very underpinnings of his society.[31] This challenge finds expression in his poetry, in his decision to abandon Spain for the land of Israel, and in his antiphilosophical philosophical work, the *Kuzari*.

Halevi substituted a deeply romantic, historically founded, revelation-centered, strikingly ethnocentric faith for the philosophically oriented religion of many of his peers. At the same time, the *Kuzari* operates within the matrix of medieval philosophical conceptions. Halevi could no more rid himself of the active intellect than a contemporary religious critic of evolution could deny the existence of atoms or DNA. More important, the antiphilosophical position of the *Kuzari* is an integral part of Halevi's revulsion at fawning courtiers, at Jewish groveling disguising itself as competitive imitation, at much of what "the exile of Jerusalem that is in Spain" stood for. It is no accident that his famous line denouncing Greek wisdom for producing flowers but no fruit and for affirming the eternity of matter is part of a poem justifying his decision to abandon Spain for the land of Israel. To the degree that Halevi's position developed in stages, there can be little doubt that the radical social critique gave birth to the philosophical revisionism; he clearly did not decide to leave Spain as a consequence of his rethinking of the role of philosophical speculation. If he did, however, the point would be even stronger. Nothing could demonstrate more clearly the degree to which the philosophic quest had become part of the warp and woof of Spanish Jewish civilization.

Halevi's insistence on the radical superiority not only of Judaism but also of the Jewish people has disturbed and perplexed many readers, particularly in light of his assertion that even proselytes can never hope to attain prophecy. His position can probably be understood best if we recognize that the roots of his revolt lay not so much in an intellectual reappraisal as in a visceral disgust with the humiliation and self-degradation that he saw in the Jewish courtier culture. He describes acquaintances who attempted to persuade him to remain in Spain as drunk and unworthy of a response.

---

[31]   For a powerful depiction of Halevi's revolt, see Gerson D. Cohen's discussion in his edition of Abraham ibn Daud, *Sefer ha-Qabbalah (The Book of Tradition)* (Philadelphia, 1967), pp. 295-300.

How can they offer him bliss/through the service of kings,/which in his eyes/is like the service of idols?/Is it good that a wholehearted and upright man/should be offered the happiness/of a bird tied up in the hands of youths,/in the service of Philistines,/of Hagarites and Hittites,/as alien gods/seduce his soul/to seek their will/and forsake the will of God,/to betray the Creator/and serve creatures instead?

I have already noted the psychological inadequacy of attempting to demonstrate that Jews are just as good as non-Jews; in such a case, the standard of comparison remains the alien culture which Jews strive to match and imitate. Though Halevi was not the only one to assert that Jewish culture was not merely equal but superior, he appears to have regarded the protestations of others as halfhearted, inadequate, even pathetic. There was certainly nothing in the philosophical enterprise in its standard form that had the potential to demonstrate the superiority of Judaism over Islam. In Christian societies, philosophical arguments offered the opportunity of establishing the implausibility, even the impossibility, of distinctive Christian dogmas; in a society with a dominant religion which Maimonides himself described as impeccably monotheistic, this option was precluded. The only way to overcome the status of "despised people," a characterization which appears in the very title of the *Kuzari*, was to cut the Gordian knot and declare one's emancipation from the usual rules of the philosophical game. Judaism rests on a unique revelation, not a common philosophic consensus; Jews are set apart and above, their status ingrained and unapproachable even through conversion. Only such a position could speak to the psychic impulses that lay at the very roots of Halevi's revolt.[32]

[32] For the poetic passage quoted, see Hayyim Schirmann, *Ha-Shirah ha-'Ivrit bi-Sefarad u-bi-Provence* 1 (Jerusalem, 1954), p. 498. For the passage about Greek wisdom, see pp. 493-494.

Several very recent studies have grappled with Halevi's position on the second class status of converts. Daniel J. Lasker's "Proselyte Judaism, Christianity, and Islam in the Thought of Judah Halevi," *Jewish Quarterly Review* 81 (1990): 75-91, addresses the issue without any effort to mitigate the sharpness of Halevi's assertion. Attempts to provide such mitigation appear in Lippman Bodoff, "Was Yehudah Halevi Racist?," *Judaism* 38 (1989): 174-184, and in Steven Schwartzschild, "Proselytism and Ethnicism in R. Yehudah HaLevy," in *Religionsgespräche im Mittelalter*, ed. by Bernard Lewis and Friedrich Niewöhner (Wiesbaden, 1992), pp. 27-41.

There is a talmudic passage which could have served as a source for Halevi's position about the denial of prophecy to proselytes. See *Kiddushin* 71b for the assertion that God rests his presence (*shekhinah*) only on families of unimpeachable Jewish lineage.

Halevi's assertion that one who accepts Judaism because of faith in the revelation is better than one who tries to approach it through the clever application of reason did not prevent him from maintaining, along with many other medieval Jews, that much of the wisdom of ancient Greece and Rome was derived from Jewish sources. Since the travails of exile have led to the loss not only of much of the Hebrew language but also of ancient Jewish wisdom, that wisdom has come to be associated with the Greeks and Romans. In the hands of rationalists, this argument served not only as an assertion of Jewish pride but as a legitimation of philosophical study. The wisdom of Solomon had to be redeemed from gentile hands. To a later figure like Nahmanides, whose attitude toward speculation was complex and ambivalent, the fact that gentiles have been influenced by ancient Jewish learning was unassailable, but the lessons to be drawn were less clear. Since the crucial Jewish wisdom had been preserved within the fold, and the material embedded in the books of the Greeks could be recovered only through explorations fraught with spiritual peril, the decision to embark on such exploration required careful, even agonizing deliberation. Despite this ambivalence, the dominant message of the conviction that philosophy was purloined from the Jews was undoubtedly to establish its Jewish legitimacy and perhaps even its standing as a component of Torah itself.[33]

The position of medieval rationalists concerning the relationship between philosophy and Torah is crucial to our entire discussion, and it explains my scrupulous avoidance of the tempting and common term "secular studies." There was nothing secular about metaphysics, and because of the preparatory character of many other disciplines, they too assumed religious value. We have already seen Saadya's arguments for the existence of a religious obligation to engage in philosophical speculation, and similar arguments recur throughout the Jewish Middle Ages. Abraham, we are told repeatedly, attained his knowledge of God through philosophical proofs. We are commanded to "*know* this day... that the Lord is God" (Deut. 4:39). David instructed Solomon, "*Know* the God of your father, and serve him with a whole heart and a willing soul" (I Chron. 28:9). Jeremiah wrote, "Let him that glories glory in

---

[33] *Kuzari* 2:26; 66. Cf., *inter multa alia*, *Guide* 1:71. Many of the relevant references have been summarized in Norman Roth, "The 'Theft of Philosophy' by the Greeks from the Jews," *Classical Folia* 22 (1978): 53-67. For Nahmanides, see *Kitvei Ramban* 1, p. 339, and see below for his overall stance.

this, that he *understands and knows me. . .* , says the Lord" (Jer. 9:23).[34] These proof-texts, of course, were not unassailable, and antirationalists argued that there are superior ways of reaching God. Halevi, for example, cleverly reversed the rationalists' argument that Abraham had attained philosophical knowledge of God. The patriarch had indeed pursued philosophical understanding, but the Rabbis tell us that when God told him to go outdoors (Gen. 15:5), he was really telling him to abandon astrology and listen to the divine promise. In this context, astrology is merely an example of "all forms of syllogistic wisdom," which are to be left behind once direct revelation has been attained.[35]

The argument for speculation, however, was not wholly dependent upon proof-texts. If love of God, clearly a quintessential religious value, was to have any real meaning, it could flow only from a knowledge of the Creator's handiwork, and this required a pursuit of the sciences. Moreover, the knowledge of God that comes from tradition alone is inherently insufficient and is in any event secondary rather than primary knowledge. Only those intellectually unfit for speculation can be excused from this obligation; others who neglect their duty are guilty of what R. Bahya ibn Paqudah called "laziness and contempt for the word of God and his Law" and will be called to account for their dereliction.[36]

A secondary argument pointed to the desirability, even the obligation, of impressing the gentiles with the wisdom and understanding of the Jewish people (cf. Deut. 4:6; *Shabbat* 75a). Bahya made this point with exceptional vigor by maintaining that gentile recognition of Jewish wisdom can come only if Jews prove the truth of their faith

> by logical arguments and by reasonable testimony. For God has promised
> to unveil the minds of the nations of their ignorance and to show His
> bright light to prove the truth of our religion, as it is said, "And many
> peoples shall go and say, Come yet and let us go up to the mountain of
> the Lord, to the House of the God of Jacob, and He will teach us of His
> ways, and we will walk in His paths. For out of Zion shall go forth the Law,

---

[34] On these and other arguments, see Herbert A. Davidson, "The Study of Philosophy as a Religious Obligation," in *Religion in a Religious Age*, ed. by S. D. Goitein (Cambridge, Mass., 1974), pp. 53-68.

[35] *Kuzari* 4:17, 27.

[36] *The Book of Direction to the Duties of the Heart*, trans. by Menahem Mansour (London, 1973), Introduction, p. 94.

and the word of the Lord from Jerusalem" (Isaiah 2:3). Thus it becomes a certainty to us, through logic, Scripture, and tradition, that we are obligated to speculate upon every matter the truth of which is conceivable to our minds.[37]

This is a remarkable formulation. The object to Bahya is not merely to cause gentiles to admire Jewish wisdom. Jewish philosophical expertise is the medium of an eschatological missionary endeavor. Non-Jews will accept the truth of Judaism at the end of days not because of a supernatural *deus ex machina* but because of the persuasive powers, aided no doubt by God, of Jewish philosophical arguments. Maimonides' well-known view that gentile recognition of the truth at the end of days will come through gradual preparation mediated by Christianity and Islam rather than through a sudden, miraculous upheaval may well be adumbrated in this strikingly naturalistic position in *The Duties of the Heart*. In any event, Bahya has assigned philosophy nothing less than a messianic function.

In a famous and controversial extended metaphor, Maimonides graphically illustrated his conviction that philosophy alone affords the highest level of religious insight. Near the end of his *Guide*, he tells us that the varying levels of people's apprehension of God can be classified by analogy with the inhabitants of a city who seek the palace of the king. People who have no doctrinal belief are like individuals who have not entered the city at all. Those who have engaged in speculation but have reached erroneous conclusions can be compared with people within the city who have turned their backs on the palace. Then there are those who seek the palace but never see it: "the multitude of the adherents of the Law,... the ignoramuses who observe the commandments." We then come to those who reach the palace but do not enter it: "the jurists who believe true opinions on the basis of traditional authority and study the law concerning the practices of divine service, but do not engage in speculation concerning the fundamental principles of religion." At long last we come to those who have "plunged into speculation." Only one "who has achieved demonstration, to the extent that that is possible, of everything that may be demonstrated... has come to be with the ruler in the inner part of the habitation."[38]

---

[37]   *The Duties of the Heart*, ch. I., p. 115.
[38]   *Guide* 3:51, pp. 618-619.

The supreme value that Maimonides attributed to philosophical speculation does not in itself demonstrate that he classified it as Torah. Several passages in the first book of his code, however, establish this clearly and reinforce the pride of place that he assigned to such speculation in his hierarchy of values. The first two chapters of the code deal in summary fashion with metaphysical questions which Maimonides then tells us represent what the Rabbis called the "account of the chariot." The next two chapters set forth the essentials of astronomy and physics which, says Maimonides, are "the account of creation." In combination, these chapters constitute what the Talmud calls *pardes*, which is clearly a term for the secrets of the Torah. Later he informs us explicitly that "the subjects called *pardes* are subsumed under the rubric *gemara*," and in the *Guide* he describes the philosophical discussion of divine attributes, creation, providence, and the nature of prophecy as the mysteries and secrets of the Torah.

This, however, is not the end of it. Alone among medieval Talmudists, Maimonides took literally a rabbinic statement that the talmudic discussions between Abbaye and Rava are considered "a small matter" compared with the account of the chariot, which is "a great matter." Since the account of the chariot means metaphysical speculation, the value judgment expressed here is wholly consistent with the palace metaphor in the *Guide* and, to many medieval observers, no less disturbing.[39]

What renders Maimonides' position all the more striking is its potential implications for talmudic study. The introduction to his code contains a famous observation that it will now be possible to study the written

---

[39] See *Hil. Yesodei ha-Torah* 2:11-12; 4:10, 13; *Hil. Talmud Torah* 1:11-12; *Guide* 1:35. Isadore Twersky has devoted a number of important studies to Maimonides' views on these questions. See especially his *Introduction to the Code of Maimonides (Mishneh Torah)* (New Haven, 1980), pp. 356-514, esp. pp. 488-507; "Some Non-Halakhic Aspects of the Mishneh Torah," in *Jewish Medieval and Renaissance Studies*, pp. 95-118; "Religion and Law," in *Religion in a Religious Age*, pp. 69-82. That Bahya regarded metaphysics as Torah may be reflected in his admonition that one must study metaphysics, but it is forbidden to do so (as in the case of Torah itself) for worldly benefit. See Safran, "Bahya ibn Pakuda's Attitude" (above, n. 26), p. 160. For a halakhic analysis of Maimonides' position on the status of philosophical inquiry as a technical fulfillment of the commandment to study Torah, see Aharon Kahn, "Li-Qevi'at ha-Hefza shel Talmud Torah," *Beit Yosef Shaul: Qovez Hiddushei Torah* 3 (1989): 373-374, 386-403. In Kahn's view, even Maimonides believed that only philosophical discussions centered on sacred texts qualify for the status of Torah. While Kahn's interesting argument is based on instincts that are (and should be) difficult to overcome, the hard evidence for the conclusion remains rather thin.

Torah, followed by "this [book]," from which the reader will know the oral Torah, so that it will be unnecessary to read any other book in between. The possibility that Maimonides meant to render the Talmud obsolete was raised in his own time, and he vigorously denied any such intention in a letter to R. Pinhas ha-Dayyan of Alexandria. Nonetheless, the tone of even this letter reveals an attitude not wholly typical of medieval Talmudists, and some of Maimonides' epistles to his student Joseph ben Judah express relatively sharp reservations about extreme preoccupation with details of talmudic discussions at the expense of other pursuits.

In the letter to R. Pinhas he testifies that he has not taught the *Mishneh Torah* for a year and a half because most of his students wanted to study R. Isaac Alfasi's legally oriented abridgment of the Talmud; as for the two students who wanted to study the Talmud itself, Maimonides taught them the tractates that they requested. Although he goes on to insist that he wrote the code only for people who are incapable of plumbing the depths of the Talmud, this description of his students certainly does not convey single-minded devotion to teaching the talmudic text.

Far more striking are the letters to Joseph ben Judah. In one section of this collection, Maimonides predicts that the time will come when all Israel will study the *Mishneh Torah* alone with the exception of those who are looking for something on which to spend their entire lives even though it achieves no end. Elsewhere he permits Joseph to open a school but urges him to pursue trade and study medicine along with his learning of Torah; moreover, he says,

> Teach only the code of R. Isaac Alfasi and compare it with the Composition [i.e., the *Mishneh Torah*]. If you find a disagreement, know that careful study of the Talmud brought it about, and study the relevant passage. If you fritter away your time with commentaries and explanations of talmudic discussions and those matters from which we have excused people, time will be wasted and useful results will be diminished.

Finally, a slightly later citation quotes Maimonides to the effect that talmudic scholars waste their time on the detailed discussions of the Talmud as if those discussions were an end in themselves; in fact their only purpose was to make the determinations necessary for proper observance of the commandments.[40]

---

40   *Iggerot le-Rabbenu Moshe ben Maimon*, ed. and trans. by Yosef Kafih (Jerusalem, 1972),

These passages do not make explicit reference to what it is that one should do with the time saved by the study of the *Mishneh Torah*. It is perfectly clear, however, that Maimonides had in mind more than the study of medicine and the merchant's trade. One of the functions of his great halakhic work was to expand the opportunities for the pursuit of philosophical speculation.

Despite the frequency, clarity, vigor, and certainty with which Maimonides affirmed the supreme value of speculation and its standing at the pinnacle of Torah, the poetry and pathos of a single powerful passage reveal how all this can sometimes be overshadowed by the unshakable instinct of which I spoke at the outset: the instinct that it is the Torah that constitutes Torah. In his correspondence with R. Jonathan ha-Kohen of Lunel, Maimonides addressed various questions about specific rulings in his code. He was clearly moved by the informed reverence toward his magnum opus that he found among the rabbis of Provence and looked back with nostalgia on the years that he devoted to its composition. His formulation is both striking and problematic:

> I, Moses, inform the glorious Rabbi R. Jonathan ha-Kohen and the other scholars reading my work: Before I was formed in the stomach the Torah knew me, and before I came forth from the womb she dedicated me to her study [cf. Jer. 1:5] and appointed me to have her fountains erupt outward. She is my beloved, the wife of my youth, in whose love I have been immersed since early years. Yet many foreign women have become her rivals, Moabites, Ammonites, Edomites, Sidonians, and Hittites. The Lord knows that they were not taken at the outset except to serve her as perfumers and cooks and bakers. Nonetheless, the time allotted to her has now been reduced, for my heart has been divided into many parts through the pursuit of all sorts of wisdom.[41]

There are no doubt ways to mitigate the incongruity of this passage. First, the allusion may well be to ancillary, propaedeutic studies whose status as "handmaidens of theology" was well established; neither metaphysics nor, arguably, even physics are necessarily included. Moreover, just a few lines later the letter concludes, "May the Lord, blessed be He, help us and you study His Torah *and understand His unity* so that we may not stumble, and let the verse be fulfilled in our own time,

pp. 126, 134, 136.

41   *Teshuvot ha-Rambam*, ed. by Jehoshua Blau, 2nd ed., 3 (Jerusalem, 1986), p. 57.

'I will put my Torah in their inward parts and write it on their hearts'"
(Jer. 31:33). Nonetheless, the passionate wistfulness of Maimonides'
tone leaves me resistant to efforts at integrating this outburst of religious
nostalgia seamlessly into the web of his thought.[42] One almost suspects
that as Maimonides recovered from the surge of emotion that overcame
him, he purposely inserted the crucial phrase into his final sentence so
that no one should suspect that he had renounced some of his central
commitments. We are witness here to a fascinating and revealing
glimpse of the capacity of an unphilosophical, almost atavistic love for
old-fashioned Torah to overwhelm, if only for a moment, the intellectual
convictions of the very paradigm of philosophical rationalism.

Aside from the special case of Halevi, we have little direct evidence
of principled opposition to philosophy in Muslim Spain. Some of the
polemical remarks in the works of Bahya, Maimonides, and others
reveal the unsurprising information that there existed Talmudists
who looked upon the enterprise with a jaundiced eye and resisted
efforts to reread rabbinic texts in the light of philosophical doctrines.
Nonetheless, there was no concerted opposition whose work has
come down to us, and Samuel ibn Nagrella is a striking, early example
of a figure of some stature in talmudic studies who represented the
full range of *adab*. Moreover, we can probably be confident that the
greatest Spanish Talmudist of the twelfth century did not maintain
a vigorous antiphilosophical stance. R. Joseph ibn Migash, who
taught Maimonides' father, did not, as far as we know, produce any
philosophical work. At the same time, given Maimonides' oft-expressed
contempt for Talmudists who opposed speculation, the great reverence
with which he described his illustrious predecessor would be difficult
to understand if ibn Migash was counted among them, and R. Abraham
Maimonides listed him among the luminaries who "strengthened
the faith that they inherited from their fathers... to know with the

---

[42]   See the attempt in Yosef Kafih, "Limmudei 'Hol' be-Mishnat ha-Rambam," *Ketavim*
2 (Jerusalem, 1989), p. 594, where the author nevertheless expresses doubts about
Maimondes' authorship of these remarks. See too Rashba's comment in Abba Mari b.
Joseph, *Sefer Minhat Qenaot* (Pressburg, 1838), p. 40=*Teshuvot ha-Rashba*, ed. by Haim
Z. Dimitrovsky 1 (Jerusalem, 1990), pp. 342-343; Profiat Duran, *Ma'aseh Efod* (Vienna,
1865), pp. 15-16. The immense religious value that Maimonides attached to philosophy
as well as his ongoing philosophical scrutiny of Jewish religious texts would render this
passage problematic even if we were to accept Kahn's conclusion that philosophical
inquiry must be based on Jewish sources in order to qualify as Torah. See above, n. 39.

eye of their intellect and the understanding of their mind" that God cannot be conceived in corporeal terms.[43] As in the case of Saadya's Baghdad, many Spanish Talmudists probably treated philosophy with salutary neglect while others, probably including ibn Migash, looked upon it with some favor even though it was not their particular field of expertise. With few significant exceptions, Spanish Jewry under Islam was unambiguously hospitable to the pursuit of philosophy, the sciences, and the literary arts.

THE GREAT STRUGGLE: PROVENCE AND NORTHERN SPAIN FROM THE LATE TWELFTH TO THE EARLY FOURTEENTH CENTURY

The great religious value of philosophy was inextricably intertwined with its great religious danger. Since reason and revelation were rooted in the same source, they could not conflict with one another;[44] at the same time, the study of philosophic texts generated a host of problems for traditional conceptions, particularly as Aristotelianism launched its triumphant march across the medieval intellectual landscape. To most believers, God had created the world out of nothing; to Aristotelians, a form of primeval matter had always existed. To the traditional believer, God's knowledge extended to the most minute details affecting the lowest of creatures, and his loving providence was over "all his handiwork" (Psalms 145:9); to the Aristotelian, he did not know particulars at all. To the person of faith, celestial reward awaited each righteous individual as a separate entity; to the Aristotelian philosopher, the soul's survival depended upon intellectual attainments and took a collective rather

---

[43] See Abraham Maimonides, *Milhamot Hashem*, ed. by Reuven Margaliyot (Jerusalem, 1953), pp. 49-50. With respect to direct evidence, however, note Israel Ta-Shema's remark that "we do not have a scintilla of information on his pursuit of philosophy, grammar, or science"; see "Yezirato ha-Sifrutit shel Rabbenu Yosef ha-Levi ibn Migash," *Kiryat Sefer* 46 (1971): 137. In light of Abraham Maimonides' statement, this formulation may be a shade too vigorous.

[44] For a sharp formulation of this point, see Norman Roth, *Maimonides: Essays and Texts, 850th Anniversary* (Madison, 1985), p. 94. He argues that from the point of view of medieval Jewish and Muslim rationalists there can be no conflict because "what prophetic revelation brings in the way of flashes of light to the masses, the philosopher sees in the full blaze of rational illumination."

than an individual form. One is tempted to paraphrase Maimonides' exalted assessment of metaphysics by observing that these are indeed not small matters.

Medieval thinkers had a wide range of options in dealing with such issues. At one end of the spectrum were those who rejected philosophical inquiry on principle. On the other were those who accepted virtually the full corpus of Aristotelian conclusions and maintained that revealed religion, which should not be consulted for the answers to ultimate questions, was intended as a political instrument for ordering the life of the masses. Ranged between these extremes were the large majority of thinkers with greater or lesser inclinations toward the preservation of traditional beliefs. In any given instance, one could argue that the philosophical position was unproven and unpersuasive or that the standard religious conception was not essential or had been misconstrued. The last approach was both controversial and fruitful because it required not only a rethinking of doctrine but a reinterpretation of classic texts. The allegorical understanding of both biblical and Talmudic material is consequently an integral and significant part of our story. The attitudes of Jews toward general culture had a profound impact on their conceptions of Judaism itself.

The battle over philosophical study became a major theme in medieval Jewish history as a result of a watershed event: the migration of many Spanish Jews to Southern France in the wake of the Almohade conquest of the late 1140s. This conquest brought the history of Andalusian Jewry to a tragic end and opened a new chapter in the relationship between Sephardic and Ashkenazic Jews. A number of the exiles moved only as far north as Christian Spain, where some of them translated scientific and philosophical works that helped to transfer the advanced culture of the Muslim world into the ever more curious Christian Europe of the twelfth century. While this dimension of cultural activity did not play a central role within the Jewish community itself, it was a development of major importance in the evolution of European civilization.[45]

---

[45] See M. Steinschneider's classic *Die Hebraeischen Uebersetzungen des Mittelalters und die Juden als Dolmetscher* (Berlin, 1893). For a readable survey of medieval translations and the Jews, see section II of Charles Singer's "The Jewish Factor in Medieval Thought," in *The Legacy of Israel*, ed. by Edwyn R. Bevan and Charles Singer (Oxford, 1927), pp. 202-245. On earlier contacts between Ashkenazim and Sephardim, see the important reassessment by Avraham Grossman, "Bein Sefarad le-Zarfat: ha-Qesharim

From an internal Jewish perspective, the major acts in this drama were to be played out in the south of France.[46] For the first time, substantial numbers of Ashkenazim and Sephardim confronted one another in the same community, and the immigrants resisted any assimilation into the cultural patterns of the native Ashkenazim. On the contrary, one senses a degree of self-confident assertiveness that borders on cultural imperialism. The Provençal Jews needed to defend even their halakhic traditions against a Sephardic effort to impose the rulings of R. Isaac Alfasi, and the Spanish Jews brought with them a feeling of almost contemptuous superiority toward those who were untrained in the broader culture of the Andalusian elite. What made this challenge particularly effective was the inability of the Jews of Provence to point to their own unambiguous superiority in Torah narrowly construed. Although the immigrants themselves could offer no Talmudists to compete with R. Abraham b. David of Posquières or R. Zerahiah HaLevi of Lunel, they could point to a substantial cohort of distinguished rabbis produced by their native culture along with its philosophical achievements.

Under such circumstances, the argument that pursuit of philosophy enhanced religion by providing insight into the nature of God was difficult to resist. At the same time, the deviations from traditional religious conceptions that philosophy brought in its wake could not but cause concern in a society that was being exposed to such ideas for the first time, and the argument from the dangers of philosophical heresy loomed large. It may well be that this dialectic was responsible for one of the most important developments in the history of Judaism: the rise of mysticism as a highly visible factor in the intellectual constellation of medieval Jewry.

The central component of Jewish mysticism in the Middle Ages was its theosophic doctrine. Without detracting from the significance of ecstatic kabbalah, there can be little doubt that one seeking to understand the

---

bein Qehillot Yisra'el she-bi-Sefarad ha-Muslemit u-bein Qehillot Zarfat," in *Galut Ahar Golah: Mehqarim be-Toledot 'Am Yisrael Muggashim li-Professor Haim Beinart*, ed. by A. Mirsky, A. Grossman, and Y. Kaplan (Jerusalem, 1988), pp. 75-101. See now his *Hakhmei Zarfat ha-Rishonim* (Jerusalem, 1995), pp. 554-571.

[46] For a characterization of Provençal Jewish culture in this period, see Isadore Twersky, "Aspects of the Social and Cultural History of Provençal Jewry," in *Jewish Society through the Ages*, ed. by H. H. Ben Sasson and S. Ettinger (New York, 1971), pp. 185-207.

attraction of esoteric lore in the initial stages of its popularity must look at its doctrinal rather than its experiential aspects. Such an examination reveals that kabbalah provided the perfect solution, at least to people with a receptive religious personality, to the critical intellectual issue that confronted Jews at precisely the time and place in which mysticism began to spread.

The essential claim made by kabbalists was that God had revealed an esoteric teaching to Moses in addition to the exoteric Torah. This secret lore uncovered the deeper meaning of the Torah, and it also taught initiates the true nature of God and creation; it is here, not in Aristotelian physics and metaphysics, that one must seek the meaning of the accounts of creation and of the chariot. Indeed, a recent study has argued that longstanding mystical doctrines were now at least partially publicized because the bearers of these doctrines could not suffer in silence the Maimonidean-style claim that the rabbis had referred to gentile disciplines as the secrets of the Torah. However that may be, kabbalah offered a revealed key to precisely the knowledge that philosophers sought. By locating that key in an inner Jewish tradition, kabbalists could argue that philosophy with all its dangers was superfluous, and even though Rabbinic tradition had attributed spiritual peril to the study of mystical secrets, one could hardly compare the potential for heresy in the pursuit of revealed truth to the dangers of studying Aristotle. Even without reference to the problem of heresy, kabbalah promised the late twelfth-century Provençal Jew all that philosophy offered and more, since human reason is fallible while the word of God is not. Small wonder that Jewish thinkers began to respond, and mysticism embarked on a path that would lead it toward a pre-eminent position in Jewish piety and religious thought by the sixteenth and seventeenth centuries.[47]

The penetration of Sephardic philosophical culture into Southern France in the late twelfth and early thirteenth centuries produced the

---

[47] I made the essential point in "Miracles and the Natural Order in Nahmanides," in *Rabbi Moses Nahmanides (Ramban): Explorations in His Religious and Literary Virtuosity*, ed. by Isadore Twersky (Cambridge, Mass. and London, England, 1983), p. 111. Cf. the citation from A.S. Halkin in note 17 there. On the suggestion that mystics were responding to the claim that Aristotelian doctrines are the secrets of the Torah, see Moshe Idel, *Kabbalah: New Perspectives* (New Haven and London, 1988), p. 253, and much more fully in sections I and II of his "Maimonides and Kabbalah," in *Studies in Maimonides*, ed. by Isadore Twersky (Cambridge, Mass. and London, England, 1990), pp. 31-50.

first great conflict over the propriety of rationalistic speculation. The Maimonidean controversy erupted in the early 1230s as a result of the perception by R. Solomon ben Abraham of Montpellier that the study of certain works of Maimonides was leading people into heresy. Though the internal Jewish dynamic that we have been examining could have set these events in motion without any external impetus, there can be little doubt that the atmosphere of early thirteenth-century Christian Languedoc aided and abetted the process. The century had begun with the Albigensian Crusade, and the decade of the Jewish controversy was also witness to the birth of an inquisition aimed at Christian heresies.

R. Solomon sent his distinguished student R. Jonah to bring the writings in question to the attention of his natural allies, the rabbis of Northern France. As a result of this initiative, the rabbis of the North proclaimed a ban against *The Guide of the Perplexed* and the first, quasi-philosophical section of the *Mishneh Torah* ("The Book of Knowledge"). At this point, the defenders of Maimonides in the South proclaimed a ban against R. Solomon and his disciples and sent the biblical commentator R. David Kimhi (Radak) to their natural allies in what was now Christian Spain to obtain support for the second ban.

Radak discovered to his surprise that a mixed reception awaited him. While some Spanish communities affirmed the ban enthusiastically, the distinguished physician R. Judah Alfakar refused to offer support and instead wrote several sharp letters expressing his reservations about Maimonides' *Guide*. The ambivalence that Radak encountered in Spain speaks volumes for the fact that the direction of influence in the Sephardi-Ashkenazi confrontation of the previous decades was not reflected exclusively in the adoption of a philosophical culture by some Ashkenazim. The Ashkenazi impact on many Sephardim was no less profound. In some cases, this influence came through Southern France; in others, it was direct. Whatever the medium, however, Radak discovered a transformed Spanish Jewry whose attitude toward the culture produced by its own forebears could no longer be predicted with confidence.

This transformation is also evident in a letter by Nahmanides that we shall have to examine later in which he attempted, with some success, to bring the controversy to a close. In the meantime, events in Montpellier overtook developments in Spain. Zealous anti-Maimonists approached local ecclesiastical authorities with what they presented as heretical Jewish books, and the churchmen obliged by burning the controversial works of Maimonides. Indignant Maimonists complained to lay authorities apparently unhappy with ecclesiastical intervention, and the anti-Maimonist delators were promptly punished by having a part of their tongues cut off. Contemporary Maimonists evinced no dismay at the harshness of the penalty; on the contrary, they regarded it as an appropriate divine retribution for an offense whose seriousness in the medieval Jewish context could hardly be exaggerated. Though the internal Jewish controversy did not end immediately after these events, it began to die down, and the works of Maimonides remained undisturbed for decades to come.[48]

The issues raised in the substantial corpus of letters written during this controversy reveal the concerns, the tactics, and the deeply held convictions of most of the parties to the dispute. Regrettably, we possess only one letter from R. Solomon ben Abraham himself. It is of no small interest that he denies requesting a ban against the *Guide* and "The Book of Knowledge" and that he makes a point of his careful, sympathetic study of Maimonides' code in his yeshivah. What concerned him, he writes, was that some Provençal Jews had affirmed extreme philosophical positions that went so far as the allegorization of the story of Cain and Abel and even of the commandments themselves. R. Meir HaLevi Abulafia, who had questioned Maimonides' view of resurrection three decades earlier, reports that R. Solomon was motivated by a concern about rationalists who "wish to break the yoke of the commandments" by denying that God really cares for ritual observances. All God wants, they maintained, is that people know him philosophically; whether the body is pure or impure, hungry or thirsty, is quite irrelevant. R. Meir's brother Yosef b. Todros speaks of Jews who argued that all the words of the Torah and rabbinic tradition are allegories, who mocked the belief in miracles, and who regarded themselves as exempt from prayer and phylacteries. To what

---

48   The clarity of this brief summary obscures the obscurity of the events. For an admirable
      effort to reconstruct the chronology of the controversy, see A. Schochet, "Berurim
      be-Parashat ha-Pulmus ha-Rishon 'al Sifrei ha-Rambam," *Zion* 36 (1971): 27-60,
      which takes account of the important sources in Joseph Shatzmiller, "Li-Temunat
      ha-Mahaloqet ha-Rishonah 'al Kitvei ha-Rambam," *Zion* 34 (1969): 126-144. Cf. the
      earlier works by Joseph Sarachek, *Faith and Reason: The Conflict over the Rationalism
      of Maimonides* (Williamsport, Penna., 1935), and Daniel Jeremy Silver, *Maimonidean
      Criticism and the Maimonidean Controversy, 1180-1240* (Leiden, 1965). The best analysis
      of significant aspects of the debates is in Bernard Septimus, *Hispano-Jewish Culture in
      Transition* (Cambridge, Mass. and London, England, 1982), pp. 61-103.

degree these assertions reflect reality is far from clear; what is clear is that the argument that rationalism has in fact produced heresy was one of the most forceful and effective weapons in the arsenal of the opposition.[49]

In addition to specific charges of disbelief and violations of law, rationalists also faced the accusation that they abandon the study of Talmud in favor of philosophical speculation. Thus, Radak found it necessary to testify that he studies Talmud assiduously and observes the commandments meticulously; the only reason that people suspected him, he tells us, is that he had indicated that the detailed exchanges in the Talmud will be rendered obsolete in the Messianic age when everything will become clear. Many Talmudists would surely have disagreed even with the assertion to which Radak admits, and Alfakar's letter to him explicitly speaks of the inclination to abolish the discussions of Abbaye and Rava in order "to ascend in the chariot."[50]

On the most fundamental level, Alfakar, whose letters evince an impressive level of philosophical sophistication, denied the controlling authority of reason. Any compelling demonstration, he wrote, requires investigation of extraordinary intensity because of the possibility of hidden sophistry, and an erroneous premise, no matter how far back in the chain of reasoning, can undermine the validity of the conclusion. Consequently, reliance on reason to reject important religious teachings is inadmissible.

Alfakar's specific examples concentrate on the denial or limitation of miracles. Maimonides, he says, regarded Balaam's talking donkey and similar biblical miracles as prophetic visions despite the Mishnah's inclusion of the donkey's power of speech among the ten things created immediately before the first Sabbath. This Maimonidean tendency is symptomatic of the deeper problem of attempting to synthesize the Torah and Greek wisdom. Radak had explicitly praised Maimonides' unique ability to harmonize "wisdom" and faith. On the contrary, says Alfakar, the attempt was a failure. Maimonides, for example, limited the number of long-lived antediluvians

> because his intention was to leave the ordinary operation of the world intact
> so that he could establish the Torah and Greek wisdom together, "coupling

---

[49] See R. Solomon's letter in *Qevuzat Mikhtavim*, pp. 51-52; R. Meir in *Qovez Teshuvot ha-Rambam* (Leipzig, 1859) 3, p. 6a; R. Yosef in *Qevuzat Mikhtavim*, pp. 6, 21.

[50] *Qovez Teshuvot ha-Rambam* 3, pp. 3a-4a.

the tent together so that it may be one" (Exod. 26:11). He imagined that the one could stand with the other "like two young roes that are twins" (Song of Songs 4:5); instead, there was "mourning and lamentation" (Lam. 2:5). "The land was not able to bear them, that they might live together" (Gen. 13:6) as two sisters, "for the Hebrew women are not like the Egyptian women" (Exod. 1:19).

As for lesser figures than Maimonides, they reduce the number of miracles because "their soul does not consider it appropriate to believe what the Creator considered it appropriate to do."[51]

Yosef ben Todros Halevi affirmed the dangers lurking in the *Guide* by arguing that no one in his generation has the capacity to read the work without exposing himself to the danger of heresy. Consequently, he can justify the action of the Northern French rabbis without forfeiting his respect for Maimonides. Both "acted for the sake of heaven, each in his place and time." Moreover, he says, the dangers of speculation have even been recognized by the kings of the Arabs, who forbade "Greek wisdom" and philosophical study. If Yosef is referring to the Almohade rulers, we would have a striking appeal by a Jewish conservative to the judgment of persecutors of his people for the sake of validating or at least lending support to a decision affecting the internal spiritual life of Judaism.[52]

The Maimonist party responded with a vigorous defense of the value of general culture. Radak succeeded in eliciting a ban against R. Solomon and his students from the Jewish community of Saragossa, the text of which contains instructive arguments for the rationalist position taken from Rabbinic literature.

> It is widely known among our people that our sages instructed and warned us to learn the wisdom concerning the unity of God as well as external forms of wisdom that will enable us to answer heretics and know the matters utilized by disbelievers to destroy our Torah. [They] also [instructed us to study] astrology and the vanities of idol-worship, [which] one cannot learn from the Torah or the Talmud, as well as the measurement of land and knowledge of solstices and calculations, as the learned teacher of wisdom said, "The pathways of the heavens are as clear to me as the pathways of

51 *Qovez Teshuvot ha-Rambam* 3, pp. 1a-2a, 3a.
52 *Qevuzat Mikhtavim*, pp. 21-22, 13-14. The term *malkhei ha-'erev*, based on I Kings 10:15, appears as *malkhei 'arav* in the parallel verse in II Chronicles (9:14) and was no doubt understood by Joseph as Arab kings despite the ambiguity introduced by the juxtaposition of the two phrases in Jeremiah 25:24.

Nehardea," and an understanding of the scope with which they measured at a distance on both land and sea. Moreover, they ruled that no one can be appointed to the Sanhedrin to decide the law unless he knows these disciplines and medicine as well.[53]

A particularly interesting aspect of this text is the distinction between "the wisdom concerning the unity of God" (*hokhmat ha-yihud*) and "external forms of wisdom" or "external disciplines" (*hokhmot hizzoniyyot*). The former requires no defense on instrumental grounds; it is part of the Torah, and the problem is just that the antirationalists do not recognize this. External wisdom, on the other hand, needs to be justified in other ways. The document provides Rabbinic authority for some of these pursuits, whose purpose is often self-evident, but the only concrete argument set forth is the need to respond to heretics. This need, which was legitimized by a Rabbinic text, was routinely cited in other contexts to defend so religiously dubious an enterprise as the study of the New Testament. Its application to our context is attested not only in the Saragossa ban but in the counterargument of Yosef ben Todros that the rabbis' intention in urging Jews to learn the appropriate response to heretics was manifestly "to reconstruct the ruins of the faith, not to destroy it." Yosef, in other words, regarded the use of this argument as the last refuge of scoundrels, a pro forma justification for a pursuit motivated by entirely different considerations.[54]

If the information of the Saragossa authorities was reliable, the text of their denunciation contributes to our knowledge of the ban issued by the antirationalists.

The earlier ban, we are told, was directed not only against the *Guide* and "The Book of Knowledge" but against "anyone who studies any of the external disciplines." R. Bahya ben Moses, the chief signatory of the Saragossa ban, repeats this information in a letter to the Jewish communities of Aragon.[55] On the one hand, we could be dealing with an exaggeration designed to facilitate the eliciting of additional counterbans; on the other, the fact that "external books" are denounced in the

---

[53] *Qovez Teshuvot ha-Rambam* 3, p. 5b.
[54] *Qevuzat Mikhtavim*, p. 14. On reading the New Testament to answer a heretic, see my comments and references in *The Jewish-Christian Debate in the High Middle Ages* (Philadelphia, 1979; rep., Northvale, N.J. and London, 1996), pp. 309-310.
[55] *Qovez Teshuvot ha-Rambam* 3, pp. 5b, 6a.

Mishnah renders it difficult to reject this report out of hand. However that may be, rationalists were clearly uncomfortable with the talmudic prohibition of "Greek wisdom," and we find efforts at redefinition that limit the meaning of the term to a kind of coded communication that has not survived and that therefore poses no limitation whatever to the philosopher's intellectual agenda. One Maimonist argued that however one understands the term, the prohibition can certainly not result from a concern with heresy since the Rabbis would never have excluded potential diplomats from the ban had the reason for it been that weighty.[56]

Defenses of rationalism and its allied disciplines appealed to other considerations as well. The argument that philosophical sophistication was necessary to impress gentiles was fairly widespread, and it occasionally took an even stronger form: the Jewish loss of Greek wisdom, which was, of course, originally Jewish wisdom, makes Jews an object of ridicule in the eyes of their educated neighbors.[57] During the Maimonidean controversy, a more fundamental argument appears in a novel formulation that may reflect the influence of a major Christian work. In the twelfth century, Peter Abelard wrote his celebrated *Sic et Non*, which challenged opponents of speculation to account for a variety of apparent contradictions in authoritative texts. The "authority" which is the presumed alternative to reason is simply not usable without its supposed rival. One Maimonist letter argues for rationalism by citing contradictions in Rabbinic sources that can be resolved only by the sort of speculation that the antirationalists eschew.[58] Patristic contradictions have become Rabbinic contradictions, but the Abelardian argument remains intact.

We have already seen that the anti-Maimonists' concern that rationalism tends to produce heresy constituted one of their most powerful arguments against philosophical study. A striking feature of

---

[56]   Samuel Saporta in *Qevuzat Mikhtavim*, p. 95. On Greek wisdom, see Saul Lieberman, *Hellenism in Jewish Palestine* (New York, 1962), pp. 100-114, and cf. the references in Davidson, "The Study of Philosophy as a Religious Obligation" (above n. 34), pp. 66-67, n. 44.

[57]   Samuel ibn Tibbon, *Ma'amar Yiqqavu ha-Mayim* (Pressburg, 1837), p. 173. On the need to impress gentiles, see Twersky, "Provençal Jewry," pp. 190, 204-205.

[58]   Joseph Shatzmiller, "Iggarto shel R. Asher be-R. Gershom le-Rabbanei Zarfat," in *Mehqarim be-Toledot 'Am Yisrael ve-Erez Yisrael le-Zekher Zevi Avineri* (Haifa, 1970), pp. 129-140. Shatzmiller was struck by the argument but not by the Abelardian parallel, which is, of course, speculative. In a recent lecture, Bernard Septimus has noted that R. Asher may well have been making a sharp allusion to the Tosafists' own use of dialectic.

the controversy is that the Maimonists argued that precisely the reverse was true: it was antirationalism that had produced a heresy more serious than the worst philosophical heterodoxy, because many naive believers worshipped a corporeal God. The issue of anthropomorphism is therefore crucial to an understanding not only of the Maimonidean controversy but of the role that philosophy played in defining the parameters of a legitimate Jewish conception of God. There can be no higher stakes than these and no better evidence of the powerful, almost controlling presence of the philosophical enterprise at the very heart of medieval Judaism.

Maimonides listed belief in the incorporeal nature of God as one of his thirteen principles constituting the sine qua non of the faith. As he indicated both in his discussion of this creed and in his code, failure to affirm this belief is rank heresy which excludes one from a portion in the world to come. Maimonides has been assigned a highly sophisticated motivation for taking this position. Survival after death requires a cleaving to God that is possible only through the development of that aspect of the soul which perceives certain abstract truths about the Deity; the belief in an incorporeal God is consequently the minimum requirement for attaining eternal life.[59] While Maimonides may well have endorsed this view, the immediate motivation for perceiving anthropomorphism as heresy was probably simpler and more fundamental: the believer in a corporeal God does not really believe in one God at all.

Maimonides drew the connection between unity and incorporeality forcefully and explicitly:

> There is no profession of unity unless the doctrine of God's corporeality is denied. For a body cannot be one, but is composed of matter and form, which by definition are two; it is also divisible, subject to partition.... It is not meet that belief in the corporeality of God... should be permitted to establish itself in anyone's mind any more than it is meet that belief should be established in the nonexistence of the deity, in the association of other gods with Him, or in the worship of other than He.[60]

Maimonides' son provided an even sharper formulation. Anthropomorphism, he writes, is an impurity like that

---

[59] See Arthur Hyman's important article, "Maimonides' 'Thirteen Principles'," in *Jewish Medieval and Renaissance Studies*, pp. 141-142.

[60] *Guide* 1:35, p. 81. Hyman is, of course, well aware of this passage but argues that the belief in incorporeality is what gives the very profession of unity its salvific value.

of idolatry. Idolaters deny God's Torah and worship other gods beside Him, while one who, in his stupidity, allows it to enter his mind that the Creator has a body or an image or a location, which is possible only for a body, does not know Him. One who does not know Him denies Him, and such a person's worship and prayer are not to the Creator of the world. [Anthropomorphists] do not worship the God of heaven and earth but a false image of Him, just like the worshippers of demons about whom the Rabbis say that they worship [such] an image, for the entity that they have in mind, who is corporeal and has stature or a particular location where he sits on a throne, does not exist at all. It was concerning those fools and their like that the prophet said, "He has shut their eyes, that they cannot see, and their hearts, that they cannot understand."[61]

It is especially noteworthy that Maimonides does not appeal to tradition to validate his declaration that anthropomorphism is heretical. On the contrary, his comments on the motivation for his stand clearly reveal the determinative role of philosophy. He tells us in the *Guide* that if he wished to affirm the eternity of the world, he could provide a figurative interpretation to biblical texts that imply the contrary just as he has interpreted anthropomorphic verses figuratively. One reason for distinguishing the case of anthropomorphism from that of eternal matter is that the latter has not been proven. On the other hand, "that the deity is not a body has been demonstrated; from this it follows necessarily that everything that in its external meaning disagrees with this demonstration must be interpreted figuratively." Alfakar, while wrestling with the same problem, pointed to the fact that the Bible itself contains contradictory verses regarding the corporeality of God and argued that this legitimates figurative interpretation. Though Alfakar and Maimonides also cited Onkelos's alleged avoidance of anthropomorphic expressions as a precedent, and Nahmanides, Abraham Maimonides, and Samuel Saporta provided a list of anti-anthropomorphic authorities beginning with the time of the Geonim, there can be little doubt that the driving force in the extirpation of a corporeal conception of God was the philosophic enterprise.[62]

---

[61]   *Milhamot Hashem*, p. 52. For a very strong (perhaps just a bit too strong) assertion of this understanding of Maimonides' motivation (without reference to *Milhamot Hashem*), see Menachem Kellner, *Dogma in Medieval Jewish Thought From Maimonides to Abravanel* (Oxford, 1986), p. 41: "Maimonides held that. . . one who conscientiously observes the halakhah while believing in the corporeality of God is, in effect, performing idolatry."

[62]   See *Guide* 2:25, p. 328; *Qovez Teshuvot ha-Rambam* 3, p. lb; *Kitvei Ramban*, 1, pp. 346-347;

The philosophers, in fact, did their job so well that contemporary Jews find it very difficult to acknowledge the existence of medieval Jewish anthropomorphism despite substantial, credible evidence. By far the best known testimony is the assertion by R. Abraham b. David of Posquières that greater Jews than Maimonides believed in a corporeal God because they were misled by the literal meaning of Rabbinic *aggadot*. Maimonist rhetoric during the controversy is replete with assertions that the anti-Maimonists believe in a corporeal God and are consequently heretics. Some of these attacks may well be exaggerated, but they play too prominent a role in the discussion for them to have been invented out of whole cloth. Abraham Maimonides reports that the prominent anti-Maimonist David ben Saul vigorously denied that he conceived of God in crudely anthropomorphic terms; at the same time, says Abraham, David affirmed his belief that God sits in heaven, where his primary grandeur is to be found, and that a partition separates the Creator from his creatures. In a particularly sharp attack, Abraham comments that Christian support for the anti-Maimonist cause is hardly surprising since the beliefs of the two groups diverge so little.[63]

Finally, we have the works of two Ashkenazic writers who explicitly express conceptions of God which are corporeal by Maimonidean standards. R. Moses Taku is the better known of these figures, and his *Ketav Tamim* is a polemic specifically directed against the Saadyanic and Maimonidean insistence on an incorporeal God. Taku, who is cited in *Tosafot* and was not an entirely marginal figure, not only affirmed a moderate kind of anthropomorphism but also accused the philosophers of heresy in terms strikingly reminiscent of Abraham Maimonides himself. In his vigorous reversal of the Maimonidean argument, Taku wrote,

> Who knows if the redemption is being delayed because of the fact that they do not know who is performing miracles for them. Moreover, if tragedy strikes, they cry out and are not answered because they direct their cries to something other than the fundamental object of faith; for this new religion and new wisdom recently came upon the scene, and its adherents maintain

---

63 *Milhamot Hashem*, pp. 49-50; *Qevuzat Mikhtavim*, pp. 85-86, 90-91.
Rabad to *Hil. Teshuvah* 3:7; *Qovez Teshuvot ha-Rambam* 3, p. 3b; the letter of the Rabbis of Lunel and Narbonne in *Zion* 34 (1969): 140-141; *Milhamot Hashem*, pp. 69, 55. Note especially Schochet's vigorous presentation of the Maimonist polemic against anthropomorphism, *Zion* 36 (1971): 54-60. See also the literature cited in Kellner, *Dogma*, p. 233, n. 159.

that what the prophets saw was the form of created beings, while from the day that God spoke to Adam and created the world through His word, we have believed it to be the Creator and not a creature.[64]

In addition to *Ketav Tamim*, we now know of a late thirteenth-century French work which maintains the bizarre belief that the substance of God is to be found in the light above the firmament and in the air. The sun is nothing more than a moving window in the firmament, and what we see when we look at it is therefore the very substance of the deity. It is more than a little disconcerting to find a medieval Hebrew text that routinely refers to "the air, blessed be it [He?] and blessed be its [His?] name," but in this case at least, the author describes himself as the object of persecution, and he was no doubt on the theological margins of Ashkenazic Judaism despite the fact that he may have been the author of a rabbinic responsum. Nonetheless, in the late fourteenth or early fifteenth century, an Ashkenazic rabbi was still asking the basic question about the corporeality of God, and there can be little doubt that Ashkenaz in the high Middle Ages did not enjoy a consensus on this most critical of theological questions.[65] Thus, the presence of anthropomorphic conceptions among some medieval Jews provided the rationalists with a powerful religious argument for philosophical inquiry and even enabled them to reverse the accusation of heresy. Ironically, as the philosophers won their greatest victory, they destroyed the most effective argument for their importance.

For Taku, the major obstacle to the rejection of anthropomorphism was not only the plain meaning of biblical expressions; he was concerned to at least an equal degree with a multitude of Rabbinic texts which he was unwilling to interpret nonliterally. In this and other contexts, conclusions drawn from philosophy and the sciences forced medieval Jews to confront the question of *aggadah* on a fundamental level, so that these pursuits once again impinged upon the study of Torah even in the narrowest sense. We have already seen that Geonim like R. Samuel b. Hofni and R. Hai had legitimated rejection of certain *aggadot*, although

---

64   *Ozar Nehmad* 3 (1860): 82-83.
65   See Israel Ta-Shema, "Sefer ha-Maskil: Hibbur Yehudi Zarfati Bilti-Yadua mi-sof ha-Me'ah ha-Yod-Gimel," *Mehqerei Yerushalayim be-Mahashevet Yisrael* 2:3 (1982-83): 416-438; Ephraim Kupfer, "Li-Demutah ha-Tarbutit shel Yahadut Ashkenaz va-Hakhameha ba-Me'ot ha-Yod-Dalet-ha-Tet-Vav," *Tarbiz* 42 (1972/73): 114.

R. Hai had insisted on the need to make the most strenuous efforts to validate all Rabbinic statements, particularly if they are incorporated in the Babylonian Talmud. The need to reinterpret rather than reject outright was especially acute with respect to an issue like anthropomorphism, where the error was too profound to allow it to stand even as a minority view among the Rabbis. Consequently, by the time of Maimonides and the Maimonidean controversy, substantial precedent existed for a variety of approaches to aggadic texts.[66]

The issue of *aggadah* had already been raised by opponents of Maimonides in the debate over resurrection just after the turn of the thirteenth century, and the Northern French rabbis in the 1230s once again expressed concern. They believed that Maimonides had undermined the traditional understanding of reward after death and specifically criticized his rejection of a literal feast of Leviathan as described in Rabbinic *aggadot*. It is of no small interest that while one defense of Maimonides argued that he had not in fact denied that this banquet would take place, Abraham Maimonides sardonically observed that the Rabbis had proffered this promise so that naïve believers like R. Solomon of Montpellier would have something to look forward to. On a more significant level, Maimonides' assertion that the biblical punishment of *cutting off* (*karet*) signifies the destruction of the soul was attacked as a contradiction of the talmudic perception that it refers to premature death. Maimonides' critics proceeded to denounce those who abandon "*halakhot* and *aggadot*, which are the source of life, to pursue Greek wisdom, which the sages forbade." The point here is not merely the choice of one pursuit over another, but the manner in which the study of the one distorts the understanding of the other. According to a Maimonist report, some of the Ashkenazim went so far as to propose that Rashi's interpretation of *aggadot* be made dogmatically binding.[67]

---

[66]   On Taku, see his *Ketav Tamim: Ketav Yad Paris H711*, with an introduction by Joseph Dan (Jerusalem, 1984), Introduction, p. 24. On the Geonim, see above, n. 16. For a survey of attitudes toward *aggadah*, see Marc Saperstein, *Decoding the Rabbis* (Cambridge, Mass., and London, England, 1980), pp. 1-20, and cf. I. Twersky, "R. Yeda'yah ha-Penini u-Perusho la-Aggadah," in *Studies in Jewish Religious and Intellectual History Presented to Alexander Altmann*, ed. by S. Stein and R. Loewe (University, Alabama, 1979), Heb. sec., pp. 63-82. See also Lester A. Segal, *Historical Consciousness and Religious Tradition in Azariah de Rossi's Meor 'Einayim* (Philadelphia, 1989), pp. 89-114.

[67]   See Saporta, *Qevuzat Mikhtavim*, p. 94; *Milhamot Hashem*, pp. 60-61; Joseph Shatzmiller, "Li-Temunat... ," *Zion* 34 (1969): 139; idem, "Iggarto... ," in *Mehqarim... Avineri*, p. 139.

The centrality of this issue is illustrated not only by the citations of various midrashic passages in the heat of the controversy but by Abraham Maimonides' special treatise on the *aggadot*, which undoubtedly emerged from these debates. This treatise not only proposes reinterpretation but recognizes the occasional need for outright rejection as well. "We are not obligated... to argue on behalf of the Rabbis and uphold the views expressed in all their medical, scientific, and astronomical statements, [and to believe] them the way we believe them with respect to the interpretation of the Torah, whose consummate wisdom was in their hands."[68] The essence of this position had already been expressed in the *Guide* itself. Although Maimonides had argued that respect for the wisdom of the Sages requires us to strive to understand even their scientific assertions as consonant with the truth, he nonetheless laid down the following principle:

> Do not ask of me to show that everything they have said concerning astronomical matters conforms to the way things really are. For at that time mathematics were imperfect. They did not speak about this as transmitters of dicta of the prophets, but rather because in those times they were men of knowledge in these fields or because they had heard these dicta from the men of knowledge who lived in those times.[69]

Despite the apparent effort to impose Rashi's presumably literal understanding of *aggadot*, even Ashkenazic Jews were not wholly inflexible on this issue. Moses Taku himself indicated that his teachers had distinguished between Rabbinic statements that appear in the Talmud and those that do not. "If a person sees a strange remark in external [Rabbinic] books, he should not be concerned about it since it does not appear in the *aggadot* in our Talmud upon which we rely." Several disagreements with the Rabbis appear in the admittedly atypical *Sefer ha-Maskil*, and under the pressure of polemics with an apostate attacking the Talmud, R. Yehiel of Paris observed, if only for the sake of argument, that the *aggadah* does not have the same binding force as talmudic law.[70]

Note too Charles Touati's remarks in, "Les Deux Conflits autour de Maimonide et des Études Philosophiques," in *Juifs et Judaism de Languedoc*, ed. by M. H. Vicaire and B. Blumenkranz (Toulouse, 1977), p. 177.

68 *Ma'amar 'al Odot Derashot Hazal*, in *Milhamot Hashem*, p. 84.
69 *Guide* 3:14.
70 *Ketav Tamim*, Paris ms., p. 7b; *Ozar Nehmad* 3, p. 63; Ta-Shema, "Sefer ha-Maskil," p.

The most famous medieval assertion that aggadic statements are not binding also emerged out of the crucible of the Jewish-Christian debate, this time from a figure who played a crucial role in the Maimonidean controversy of the 1230s. In 1263, Nahmanides faced a different apostate who attempted to utilize Talmudic evidence for the purpose of demonstrating the truth of Christianity; in their disputation, Nahmanides argued that midrashic statements should be treated as sermons which command respect but not unqualified assent. The sincerity of that argument has been the subject of controversy to our own day, but an analysis of Nahmanides' commentary to the Torah leaves little doubt that he meant what he said.[71] Many medieval Jews wished to preserve considerable latitude in dealing with *aggadah*, and although a variety of motives were at work, philosophical considerations took pride of place.

Nahmanides' role in the controversy and his stand regarding philosophical speculation are especially important both because his efforts appear to have effectively ended the Northern French intervention and because he represents a crucial transitional type in the evolution of medieval Jewish attitudes toward general culture. On the one hand, he was hardly typical of the Andalusian-style Jewish philosopher. He expressed considerable hostility toward "the accursed Greek" Aristotle, described himself as a disciple of the Northern French Tosafists, and fully embraced the "hidden wisdom" of the kabbalah. On the other hand, he mastered the corpus of Jewish philosophical and scientific literature, practiced

429; *Vikkuah R. Yehiel mi-Paris*, ed. by S. Gruenbaum (Thorn, 1873), p. 2. See also the citation in Avraham Grossman, *Hakhmei Ashkenaz ha-Rishonim* (Jerusalem, 1981), p. 96, for Rabbenu Gershom's opposition to a deviation from a rabbinic interpretation on a nonlegal matter in a liturgical poem by a distinguished colleague. This may be at least a faint indication that some Jews in early Ashkenaz considered such deviations legitimate. It is, of course, a commonplace that twelfth-century Northern French exegetes proposed interpretations that deviated from those of the rabbis even on matters of law.

[71] See *Kitvei Ramban* I, p. 308, and Bernard Septimus's excellent, though preliminary discussion in "'Open Rebuke and Concealed Love': Nahmanides and the Andalusian Tradition," in *Rabbi Moses Nahmanides*, pp. 20-22. Marvin Fox, "Nahmanides on the Status of Aggadot: Perspectives on the Disputation at Barcelona, 1263," *Journal of Jewish Studies* 40 (1989): 95-109, reaches a conclusion with which I am in fundamental agreement, although I cannot endorse several of his arguments. On one occasion (p. 101), he perpetuates a blurring of the distinction between rejection of *aggadah* and its allegorization; see my remarks in "Maccoby's *Judaism on Trial*," *Jewish Quarterly Review* 76 (1986): 255, n. 2.

medicine, and pursued a sort of golden mean during the Maimonidean controversy. His extraordinary commentary on the Pentateuch, which mobilized the full range of his diverse interests, defies neat classification into any prior category of Jewish exegesis or thought.

In an oft-quoted passage from his *Sha'ar ha-Gemul*, a work that addresses the problem of theodicy, he denounces people who oppose any inquiry into the nature of divine justice as "fools who despise wisdom. For we shall benefit ourselves in the above-mentioned study by becoming wise men who know God in the manner in which He acts and in His deeds; furthermore, we shall become believers endowed with a stronger faith in Him than others." Despite the vigor of this formulation and its similarity to arguments for philosophical study in general, it is important to recognize that in Nahmanides' case it is narrowly focused. Speculation about theodicy differs from investigation into the existence or unity of God in a way that illuminates Nahmanides' fundamental approach to philosophical pursuits. A good philosopher speculates on the basis of empirical data. But the revelation of the Torah is an empirical datum par excellence; consequently, there is no more point in constructing proofs for doctrines explicitly taught in the revelation than for the proposition that the sun rises in the morning. At the same time, philosophical reasoning for the purpose of clarifying those doctrines is not only sensible but critically important. Although Nahmanides never formulated this position explicitly, I think that it emerges from the pattern of his work and the issues that he addressed. It surely helps to explain why he wrote his magnum opus as a commentary to the revelation and why he was attracted to kabbalah, which provided, as we have seen, revealed information about key philosophical questions.

This nuanced approach placed Nahmanides in a difficult position during the controversy of the 1230s. He opposed both untrammeled speculation and "fools who despise wisdom"; he admired both Maimonides and the rabbis of Northern France; he felt unreserved enthusiasm for "The Book of Knowledge" and mixed emotions about the *Guide*. His own sophisticated synthesis of speculation and revelation, even in its exoteric form, could not be mechanically prescribed to the masses or, for that matter, to ordinary intellectuals. Consequently, the proposal that he made is a combination of tactful diplomacy and an effort to implement the values that he considered particularly important under the trying circumstances of the dispute.

His most important letter was directed to the rabbis of Northern France. It expresses great admiration for the addressees, defends Maimonides' orthodoxy with respect to key theological issues, explains the purpose of the *Guide*, whose intended audience needs to be appreciated by the Ashkenazim, and launches into a vigorous, even impassioned encomium to "The Book of Knowledge." At this point, Nahmanides was prepared to offer a concrete proposal: The ban against "The Book of Knowledge" should be annulled, and the ban against the *Guide* should be reformulated to include public study only, which Maimonides himself had disapproved. In the spirit of R. Hai Gaon's letter, the pursuit of philosophy should be discouraged entirely, but since such a level of piety cannot be enforced for all of Israel, no broader ban is advisable.

The distinction between "The Book of Knowledge" and the *Guide* accords well with Nahmanides' fundamental outlook because the former operates within the context of the revelation while the latter raises questions that approach the tradition from the outside. The difference, then, is as much one of structure as of content. The discouragement of any philosophical study even for the elite goes beyond Nahmanides' position as it appears in his other writings, and it is likely that he adopted it because of the needs of the moment. Nonetheless, this proposal too reflects a genuine uneasiness with speculation and hostility toward the dominant form of Aristotelianism. Nahmanides, who sought not so much a religious philosophy as a philosophical religion, embodies an approach that is reflected to a greater or lesser degree in figures like R. Meir Abulafia and R. Judah Alfakar and in some of his great successors among the Talmudists of Christian Spain.[72]

---

[72] For a full exposition of my perception of Nahmanides' position, see my master's essay, *Nahmanides' Attitude Toward Secular Learning and Its Bearing Upon his Stance in the Maimonidean Controversy* (Columbia University, 1965). See also my "Miracles and the Natural Order in Nahmanides" (above, n. 47), pp. 110-111, and Septimus, "'Open Rebuke and Concealed Love'" (above, n. 71). For brief characterizations of Nahmanides, see my articles in *The Encyclopedia of Religion* 10 (New York, 1987), pp. 295-297, and in *Great Figures in Jewish History* (in Russian [translated by the editorial staff]), ed. by Joseph Dan and Judy Baumel (Tel Aviv, 1991), pp. 77-84. On Abulafia, see Septimus, *Hispano-Jewish Culture in Transition*, which also contains an insightful typology of approaches to philosophical study in this period. See also his "Piety and Power in Thirteenth-Century Catalonia," *Studies in Jewish History and Literature* [1], pp. 197-230, for an effort to reconstruct a struggle between rationalists and Talmudists of Nahmanides' type for political control of a Jewish community.
The interpretation of Nahmanides' proposal is dependent on the resolution of textual

The waning of this phase of the controversy used to be attributed primarily to nearly universal revulsion at the burning of Maimonides' works. We now have reason to believe that Nahmanides' letter played a major role by persuading the Northern French rabbis to withdraw from the fray.[73] In any event, despite an eruption in the 1280s involving a relatively minor anti-Maimonist agitator, the dispute about philosophical study did not regain its status as a cause célèbre until the first decade of the fourteenth century, when the issue was joined again. In many ways, the debate was unchanged, but in some respects it had been transformed in significant and revealing fashion.

The controversy began when R. Abba Mari of Lunel initiated a correspondence with R. Solomon ibn Adret (Rashba) to complain about the inroads made by extreme rationalism in Provence, especially in the person of Levi b. Abraham of Villefranche, who advocated an allegorical understanding of some biblical narratives. The first thing that strikes the reader of Abba Mari's work is the impact of philosophy in general and Maimonides in particular on this "antirationalist." Science and metaphysics should be studied only by one

> who has filled his stomach with bread and meat, as we have learned from the Rabbi, the teacher of righteousness, from whose mouth we live through his true statements... built upon the foundation of the Torah in "The Book of Knowledge" and *Guide of the Perplexed*, which illuminate the path of those who have been in darkness and cannot adequately be evaluated by the greatest of assessors.[74]

It is true that even in the 1230s, many antirationalists treated Maimonides himself with considerable respect. We have already noted R.

---

    problems in the letter. This is not the place for a detailed discussion. Suffice it to say that the emendation of *tehazzequ* to *lo tehazzequ* (*Kitvei Ramban* 1, p. 349), which eliminates the ban entirely, is, in my view, insupportable. For details, see chapter 5 of my master's essay and my forthcoming article, "How did Nahmanides Propose to Resolve the Maimonidean Controversy?" [reprinted in this volume].

73   See the letter of the Maimonists in Lunel and Narbonne, *Zion* 34 (1969): 142, and the discussion by Schochet, *Zion* 36 (1971): 44.

74   *Minhat Qenaot*, Preface, p. 4 (unpaginated)=Dimitrovsky, 1, p. 228. For a summary of the events and arguments of the early fourteenth-century controversy, see Joseph Sarachek, *Faith and Reason* (Williamsport, Pennsylvania, 1935), pp. 167-264. Despite a variety of subsequent studies that will be noted later, Sarachek's work can still serve as a useful orientation to the dispute.

Solomon b. Abraham's reference to the study of the *Mishneh Torah* in his yeshivah, and Judah Alfakar had distinguished rather sharply between the author of the *Guide* and those who had made it into a new Torah. At the same time, Alfakar had written that he wished that the *Guide* had never seen the light of day, and Abba Mari's encomium to precisely the two works that were at issue in the earlier controversy is striking testimony to the status that Maimonides himself had attained among all parties to the new dispute.[75]

Not only did Abba Mari express unqualified admiration for Maimonides; he even defended no less a rationalist than Aristotle himself. In a passage about the importance of the belief in creation out of nothing, where Abba Mari was clearly echoing an argument of Nahmanides, he defended his predecessor's "accursed Greek" by noting that in the absence of the information provided by revelation, a gentile in antiquity could not have been expected to achieve an adequate level of understanding with respect to this issue. On the contrary, Aristotle deserves great credit for disseminating an accurate conception of the one God to a world rife with paganism. Moreover, Abba Mari's endorsement of Maimonides' assertion that creation from nothing cannot be proved philosophically served him as an explanation for the use of the term *hoq* as a designation of the law of the Sabbath. The term is usually used for regulations whose reasons are unfathomable; in this case, the purpose of the law, which is to remind us of creation *ex nihilo*, is clear, but the belief itself cannot be demonstrated by human reason. Maimonidean philosophy has been integrated by a Provençal conservative into the warp and woof of his study of Torah.[76]

---

[75] For Alfakar, see *Qovez Teshuvot ha-Rambam* 3, pp. 2b-3a. On respect for Maimonides during the controversy of the early fourteenth century, see the remarks by Charles Touati, "La Controverse de 1303-1306 autour des études philosophiques et scientifiques," *Revue des Études Juives* 127 (1968): 23-24.

[76] *Minhat Qenaot*, Introduction, ch. 13-14, pp. 14-15=Dimitrovsky, pp. 255-258. On Abba Mari's philosophical orientation, see A. S. Halkin, "Yedaiah Bedershi's Apology," in *Jewish Medieval and Renaissance Studies*, ed. by Altmann, p. 178; "Ha-Herem 'al Limmud ha-Pilosofiah," *Peraqim* 1 (1967-8): 48-49.

The intriguing transformation of Nahmanides' argument into a defense of Aristotle deserves brief elaboration. The original point was that miracles demonstrate creation *ex nihilo* because God would not have limitless control over matter as primeval as He. Since miracles are an empirical datum that became well known throughout the world, the affirmation of the eternity of matter by "the accursed Greek" is a denial of his own vaunted empiricism. Abba Mari accepts the argument with one small correction: miracles

Abba Mari provoked sharp disagreement from Rashba when he asserted that gentile philosophical works are not harmful since everyone recognizes their provenance. Since the legitimacy of Maimonides' treatises was surely not at issue, Abba Man's ire was narrowly focused on what he perceived as the heretical teachings of the Jewish hyperrationalists. As he reports the situation, people like Levi b. Abraham understood Abraham and Sarah as matter and form, the twelve tribes as the twelve constellations, the alliances of four and five kings in Genesis 14 as the four elements and the five senses, and Amalek as the evil inclination.[77]

Such accusations about rationalist allegorization appear in various works during the thirteenth and fourteenth centuries. Even more seriously, we find the assertion that certain rationalists regarded verbal prayer as superfluous and did not observe various commandments either because they allegorized them or thought that they could fulfill their underlying purpose in a different manner. Thus, R. Jacob b. Sheshet maintained that contemporary heretics, in a fashion strikingly reminiscent of Christian polemic against Judaism, argued, "What is the purpose of this particular commandment? Reason cannot abide it. It must have been nothing but an allegory." Elsewhere, Jacob is quoted to the effect that in addition to heresies regarding primeval matter, divine providence, and reward and punishment, these rationalists assert that the purification of one's thoughts is a more than adequate substitute for prayer. Moses de Leon alleged that the adherents of "the books of the Greeks" do not observe the commandment of taking the four species on the festival of Sukkot because, they say, the reason the Torah provides is that this will enhance the joy of the holiday; well, they are happier with their gold, silver, and clothing than they could possibly be with the four species.[78]

---

are attested in a revelation granted to the Jewish people that was not in fact widely known in Aristotle's world. Hence, although Nahmanides is correct that creation *ex nihilo* can be proven, the demonstration depends on the knowledge of miracles, which is, or at least was, specifically Jewish knowledge; Maimonides is correct that the doctrine cannot be proven in a philosophical system uninformed by revelation. From this perspective, Nahmanides' position is not an indictment of Aristotle but an exculpation. For a similar view of Aristotle by a somewhat earlier figure, see Septimus's citation of Judah ibn Matka's *Midrash Hokhmah*, in *Hispano-Jewish Culture in Transition*, p. 97.

77   *Minhat Qenaot*, letter 7, pp. 40-41=Dimitrovsky, ch. 25, pp. 343-344, and elsewhere.

78   For Jacob b. Sheshet, see his *Meshiv Devarim Nekhohim*, ed. by Georges Vajda (Jerusalem, 1968), p. 145, and the citation in Isaac of Acre, *Sefer Me'irat 'Einayim*, ed. by Goldreich, pp. 58-61. For de Leon, see his *Book of the Pomegranate*, ed. by Elliot Wolfson (Atlanta, 1988), p. 391.

During the controversy, we hear occasional references to a refusal to wear *tefillin* because of a philosophically motivated rejection of the commandment's literal meaning and even to wholesale allegorization of biblical law. In these extreme cases, however, the indictments appear to reflect the behavior of isolated individuals or even what the critic perceived as the logical consequence or underlying intention of the philosophical position. One allegation about *tefillin* refers to a single person, and Rashba is clearly describing a teaching that was not made explicit when he observes that "it is evident that their true intention is that the commandments are not to be taken literally, for why should God care about the difference between torn and properly slaughtered meat? Rather, all is allegory and parable." Although such claims are not entirely unfounded, the statement that the villains in this indictment "have regarded the Torah and its commandments as false, and everything has become permitted to them" was clearly a deduction. Indeed, Rashba explicitly asserts that the hyperrationalists maintain that everything in the Torah is allegory from Genesis until—but not beyond—the revelation at Sinai; nonetheless, he says, it is evident that they really have no faith in the plain meaning of the commandments either.[79]

As a result of these concerns, Rashba issued a ban which itself reflects the changes in this issue since the 1230s. Unlike Nahmanides, Rashba was sufficiently concerned by the spread of rationalist extremism that he was prepared to go beyond the very narrow ban advocated by his

---

[79] On *tefillin*, see *Minhat Qenaot*, letter 79, p. 152=Dimitrovsky, ch. 88, p. 721, which bans anyone who understands the commandments in a purely spiritual sense, and cf. letter p. 153=Dimitrovsky, ch. 101, p. 735, where it is fairly clear that the concern was based on a specific statement made by a particular rationalist. Cf. also letter 7, p. 41=Dimitrovsky, ch. 25, p. 344. The passage in *The Book of the Pomegranate* cited in the previous note continues with the allegation that these reprobates also fail to wear *tefillin* because they understand the commandment in a spiritual sense. For the more general assertions, see *Minhat Qenaot*, letter 20, p. 60=Dimitrovsky, ch. 38, pp. 411-412, and letter 10, p. 45=Dimitrovsky, ch. 28, p. 360. The last assertion is in a text that was distributed in connection with the ban; see Dimitrovsky, ch. 100, p. 727. On neglect of *tefillin*, see the references in Isadore Twersky, *Rabad of Posquières* (Cambridge, Mass., 1962), p. 24, n. 20. See also Ephraim Kanarfogel, "Rabbinic Attitudes toward Nonobservance in the Medieval Period," in *Jewish Tradition and the Nontraditional Jew*, ed. by Jacob J. Schacter (Northvale, New Jersey and London, 1992), pp. 3-35, esp. 7-12; the issues there, however, are not philosophical. At the eleventh World Congress of Jewish Studies in 1993, Aviezer Ravitsky described a hitherto unknown commentary on the *Guide* by a Samuel of Carcassonne, who indicated quite clearly that the philosopher need not observe commandments whose purpose he regards as no longer relevant.

predecessor and to forbid the study of philosophy and some sciences by anyone who had not reached the age of twenty-five. On the other hand, the works of Maimonides were entirely exempted from the prohibition during subsequent discussions clarifying its scope; the only reason this remains in some sense a "Maimonidean controversy" is that the targets of the ban made what Rashba and Abba Mari considered blatantly illegitimate use of Maimonides' works to justify their heresies. Though the distinction between Maimonides and his followers had been made earlier, it is now far sharper and more fundamental. Thus, when modern scholars who see Maimonides as a philosophical radical tell us that the people attacked by Abba Mari were no more dangerous than Maimonides himself, they impose a reading of the Maimonidean corpus which the proponents of the ban did not share.[80]

The validity of the conservatives' perception of Maimonides is, of course, only one side of the coin; the other is the validity of their perceptions of the Maimonists. We have already seen that even the evidence of the antirationalist pronouncements suggests that assertions of wholesale rejection of the commandments by more than a handful of rationalists may be exaggerated. The vigorous response to the ban provides us with a substantial set of arguments for the religious orthodoxy of the philosophers and for the value of the maligned philosophical enterprise. The most extensive of these polemics that remains extant is the apology for philosophy addressed to Rashba himself by R. Yedaiah Bedershi.[81]

Though the work is written in a tone of extreme reverence for the addressee, it concedes virtually nothing to the allegations leveled in the ban. A handful of Provençal Jews may deserve censure for publicizing philosophical teachings best left to the elite, but the content of these teachings is untainted by heresy. The reports of allegorization of biblical narratives and commandments are wholly false; at most, one philosopher is known to have argued that the correspondence between the number of tribes and the number of constellations demonstrates that the Jewish people is bound by the stars, but even this deplorable position takes the reality of the twelve tribes for granted.

---

[80] Touati, "La Controverse," pp. 23-24; A. S. Halkin, "Why Was Levi ben Hayyim Hounded?," *Proceedings of the American Academy for Jewish Research* 24 (1966): 65-77.

[81] See Halkin's articles cited in n. 76. The text appears as *Ketav Hitnazzelut, She'elot u-Teshuvot ha-Rashba* (Bnei Braq, 1958), 1:418, pp. 154-174, and was separately edited by S. Bloch (Lvov, 1809).

Moreover, says Yedaiah, the study of philosophy has overwhelming religious value. It provides proof of the existence and unity of God; demonstrates the falsehood of determinism, magic, and metempsychosis; establishes the truth of prophecy and the spiritual character of the immortal soul; and distinguishes between impossibilities that can be rendered possible through miracles and those which even divine omnipotence itself cannot overturn. First and foremost, philosophy has extirpated what was once the epidemic of anthropomorphism. Here Yedaiah's formulation is extraordinarily strong:

> In the early generations, the corporeal conception of God spread through virtually the entire Jewish exile... ; however, in all the generations there arose Geonim and wise men in Spain, Babylonia, and the cities of Andalusia, who, because of their expertise in the Arabic language, encountered the great preparatory knowledge that comes with smelling the scent of the various forms of wisdom, whether to a greater or lesser degree, which have been translated into that language. Consequently, they began to clarify many opinions in their study of Torah, especially with respect to the unity of God and the rejection of corporeality, with particular use of philosophical proofs taken from the speculative literature.[82]

The issue of tradition versus philosophical innovation emerges in even bolder relief than it did in Maimonides' discussion of anthropomorphism. Although Yedaiah explicitly denies that the ancient Rabbis were anthropomorphists, he sees the attaining of a purified conception of God in the Middle Ages as an achievement of a philosophical enterprise unaided by tradition but crucially dependent upon familiarity with Arabic texts. The very essence of the Torah, largely lost through the travails of exile, was restored through the discipline which the antirationalists would now undermine.

Once again we find the advocates of philosophy referring to non-Jews in an effort to legitimate speculation. Jacob ben Makhir pointed to

> the most civilized nations who translate learned works from other languages into their own... and who revere learning.... Has any nation changed its religion because of this?... How much less likely is that to happen to us, who possess a rational Torah.[83]

---

[82] *She'elot u-Teshvot ha-Rashba* 1, p. 166.
[83] Cited in Yitzhak Baer, *A History of the Jews in Christian Spain* 1 (Philadelphia, 1961), p. 296.

Jacob's reference to the rationality of Judaism carries significance that goes beyond the specific point in this text. The fact that these discussions now take place in a Christian rather than a Muslim context means that the conviction that Judaism is more rational than its rival can be mobilized to enhance the importance of philosophical study by pointing to its value as a polemical tool. When a Jew justified speculation on the grounds of its usefulness in replying to heretics, the reference was not necessarily to Christians; nonetheless, when Bedershi tells us that one advantage of setting criteria for the possibility of miracles is that it enables us to rule out God's ability to make Himself corporeal, the implications for anti-Christian polemic are self-evident. R. Israel b. Joseph, a fourteenth-century Spanish rabbi who studied with R. Asher ben Yehiel, vigorously supported the study of "external disciplines" solely on the basis of their value in supplying "answers to those who err" and providing the ability "to defeat them in their arguments." Here too, while those who err no doubt included philosophical heretics, it is hard to imagine that R. Israel was not also thinking of the utility of philosophy for vanquishing the arguments of Christian missionaries. Hasdai Crescas' *Bittul 'Iqqarei ha-Nozerim* constitutes eloquent testimony to the importance of philosophical sophistication for the late medieval Jewish polemicist in Spain, and it can be asserted with full confidence that no Jewish reader of that work could have come away from it with the slightest doubt that at least some Jews ought to study philosophy.[84]

In light of the usefulness of philosophy for anti-Christian polemic, it is ironic and intriguing that the desire to convert Jews impelled the governor of Montpellier to take the side of the rationalists at the height of the controversy. The advocates of philosophy had issued a counterban against

[84]   For R. Israel b. Joseph ha-Yisre'eli's remarks, see his commentary to *Avot* 2:14, cited in Israel Ta-Shema, "Shiqqulim Pilosofiyyim be-Hakhra'at ha-Halakhah bi-Sefarad," *Sefunot* 18 (1985): 105. R. Israel noted that these external disciplines cannot be approached safely before the reader has become a mature Talmudic scholar; hence, the rabbis forbade one to teach *higgayon* or Greek wisdom to one's son. The thrust of his observation, however, is permissive: It is prohibited for the father to teach his son, but it is permissible for the father to study on his own. See Saul Lieberman, *Hellenism in Jewish Palestine* (New York, 1962), pp. 102-104. On Crescas, see *Bittul 'Iqqarei ha-Nozerim*, ed. by Daniel J. Lasker (Ramat Gan, 1990), or Lasker's *Jewish Philosophical Polemics Against Christianity in the Middle Ages* (New York, 1977). On the use of more rigorous philosophical arguments for polemical purposes, see also Shalom Rosenberg, *Logiqah ve-Ontologiah ba-Pilosophiah ha-Yehudit ba-Me'ah ha-Yod-Dalet* (Hebrew University dissertation, 1974), p. 44. On answering heretics, see also n. 54 above.

anyone who would refuse to teach the banned disciplines to people under the age of twenty-five in obedience to the antirationalists' proclamation, and they sought legal backing from the civil authorities. Abba Mari informs us that although the governor did not grant all their requests, he lent some support because he was convinced that if Jews were to prohibit anything but Talmudic study for a substantial period of a person's life, this would create a situation in which no Jew would ever convert to Christianity.[85]

There is strong reason to believe that a majority of the Jews in Montpellier sided with the rationalists.[86] The philosophical culture of

[85] The phrase that I have translated "talmudic study" literally means "the discipline (*hokhmah*) that you call Gamaliel" (*Minhat Qenaot*, letter 73, p. 142=Dimitrovsky, ch. 92, p. 701). For the identification of "Gamaliel" with Talmud, see Heinrich Graetz, *Geschichte der Juden* (Leipzig, 1863), 7, p. 276; Ch. Merchavia, *Ha-Talmud bi-Re'i ha-Nazrut* (Jerusalem, 1970), p. 211, and Dimitrovsky, ad loc. ("apparently this refers to the Talmud"). For the view that "Gamaliel" means medicine, see David Kaufmann, *Die Sinne* (Budapest, 1884), p. 7, n. 12; D. Margalit, "'Al Galenus ve-Gilgulo ha-'Ivri Gamliel," *Sinai* 33 (1953) : 75-77; Judah Rosenthal's review of Merchavia, *Kiryat Sefer* 47 (1972): 29; Joseph Shatzmiller, "Bein Abba Mari la-Rashba: ha-Massa ve-ha-Mattan she-qadam la-Herem be-Barcelona," *Mehqarim be-Toledot 'Am Yisrael ve-Erez Yisrael* 3 (Haifa, 1974), p. 127. I cannot see why a Christian would find it necessary to describe medicine by its presumed Jewish name, especially since the ban does not call it Gamaliel, or even why the exclusion of medicine would need to be mentioned at all in this context. The fact that this would constitute the only attested use of Gamaliel in so broad a sense also militates against the identification. It is true that Talmud was not normally called a *hokhmah*, but in the context of this ban, I can easily see a Christian using the equivalent term, presumably *scientia*. Moreover, the Christian argument that the study of rabbinic literature is an impediment to conversion is attested as far back as Justinian's Novella 146 and was reiterated in the 1240s by Odo of Chateauroux. For Justinian, see the text and translation in Amnon Linder, *The Jews in Roman Imperial Legislation* (Jerusalem, 1987), pp. 405-410; for Odo, see the text in Merchavia, p. 450 (". . . hanc esse causam precipuam que iudeos in sua perfidia retinet obstinatos"). Because the motive assigned by Abba Mari is so congenial to his own position in the controversy, we must read it with some skepticism; note Kaufmann's remark (loc. cit.) that the antirationalist Yosef Yavetz would have given a great deal to have known this quotation. In light of Odo's assertion, however, the report is entirely plausible.
Note too Kaufmann's argument that philosophical allegory may have been influenced by Christian allegory and that this connection led to the hope for conversion through philosophical study; see his "Simeon b. Josefs Sendschreiben an Menachem b. Salomo," in *Jubelschrift zum Neunzigsten Geburtstag des Dr. L. Zunz* (Berlin, 1884), German section, p. 147. I doubt that Christian influence on rationalist allegorizarion was decisive, and the main point appears to have been that talmudic study retards conversion.
On the counterban and the governor, see the references in Marc Saperstein, "The Conflict over the Rashba's Herem on Philosophical Study: A Political Perspective," *Jewish History* 1:2 (1986): 37, n. 19.

[86] Shatzmiller has argued this point persuasively in "Bein Abba Mari la-Rashba," pp. 128-130.

Provençal Jewry was so pervasive that rationalist sermons were delivered in synagogues and even at weddings. Opposition to the ban came from the distinguished Perpignan Talmudist R. Menahem ha-Meiri, who argued that spiritual damage to a handful of people cannot be allowed to undermine entire fields of study, that even the books of the Greeks have great religious value, that Jews cannot allow gentiles to mock them for their intellectual backwardness, and that Provence can boast a variety of figures who have distinguished themselves in both talmudic and philosophical learning. Here again the antirationalist party demonstrated how much the atmosphere had changed since the 1230s: The reply to ha-Meiri by a disciple of Abba Mari fully conceded the great value of philosophy and pointed out that the ban was directed only at the young.[87]

Ha-Meiri himself was a paradigm of the ideal toward which moderate rationalists strove and to which even extreme rationalists paid lip service: a Talmudist of standing who valued philosophy and the sciences and devoted himself to their study. Ha-Meiri's openness to general culture combined with his well-known attitude of toleration toward Christianity suggests an additional dimension of the issue that we have been addressing. Intellectual involvement with the dominant society often goes hand in hand with social involvement of a relatively benign sort. By this time, Christian intellectuals had attained an impressive level of philosophical sophistication to the point where ha-Meiri could express concern about their contempt for ignorant Jews; consequently, familiarity began to breed respect. In ha-Meiri's case, this respect led to the formulation of a wholly novel halakhic category which roughly means civilized people, a category which helped to exempt Christians from a series of discriminatory Talmudic statements. While this is not a case of incorporating an external value or doctrine into Rabbinic law— the Christendom that ha-Meiri knew had hardly developed a theory of religious toleration—it probably is an instance of reexamining *halakhah* and Jewish values in light of habits of mind developed by exposure to a culture shared with the gentile environment. Once again, the core of the Torah was touched—or its deeper meaning revealed—through insights inspired by involvement in general culture.[88]

---

[87] See "Hoshen Mishpat," *Jubelschrift... Zunz,* Hebrew section, pp. 142-174. For the last point, see especially pp. 162-164.

[88] On ha-Meiri and Christianity, see Yaakov Blidstein, "Yahaso shel R. Menahem ha-Meiri la-Nokhri—Bein Apologetiqah le-Hafnamah," *Zion* 51 (1986): 153-166, and the earlier

THE SEPHARDIM OF THE LATE MIDDLE AGES

The affirmation of the value of philosophy even by the conservatives in this dispute reflects a critically important characteristic of late medieval Jewish culture in Provence and in Spain. Virtually without exception, rabbinic figures of the first rank, whose pursuit of Talmudic study was their central preoccupation, either devoted some time to the study of "wisdom" or expressed no opposition to its cultivation.[89]

Rashba himself was not uninfluenced by philosophical ideas. This would be evident even from Bedershi's apology, which clearly assumed that its recipient was receptive to the major thrust of the argument, but it is also explicit in Rashba's own writings. In one elaborate responsum, for example, he analyzed the parameters within which philosophical arguments can be brought to bear on the reinterpretation of sacred texts, and he staked out a position that we would expect from a disciple of Nahmanides: there is a legitimate place for such arguments as long as the critical demands of tradition are accorded unchallenged supremacy.[90] R. Yom Tov Ishbili (Ritba), perhaps the greatest rabbinic figure in the generation following Rashba, wrote a work exemplifying the same general posture. He defended Maimonides against the strictures in Nahmanides'

studies cited there. See now the important analysis by Moshe Halbertal, "R. Menahem ha-Meiri: Bein Torah le-Hokhmah," *Tarbiz* 63 (1994): 63-118, which points to a specific philosophical context for ha-Meiri's position.

[89] See Israel Ta-Shema's "Rabbi Yona Gerondi: Spiritualism and Leadership," presented at the Jewish Theological Seminary's 1989 conference on "Jewish Mystical Leadership, 1200-1270," esp. p. 11. A bound volume of typescripts of the proceedings is available in the Mendel Gottesman Library, Yeshiva University. See also Ta-Shema's "Halakhah, Kabbalah u-Pilosophiah bi-Sefarad ha-Nozerit—le-Biqqoret Sefer 'Toledot ha-Yehudim bi-Sefarad ha-Nozerit'," *Shenaton ha-Mishpat ha-'Ivri* 18-19 (1992-94): 479-495. For a balanced, moderate defense of a broad curriculum in fourteenth-century Spain, see Profiat Duran's introduction to *Ma'aseh Efod*, pp. 1-25.

[90] *She'elot u-Teshuvot ha-Rashba* (1958) 1:9, also edited by L. A. Feldman, *Shnaton Bar-Ilan* 7-8 (1970): 153-161. For a thorough analysis of Rashba's stance, see the unpublished master's thesis by David Horwitz, *The Role of Philosophy and Kabbalah in the Works of Rashba* (Bernard Revel Graduate School, Yeshiva University, 1986). See also Carmi Horowitz, "'Al Perush ha-Aggadot shel ha-Rashba—Bein Qabbalah le-Pilosophia," *Da'at* 18 (1987): 15-25, and Lawrence Kaplan, "Rabbi Solomon ibn Adret," *Yavneh Review* 6 (1967): 27-40. (I should probably not press the argument from Bedershi's perception too hard since *Ktav Hitnazzelut* takes for granted the questionable proposition that Rashba would recognize the value of philosophy because of its ability to refute the belief in metempsychosis, a kabbalistic doctrine that Rashba probably endorsed.)

commentary to the Pentateuch while at the same time affirming that in the final analysis Nahmanides is usually correct.[91]

The endorsement of at least a moderate level of rationalism no doubt resulted from the importance of philosophy in traditional Spanish Jewish culture, but we should not underestimate the impact of the heroic image of Maimonides. Just as Nahmanides' embrace of kabbalah made it very difficult to reject mysticism as a heresy, Maimonides' devotion to philosophy rendered its thorough delegitimation by Sephardic Jews almost impossible. Even some kabbalists attempted to synthesize their discipline with a reinterpreted Maimonidean corpus, though others went so far as to assert that the author of the *Guide* had seen the error of his ways once the secrets of the hidden wisdom were revealed to him. This last example is a rare case of the exception that really proves the rule, because it demonstrates that Maimonides' position stood as such a hallmark of legitimacy that some Jews could comfortably maintain a contrary position only by forcibly redefining the Maimonidean stance.[92]

Moderate rationalism was, of course, not the only approach endorsed by Provençal and Spanish Jews in the later Middle Ages. Despite the exaggerated nature of the conservative manifestoes issued during the controversy, some late medieval thinkers really did espouse radical positions with respect to many philosophical and exegetical issues. When Jacob b. Sheshet denounced rationalists who "assert that the world is primeval... , that divine providence does not extend below the sphere of the moon... , that there is no reward for the righteous or punishment for the wicked... and that there is no need to pray but only to purify one's thoughts,"[93] he was engaging in hyperbole but not in fantasy. The

---

[91]   See his *Sefer ha-Zikkaron*, ed. by Kalman Kahana (Jerusalem, 1956), pp. 33-34.

[92]   For Abraham Abulafia's effort to create a Maimonidean kabbalah, see sections IV-VI of Moshe Idel's "Maimonides and Kabbalah," in Twersky, *Studies in Maimonides*, pp. 54-78. On Maimonides as a kabbalist, see Gershom Scholem, "Me-Hoqer li-Mequbbal: Aggadot ha-Mequbbalim 'al ha-Rambam," *Tarbiz* 6 (1935): 90-98, and Michael A. Shmidman, "On Maimonides' 'Conversion' to Kabbalah," in *Studies in Medieval Jewish History and Literature*, ed. by Twersky, 2, pp. 375-386. For a discussion of this and similar legends in the broader context of folk conceptions about Maimonides, see the study by my father Isaiah Berger, "Ha-Rambam be-Aggadat ha-'Am," in *Massad: Me'assef le-Divrei Sifrut* 2, ed. by Hillel Bavli (Tel Aviv, 1936), pp. 216-238; and compare his eloquent observations on the contrast between the folk images of Maimonides and Rashi in his "Rashi be-Aggadat ha- 'Am," in *Rashi: Torato ve-Ishiyyuto*, ed. by Simon Federbush (New York, 1958), pp. 147-149.

[93]   Cited in *Me'irat 'Einayim*, ed. by Goldreich, p. 58.

rationalist propensity toward allegorization undoubtedly went beyond anything that rabbis like Rashba would countenance, and we should not allow the Maimonist arguments of Bedershi and his colleagues to blind us to this reality. The works of Samuel ibn Tibbon, Moses Narboni, Joseph ibn Kaspi, Gersonides, and Isaac Albalag constitute but part of a corpus of literature attesting to a flourishing tradition of vigorous rationalism that severely tested the prevailing boundaries of religious orthodoxy.

Philosophers of this stripe were often prepared to make an explicit case against excessive concentration in Talmudic study. The most famous example of this attitude is the story ibn Kaspi tells in his will about the problem that arose during a party in his home when "the accursed maid" placed a dairy spoon in a pot of meat. Poor ibn Kaspi had to go to the local rabbi, who kept him waiting for hours in a state of near starvation before apprising him of the *halakhah*. Nonetheless, he tells us, he was not embarrassed by his ignorance, since his philosophical sophistication compensated for the shortcomings in his halakhic expertise. "Why," he asks, "should a ruling or directive regarding the great existence or unity of God be inferior to a small dairy spoon?"[94]

Other expressions of this approach are less amusing but no less striking. Some Jews demonstrated the obscurantism of those who devote their lives to talmudic study by pointing to the Talmud's own assertion that the phrase "He has set me in dark places like the dead of old" (Lamentations 3:6) refers to the Talmud of Babylon. R. Judah ibn Abbas maintained that people who study Talmud constantly "neglect the proper service and knowledge of God" and described Talmudic novellae and *Tosafot* as a waste of valuable time. It is a matter of no small interest that Hasdai Crescas wrote his philosophical refutation of Christianity in Aragonese or Catalan so that Jews could have ready access to his arguments; there was thus a substantial, sophisticated Jewish audience in late medieval Spain who could follow a difficult vernacular text but not a difficult Hebrew one.

---

[94]   Israel Abrahams, *Hebrew Ethical Wills* 1 (Philadelphia, 1926), pp. 151-152. The somewhat awkward use of the term "great," which technically modifies *unity* in the original, is clearly intended to evoke Maimonides' straightforward understanding of the Talmudic contrast between great and small matters. See above, n. 39. On Ibn Kaspi's intellectual stance, see Isadore Twersky, "Joseph ibn Kaspi: Portrait of a Medieval Jewish Intellectual," in *Studies in Medieval Jewish History and Literature* [1], pp. 231-257.

Ibn Kaspi himself, in a work marked by the arresting assertion that Job's suffering was a just consequence of his failure to pursue a philosophical understanding of his faith, utilized the traditionalists' affirmation of the importance of Talmudic study to support the indispensability of philosophy. After all, he argued, there exist both physical commandments and commandments of the heart or intellect. Everyone agrees that with respect to the former, an understanding of the intellectual underpinning is eminently desirable. "Why else should we toil to study the Talmud? We might just as well be satisfied with the rulings of Maimonides and R. Isaac Alfasi." Now there is surely no basis for distinguishing the latter commandments from the former with respect to this principle, and books of physics and metaphysics stand in the same relationship to the commandments of the heart as the Talmud does to the physical commandments. Originally, such philosophical works were written by Jewish sages like Solomon, but "we were exiled because of our sins, and those matters have now come to be attributed to the Greeks" except for scattered references in the Talmud. In other words, one cannot affirm the critical importance of Talmudic study without being logically compelled to grant at least equal value to the pursuit of philosophy and the sciences.[95]

On the other side of the ledger, R. Asher b. Yehiel, who was born and trained in Germany, brought with him a pejorative attitude toward the value of general culture. In responding to the suggestion that no one without expertise in Arabic should render a legal decision, he maintained that his reasoning powers in Torah were in no way inferior to those

---

[95] On the "dark places" and the Talmud, see *Me'irat 'Einayim*, p. 62; Isadore Twersky, "Religion and Law," in *Religion in a Religious Age*, p. 77, and Twersky, "R. Yeda'yah ha-Penini," Altmann Festschrift, p. 71. The Talmudic passage is in *Sanhedrin* 24a. For Ibn Abbas, see Goldreich's quotations from the manuscript of *Ya'ir Nativ* (Oxford 1280, p. 50a) in *Me'irat 'Einayim*, pp. 412-413. The oft-quoted curriculum in ibn Abbas's work, which culminates with the study of metaphysics, was published by Asaf, *Meqorot* 2, pp. 29-33. On the vernacular original of *Bittul 'Iqqarei ha-Nozerim*, see Lasker's edition, pp. 13, 33. Note too the Castilian *Proverbos Morales* by the fourteenth-century R. Shem Tov ibn Ardutiel, *The Moral Proverbs of Santob de Carrion: Jewish Wisdom in Christian Spain*, ed. by T. A. Perry (Princeton, 1988).

If we contemplate for a moment the magnitude of Job's suffering, we can begin to appreciate the importance attached to the philosophic quest by a man willing to propose ibn Kaspi's explanation for such torment. This explanation appears along with the very clever argument linking Talmudic and philosophical study in *Shulhan Kesef: Be'ur 'al Iyyov*, in *'Asarah Kelei Kesef*, ed. by J. Last (Pressburg, 1903), pp. 170-172.

of Spanish Rabbis, "even though I do not know your external wisdom. Thank the merciful God who saved me from it." The pursuit of such wisdom, he said, leads people away from the fear of God and encourages the vain attempt to integrate alien pursuits with Torah. Still, even R. Asher describes philosophers as very wise men, and an assessment of Spanish Jewish attitudes would have to assign greater weight to the remarkable suggestion that he rejected than to the negative reaction that he expressed.[96]

That suggestion reflects a real and significant phenomenon: the halakhic decision-making and Talmudic study of Provençal and Spanish rabbis were sometimes affected by philosophical considerations. To begin with the most famous example in Maimonides himself, the omission in the *Mishneh Torah* of talmudic laws based on the intervention of the creatures that the rabbis called *shedim* was almost certainly the result of philosophically motivated skepticism. R. Zerahiah Halevi cited technical logical terminology and philosophical references in a halakhic discussion. Conceptions of providence were brought to bear on decisions regarding the remarriage of a woman whose first two husbands had died. A more general illustration of the pervasiveness of the philosophical atmosphere emerges from the first sentence of R. Yeruham b. Meshullam's introduction to a work of Talmudic scholarship, where he informs us how "the scholars of [philosophical] research" have classified the considerations leading to the pursuit of wisdom.[97]

---

[96]   See *She'elot u-Teshuvot ha-Rosh* (Venice, 1603), 55:9. Cf. Israel Ta-Shema, "Shiqqulim Pilosofiyyim," *Sefunot* 18 (1985): 100-108.

[97]   On the impact of Maimonides' attitude toward "popular religion" on the *Mishneh Torah*, see Twersky, *Introduction to the Code of Maimonides*, pp. 479-484; see especially Marc B. Shapiro's forthcoming essay in *Maimonidean Studies*. I am unpersuaded by Jose Faur's effort in his generally perceptive *'Iyyunim be-Mishneh Torah le-ha-Rambam: Sefer ha-Madda* (Jerusalem, 1978), pp. 1-2 n. 1, to minimize the philosophical motivation for the omission of *shedim*. For some observations on the impact of Maimonides' scientific posture on his halakhic approach, see Isadore Twersky, "Aspects of Maimonidean Epistemology: Halakhah and Science," in *From Ancient Israel to Modern Judaism: Intellect in Quest of Understanding. Essays in Honor of Marvin Fox*, ed. by Jacob Neusner, Ernest S. Frerichs, and Nachum M. Sarna (Atlanta, Georgia, 1989) 3, pp. 3-23. For R. Zerahiah Halevi, see I. Ta-Shema, "Sifrei ha-Rivot bein ha-Ravad le-bein Rabbi Zerahiah Halevi (ha-Razah) mi-Lunel," *Qiryat Sefer* (1977): 570-576. On the problem of remarriage, see Ta-Shema, *Sefunot* 18, p. 110, and Y. Buxbaum, "Teshuvot Hakhmei Sefarad be-Din Qatlanit," *Moriah* 7 [78/79] (1977): 6-7. R. Yeruham's comments are in *Sefer Mesharim* (Venice, 1553; rep., Jerusalem, 1975), p. 2a.

Most strikingly, it now appears that an innovative methodology of Talmudic study which conquered Spain in the fifteenth century and dominated the approach of Sephardic communities for two hundred years was rooted in philosophical logic. R. Isaac Kanpanton produced guidelines which required the student to investigate the correspondence between the language and meaning of a Talmudic text with exquisite care and to determine the full range of possible interpretations so that the exegetical choices of the major commentators would become clear. In setting forth this form of investigation, or *'iyyun*, Kanpanton made explicit reference to logical terminology, and Daniel Boyarin has recently made a compelling argument that the system as a whole and all its major components originated in the medieval philosophical milieu. He maintains that

> Jewish scholars in the final days of the Spanish Jewish community saw logic as the road to attaining truth in all sciences, including that of the Torah. Any argument which did not qualify under the canons of logical order was faulty in their eyes. Logical works and principles served as the foundation for scientific and philosophical investigation, and they pointed the way toward valid proof and the avoidance of error in these fields. Since the science of the Talmud differed in its language and its problems from the other sciences—mainly because it is essentially exegetical—the need was felt for general works specific to this field which would direct investigation there.[98]

These were indeed the final days of Spanish Jewry, and the connection between philosophical pursuits and the behavior of the community in extremis has exercised analysts both medieval and modern. Conservatives like R. Isaac Arama renewed the attack against allegorists by asking why they need the Torah at all. When it corresponds to philosophical truths, they accept it literally, and when it does not, they explain it figuratively; in either case, the knowledge they had before the revelation is coterminous with what they know after it. R. Yosef Yavetz attributed the relatively large number of conversions around the time of the expulsion to the corrupting influence of philosophical relativism, a

---

[98] Daniel Boyarin, *Ha-'Iyyun ha-Sefaradi* (Jerusalem, 1989), pp. 48-49. The main documentation of Boyarin's general thesis is on pp. 47-68. For a similar development in the field of biblical exegesis, see Shimon Shalem, "Ha-Metodah ha-Parshanit shel Yosef Taitazak ve-Hugo," *Sefunot* 11 (1971-77): 115-134.

judgment endorsed in the twentieth century by Yitzhak Baer. R. Abraham Bibago, on the other hand, writing in the middle of the fifteenth century, denied that philosophically oriented Jews were any less steadfast than pure Talmudists; spiritual weakness is not dependent upon intellectual orientation. More generally, Bibago's attack against extreme rationalists and especially against opponents of philosophy tends to demonstrate that both groups were active in late medieval Spain. Bibago himself was a relatively moderate rationalist who fits well into the category of Spanish Jews like R. Isaac Abravanel who studied philosophy but attempted to counter rationalist extremism through a conservative interpretation of Maimonides and his legacy. When such a person denounces fools who call "people of intellect and reason" heretics, his remarks deserve special notice; apparently, Spain too was not without thoroughgoing critics of the philosophical enterprise for whom even the rationalism of Bibago was an impermissible deviation from pristine Judaism.[99]

There is little evidence for the outright Averroist-style skepticism that Yitzhak Baer blames for the apostasy of beleaguered Iberian Jews. Nevertheless, it seems fair to say that an acculturated community is a less likely candidate for martyrdom than an insular one. Imagine two people with equal faith in the truth of Judaism confronting the executioner's sword. The first is an admiring participant in the culture he is being told to embrace, however much he rejects its religion; the second responds to that environment with visceral revulsion. While there are no easy formulas for determining the willingness to be martyred, the second type, who represents the Ashkenazic Jew of the first crusade, is surely more likely to choose death. On this level, the Jews of Spain paid a spiritual price for integration into the cultural milieu of their potential persecutors.

---

[99] See Yavetz's *Sefer Or ha-Hayyim* (Lemberg, 1874), ch. 2, and the references in Baer, *A History of the Jews in Christian Spain* 2, p. 509, n. 12, and in Isaac E. Barzilay, *Between Reason and Faith: Anti-Rationalism in Italian Jewish Thought, 1250-1650* (The Hague, 1967), p. 148. For Baer's citation of Arama and indictment of Jewish Averroism, see his *History* 2, pp. 253-259. Baer's position was rejected by Haim Hillel Ben Sasson, "Dor Golei Sefarad 'al 'Azmo," *Zion* 26 (1961): 44-52, 59-64. On Bibago, see Joseph Hacker, "Meqomo shel R. Avraham Bibag ba-Mahaloqet 'al Limmud ha-Pilosophiah u-Ma'amadah bi-Sefarad ba-Me'ah ha-Tet-Vav," *Proceedings of the Fifth World Congress of Jewish Studies* 3 (Jerusalem, 1972), Heb. sec., pp. 151-158. Cf. also the oft-quoted anti-philosophical responsum by R. Isaac ben Sheshet, *She'elot u-Teshuvot Bar Sheshet* (Vilna, 1878), no. 45.

As we have seen in various contexts, the pursuit of the natural sciences went hand in hand with philosophical study, and their status as a mere handmaiden of metaphysics did not prevent them from being investigated with intensity and sophistication. Jewish physicians remained prominent throughout the Middle Ages, and Maimonides' medical treatises contain insights of lasting value. Gersonides made impressive contributions to astronomy, including the preparation of astronomical tables at the request of influential Christians, and fourteenth-century Provençal Jews continued to translate numerous scientific texts. Ibn Kaspi took pleasure in the unvarnished meaning of a Talmudic text which asserted that gentile scholars had defeated the sages of Israel in a debate about astronomy; this, he said, demonstrates that non-Jews have something to teach us and that their works should not be ignored.[100]

The relationship between astronomy and astrology raised scientific and theological questions which confound the usually predictable boundaries between rationalists and their opponents. From a modern perspective, Maimonides' vigorous opposition to astrology seems precisely what we ought to expect from a person of his intellectual bent. To many medievals, however, astrology was not only validated by Rabbinic texts; it was a science like all others. Gersonides, for example, argued that the discipline was often empirically validated, and it was taken for granted that miracles must overcome not only the regularities of physics but the astrological order as well. At the same time, nonrationalist religious considerations could produce opposition

---

[100] For a succinct summary of Maimonides' contributions to medieval medicine, see S. Muntner, "Gedulato ve-Hiddushav shel ha-Rambam bi-Refuah," in *Ha-Ram Bamza"l* [sic]: *Qovez Torani-Madda'i*, ed. by Y. L. Maimon (Jerusalem, 1955), pp. 264-266. On Jewish physicians in general, see inter alia, I. Munz, *Die Jüdische Ärzte im Mittelalter* (Frankfurt am Main, 1922), and D. Margalit, *Hakhmei Yisrael ke-Rofe'im* (Jerusalem, 1962). On science in general and astronomy in particular, see Bernard R. Goldstein, "The Role of Science in the Jewish Community in Fourteenth-Century France," *Annals of the New York Academy of Sciences* 314 (1978): 39-49, reprinted in his *Theory and Observation in Ancient and Medieval Astronomy* (London, 1985); L. V. Berman, "Greek into Hebrew: Samuel b. Judah of Marseilles, Fourteenth-Century Philosopher and Translator," in *Jewish Medieval and Renaissance Studies*, pp. 289-320; Twersky, "Joseph ibn Kaspi" (above n. 94), p. 256, n. 52, where he cites a variety of references to divergent Jewish interpretations of the passage in *Pesahim* 94b concerning the victory of the gentile astronomers. On continuing astronomical study by sixteenth- and seventeenth-century Jews in the Eastern Mediterranean, see Goldstein, "The Hebrew Astronomical Tradition: New Sources," *Isis* 72 (1981): 237-251, also reprinted in *Theory and Observation*.

to astrology, so that on this issue the Maimonidean legacy found itself in the unaccustomed company of R. Moses Taku. In the case of Gersonides, astronomy and astrology were kept rigorously separated, so that the affirmation of astrological truths had no adverse effect on his important astronomical studies.[101]

Although Spain and Provence were the major centers of philosophical and scientific pursuits among the Jews of the high and late Middle Ages, they did not enjoy a monopoly. Byzantine Jewry lived in a culture which preserved much of the Greek legacy of antiquity, and its intellectual profile has been described as "catholic in outlook and integrated with its environment. Secular studies were pursued as much as traditional religious studies."[102] Israel Ta-Shema, who has read substantial portions of the massive, unpublished works of Byzantine Jews available in the Institute of Microfilmed Hebrew Manuscripts in Jerusalem, has spoken to me with wonderment of the immense size and scope of the encyclopedic compositions produced by that Jewry, although he is less impressed by their depth or creativity.

Yemenite Jews, in part because of the influence of the Muslim environment and in large measure because of the inspiration provided by Maimonides, produced works reflecting familiarity with the full range of

[101] For Maimonides' position, see his letter in Alexander Marx, "The Correspondence between the Rabbis of Southern France and Maimonides about Astrology," *Hebrew Union College Annual* 3 (1926): 311-358. (This letter [p. 351] also contains Maimonides' well-known remark that he had read a multitude of Arabic works on idolatry, an observation which has been regarded as problematic in light of *Hil. 'Avodah Zarah* 2:2. For a discussion of the passage in *Hil. 'Avodah Zarah*, see Lawrence Kaplan and David Berger, "On Freedom of Inquiry in the Rambam—and Today," *The Torah U-Madda Journal* 2 [1990]: 37-50.) For Nahmanides' arguments from Talmudic texts, see his responsum in *Kitvei Ramban* 1, pp. 378-381; see also his *Commentary to Job, Kitvei Ramban* 1, p. 19, for the assumption that overturning someone's astrological fate requires miraculous divine intervention. Gersonides presented his argument on dreams, divination, prophecy, and astrology in *Milhamot Hashem* 2:1-3 (Leipzig, 1866), pp. 92-101; Levi ben Gershon (Gersonides), *The Wars of the Lord*, trans. by Seymour Feldman, 2 (Philadelphia, 1987), pp. 27-41. On the frequent but imperfect success of astrologers, see p. 95; Feldman, p. 33. For his separation of astronomy and astrology, see Goldstein, "The Role of Science," p. 45. On Moses Taku, see *Ketav Tamim, Ozar Nehmad* 3, pp. 82-83. (I do not mean to imply that Taku's position, which is reflected in a fleeting remark, was fully identical with that of Maimonides.)

[102] Steven B. Bowman, *The Jews of Byzantium: 1204-1453* (University, Alabama, 1985), p. 168. Bowman goes on to suggest that this integration into Byzantine culture may have served to undermine the cultural independence of the established Jewish community in the face of the Ottoman conquest and Sephardi immigration.

the medieval sciences. In an exceptionally strong formulation, R. Perahiah b. Meshullam wrote that "without the sciences of the intelligibles there would be no Torah," and Hoter b. Shlomoh reiterated the standard justification of scientific study as a preparation for metaphysical speculation.[103]

Similarly, the successor culture of medieval Spain was largely true to its heritage. The relative decline and stagnation of Muslim culture in the late Middle Ages had taken its toll on the intellectual creativity of Eastern Jewry, but under the stimulus of the Spanish immigration, the Jews of the Ottoman Empire displayed a renewal of cultural ferment. While this activity was mainly exegetical and homiletical, it included the study and translation of philosophical works. A recently published text provides a striking glimpse into a cast of mind which takes all learning as its province. A young scholar felt insulted when his town was denigrated as climatically unfit for the production of intellectuals. In an indignant response, he challenged the critic to do battle:

> Come out to the field and let us compete in our knowledge of the Bible, the Mishnah, and the Talmud, *Sifra* and *Sifrei* and all of Rabbinic literature; in the external sciences—the practical and theoretical fields of science, the science of nature, and of the Divine; in logic... , geometry, astronomy, and law; in the natural sciences—the longer commentary and the shorter commentary, *Generatio et Corruptio*, *De Anima* and *Meteora*, *De Animalia* and *Ethics*. . . Try me, for you have opened your mouth and belittled my dwelling-place, and you shall see that we know whatever can be known in the proper manner.[104]

---

[103] The first major scientific work by a Yemenite Jew was Netanel al-'Fayyumi's *Bustan al-'Uqul*, and interest in these disciplines persisted into the seventeenth century. See, inter alia, Y. Tzvi Langermann, *Ha-Madda'im ha-Meduyyaqim be-Qerev Yehudei Teiman* (Jerusalem, 1987); Yosef Kafih, "Arba'im She'elot be-Pilosophiah le-Rav Perahiah be-R. Meshullam," *Sefunot* 18 (1985): 111-192; David R. Blumenthal, *The Commentary of R. Hoter ben Shelomo to the Thirteen Principles of Maimonides* (Leiden, 1974); Meir Havazelet, "'Al ha-Parshanut ha-Allegorit-ha-Pilosofit be-Midrash ha-Hefez le-Rabbi Zekharyah ha-Rofe," *Teima* 3 (1993): 45-56; and the references in Amos Goldreich, "Mi-Mishnat Hug ha-'Iyyun: 'Od 'al ha-Meqorot ha-Efshariyyim shel 'ha-Ahdut ha-Shavah'," *Mehqerei Yerushalayim be-Mahashevet Yisrael* 6 (3 -4) (1987): 150, n. 35.

[104] Joseph Hacker, "The Intellectual Activity of the Jews of the Ottoman Empire during the Sixteenth and Seventeenth Centuries," in *Jewish Thought in the Seventeenth Century*, ed. by Isadore Twersky and Bernard Septimus (Cambridge, Mass., and London, England, 1987), p. 120. (Hacker's translation was printed in a somewhat garbled form, and so I have modified it slightly on the basis of the Hebrew version of

The polemical vigor and unmitigated pride in such remarks reflect a mentality that does not harbor the slightest twinge of doubt about the legitimacy and significance of all these pursuits.

At the same time, we have interesting evidence of opposition to philosophical study in this community. R. Menahem de Lonzano published an attack against philosophy which pointed to serious religious errors that it had inspired even in great figures of the past including Maimonides, R. Joseph Albo, and, strikingly, R. Bahya ibn Pakuda. We have already seen that Bahya decidedly belonged among the strongest advocates of speculation, but the piety that suffuses the bulk of his ethical work served to mute his rationalistic message and insulate him from serious attack by most anti-rationalists. De Lonzano was sensitive to this message and complained that Bahya, like Maimonides, placed metaphysics at the pinnacle of human endeavor despite the implications for the status of straightforward study of the Torah; indeed, the broadside cites a nameless rabbinic contemporary in Istanbul who wondered why the *Guide* had been burned while *The Duties of the Heart* had remained untouched. On the one hand, it is clear that de Lonzano's attack reflected the view of an influential circle of Talmudists. It is equally clear, however, that he was deeply concerned about the likelihood that he would be subjected to scathing criticism for his position, and he describes contemporaries who advocated the study of halakhic codes rather than the Talmud so that they could devote their time to other disciplines. While we cannot know with any certainty why this critique of philosophy was omitted from the second, early seventeenth-century version of de Lonzano's book, the opposition that it no doubt engendered is as likely an explanation as any.[105] Ottoman Jewry, though on the verge of cultural decline and by no means univocal in its attitude to general culture, remained generally loyal to the legacy of medieval Sephardic thought.

his article, "Ha-Pe'ilut ha-Intelleqtualit be-qerev Yehudei ha-Imperiah ha-'Ottomanit ba-Me'ot ha-Shesh-'Esreh ve-ha-Sheva'-'Esreh," *Tarbiz* 53 [1984]: 591.) Note also Hacker's citations from Solomon le-Beit ha-Levi and Abraham ibn Migash on pp. 123-126.

105   See Joseph Hacker, "Pulmus ke-neged ha-Pilosophiah be-Istanbul ba-Me'ah ha-Shesh-'Esreh," *Mehqarim be-Qabbalah be-Pilosophiah Yehudit u-be-Sifrut ha-Musar ve-he-Hagut Muggashim li-Yesha'yah Tishbi bi-Melot lo Shiv'im ve-Hamesh Shanim* (Jerusalem, 1986), pp. 507-536.

ASHKENAZ

The Northern European heartland of medieval Ashkenazic Jewry had a complex relationship with the dominant Christian civilization that defies the often simplistic characterizations describing the Ashkenazim as insular and narrow. There is no question that Northern French and German Jews, unlike their Sephardi counterparts, were deeply resistant to philosophical inquiry, largely because of the absence of a surrounding philosophical culture during their formative period; a Jewish civilization which reached maturity unaccustomed to speculation will be particularly sensitive to its alien dangers. Certainly the image of the Ashkenazim among Spanish and Provençal advocates of philosophy was that of benighted obscurantists. Radak wrote to Alfakar, "You and other wise men engage in the pursuit of wisdom and do not follow the words of the Ashkenazim, who have banned anyone who does so." R. Isaac of Acre, who became an advocate of such inquiry late in his life, reacted with disdain to those who refuse to examine

> a rational argument or to accept it. Rather, they call one to whom God has given the ability to understand rational principles... a heretic and non-believer, and his books they call external books, because they do not have the spirit needed to understand a rational principle. This is the nature of the rabbis of France and Germany and those who are like them.

During the controversy of the 1230s, Maimonists in Narbonne sent a letter to Spain with a particularly vitriolic denunciation of the French rabbis as fools and lunatics with clogged minds, who are devoted to superstitious nonsense and immersed in the fetid waters of unilluminated caves.[106]

Even in the context of philosophical speculation narrowly defined, the situation was not quite so simple. A paraphrase of Saadya's *Beliefs and Opinions* that made its way to early medieval Ashkenaz had a profound effect on the theology of significant segments of that Jewry. Unusual works like *Ketav Tamim* and *Sefer ha-Maskil* demonstrate familiarity with some speculative literature, and the author of the latter treatise

---

[106] For Radak, see *Qovez Teshuvot ha-Rambam*, p. 3b. For Isaac of Acre, see Goldreich's quotation from Oxford ms. 1911 in *Me'irat 'Einayim*, p. 412. The letter from Narbonne was published by Shatzmiller in *Zion* 34 (1969): 143-144.

was conversant with a variety of up-to-date scientific theories and experiments. In general, technological advances, experimental results, and observations of nature raised no serious religious problems, and there was no intrinsic reason for people unaffected by a theory of propaedeutic studies to connect them to philosophy. We should not be surprised, therefore, that Ashkenazic literature, probably even more than that of the Sephardim, reflects the keen interest and penetrating eye of Jews evincing intense curiosity about the natural and mechanical phenomena that surrounded them.[107] Moreover, the moment we broaden the question to include the Jewish response to the surrounding culture in general, we discover the possibility of creative interaction that may have transformed important aspects of Ashkenazic piety and thought.

First of all, the religious confrontation with the Christian world impelled some Jews to study Latin as a polemical tool. More important, the ruthless pursuit of straightforward interpretation, or *peshat,* by twelfth-century Jewish commentators in France can plausibly be seen as a Jewish reaction to nonliteral Christian exegesis. A Jewish polemicist insisting

---

[107] On the paraphrase of Saadya and its influence, see Ronald C. Kiener, "The Hebrew Paraphrase of Saadiah Gaon's *Kitab al-Amanat Wa'l-I'tiqadat,*" *AJS Review* 11 (1986): 1-25, and Yosef Dan, *Torat ha-Sod shel Hasidut Ashkenaz* (Jerusalem, 1986), especially pp. 22-24. On science and philosophy in *Sefer ha-Maskil,* see Ta-Shema, "Sefer ha-Maskil," pp. 435, 437-438.

Though the observation about propaedeutic studies is mine, I owe the vigorous formulation about the Ashkenazim's keen interest in the world around them to a conversation with Ta-Shema; cf. Noah Shapira, "'Al ha-Yeda' ha-Tekhni ve-ha-Tekhnologi shel Rashi," *Korot* 3 (1963): 145-161, where Rashi's extensive technological information is treated, probably wrongly, as exceptional. See now the brief but very important note by Y. Tzvi Langermann, "Hibbur Ashkenazi Bilti Noda' be-Madda'ei ha-Teva'," *Kiryat Sefer* 62 (1988-89): 448-449, where he describes a scientific treatise by a fourteenth-century French Jew who was particularly interested in practical science, including various instruments, and who reported that he had written a different work demonstrating how scientific knowledge sheds new light on the understanding of Torah. See also n. 131 below.

The warm, respectful welcome extended to R. Abraham ibn Ezra by prominent Tosafists certainly does not bespeak instinctive hostility to bearers of a broader cultural orientation. For Ta-Shema's more problematic assertion that Ashkenaz boasted full-fledged rationalist allegorizers, see his "Sefer ha-Maskil," 421; if such an approach had really attained an appreciable level of visibility in Northern Europe, it is hard to imagine that we would not find more substantial criticisms of it in the extant literature. Finally, it is worth noting an oral observation by Haym Soloveitchik that the major rabbinic luminaries of Northern France are not among the signatories of the ban against the *Guide* and *Sefer ha-Madda.*

upon *peshat* in a debate with a Christian could not easily return home and read the Bible in a way that violated the very principles of contextual, grammatical interpretation that he had just been passionately defending. Even explanations that are not labeled as anti-Christian can be motivated by the desire to avoid Christological assertions. There is, moreover, substantial evidence of scholarly interchange of a cordial, nonpolemical sort among Jews and Christians attempting to uncover the sense of the biblical text, and the Jewish approach had a considerable impact on the churchmen of St. Victor and other Christian commentators. Finally, the fact that the explosion of Jewish learning and literary activity took place in twelfth-century France may well be related to the concomitant "renaissance of the twelfth century" in the larger society.[108]

The stereotype of the narrow Ashkenazi sometimes included the assertion that even biblical study was ignored, and there is a degree of validity in this image, particularly in the later Middle Ages.[109] Nonetheless,

[108] See Aryeh Grabois, "The *Hebraica Veritas* and Jewish-Christian Intellectual Relations in the Twelfth Century," *Speculum* 50 (1975): 613-634; David Berger, "Mission to the Jews and Jewish-Christian Contacts in the Polemical Literature of the High Middle Ages," *The American Historical Review* 91 (1986): 576-591; Berger, "Gilbert Crispin, Alan of Lille, and Jacob ben Reuben: A Study in the Transmission of Medieval Polemic," *Speculum* 49 (1974): 34-47 (on the use of Latin texts by a Jewish polemicist); Avraham Grossman, "Ha-Pulmus ha-Yehudi-ha-Nozri ve-ha-Parshanut ha-Yehudit la-Miqra be-Zarfat ba-Me'ah ha-Yod-Bet (le-Parashat Ziqqato shel Ri Qara el ha-Pulmus)," *Zion* 51 (1986): 29-60 (for persuasive examples of unlabeled anti-Christian commentaries); Grossman, *Hakhmei Zarfat ha-Rishonim*, 473-504; Beryl Smalley, *The Study of the Bible in the Middle Ages* (Notre Dame, 1964); Elazar Touitou, "Shitato ha-Parshanit shel ha-Rashbam 'al Reqa' ha-Meziut ha-Historit shel Zemanno," in *'Iyyunim be-Sifrut Hazal ba-Miqra u-be-Toledot Yisrael: Muqdash li-Prof. Ezra Zion Melamed* (Ramat Gan, 1982), ed. by Y. D. Gilat et al., pp. 48-74 (on the impact of the twelfth-century Renaissance). For the possible influence of Christian art on Ashkenazic Jews, see Joseph Gutmann's presentation and my response in J. Gutmann, et al., *What Can Jewish History Learn From Jewish Art?* (New York, 1989), pp. 1-18, 29-38. Gabriele L. Strauch's *Dukus Horant: Wanderer Zwischen Zwei Welten* (Amsterdam and Adanta, 1990) analyzes a fairly typical medieval German romance written or copied by a fourteenth century German Jew in Yiddish (or at least in Hebrew characters with some specifically Jewish terminology). Note also Dan, *Torat ha-Sod*, pp. 37-39, for some general observations on the impact of folk beliefs about magic, astrology, and the like on Ashkenazic Jewry. Finally, Ivan G. Marcus has now presented an analysis of an Ashkenazic ritual for the purpose of illuminating the manner in which responses to Christian society can make their way into the religious life of both scholars and the laity; see his *Rituals of Childhood: Jewish Acculturation in Medieval Europe* (New Haven and London, 1996).

[109] See Profiat Duran's introduction to *Ma'aseh Efod*, p. 41, and the discussion in Isadore Twersky, "Religion and Law," in *Religion in a Religious Age*, ed. by Goitein, pp. 74-77.

the innovative biblical exegesis in twelfth-century France demonstrates that this perception is selective and skewed. Not only did Ashkenazic Jews study Bible; biblical exegesis served as both a battleground and a bridge where Jews and Christians came into frequent, creative contact as enemies and as partners.

In the field of biblical study, interaction is firmly established; what requires elucidation is the extent and nature of its effects. We face a more fundamental problem with respect to the most intriguing question of all: Did the revolutionary use of dialectic in the Talmudic methodology of the Northern French Tosafists owe anything to the intellectual upheaval in the larger society? There is hardly any evidence of Jewish familiarity in Ashkenaz with the study of canon law and philosophy, which were the two major areas in which the search for contradictions or inconsistencies and their subsequent resolution began to play a central role. It is even more difficult to imagine that Christians, whose familiarity with the Talmud was virtually nil, could have been much influenced by Tosafists. At the same time, the very individuals who pursued the new methodologies in fields unknown by the members of the other faith met on the terrain of biblical studies. Rashbam, who was a Tosafist as well as a *peshat*-oriented biblical exegete, is a good Jewish example. In light of these well-documented contacts, it surely cannot be ruled out—indeed, it seems overwhelmingly likely—that some taste of the exciting new approaches was transmitted. When the German pietists wanted to criticize the Tosafist approach, they denounced the utilization of "Gentile dialectic" (*dial tiqa* [*dialeqtiqah*] *shel goyim*); though we are under no obligation to endorse the historical judgment of the pietists, the criticism establishes at least a threshold level of familiarity with the term and its application.[110]

See also Mordechai Breuer, "Min'u Beneikhem min ha-Higgayon," in *Mikhtam le-David: Sefer Zikhron ha-Rav David Ochs*, ed. by Yitzhak Gilat and Eliezer Stern (Ramat Gan, 1978), pp. 242-264, and Frank Taimage, "Keep Your Sons From Scripture: The Bible in Medieval Jewish Scholarship and Spirituality," in *Understanding Scripture: Explorations of Jewish and Christian Traditions of Interpretation*, ed. by Clemens Thoma and Michael Wyschogrod (New York, 1987), pp. 81-101. On evidence for Ashkenazic biblical study in the pre-crusade period, see Avraham Grossman, *Hakhmei Ashkenaz ha-Rishonim*, pp. 240, 288-289, 323 (inter alia), and cf. my review, "Heqer Rabbanut Ashkenaz ha-Qedumah," *Tarbiz* 53 (1984): 484, n. 7. For an overall analysis of the evidence, see Ephraim Kanarfogel, *Jewish Education and Society in the High Middle Ages* (Detroit, 1992), pp. 79-85.

[110] See Kanarfogel, *Jewish Education*, pp. 70-73. The pietists' denunciation of dialectic is in *Sefer Hasidim*, ed. by J. Wistinetsky, 2nd ed. (Frankfurt am Main, 1924), par.

The relationship of these pietists to the surrounding culture is itself highly suggestive. The system of penances that they introduced into the process of repentance is no longer regarded as a defining characteristic of their movement; nonetheless, that system remains a major development in the history of Jewish piety, and despite a smattering of antecedents in rabbinic literature, it is overwhelmingly likely that the influence of the Christian environment was decisive.[111] With respect to quintessentially religious behavior, the inhibition against following Christian models should have been overwhelming, and I think that the psychological factor that overcame it was analogous to the competitive imitation that we have already seen in Muslim Spain. It was critically important for the Jewish self-image that Jews not be inferior to the host society. In Spain, the competition was cultural and intellectual; in Ashkenaz, given the different complexion of both majority and minority culture, it was a competition in religious devotion. I have suggested elsewhere that this consideration may account in part for the assertions by Jewish polemicists that the chastity of monks and nuns is more apparent than real. Celibacy was an area in which Jewish law did not allow competition, and so the problem was resolved by the not entirely unfounded allegation that the religious self-sacrifice of Christians was illusory. With respect to self-mortification for sin, Jewish law was not quite so clear, and Ashkenazi pietists set out to demonstrate that they would not be put to shame by Christian zeal in the service of God.[112]

In the late Middle Ages, Northern European Jewry was subjected to expulsions, persecutions, and dislocations which disrupted its cultural

752, p. 191. Note too the citation of some parallel methods in *Tosafot* and Christian works in Jose Faur, "The Legal Thinking of Tosafot: An Historical Approach," *Diné Israel* 6 (1975): xliii-lxxii. For intimate familiarity with Christian works in the writings of the probably atypical R. Elhanan b. Yaqar of London, see G. Vajda, "De quelques infiltrations chrétiennes dans l'oeuvre d'un auteur anglo-juif du XIIIe siècle," *Archives d'Histoire Doctrinale et Littéraire du Moyen Age* 28 (1961): 15-34.

[111]   On the Christian analogues to the penances of Hasidei Ashkenaz, see Yitzhak Baer, "Ha-Megammah ha-Datit ve-ha-Hevratit shel Sefer Hasidim," *Zion* 3 (1938): 18-20. For the new evaluation of the movement's center of gravity, see Haym Soloveitchik, "Three Themes in the Sefer Hasidim," *AJS Review* 1 (1976): 311-357. See also Ivan Marcus, *Piety and Society: The Jewish Pietists of Medieval Germany* (Leiden, 1981).

[112]   On celibacy, see my observations in *The Jewish-Christian Debate in the High Middle Ages*, p. 27. I have elaborated somewhat in a forthcoming essay, "Al Tadmitam ve-Goralam shel ha-Goyim be-Sifrut ha-Pulmus ha-Ashkenazit," in [*Yehudim mul ha-Zelav*], ed. by Yom Tov Assis, et al.

life and moved its center of gravity eastward. By the late fourteenth and early fifteenth centuries, a figure like R. Yom Tov Lipmann Mühlhausen of Prague demonstrates that some Jewish intellectuals had achieved familiarity with philosophy and general culture. In 1973, Ephraim Kupfer published a seminal article which attempted to establish the substantial presence of rationalism in Ashkenaz during this period. There can be no question that much of the evidence that he adduced is significant and stimulating. We can hardly fail to be intrigued, for example, by an argument in an Ashkenazic text that ancient shifts in the *halakhah* of levirate marriage resulted from a rejection of metempsychosis by increasingly sophisticated rabbis. At the same time, it is far from clear that this material reflects the views and interests of substantial segments of Ashkenazic society, and it is very likely that one of the important figures in the article came to Europe from Israel bearing texts and ideas that stem from the Jewish communities of the Muslim East. Both the dissemination and the rootedness of philosophical study in fourteenth- and fifteenth-century Ashkenaz remain an open question, and I am inclined to think that it stood considerably closer to the periphery than to the center.[113]

The question of the standing of philosophy among fifteenth-century Ashkenazim has a significant bearing on the proper evaluation of major

---

[113] See Kupfer, "Li-Demutah," *Tarbiz* 42 (1973): 113-147. It is noteworthy that one of the texts cited by Kupfer (p. 129) takes it for granted that the ancient rabbis learned proper methods of demonstration from the works of Aristotle, a position which reverses the standard medieval Jewish assertion about the source of Greek philosophy. See also Kupfer's brief supplementary notes in his "Hassagot min Hakham Ehad 'al Divrei he-Hakham ha-Rav R. Yosef b. ha-Qadosh R. Yosef ha-Lo'azi she-Katav ve-Qara be-Qol Gadol neged ha-Rambam," *Qovez 'al Yad* n.s. 11 [21] (1985): 215-216, nn. 2, 4. For some evidence of interest in philosophy outside the "Mühlhausen circle," particularly in *Sefer Hadrat Qodesh* written in Germany shortly before the middle of the fourteenth century, see Davis, *R. Yom Tov Lipman Heller*, pp. 88-103, and see now his "Philosophy, Dogma, and Exegesis in Medieval Ashkenazic Judaism: The Evidence of *Sefer Hadrat Qodesh*," *AJS Review* 18 (1993): 195-222. For an early, brief expression of reservations about Kupfer's thesis, see Joseph Dan, "Hibbur Yihud Ashkenazi min ha-Me'ah ha-Yod-Dalet," *Tarbiz* 44 (1975): 203-206. For a more detailed critique, see Israel Jacob Yuval, *Hakhamim be-Doram* (Jerusalem, 1988), 286-311. In an oral communication, Moshe Idel has noted several considerations pointing to the likelihood that Menahem Shalem came from Israel: His non-Ashkenazic name usually refers to a Jerusalemite; he makes reference to Emmaus, which he identifies as Latrun; he had a text by Abraham Abulafia and a translation of an Arabic text by Abraham Maimonides. If Idel is correct, and if Kupfer's suggestion that the two Menahems in his study are really one and the same is also correct, then the dominant personality in the article was not an Ashkenazic Jew.

trends and figures in the intellectual life of the burgeoning new center in sixteenth-century Poland. R. Moses Isserles and R. Mordecai Jaffe are the two most prominent examples of distinguished Talmudists who maintained a position of moderate rationalism in which a conservative understanding of Maimonides and a philosophical interpretation of kabbalah served to unite diverse strands of Jewish piety and theology in a manner that removed any threat to traditional religious affirmations.[114] If Kupfer is correct, then this position can be seen as a natural continuation of intellectual trends in late medieval Ashkenaz, and the approach of Isserles and Jaffe would fit well into their generally conservative posture. If he is not, then we must seek other sources for the penetration of philosophical ideas into Polish Jewish thought.

The first of these is the Northern European Renaissance, which affected both Poland and Bohemia and can consequently help to account not only for the elements of rationalism in the works of Polish rabbis but for the significant scientific and philosophical activity among the Jews of late sixteenth and early seventeenth-century Prague. In the case of David Gans of Prague, the relationship with Christian society is crystal-clear: Gans was the first influential Jew to confront Copernicanism, and he did so as a personal associate of Tycho Brahe and Johann Kepler. Gans's illustrious contemporary, R. Judah Loew (Maharal), produced an impressive theological corpus which made extensive, though cautious use of the Jewish philosophical tradition, and described astronomy as "a ladder to ascend to the wisdom of the Torah," while his student R. Yom Tov Lipman Heller, best known for his standard commentary to the Mishnah, displayed considerable interest in the pursuit of mathematics and astronomy. The period from 1560 to 1620 saw a significant increase in works of a philosophical and scientific nature throughout the Ashkenazic orbit, and the contacts between the Jewish communities of Prague and Poland no doubt contributed to the spread of these pursuits. A second significant source of cultural stimulation for Polish Jewry may well have been Renaissance Italy. Polish Jews were in continual contact with Italy in a multitude of contexts; numerous Padua-trained

---

[114] See Lawrence Kaplan, "Rabbi Mordekhai Jaffe and the Evolution of Jewish Culture in Poland in the Sixteenth Century," in *Jewish Thought in the Sixteenth Century*, ed. by Bernard D. Cooperman (Cambridge, Mass., and London, England, 1983), pp. 266-282. On Isserles' thought, see Yonah Ben Sasson, *Mishnato ha-'Iyyunit shel ha-Rama* (Jerusalem, 1984).

physicians came to Poland, and a constant stream of literary material crossed the border.[115]

The use of this material would have been legitimated in the eyes of some conservatives by the heroic image of Maimonides, whose orthodoxy was now beyond reproach. Once again, we find an exception, which genuinely proves this rule. In midsixteenth-century Posen, the extreme and eccentric anti-rationalist R. Joseph Ashkenazi persuaded his father-in-law R. Aaron to deliver an uncompromising attack against the study of philosophy. Ashkenazi, as we know from a later work of his, attacked Maimonides with startling vitriol as an outright heretic who deserves no defense and who is largely responsible for popularizing the allegorization of the Bible and of *aggadah* that has undermined authentic Judaism. Nevertheless, he himself cited with disgust the unanimity of the admiring chorus of Maimonides' supporters, and R. Avraham Horowitz's attack on Ashkenazi demonstrates further the passionate reaction inspired by unrestrained criticism of the author of the *Guide*. Horowitz's work, which contains a vigorous defense of philosophical study, also reflects the presence in sixteenth-century Poland of unabashed exponents of speculation, although the author's partial revision of his rationalist views years later points to the countervailing forces that may well have been dominant even at that time, as they surely were by the dawn of the Jewish enlightenment.[116]

---

[115] On Gans in particular and Prague in general, see Mordecai Breuer, "Qavvim li-Demuto shel R. David Gans Ba'al Zemah David," *Bar Ilan* 11 (1973): 97-103, and his edition of *Sefer Zemah David le-Rabbi David Gans* (Jerusalem, 1983), esp. pp. 1-9. On Heller, see Davis, *R. Yom Tov Lipman Heller*, pp. 339-517; for documentation on the upsurge in Ashkenazic works of a philosophical and scientific nature, see Davis, pp. 121-129. On the contacts between Ashkenaz and Italy, see Jacob Elbaum, "Qishrei Tarbut bein Yehudei Polin ve-Ashkenaz le-bein Yehudei Italia ba-Me'ah Ha-Tet-Zayin," *Gal'ed* 7-8 (1985): 11-40, and, more briefly, his *Petihut Ve-Histaggerut* (Jerusalem, 1990), 33-54. On Jews in the medical school at Padua, see Daniel Carpi, "Yehudim Ba'alei Toar Doctor li-Refuah mi-Ta'am Universitat Padua ba-Me'ah ha-Tet-Zayin u-be-Reshit ha-Me'ah ha-Yod-Zayin," in *Sefer Zikkaron le-Natan Cassutto (Scritti in Memoria di Nathan Cassuto)*, ed. by Daniel Carpi, Augusto Segre, and Renzo Toaff (Jerusalem, 1986), pp. 62-91.

[116] Lawrence Kaplan has pointed out that despite the impression given by some earlier scholarship, Horowitz's revision does not represent a radical rejection of his earlier views; see "Rabbi Mordekhai Jaffe," p. 281, n. 8. Horowitz's attack was published and discussed by Ph. Bloch, "Der Streit um den Moreh des Maimonides in der Gemeinde Posen um die Mitte des 16 Jahrh.," *Monatsschrift für Geschichte und Wissenschaft des Judenthums* 47 (1903): 153-169, 263-279, 346-356. For an analysis of Joseph Ashkenazi and selections from his work, see Gershom Scholem, "Yedi'ot Hadashot 'al R. Yosef Ashkenazi, ha-'Tanna'

Isserles' conservative philosophical treatise contained considerable scientific discussion as well, and he also wrote a separate astronomical work in the form of a commentary to the standard textbook in that field, Georg Peurbach's *Theoricae Novae Planetarum*. R. Solomon Luria, in an oft-quoted exchange with Isserles, denounced him for citing scientific information derived from gentile sources in a halakhic decision about the *kashrut* of a particular animal and for reading philosophical works at all, and he blames such attitudes for the bizarre and otherwise unattested phenomenon of young Polish Jews who recite an Aristotelian prayer in the synagogue. Isserles' response is revealing. He justified his actions, but made it clear that he gained his scientific knowledge only from Jewish books and that he pursued these studies only at times when most people are out taking walks on Sabbaths and holidays.

Recent research has tended to portray a greater openness to rationalism and science than we had been accustomed to ascribe to this Jewry. Nevertheless, it remains difficult to take the pulse of sixteenth-century Polish Jewish intellectuals with respect to our question: probably a small group of full-fledged rationalists, a substantial number of conservative advocates of a tamed philosophy, and a significant group of rabbis who either shied away from speculation or actively opposed it.[117]

mi-Zefat," *Tarbiz* 28 (1959): pp. 59-89, 201-235. A detailed response to Ashkenazi by a contemporary Italian Jew was published by Kupfer, "Hassagot min Hakham Ehad," *Qovez al Yad* n.s. 11 [21] (1985): 213-288. On Ashkenazi's denunciation even of Maimondes' code, see I. Twersky, "R. Yosef Ashkenazi ve-Sefer Mishneh Torah la-Rambam," *Sefer ha-Yovel li-Kevod Shalom Baron*, ed. by Saul Lieberman (Jerusalem, 1975), pp. 183-194. The moderate rationalism of R. Eliezer Ashekenazi of Posen also deserves mention, although the fact that he spent many years in the East mitigates his significance for a characterization of Polish Jewry; see the analysis of Ashkenazi's exegetical independence in Haim Hillel Ben Sasson, *Hagut ve-Hanhagah* (Jerusalem, 1959), pp. 34-38.

[117] On Isserles' astronomical treatise, see Y. Tzvi Langermann, "The Astronomy of Rabbi Moses Isserles," in *Physics, Cosmology, and Astronomy, 1300-1700: Tension and Accommodation*, ed. by S. Unguru (Dordrecht and Boston, 1991), pp. 83-98. For the exchange between Isserles and R. Solomon Luria, see *She'elot u-Teshuvot ha-Rama*, ed. by Asher Siev (Jerusalem, 1971), nos. 5-7, pp. 18-38, and cf. the summary in Ben Zion Katz, *Rabbanut, Hasidut, Haskalah* 1 (Tel Aviv, 1956), pp. 32-33. It is worth noting that even Luria maintains that he is as familiar with the disputed literature as Isserles (Siev, p. 26). On Poland specifically and sixteenth-century Ashkenazic Jewry in general, see Jacob Elbaum, *Zeramim u-Megammot be-Sifrut ha-Mahashavah ve-ha-Musar be-Ashkenaz u-be-Polin ba-Me'ah ha-Tet-Zayin* (Hebrew University dissertation, 1977), pp. 120-135; Elbaum, *Petihut ve-Histaggerut*, esp. chapter 5; Davis, *R. Yom Tov Lipman Heller*; and the still useful survey by Lawrence H. Davis, "The Great Debate: Secular Studies and the Jews in Sixteenth Century Poland," *Yavneh Review* 3 (1963): 42-58.

ITALIAN SYMBIOSIS

With respect to Poland and the Ottoman Empire, we could legitimately speak of successor cultures to Ashkenaz and Spain respectively, despite the fact that Middle Eastern Jewry had its own intellectual tradition before the Iberian immigration. Italy is a more complex and more interesting story. Despite their Christian environment, the Jews of medieval Italy appear to have maintained a greater degree of openness to the surrounding culture than did Ashkenazic Jewry. Shabbetai Donnolo is a well-known, early example of the sort of learned physician and scientist that we usually associate with Jews in the Muslim orbit. To some degree, this phenomenon may have resulted from the significant Muslim impact on Southern Italy, but I am inclined to attribute even greater importance to the fact that pre-twelfth-century Southern Europe maintained a greater continuity with the classical past than did the Christian communities of the North. A case in point is the familiarity of the anonymous tenth-century Italian Jew who wrote *Josippon* with earlier Latin works. By the thirteenth century, Italian Jews displayed a level of sophistication in philosophical and literary pursuits that owed something to contacts with Iberia but at least as much to a receptivity to the cultural developments in their immediate environment. Thus, easily the most philosophically sophisticated anti-Christian polemicist of the thirteenth century was Moses ben Solomon of Salerno, and the often secular, sometimes ribald poetry of Immanuel of Rome could not have been composed in any other Jewry in the medieval Christian world.[118]

Toward the end of the Middle Ages, both Sephardi and Ashkenazi immigrants introduced a mixture of new influences. Elijah del Medigo's late fifteenth-century *Behinat ha-Dat* is a clear-cut example of the impact of rationalism, but the fate of Aristotelian philosophy among the Jews of Renaissance Italy is bound up with central questions about their

---

[118] On Donnolo, see the discussion and references in A. Sharf, *The Universe of Shabbetai Donnolo* (New York, 1976). For the greater cultural continuity in Southern Europe, see R. W. Southern's observations in *The Making of the Middle Ages* (New Haven and London, 1953), pp. 20-25. On *Josippon*, see *Sefer Yosifon*, ed. by David Flusser, 2 vols. (Jerusalem, 1978, 1980); in particular, note Flusser's well-documented observation that the author knew Latin works better than rabbinic literature. Moses of Salerno's philosophical polemic was published by Stanislaus Simon, *Mose ben Salomo von Salerno und seine philosophischen Auseinandersetzung mit den Lehren des Christentums* (Breslau, 1931). For Immanuel, see *Mahberot Immanuel*, ed. by A. M. Haberman (Tel Aviv, 1946).

cultural posture. Lists of books in Italian Jewish libraries in the fifteenth and early sixteenth centuries appear to reflect a decline of interest in philosophy from the beginning to the end of that period, with the important and unsurprising exception of Maimonides' *Guide* and some of its commentators. This impression is reinforced by a complaint leveled by R. Isaac Abravanel in Venice as early as the late fifteenth century about the unavailability of Averroes' *Epistle on the Conjunction* and Moses Narboni's commentary on it. If the requisite work were "*tosafot* or codes, I would borrow it from one of the natives, but in philosophy this is impossible." The declining philosophical content of Jewish sermons in the first half of the sixteenth century provides further evidence of the same significant development.[119]

The diminution of interest in metaphysics does not bespeak the end of Italian Jewish acculturation. First of all, the continuing use of the scholastic philosophical approach by no less a figure than R. Ovadiah Seforno demonstrates the persistent vitality of that tradition within important rabbinic circles. More important, Renaissance Christians were themselves engaged in disputes about the value of philosophy and tended to emphasize the scientific, ethical, and political dimensions of the Aristotelian corpus rather than its metaphysical component; in a sense, then, the very de-emphasis of the philosophical tradition can be seen not as a turning inward but as a reflection of a larger cultural trend. There is no denying that the gradual displacement of Aristotelianism by kabbalah in the minds of many Italian Jews reflected a desire to emphasize the uniqueness of the Jewish people and its culture in a manner reminiscent of Halevi, whose *Kuzari* underwent something of a popular revival; nonetheless, even R. Yehiel Nissim of Pisa, who produced the most impressive reasoned argument for this displacement, recognized the value of philosophical investigations, not to speak of scientific inquiry, provided that they were not assigned primacy in a rivalry with the Torah.[120]

---

[119]   For del Medigo, see his *Sefer Behinat ha-Dat*, ed. by Jacob Ross (Tel Aviv, 1984), and D. Geffen, "Insights into the Life and Thought of Elijah del Medigo Based on his Published and Unpublished Works," *Proceedings of the American Academy for Jewish Research* 41-42 (1973-74): 69-86. On, libraries, sermons, and the overall phenomenon, see Reuven Bonfil, *Ha-Rabbanut be-Italia bi-Tequfat ha-Renaissance* (Jerusalem, 1979), pp. 173-206; *Rabbis and Jewish Communities in Renaissance Italy* (Oxford and New York, 1990), pp. 270-323. For the citation from Abravanel, see Hacker, "The Intellectual Activity of the Jews of the Ottoman Empire" (above, n. 104), n. 47 (pp. 117-118).

[120]   See Bonfil, *Ha-Rabbanut*, pp. 179-190; *Rabbis*, pp. 280-298.

Once we step outside the four ells of Aristotelian metaphysics, the evidence for Renaissance Jewry's immersion in the surrounding culture becomes overwhelming. Indeed, to an observer coming to the subject from the study of another Jewish community, including that of Iberia, the lively and genuinely significant historians' debate over the inner or outer directedness of fifteenth- and sixteenth-century Italian Jews takes on a surreal quality. This is a community with intellectuals entranced by the rhetorical works of Cicero and Quintilian and with preachers who lace their sermons with references to classical authors while insisting that the Bible cannot be properly understood without a literary sensitivity nurtured by careful study of gentile as well as Jewish literature. It is a community with thinkers who set up the Renaissance ideal of *homo universalis* or *hakham kolel* as a paradigm of intellectual perfection attained by King Solomon and sought by anyone with healthy educational priorities. It is a community that produced a plan, at least on paper, of setting up what one observer has described as a Yeshiva University, where the primary emphasis would be on the study of "the written and oral Torah, laws, *tosafot*, and decisors," but instruction would also be provided in the works of Jewish philosophers, Hebrew grammar, rhetoric, Latin, Italian, logic, medicine, non-Jewish philosophical works, mathematics, cosmography, and astrology. It is a community with vigorous, ongoing exchanges with the contemporary Christian elite. Not only did Elias Levita teach Hebrew to Christian scholars; not only did kabbalah itself, which was sometimes taught by Jews, inspire the speculative creativity of Christian thinkers; it now appears likely that Pico della Mirandola's version of the quintessentially Renaissance definition of man as a median creature with the power to fashion himself in freedom owes much to a medieval Muslim formulation mediated by Pico's Jewish associate Yohanan Alemanno.[121]

---

[121] On rhetoric, see The *Book of the Honeycomb's Flow. Sefer Nofeth Suphim by Judah Messer Leon.* A Critical Edition and Translation by Isaac Rabinowitz (Ithaca and London, 1983). See also R. Bonfil's introduction to the facsimile edition of *Nofet Zufim* (Jerusalem, 1981). Like del Medigo, Messer Leon was interested in philosophy as well. On *homo universalis* and King Solomon, see Arthur M. Lesley, *The Song of Solomon's Ascents* (University of California at Berkeley dissertation, 1976), and the citation from David Messer Leon's *Shevah Nashim* in Hava Tirosh-Rothschild, "In Defense of Jewish Humanism," *Jewish History* 3 (1988): 54 (n. 55); note also her remarks on p. 33.

On the proposal in 1564 to set up an academy for Torah and general studies in Mantua, see the text in Asaf, *Meqorot* 2, pp. 116-120; Asaf noted (p. 115) that only an Italian

At the same time, vigorous opposition to philosophy and the humanist agenda produced a continuing debate. The fact that Joseph Ashkenazi wrote his vitriolic attack against Maimonides while in Italy is no doubt fortuitous, but it made enough of an impact there to have elicited an elaborate refutation. Yosef Yavetz's *Or ha-Hayyim* is the work of a Spanish exile in Naples who rejected philosophical pursuits as damaging to faith and did battle with the hallowed rationalist understanding of the biblical admonition to "know" God as a philosophical imperative; a pious individual needs to be rescued from "the ambush of human reason, which lurks in wait... at all times." R. David Proventzalo advised the young David Messer Leon to follow the ways of distant Talmudists rather than the philosophical agenda of local rabbis, who appear to assign no value to the Torah and Talmud. R. Ovadiah of Bertinoro denounced the study of Aristotle in particular and philosophy in general in both his commentary to the Mishnah and his correspondence, writing approvingly of the untainted piety that he found in the land of Israel in contrast to the deplorable situation in Italy. In the introduction to his halakhic work *Giddulei Terumah*, R. Azariah Figo lamented his youthful pursuit of general culture in the late sixteenth century and described his decision to "expel this maidservant" and return to the Talmud, although it is noteworthy that he berated himself only for reversing the proper order of priorities, not for pursuing a forbidden path.[122]

Jew could have thought of such a project. The apt analogy to Yeshiva University was made by Yehezkel Cohen, "Ha-Yahas le-Limmudei Hol me-Hazal ve-'ad Yameinu— Seqirah Historit-Sifrutit,'" in *Yahas ha-Yahadut le-Limmudei Hol* (Israel, 1983), p. 20. Although this would not have been a degree granting institution, the plan envisioned a preparatory program that would enable the student to enroll subsequently in a formal *studio* and receive a secular degree (*semikhah*) in a very short time. On Elias Levita and the teaching of Hebrew and kabbalah to Christians, see the discussion in Yitzhak Penkower, "'Iyyun Mehuddash be-Sefer Masoret ha-Masoret le-Eliyyahu Bahur: Ihur ha-Niqqud u-Biqqoret Sefer ha- Zohar," *Italia* 8 (1989): 36-50, and the references in n. 93 (pp. 37-38).

For Alemanno's likely influence on Pico's crucial conception of man, see Moshe Idel, "The Anthropology of Yohanan Alemanno: Sources and Influences," *Topoi* 7 (1988): pp. 201-210. David Ruderman has recently argued that Pico's replacement of a narrow vision of Christian culture with one that was more broadly human created a new challenge and a new opportunity for Renaissance Jews confronting their intellectual environment; see his very useful summary article, "The Italian Renaissance and Jewish Thought," in *Renaissance Humanism: Foundations, Forms, and Legacy, Volume I: Humanism in Italy*, ed. by Albert Rabil Jr. (Philadelphia, 1988), pp. 382-433.

[122] On the response to Ashkenazi, see Kupfer, "Hassagot min Hakham Ehad" (above,

Despite the advice that he received, David Messer Leon ultimately opted for humanist pursuits to the point of arguing that the Talmudist who is also a *hakham kolel* is more deserving of rabbinic ordination than an ordinary Talmudist. When he left Italy for Constantinople, he found himself under attack for his frequent citation of classical literature in his sermons; in response, he produced a passionate defense of the humanist enterprise, arguing for the value of classical poetry and rhetoric in achieving human perfection, which is bound up with the quest for religious perfection. Two Jewish biographies, one of King Solomon, the other of Isaac Abravanel, written in Italy between the late fifteenth and mid-sixteenth centuries, clearly reflect Renaissance literary trends and further illustrate Jewish involvement in humanistic study and creativity. The seventeenth-century autobiography of Leone da Modena, which can be seen as an extension of this genre, is but one of many indications not only of its author's extraordinary range of interests but of the continuing, even growing Jewish familiarity with the broader culture well into the Baroque period. The glorification of Hebrew reached its peak at the height of the Renaissance, while in the post-Renaissance period even Jewish authors with an excellent command of Hebrew were ever more likely to write in the vernacular.[123]

n. 113). For the translation from Yavetz's *Or ha-Hayyim* (Lublin, 1910), pp. 74-76, see Arthur M. Lesley, "The Place of the *Dialoghi d'amore* in Contemporaneous Jewish Thought," in *Ficino and Renaissance Neoplatonism*, ed. by K. Eisenbichler and O. Z. Pugliese (University of Toronto Italian Studies I, Ottawa, 1986), p. 75, and cf. Barzilay's discussion, *Between Reason and Faith*, pp. 133-149. For R. Ovadiah of Bertinoro, see his commentary to *Sanhedrin* 10:1 and the letter published in A. Kahana, *Sifrut ha-Historiah ha-Yisre'elit* 2 (Warsaw, 1923), p. 47, and cf. the commentary to *Avot* 5:22. Cf. also Immanuel Benevento's kabbalistically motivated hostility to philosophy; see the references in Segal, *Historical Consciousness and Religious Tradition*, pp. 61-62 (n. 20). On Proventzalo's advice, see Bonfil, *Ha-Rabbanut*, pp. 173-174; *Rabbis*, p. 270. For Figo, see *Sefer Giddulei Terumah* (Venice, 1643), and Barzilay, pp. 192-209. A similar statement of regret at excessive attention to works of general culture appears in the early seventeenth-century *Shiltei ha-Gibborim* of Abraham Portaleone, but the book itself, despite its presumed character as an act of penitence for these intellectual indiscretions, is replete with references to the classics; see Segal, p. 52, and the references in n. 23. In a personal communication, David Ruderman has underscored his view of Portaleone and Figo as anti-Aristotelians who nevertheless maintained a positive attitude toward empirical science.

123 Messer Leon's observation on the qualifications for ordination is reminiscent of the assertion that angered R. Asher b. Yehiel about the connection between knowledge of Arabic and the right to render a decision in Jewish law. The apologia for humanism is in Messer Leon's unpublished *Shevah Nashim*; for a summary and analysis, see

In her study of David Messer Leon's work, Havah Tirosh-Rothschild observes that

> by the end of the fifteenth century, Jewish rationalist tradition had so absorbed Greek philosophy that it had become far less subversive and was even palatable. By David ben Judah's day, however, no such absorption had yet occurred of the poetry, oratory, geography, history and letters of classical antiquity—all introduced to Jews through Renaissance humanism. These subjects, if not philosophy, still seemed to threaten Jewish traditional values, at least in Constantinople if not in Italy.[124]

The point is an important one; nevertheless, most of these pursuits did not have the potential to challenge Judaism in the manner of Aristotelian philosophy. The one which did was history, and the Italian Jew who utilized the discipline dangerously generated a brief but revealing cause célèbre.

In its most common mode, history was a humanistic endeavor no more dangerous than poetry or rhetoric, and some sixteenth- and

Tirosh-Rothschild, "In Defense of Jewish Humanism." On the biographies, see Arthur M. Lesley, "Hebrew Humanism in Italy: The Case of Biography," *Prooftexts* 2 (1982): 163-177. Da Modena was a multifaceted figure who continues to fascinate. See *The Autobiography of a Seventeenth-Century Venetian Rabbi: Leon Modena's The Life of Judah*, trans. and ed. by Mark R. Cohen (Princeton, 1988), and cf. Cohen's "Leone da Modena's *Riti*: A Seventeenth-Century Plea for Social Toleration of Jews," *Jewish Social Studies* 34 (1972): 287-321. On the persistence and growth of certain forms of acculturation, including use of the vernacular, in the Baroque period, see Robert Bonfil, "Change in the Cultural Patterns of a Jewish Society in Crisis: Italian Jewry at the Close of the Sixteenth Century," *Jewish History* 3 (1988): 11-30. For some observations on Italian Jewish familiarity with Christian philosophy and, more generally, on the relatively painless absorption by this Jewry of a multitude of diverse disciplines and approaches, see Yosef Sermoneta's review of Barzilay's *Between Reason and Faith* in *Kiryat Sefer* 44 (1970): 539-546.

Despite changes in orientation and advances in methodology, the material accumulated in Cecil Roth, *The Jews in the Renaissance* (Philadelphia, 1959), and Moses Shulvass, *The Jews in the Life of the Renaissance* (Leiden, 1973), retains its value and documents Jewish activity in fields like art, drama, music, and printing, which I have been unable to treat in this survey. The most vigorous and influential argument for a new perspective is Bonfil's "The Historian's Perception of the Jews in the Italian Renaissance. Towards a Reappraisal," *Revue des Études Juives* 143 (1984): 59-82, which sees Italian Jewish acculturation as part of a competitive struggle affirming Jewish identity in the face of pressure rather than a reflection of an idyllic cultural symbiosis. See now Bonfil's synthetic treatment, *Jewish Life in Renaissance Italy* (Berkeley, Los Angeles, and London, 1994).

[124] "In Defence of Jewish Humanism," p. 39.

seventeenth-century Jews in Italy and elsewhere utilized it to provide religious consolation, to place the Jewish experience in a broader context, to validate the tradition, to set the stage for the end of days, to ponder the causes of the Jewish condition, or simply to entertain. Some of these purposes had been pursued even in the Middle Ages by the few Jews who had engaged in the enterprise of setting down events that had, after all, already taken place and whose utility was consequently viewed with considerable skepticism. R. Sherira's epistle took the form of a standard responsum; *Josippon* provided a basic historical survey as well as implicit advice about appropriate Jewish behavior in the face of superior force; R. Abraham ibn Daud's *Book of Tradition* validated the tradition, defended the glories of Andalusian Jewry, and may have pointed esoterically to the date of the redemption; the crusade chronicles provided emotional release and religious inspiration in the wake of unspeakable tragedy.[125]

Whether or not the historical writings of sixteenth- and seventeenth-century Jews reflect a significant historiographical movement has recently become a disputed question. On the one hand, Jewish authors produced ten books of a roughly historical character in the course of about a century, a number that exceeds the entire output of the Middle Ages, and some of these are clearly indebted to the historiographic corpus that emerged in Renaissance society. On the other hand, a rigorous definition of history would exclude many, perhaps most, of these works, and even if they are all counted, they do not approach the number that one might reasonably expect in light of the proportion of Christian Renaissance works devoted to historiography.[126] In any

---

[125] See *Sefer Yosifon*, ed. by Flusser; ibn Daud's *Sefer Ha-Qabbalah*, ed. by Cohen; Shlomo Eidelberg, *The Jews and the Crusaders* (Madison, Wisconsin, 1977), and Robert Chazan, *European Jewry and the First Crusade* (Berkeley and Los Angeles, 1987), pp. 223-297. On R. Sherira, see above, n. 19. For an example of medieval Jewish denigration of the value of history, see Maimonides' *Commentary to the Mishnah, Sanhedrin* 10:1 (almost immediately before the list of the thirteen principles of faith).

[126] See Yosef Hayim Yerushalmi's *Zakhor: Jewish History and Jewish Memory* (Seattle and London, 1982), pp. 55-75, and his "Clio and the Jews: Reflections on Jewish Historiography in the Sixteenth Century," *American Academy for Jewish Research Jubilee Volume* (*PAAJR* 46-47 [1979-80]): 607-638; Robert Bonfil, "How Golden Was the Age of the Renaissance in Jewish Historiography?" *History and Theory* 27 (1988): 78-102. Bonfil accounts for what he regards as the relative paucity of Jewish historical works on the grounds that diaspora Jews did not have the sort of political and military history that lent itself to the narrative style most characteristic of Renaissance historiography.

event, despite the great interest of several of these books and despite their frequent debt to Christian models, they do not challenge Jewish tradition.

Except one. Azariah de' Rossi's *Me'or 'Einayim*, which is not a narrative history but a series of historical studies, utilized non-Jewish sources to test the validity of historical assertions in Rabbinic texts to the point of rejecting the accepted chronology of the Second Temple and modifying the Jewish calendar's assumptions about the date of creation. The author was clearly sensitive to the prospect of opposition, and he defended the study of history on the grounds of religious utility and the intrinsic value of the search for truth. There is, however, considerable irony in his argument for rejecting historical statements of the Rabbis in favor of gentile authorities. The Sages, he writes, were concerned with important matters; with respect to trivial concerns like history, we should expect to find a greater degree of reliability in the works of gentiles, who after all specialize in trivialities.[127] The difficulty of distinguishing the strands of sincerity and disingenuousness in this assertion speaks volumes for the problematic nature of de' Rossi's undertaking. He can justify his methodology only by minimizing the significance of his discipline.

Contemporary histories differ about the novelty of de' Rossi's challenge. Since the reinterpretation and even rejection of *aggadah* had respectable medieval precedent, Salo Baron and Robert Bonfil have argued that Azariah did little more than broaden the grounds for such a step to embrace historical as well as philosophical or kabbalistic considerations. Yosef Yerushalmi, on the other hand, sees a more radical and significant innovation in *Me'or 'Einayim*; philosophy and kabbalah, he argues, had long been regarded as sources of truth, while Azariah was willing to utilize "profane history... drawn from Greek, Roman and Christian writers" to judge the validity of rabbinic statements.[128] The distinction is important and the formulation can, I think, be sharpened. Philosophical truth was not based on the authority of Aristotle; it rested on arguments that Aristotle may have formulated

---

[127] *Sefer Me'or 'Einayim*, ed. by David Cassel (Vilna, 1866), p. 216.

[128] See Baron, *History and Jewish Historians* (Philadelphia, 1964), pp. 167-239, 405-442; Bonfil, "Some Reflections on the Place of Azariah de' Rossi's *Me'or 'Einayim* in the Cultural Milieu of Italian Renaissance Jewry," in *Jewish Thought in the Sixteenth Century*, pp. 23-48, esp. 23-25; Yerushalmi, "Clio and the Jews," pp. 634-635, and *Zakhor*, p. 72.

but were now available to any thinker in an unmediated fashion. It was reason, not Aristotle, that required the reinterpretation of whatever Rabbinic text was at issue. History is different. Although reason is very much involved and the decision to follow a gentile account instead of a rabbinic one does not result from a simple preference for Tacitus over Rabbi Yosi, the fact remains that on some level one is accepting the testimony of gentiles rather than that of the Talmudic sages. This may be a legitimate extension of the medieval precedent, but it is hardly a straightforward one.

This point tells us something significant about Italian Jewry and not merely about de' Rossi. Bonfil has demonstrated convincingly that the Italian attack on *Me'or 'Einayim* was much more limited in both its ideological scope and its degree of support than historians used to think. Since Bonfil himself does not see the work as radically innovative, he regards the relatively mild opposition as roughly the sort of reaction that we might have expected. Yerushalmi, writing before Bonfil's study, made the cautious observation that "it is perhaps a token of the flexibility of Italian Jewry that the ban upon the book, [which] only required that special permission be obtained by those who wanted to read it, was not always enforced stringently." If we accept, as I think we should, both Yerushalmi's perception of the book and Bonfil's findings about the ban, the implications for Italian Jewry become more striking. A substantial majority of the rabbinic leadership accepted with equanimity a work which treated the historical statements of the ancient Sages with startling freedom. The contrast with the intense opposition to *Me'or 'Einayim* from R. Joseph Caro in Safed and R. Judah Loew (Maharal) in Prague highlights the openness of sixteenth-century Italian Jews to non-Jewish sources and the willingness to utilize them even in the most sensitive of contexts.[129]

---

[129] See Yerushalmi, "Clio," p. 635; *Zakhor*, pp. 72-73. On R. Joseph Caro, see the references in Segal, *Historical Consciousness*, p. 68, n. 51; on the Maharal, see Segal, pp. 133-161. Another, perhaps fairer way to make the point would be to say that Italian Jewry agreed with Bonfil while the Maharal and R. Joseph Caro agreed with Yerushalmi, but this alone would fail to convey the significance of the Italian position. For a nuanced discussion of major features of de' Rossi's work, see now Bonfil's elaborate introduction to his anthology, *Kitvei 'Azariah min ha-Adummim: Mivhar Peraqim mi-tokh Sefer Me'or 'Einayim ve-Sefer Mazref la-Kesef* (Jerusalem, 1991).

THE SCIENTIFIC REVOLUTION
AND THE TRANSITION TO MODERN TIMES

Apart from the humanistic pursuits that characterized the Renaissance, early modern Europe also witnessed an increasing interest in the natural world. Though the most significant manifestation of this interest was the Copernican revolution and its aftermath, scientifically oriented Jews in the sixteenth, seventeenth, and early eighteenth centuries evinced greater interest in new approaches to chemistry, medicine, zoology, botany, mineralogy, and geography. Hundreds of Jews graduated from the medical school in Padua. Various Jewish works demonstrate familiarity with Paracelsian chemical medicine and Cartesian mechanics, and they display an insatiable curiosity about wondrous beasts and other natural marvels widely reported in an age of exploration. We find a revival and elaboration of the medieval arguments for the Jewish origin of the sciences and their religious utility along with a recognition that the ancient philosophers had attained important religious truths unaided by Jewish instruction.[130]

Jewish enthusiasm for these new scientific pursuits was greatly facilitated by a critically important conceptual change. In the Middle

---

[130] See David B. Ruderman, *Science, Medicine, and Jewish Culture in Early Modern Europe. Spiegel Lectures in European Jewish History* 7 (Tel Aviv, 1987), and his overlapping article, "The Impact of Science on Jewish Culture and Society in Venice," in *Gli Ebrei e Venezia* (Milan, 1987), pp. 417-448. See also his *Kabbalah, Magic, and Science: The Cultural Universe of a Sixteenth-Century Jewish Physician* (Cambridge, Mass., and London, 1988). In light of Abba Mari of Lunel's salute to Aristotle for achieving genuine monotheism in the absence of revelation, Ruderman's description of Abraham Yagel's "remarkable" assertion that pagan philosophers "discovered their faith independently of Jewish revelation" (p. 146) needs to be toned down a bit; see above, n. 76. For Jews at the medical school in Padua, see above, n. 115.

On the Jewish origins of the sciences, see, in addition to the references in n. 37 of Ruderman's lecture, the introduction to David Kaufmann's *Die Sinne*, and D. Margalit, "'Al Galenus ve-Gilgulo ha-'Ivri Gamliel," *Sinai* 33 (1953): 75-77. On geography, see L. Zunz, "Essay on the Geographical Literature of the Jews from the Remotest Times to the Year 1840," in *The Itinerary of R. Benjamin of Tudela*, trans. by A. Asher, 2 (London, 1841), pp. 230-317; Ruderman, *The World of a Renaissance Jew: The Life and Thought of Abraham ben Mordecai Farissol* (Cincinnati, 1981), pp. 131-143; André Neher, *Jewish Thought and the Scientific Revolution of the Sixteenth Century: David Gans (1541-1613) and His Times* (Oxford and New York, 1986), pp. 95-165.

For a major synthesis and analysis of the entire subject, see now Ruderman's *Jewish Thought and Scientific Discovery in Early Modern Europe* (New Haven, 1995).

Ages, the natural sciences were part of a larger tapestry whose dominant element was metaphysics. During the Renaissance and beyond, philosophy and certain kinds of science grew apart, and the scientific domain itself came to be divided between empiricist and rationalist-mathematical spheres. In this environment, certain scientific fields were uncontaminated by the philosophical baggage associated in some Jewish minds with Aristotelianism, and a Jew could remain a staunch opponent of rationalism in its medieval mode while retaining an intense interest in the new science.[131]

The Jewish absorption of the monumental revolution in astronomy was far more problematic. David Gans of late sixteenth-century Prague, though best known for his historical work *Zemah David*, was the first influential Jew to confront Copernicanism, and his attitude to the new astronomy is characteristic of what was probably the dominant reaction by knowledgeable Jews through the early eighteenth century: interested awareness but ultimate rejection.[132] Although Yosef Shlomo Delmedigo, who studied with Galileo and ended his days in Prague, spoke very highly of Copernicus, two major compendia at the very end of our period still reject the heliocentric theory in sharp terms. Toviah Katz described Copernicus's position with some care and even presented a series of Copernican arguments; at the same time, he called him "the firstborn of Satan" and described the adherents of his view as heretics.[133] Similarly,

---

[131]   David Ruderman is largely responsible for sharpening my awareness of this point. On the division within the sciences, see Thomas S. Kuhn, "Mathematical vs. Experimental Traditions in the Development of Physical Science," *Journal of Interdisciplinary History* 1 (1976): 1-31. As I indicated above, it is important to note that for medieval Ashkenazic Jews, the link between empirical science and rationalist philosophy had never been made, and so their interest in the physical world was never encumbered by this complication.

[132]   See Neher, *Jewish Thought and the Scientific Revolution*.

[133]   *Ma'aseh Toviah* (Krakau, 1908), pp. 43b-44b ("'Olam ha-Galgalim," ch. 4). Ruderman (*Science, Medicine, and Jewish Culture*, p. 21) notes correctly that the chapter ends "limply," without any refutation of the Copernican arguments noted. Nonetheless, the conclusion is slightly more forceful than he indicates. Toviah does not assert that the unspecified counterarguments "are easily confusing [even] to one who understands them"; he says that their validity is easily evident to such a person (*benaqel nekhohot*, not *nevukhot*). Moreover, the previous chapter sets forth six standard arguments against the Copernican theory.

On Delmedigo, see Isaac Barzilay, *Yosef Shlomo Delmedigo, Yashar of Candia: His Life, Works, and Times* (Leiden, 1974), and Yosef Levi, "Aqademiah Yehudit le-Madda'im be-Reshit ha-Me'ah ha-Sheva-'Esreh: Nisyono shel Yosef Shlomoh Delmedigo," *Proceedings of the Eleventh World Congress of Jewish Studies*, Division B, vol. 1, Hebrew section, pp. 169-176.

David Nieto dismissed the Copernican conception as an abomination.[134] By this time, the scientific defense of the Ptolemaic system had become very difficult, but Copernicus had still not carried the day among all intellectuals, let alone among the masses. Since most seventeenth- and early eighteenth-century European Jews, especially outside Italy, were relatively isolated from the burgeoning scientific community, and since they had rabbinic as well as biblical texts to inhibit their receptivity to the new astronomy, it is not surprising that they generally cast their lot with the rear guard action aimed against the Copernican revolution.

During the centuries in which modern Europe was being formed, the major Jewish cultural centers turned inward despite the growing Jewish involvement in national and international commerce. In a recent revisionist work, Jonathan Israel has argued that the period from 1550 to 1713, and particularly from 1650 to 1713, saw "the most profound and pervasive impact on the west which [the Jews] were ever to exert while retaining a large measure of social and cultural cohesion." To the extent that he applies this observation to economics and politics, including the ascendancy of Court Jews in Central Europe and elsewhere and the rough synchronism of Ashkenazi and Sephardi influence on finance and trade, he provides an important new perspective on early modern Jewry. On the other hand, he underestimates and misconceives much of medieval Jewish culture and considerably overrates the achievements of early modern Jews when he writes that "the radical transformation of Jewish culture which occurred during the middle decades of the sixteenth century was, assuredly, one of the most fundamental and remarkable phenomena distinguishing post-Temple Jewish history" and then extends his enthusiastic evaluation into the following century as well.[135]

As we have seen, Italian Jewish culture was indeed marked by an impressive synthesis of Jewish pride and openness to the surrounding

---

[134] This translation may be a trifle too strong for *piggul*, but Neher's effort to soften Nieto's anti-Copernicanism by taking "piggul hu lo yerazeh" in the narrow legalistic sense determined by the phrase's biblical context ("a sacrifice which would not be acceptable in the Temple") is an apologetic distortion of a very strong expression; see *Jewish Thought and the Scientific Revolution*, p. 256. On Delmedigo, Katz, Nieto, and others, see Hillel Levine, "Paradise Not Surrendered: Jewish Reactions to Copernicus and the Growth of Modern Science," in *Epistemology, Methodology, and the Social Sciences*, ed. by Robert S. Cohen and Mark W. Wartofsky (Dordrecht, Boston, and London, 1983), pp. 203-225.

[135] Jonathan I. Israel, *European Jewry in the Age of Mercantilism, 1550-1750*, 2nd ed. (Oxford, 1989). The quotations are from pp. 1 and 70.

culture. In the new Jewish community of seventeenth-century Holland, Sephardic Jews, including some with a Marrano past that made them fully conversant with Christian civilization, contributed philosophical, polemical, and scientific works that utilized wide learning and, when written or available in the vernacular, sometimes influenced European intellectuals. It was not only in Italy that Christian Hebraists held discussions with Jews about scholarly and religious issues. Court Jews were necessarily conversant with the surrounding culture while remaining, at least in many cases, loyal members of the Jewish community.[136]

At the same time, the major seventeenth-century Jewish centers outside Italy were either in a state of cultural decline or evinced relatively little concern with intellectual trends in the surrounding society. Jewry under Islam confronted a Muslim world that was itself culturally stagnant and consequently failed to provide the stimulus that Jewish thinkers needed for creative engagement with disciplines outside of Torah. Theoretically, this Jewry continued to value the sort of intellectual described in an early seventeenth-century chronicle from Fez as

> a complete scholar thoroughly familiar with all the sciences: the science of speculation (*'iyyun*) to an infinite degree, the science of grammar, the science of philosophy, the science of metrical poetry. There was no one like him among all the scholars of Israel.... If anyone had an uncertainty regarding a passage in *Tosafot* or the work of R. Elijah Mizrahi or the Talmud, he would come to this scholar and would not leave until those uncertainties would be fully resolved.[137]

Nevertheless, such scholarship, at least with respect to philosophy, meant mastery of an existing corpus rather than the production of original, creative work.

Ashkenazic Jewry had always felt more of an adversarial relationship with the surrounding society, and even the examples of cultural interaction

---

[136] Israel, *European Jewry*, pp. 70-86, 142-144, 216-231. On the former Marranos, see Yosef Kaplan, "The Portuguese Community of Amsterdam in the Seventeenth Century between Tradition and Change," in *Society and Community*, ed. by Abraham Hain (Jerusalem, 1991), pp. 141-171, and Kaplan, "Die Portugiesischen Juden und die Modernisierung: zur Veränderung jüdischen Lebens vor der Emanzipation," in *Jüdische Lebenswelten: Essays*, ed. by Andreas Nachama et al. (Frankfurt a.M., 1991), pp. 303-317.

[137] *Divrei ha-Yamim*, in *Fez va-Hakhameha*, ed. by David Ovadia, 1 (Jerusalem, 1979), pp. 47-48. Cf. Elazar Touitou, *Rabbi Hayyim Ibn 'Attar u-Perusho Or ha-Hayyim 'al ha-Torah* (Jerusalem, 1981), p. 28.

that we examined earlier were often characterized by an element of reserve or competition. With the removal of the Ashkenazic center to the alien environment of Poland, the sense of existential separateness was reinforced, and Jacob Katz has noted that even the martyrdoms in seventeenth-century Poland differ from those of the Crusades as defiant confrontation gave way to a sense of isolation from a hostile environment.[138] Although sixteenth-century Poland was not unaffected by the intellectual currents inspired by humanism and the Reformation, the rationalism that found lukewarm expression in R. Moses Isserles and some of his contemporaries essentially came from a culture outside the immediate environment. As Poland became a cultural backwater in seventeenth- and eighteenth-century Europe, this mild philosophical interest found no reinforcement either in the surrounding society or the indigenous Ashkenazic tradition, and without such reinforcement it largely faded away.

Even in seventeenth-century Germany, which was closer to the center of European creativity, there was insufficient impetus for Ashkenazic Jews to overcome the cultural legacy of their formative period without substantial struggle and considerable delay. In many cases, the communities were being reconstituted in the wake of expulsions and persecutions. The gradual opening of Christian society to some Jews began to undermine the observance of Jewish individuals rather than inspire an intellectual transformation and Renaissance.

Profound differences separated the medieval Iberian experience of a culturally stimulating environment from the situation of early modern Ashkenazim. First, the Jews of Northern Europe came to modernity with a deeply entrenched, fully formed approach that was highly suspicious of external wisdom. Second, the challenges of modern science and philosophical skepticism could not be faced in the kind of partnership with the dominant society that medieval Jews had enjoyed. It is true that Christianity had to face these challenges quite as much as Judaism, but the challenges emanated from Christian society itself, not from a philosophy inherited from classical antiquity. Thus, the search for intellectual allies was severely complicated. Traditional Christians were for the most part heirs to a fully developed, millennial legacy of

---

[138] Katz, *Exclusiveness and Tolerance* (Oxford, 1961), pp. 131-155, and "Bein Tatnu LeTah-Tat," *Sefer Yovel le-Yitzhak Baer*, ed. by S. Ettinger et al. (Jerusalem, 1961), pp. 318-337.

contempt for Judaism; seventeenth-century skeptics and eighteenth-century *philosophes* regarded Judaism with at least as much disdain as they felt for Christianity and were in any event the authors of the very challenge that had to be faced. When medieval philosophers were called heretics, they usually denied the charge; the moderns often embraced it, indeed, shouted it from the rooftops. The pursuit of speculative thought became associated with irreligion to a far more profound and extensive degree than it had in the Middle Ages.

Moreover, the nature of modern philosophy was so different from that of the medieval past that the religious attractiveness of the discipline was severely undermined. To the medievals, if philosophy posed serious challenges to religious faith, it also provided indispensable insights into the nature of God. Modern philosophy seemed to supply little more than the problems. At best, religious philosophers could refute attacks against the faith, but they would probably not emerge with new insights about the issues that they were accustomed to regard as the classic subject matter of philosophy. They would find little but heresy on divine providence, hardly anything on attributes or incorporeality, and nothing at all about the recently deceased active intellect and celestial spheres. If all philosophy could achieve was the neutralizing of its own evil influence, then ignoring the enterprise could achieve the same result at a great saving of time and effort, not to speak of averting danger to one's faith. The imperative of answering the heretic was rarely sufficient in itself to inspire philosophical study. In addition to these critical considerations, the religious value of philosophical inquiry was radically diminished by the conviction of many traditional Jews at the dawn of the Enlightenment that the crucial information about God was available through kabbalah.

For the sake of sharpening the analysis, I have intentionally formulated these points with one-dimensional vigor. If modern philosophy did not provide solutions to medieval questions about God and creation, it might nevertheless suggest new areas of fruitful inquiry. The medieval argument that studying the world inspires love of God seemed all the more persuasive to believers beholding the mathematically elegant universe of the new science. We cannot, however, expect the rabbinic leadership of Ashkenazic Jewry to have known the evolving new approaches well enough to have formulated an innovative positive response; indeed, in the early stages they did not know them well enough even to have fully appreciated the new dangers.

Thus, when we do find an interest in philosophical inquiry among the rabbis of early modern Ashkenaz, it tends to take a very traditional form. R. Yair Hayyim Bacharach, for example, laid great emphasis on the practical primacy of talmudic study and the theoretical primacy of kabbalah, while demonstrating considerable familiarity with Jewish philosophical literature. In a study of Bacharach, Isadore Twersky observes that "philosophic literature was studied for religious reasons, as part of a spiritual quest, totally separate from external contacts and influences." R. Jacob Emden reports in his autobiography that his father Hakham Zevi Ashkenazi read secular works "in his spare time" and studied "other knowledge" with the scholars who attended the *Klaus* that he headed in late seventeenth-century Hamburg "until they achieved perfection in Torah and wisdom"; here too we are undoubtedly dealing with something other than a fresh and creative confrontation with the world of modern wisdom.[139]

By the mid-eighteenth century, Emden's own ambivalent attitude to the study of the "external" disciplines reflects the growing impact of the European opening to the Jews. His essential position is quite negative; at the same time, he speaks of a yearning for the sciences which he fulfilled in part by reading Hebrew books in fields like history and geography and in part by studying the works of non-Jews in the bathroom. His familiarity with the New Testament is striking, and it comes together with a relatively favorable attitude to Jesus and even to Paul. What is most interesting is a recurring justification for secular study that does not appear in premodern times. Jews, says Emden, must achieve some familiarity with gentile language and culture for the sake of mingling comfortably with people. This is a striking reflection of a changed social atmosphere with far-reaching importance for the integration of Jews into European society.[140]

Outside of rabbinic circles, incipient social integration in a world of growing religious skepticism gradually eroded the loyalties of some Ashkenazic Jews. Beginning around the end of the seventeenth century,

---

[139]   On Bacharach, see I. Twersky, "Law and Spirituality in the Seventeenth Century: A Case Study in R. Yair Hayyim Bacharach," in *Jewish Thought in the Seventeenth Century*, pp. 447-467 (quotation from p. 455). On Hakham Zevi, see Emden's *Megillat Sefer*, ed. by D. Kahana (Warsaw, 1897), pp. 11, 16-17, cited in Jacob J. Schacter, *Rabbi Jacob Emden: Life and Major Works* (Harvard University dissertation, 1988), pp. 587-588.

[140]   See chapter 6 of Schacter's dissertation for a discussion of Emden's general stance, and see especially p. 505, where he notes the novelty of the argument from social interaction.

substantial numbers of Jews began to drift away from accepted religious norms, and a smaller number may even have rejected traditional beliefs under the influence of Enlightenment thought. The official community, however, did not begin to change until the second half of the eighteenth century, when leaders of the Jewish Enlightenment began to demand curricular reform and social accommodation.[141]

Despite the fact that these demands were often made in the name of the well-attested rationalist tradition that we have examined throughout this study, the timing, the context, and the orientation of the new movement made it a threat to the established order both politically and religiously. European Jewry, like European Christendom, faced a world in which religion itself could no longer be taken for granted. In the new, largely secular order that established itself in the eighteenth century and continues to our own day, the legitimacy of general culture remained an issue only for the traditionalist segment of the Jewish people, and the terms of the debate were narrowed and transformed. For some, the overwhelming new dangers required an ever more stringent isolation from the evils of modernity. For others, these dangers could be tamed by selective admission of the religiously neutral elements of the new society and culture. For a few, the Torah itself required a heroic confrontation with modernity in all its fullness, a confrontation that would enrich both Judaism and the world.

ACKNOWLEDGMENTS

This essay was written when I was a fellow at the Annenberg Research Institute during the academic year 1989-1990. It is a pleasure to thank the staff of the Institute and of its library for their courtesy and

---

[141] On the timing and extent of these transformations, see the debate between Azriel Schochet, *'Im Hillufei Tequfot* (Jerusalem, 1960), and Jacob Katz, *Out of the Ghetto* (Cambridge, 1973). Cf. Schochet's "Reshit ha-Haskalah ba-Yahadut be-Germania," *Molad* 23 (1965): 328-334. See also Israel, who argues very strongly that there was widespread abandonment of tradition, including outright conversion (*European Jewry*, pp. 254-256). On apostasy in the wake of Sabbatianism, see Elisheva Carlebach, "Sabbatianism and the Jewish-Christian Polemic," *Proceedings of the Tenth World Congress of Jewish Studies*, Division C, 2 (1990): 6-7. For a relevant analysis that focuses primarily on a later period, see David Sorkin, *The Transformation of German Jewry*, 1780-1840 (New York, 1987).

professionalism. It is a particular pleasure to thank Professor Daniel J. Lasker, who occupied the office next to mine and served as an unfailing source of sound advice and refreshing good humor. I no doubt invaded the offices of two additional fellows of the institute far too frequently, but Professors Anita Shapira and William C. Jordan provided such intellectual stimulation that any expression of regret that I might offer for those interruptions would be insincere. Please forgive me, but I confess that I would do it again.

Outside the institute, Professors Menahem Ben Sasson and David Ruderman read the entire manuscript and provided illuminating, significant suggestions, many of which I had the good sense to incorporate. I am very grateful to Dr. Jacob J. Schacter for his meticulous editorial supervision, which was often substantive as well as technical. After my return from Annenberg, I benefited from the welcoming atmosphere, extraordinary resources, and knowledgeable staff at the Mendel Gottesman Library of Yeshiva University in preparing the final version of the study. While I have added references to more recent scholarship and included many observations reflecting subsequent research, the 1990 text remains at the core of this work.

Finally, my wife Pearl as well as Miriam, Elie, Yitzhak, and Gedalyah not only endured my weekly absences during preparations for the marriage which brought Elie into the family, but, together with Ditza and Miriam, who have joined us more recently, provided love, encouragement, and the inspiration that comes from their own embodiment of Torah and the best of general culture.

HOW DID NAHMANIDES PROPOSE TO RESOLVE
THE MAIMONIDEAN CONTROVERSY?

From: *Meah She'arim: Studies in Medieval Jewish Spiritual Life in Memory of Isadore Twersky*, ed. by Ezra Fleischer et al. (Magnes: Jerusalem, 2001), pp. 135-146.

The permissibility of pursuing "external wisdom" became a major motif in the intellectual history of the Jews during the Middle Ages, and in the 1230's it exploded into the greatest controversy that had ever shaken European Jewry, cutting across the three major cultural centers of Northern Europe, Southern France, and Iberia. Concerned by allegorization of Scripture and other manifestations of philosophical radicalism, R. Solomon b. Abraham of Montpellier dispatched his distinguished student R. Jonah Gerondi to Northern France with copies of Maimonides' *Guide of the Perplexed* and *Sefer ha-Madda* so that he might alert the Northern Rabbis to the sort of works that had been used and misused by the radical allegorizers.

Whatever Rabbi Solomon's intentions, the result was a ban prohibiting the study of both books. Enraged, Provencal advocates of philosophical study proclaimed a counterban against R. Solomon and his disciples and sent their own distinguished representative, the aged R. David Kimhi, to solicit support for the counterban among their presumed natural allies in Northern Spain. Radak's mixed reception speaks volumes for the intellectual and religious changes in certain segments of the Sephardic elite during the early thirteenth century. In some circles he received the unalloyed support that he expected; elsewhere, however, for reasons ranging from the ideological to the personal, he encountered reluctance, ambivalence, even hostility.[1] With the benefit of hindsight,

---

[1] The best reconstruction of the course of events remains that of Azriel Schochet, "Berurim be-Parashat ha-Pulmus ha-Rishon 'al Sifrei ha-Rambam," *Zion* 36 (1971): 27-60. For a recent analysis, see my discussion in Gerald J. Blidstein, David Berger, Sid Z. Leiman and Aharon Lichtenstein, *Judaism's Encounter with Other Cultures: Rejection or*

we can unhesitatingly identify Nahmanides as the most distinguished Spanish Rabbi in the 1230's, indeed, in the entire history of Christian Spain. At the time, his preeminence was not quite so unambiguous, but all sides surely recognized that his stand in the controversy would loom large. It was hardly a simple matter, however, to predict the position of a figure who exemplified in striking fashion the kaleidoscopic variety of intellectual and spiritual currents which swirled through Provencal and Spanish Jewish communities during those decades. Talmudic exegete and codifier, mystic, physician, theologian, poet, biblical commentator, communal leader, and future polemicist, Nahmanides absorbed and reshaped the influence of Tosafist dialectic, of Southern French Rabbinics and kabbalah, and of indigenous Spanish traditions. Nahmanides' attitude toward philosophical study reflected the complexity of his intellectual and spiritual legacy. He studied the philosophical corpus of his Jewish predecessors, greatly admired Maimonides, and insisted on the value of theological investigation in his work on theodicy. At the same time, he despised Aristotle, vigorously rejected many of Maimonides' rationalistic assertions, and believed the secrets of the Torah to be embodied in mysticism rather than metaphysics. As I have noted elsewhere, Nahmanides regarded the revelation as an empirical datum *par excellence*, so that philosophical inquiry could build upon it without struggling by unaided reason to reach conclusions already provided by God. Consequently, Nahmanides expressed his central views in the form of a commentary to the revelation, and his attraction to kabbalah was itself an expression of his search for a revealed source of theological truths.[2] This presentation of Nahmanides' position hardly reflects the unvarying consensus of modern scholarship. Because of the great variety of strands which formed his religious persona, students of medieval history and philosophy, of the Maimonidean controversy, and of Nahmanides himself have perceived him in strikingly different ways. Until quite recently, most scholars placed

---

Integration?, ed. by Jacob J. Schacter (Northvale, N.J., and Jerusalem, 1997), pp. 85-100.

[2]   See my "Miracles and the Natural Order in Nahmanides," in *Rabbi Moses Nahmanides (Ramban): Explorations in his Religious and Literary Virtuosity*, ed. by Isadore Twersky (Cambridge, Mass., 1983), pp. 110-111, and my discussion in *Judaism's Encounter*, pp. 99-100. See too my unpublished Master's essay (which analyzes more briefly the letter which stands at the center of this article), *Nahmanides' Attitude toward Secular Learning and Its Bearing upon his Stance in the Maimonidean Controversy* (Columbia University, 1965), chapter 1 (pp. 2-23).

him squarely in the anti-philosophical camp, and some of these regarded his expressions of admiration for Maimonides and his works as tactical stratagems that did not reflect his deepest convictions.[3] Other scholars understood that this one-sided picture of Nahmanides was a caricature, but presenting a balanced, integrated portrait of his multi-faceted genius remained a daunting task.[4] As we shall see, all students of Nahmanides face a difficult challenge in describing and accounting for his position during the Maimonidean controversy. Though a full characterization of his stand requires the analysis of more than one document, by far the most important source is a much-discussed letter that he wrote to the rabbis of Northern France. Here, textual uncertainties and ideological perplexities have produced contradictions and confusion in the scholarly literature. My limited purpose in this essay is to examine some of these uncertainties with the hope that confusion will give way to clarity. The bulk of this

---

[3]   Note, inter alia, Salo Baron, *A Social and Religious History of the Jews*, first edition (New York, 1937), vol. 2, p. 140 ("With the growth of antirationalist forces, most kabbalists rejected Maimonides and all scholasticism. With Nahmanides, the antiphilosophical reaction received the stamp of approval from a revered authority."); J. Newman, *The Commentary of Nahmanides on Genesis Chapters 1-6:8* (Leiden, 1960), pp. 13-14; the references to Y. Baer, H.H. Ben Sasson, Y. Kaplan, S. Krauss and others in Bernard Septimus, "'Open Rebuke and Concealed Love': Nahmanides and the Andalusian Tradition," in Twersky, *Rabbi Moses Nahmanides*, p. 14, n. 12. Krauss (*Ha-Goren* 5 [1905]: 84, 88) affirms that Nahmanides was insincere even in his limited defense of philosophy and goes so far as to ascribe to him a belief in the corporeality of God; for a more recent affirmation of the erroneous view that Nahmanides was an anthropomorphist, see Martin A. Cohen, "Reflections on the Text and Context of the Disputation of Barcelona," *Hebrew Union College Annual* 35 (1964): 169, 176.

[4]   Though leaving much to be desired, the most successful effort in the nineteenth century was Joseph Perles, "Über den Geist des Commentars des R. Moses ben Nachman zum Pentateuch und über sein Verhältniss zum Pentateuch-Commentar Raschis," *Monatsschrift für Geschichte und Wissenschaft des Judenthums (MGWJ)* 7 (1858): 81-97, 117-136. The best characterization to date is Septimus, "'Open Rebuke and Concealed Love'" (n. 3). See too Ch. Henoch, *Ha-Ramban ke-Hoqer ve-ki-Mequbbal* (Jerusalem, 1978); Moshe Idel, "R. Mosheh ben Nahman—Kabbalah, Halakhah, u-Manhigut Ruhanit," *Tarbiz* 64 (1995): 535-580; Y. Tzvi Langermann, "Acceptance and Devaluation: Nahmanides' Attitude toward Science," *Journal of Jewish Thought and Philosophy* 1(1992): 223-245; David Novak, *The Theology of Nahmanides Systematically Presented* (Atlanta, 1992); Josef Stern, "Nachmanides's Conception of Taʿamei Mitzvot and its Maimonidean Background," in *Community and Covenant: New Essays in Jewish Political and Legal Philosophy* ed. by Daniel Frank (Albany, 1995), pp. 141-171; Stern, "The Fall and Rise of Myth in Ritual: Maimonides versus Nahmanides on the *Huqqim*, Astrology, and the War against Idolatry," *The Journal of Jewish Thought and Philosophy* 6 (1997): 185-263.

highly respectful, even deferential letter explains that the rabbis of the North do not fully understand the cultural circumstances that produced Maimonides' *Guide* and indicates why his purportedly objectionable views are either correct or at least well within the framework of normative Judaism. The *Mishneh Torah*, including *Sefer ha-Madda*, receives unstinting praise; while one may challenge specific points, the work itself is Torah pure and simple. Finally, as he concludes his lengthy, eloquent defense of "the great rabbi," Nahmanides sets forth a concrete proposal. The first element of this proposal is crystal clear: the ban against both books must be revoked. At this point, however, textual problems begin to muddy the waters. Nahmanides' letter is extant in three versions. Chaim Dov Chavel reproduced the poorest of these in the first two printings of his standard *Kitvei Ramban*; beginning with the third printing, he published a better one based on the first printed edition. The best text was published in 1860 from a Saraval manuscript by Joseph Perles, who supplied variant readings from the other versions.[5] Because Chavel's text is by far the most widely used and hence the most influential, our story must begin there. After the vigorous recommendation that the ban against the *Guide* and the *Sefer ha-Madda* be revoked, the letter in the current printings of *Kitvei Ramban* continues as follows:

ויצא דבר מלכות מלפניכם ותהיו לאגודה ולקשר של קיימא לאבד זרוע רמה להחרים לנדות
ולשמת כל לשון מדברת גדולות אשר האלוהים יצמת המליעיג על ההגדות או מרחיב פה על
האסמכתות ואל עוסקי ספר מורה הנבוכים כתות כתות תשימו יד מוראכם אל פיהם, (והיא מן
המדה) כי מצות הרב הגדול המחברו הוא לאמור: 'לא תפרשוהו ולא תפרסמוהו'.

Let a royal command issue forth from you as you become a single group and a lasting bond to destroy an upraised arm, to excommunicate, ban, and place under a curse every tongue speaking arrogantly which God will destroy, one who mocks the *aggadot* or opens his mouth against *asmakhtot*. As for those who study the *Guide of the Perplexed* in groups, place your fearsome hand to their mouth, for the command of the great rabbi who wrote it was, "Do not

---

5   See C.D. Chavel, *Kitvei Ramban* (Jerusalem, 1963), vol. 1, pp. 333-351; Joseph Perles, "Nachträge über R. Moses ben Nachman," *MGWJ* 9 (1860): 175-195. For the publication history of the various versions, see Mauro Perani, "Mistica e Filosofia: La Mediazione di Nahmanide nella Polemica sugli Scritti di Maimonide," in *Correnti Culturali e Movimenti Religiosi del Giudaismo*, ed. by Bruno Chiesa (Rome, 1987) (*Atti del V Congresso internazionale dell' Associazione Italiana per lo Studio del Giudaismo* [AISG Testi e Studi 5]), p. 239, n. 35.

interpret or publicize it."[6]

This appears to be perfectly clear, and indeed it is. The ban on private study of the *Guide* should be revoked, but a ban on group study should remain (or be instituted). Nonetheless, Chavel, following Ze'ev Jawitz, was persuaded by a later passage (which we shall examine presently) that Nahmanides did not want any ban at all against the *Guide*. A reader who regards such a conclusion as firmly established can force this text to conform to it. Thus, the ban might apply to those who speak arrogantly and who mock Rabbinic texts, but for those who study the *Guide* in groups, a fearsome hand (without a ban) is sufficient. Chavel himself goes even further than this. His English translation of the letter reads as follows:

> ...to excommunicate, ban, and desolate every "tongue that maketh great boasts," while God will crush whoever mocks the Agadoth (homilies) or speaks boldly [and disparagingly] about the Scriptural supports [for Rabbinic interpretations]. Concerning those who engage [themselves] in group study of the book Moreh Nebuchim, lay the hand of your fear upon their mouth.[7]

This translation appears to limit the ban to those who make unspecified "great boasts" without applying it even to those who mock the Rabbis. As for group study of the *Guide*, Chavel explains in his note to the last line that "lay the hand of your fear upon their mouth" means, "Your fear will leave them awestricken, unable to contravene your word." Any formal ban against organized study of the *Guide* has been made to disappear.[8] The language of the Saraval manuscript, however, links the

---

6   *Kitvei Ramban* I, p. 349. *Aggadot* are the non-legal pronouncements of the Rabbis; *asmakhtot* are Scriptural citations used to buttress Rabbinic laws. On the parenthetical phrase והיא מן המידה, which I have left untranslated, see n. 8.

7   Nahmanides, *Writings and Discourses*, translated by Charles B. Chavel (New York, 1978), vol. 2, p. 409.

8   Two additional points make the story of Chavel's understanding of this passage even more interesting. 1. His translation continues, "This is the proper measure [of action], for the charge of the great Rabbi [Maimonides], its author, was as follows: 'Do not explain it or publicize it.'" Presumably, he takes the first clause to mean that striking fear without a ban is the proper measure of action. The clause itself, however (והיא מן המידה), does not appear in the text utilized in the later printings of *Kitvei Ramban*, a text which forms the basis for Chavel's translation of the letter as a whole; it is, rather, borrowed from the text he used in the first two printings (see the end of this note), where it substitutes for a line in the current text and, as Perles remarked in his apparatus (*MGWJ* 9 (1860): 193, n. 15), defies comprehension. Chavel has not only

treatment of those who study the *Guide* in groups even more tightly to those who mock the Rabbis and speaks unambiguously of a ban.

ויצא דבר מלכות לפניכם ותהיו לאגודה ולקשר של קיימא לנדות ולשמת על לשון מדבר גדולות אשר אלהים יצמת, המלעיג על ההגדות או מרחיב פה על האסמכתות ועל עוסקי בספר מורה הנבוכים כתות כתות. כי מצות הרב הגדול המחבר היא לא תפרסמוהו ולא תפרשוהו.

Thus, the Rabbis should ban "the tongue speaking arrogantly which God will destroy, one who mocks the *aggadot* or opens his mouth against the *asmakhtot*, and those who study the *Guide of the Perplexed* in groups." Here there is no room for maneuver. Group study of the *Guide* is to be placed under a ban.[9] Let us now continue with Chavel's text:

ואם אתם רבותינו תסכימו עם חכמי פרובינצה וגם אנחנו נצא בעקבותיכם, תחזקו הדבר הזה בחרם ואלה, ברעם וברעש ובקול המולה גדולה ולהב אש אוכלה ובמלחמת תנופה עבדותו הרדפה הן למות הן לשרושי הן לענוש נכסין ולאסורין הלא די בזה תקנה וגרר.

And if you our Rabbis will agree with the Provencal sages and we too will follow in your footsteps, you will strengthen this matter with an excommunication and curse, with thunderous noise, a great roaring sound, the blaze of consuming fire, and sweeping warfare, engaging in pursuit unto death, uprooting, confiscation of possessions, or imprisonment [cf. Ezra 7:26]; with this step there will be a sufficient enactment and restraint.[10]

borrowed it from the other version; he has changed its location in order to provide the necessary transition. (In the current Hebrew printings, it appears in parentheses in its new location.) 2. In the version published in the first two printings, we find the erroneous reading תשימו יד מוראכם אל פיכם ("place your fearsome hand to your [not "their"] mouth"). In his note to that line, Chavel commented, "The intention is that you should place your hand to your mouth by refraining from issuing a curse and an excommunication, but only an enactment and restraint, as he explains later." In the later printings, this note has, of course, disappeared, but the overall interpretation which it presumably supported remains intact. (The truth is that even in the first version this reading was virtually impossible to sustain because of the immediate continuation.) To clarify these two points, let me present the relevant lines in Chavel's first printings, which correspond to the text in *Qovez Teshuvot ha-Rambam* (Leipzig, 1859), sec. 3, p. 10a:

ויצא דבר מלפניכם ותהיו לאגודה ולקשר של קימא והיא קימא מן המדה. ואל עוסקי ספר מורה הנבוכים כתות כתות תשימו יד מוראכם אל פיכם כי מצות הרב הגדול המחברו הוא לאמר: לא תפרשוהו ולא תפרסמוהו.

9   Perles' ed., p. 193. The point is that this text leaves us no syntactic option at all. ועל לנדות ולשמת עוסקי בספר מורה הנבוכים כתות כתות can only be governed by.

10   *Kitvei Ramban*, p. 349. The word that I have translated "pursuit" (*hardafah*) is actually

The last part of this sentence is the crux of our problem. As I have translated it, it means that a stringent ban against those who mock the Sages and study the *Guide* in groups is sufficient to address the legitimate concerns of the Northern French Rabbis; there is no need for a general ban against the *Guide*, let alone the *Sefer ha-Madda*ᶜ. The exaggerated rhetoric is there to persuade the Rabbis of the North that the narrow ban Nahmanides proposes is more than a symbolic gesture; at the same time, no one took literally the references to death and imprisonment taken from Ezra 7:26. This rhetoric does not obscure the main thrust of the proposal, which is the abolition of the key ban. Thus, Nahmanides can continue, as we shall see, with a description emphasizing the irenic character of his recommendation.

Jawitz, however, and Chavel after him, did not see the possibility of this reading or did not find it plausible in light of the continuation emphasizing peaceful persuasion. Thus, Chavel translates, "An ordinance and safeguard will suffice for this [problem]."[11] In other words, this clause explicitly rules out any ban. How, then, can this be reconciled with the categorical statement, "You will strengthen this matter with an excommunication..."? There is only one solution to the problem, and it was proposed as self-evident by Jawitz. The little word "not" (*lo*) is missing from the text. Hence, read, "*Do not* strengthen this matter with an excommunication."

Jawitz was so certain of this that in his critique of Graetz's understanding of the letter, he wrote the following remarkable footnote:

> It may well be that a little word, the word *lo* which is missing between 'footsteps' and 'strengthen' in the *Qovez Teshuvot ha-Rambam* before me, is also missing in the other versions of the letter to which I do not currently have access; perhaps (*sic!*) this is what caused Graetz to err. But who can fail to see that every word in the remainder of this passage demonstrates its [erroneous] omission, indeed proclaims that omission in the loudest tones?"[12]

the Talmud's explanation of the word I have translated "uprooting" (*sheroshi*); *hardafah* is in turn defined as excommunication. See *Bav. Moᶜed Qatan* 16a.

11 *Writings and Discourses*, p. 411.

12 Zeʾev Jawitz, *Toledot Yisrael*, vol. 12 (Tel Aviv, 1954), p. 183. Jawitz's conviction was certainly reinforced by the fact that he was working with the text that reads, "Place your fearsome hand to *your* mouth." (See above, n. 8.)

Although Chavel did not incorporate this emendation into his text, he cited it in a note, inserted it in brackets into his English translation, and predicated his entire understanding of the letter upon its validity. In the most recent study of the letter, Mauro Perani does not address this textual issue directly; nonetheless, his unqualified assertion that Nahmanides simply proposed the annulling of the ban indicates quite clearly that he reads the passage along the same lines.[13] I hesitate to say that this reading is the current state of the question—despite the crucial role of this letter in the controversy, there probably is no state of the question. What is certain is that this is a central position in current scholarship and the reigning impression among lay readers of the standard edition.[14]

I have already alluded to the irenic continuation of the letter and its impact on the deletion of the ban from the text by some scholars. Here, then, is that continuation, again following Chavel's text:

במרעה השלום תנהלו הצאן ובנאות האהבה תרביצו העדר, ועוד ראוי לכם להזהיר בנחת את

---

13   "Mistica e Filosofia" (n. 5), p. 251.

14   Neither Schochet nor Septimus clearly articulates his understanding of Nahmanides' position, though both properly refer the reader to Perles' edition. Schochet discusses only Nahmanides' proposal to annul the ban and tells his reader nothing about the concomitant recommendation to ban group study of the *Guide*; see "Berurim" (n. 1), p. 44.

In his *Maimonidean Criticism and the Maimonidean Controversy 1180-1240* (Leiden, 1965), Daniel Jeremy Silver, who used the edition in *Qovez Teshuvot ha-Rambam*, reported that Nahmanides "suggests peace and a withdrawal of the ban as the sole remedy; if not the withdrawal of the whole ban, at least of that part which subjects the *Mishneh Torah*" (p. 171). This summary, which misses the distinction between private and public study of the *Guide* while accurately reflecting Nahhmanides' far greater enthusiasm for the *Mishneh Torah*, is an indication of Silver's own struggle to determine the bottom line of this text.

The other book-length treatment of the controversy (Joseph Sarachek, *Faith and Reason: The Conflict over the Rationalism of Maimonides* [Williamsport, Penn., 1935]) maintains that Nahmanides urged that the ban be revoked. "In the first place, it should never have been enacted.... Under no circumstances...should the Book of Knowledge, a part of the Code, have been prohibited because it could not be put in the same category as the Guide.... On the other hand, extreme caution must be exercised in using the Guide. Maimonides himself urged that it not be studied save under certain stipulations, particularly, that people occupying themselves with it be mature in age and steeped in rabbinic literature" (pp. 116-118). In other words, no ban at all should remain, even against the *Guide*, although the latter should be studied only by properly qualified readers. Here again, the author's struggle to make sense of a challenging text is painfully evident.

הכל להניח העסק מכל וכל, ירא שמים ישוב וישקוד על ספר תורה שבכתב ותורה שבעל פה,
כי הוא בית חיינו ובזה מעלתנו תגדל, השומע ישמע והחדל יחדל, שאי אפשר לכם להוכיח
לכוף כל ישראל להיות חסידים. ובזה נהגו אבות העולם ליסר מזה חכמים גדולים, אף כי
למנוע מן ההגיון התלמידים המתחילים ללמוד, כמו שמצאתי בתשובת רבינו האי גאון ז"ל
לנגיד מ"כ שכתב לו בלשון הזה: 'תקון הגוף ומישור הנהגת האדם הוא עסק המשנה והתלמוד,
ואשר טוב לישראל... ואשר יסיר יסיר לבו מזה ויתעסק בדברים ההם בלבד, יסיר מעליו תורה
ויראת שמים, ויפסיד עצמו באותן העניינים הכתובים בספרים החצונים, ויסיר מעליו כל דברי
תורה לגמרי. ומזאת ההסרה יארע לאדם שישבש דעתו עד שלא יחוש לעזיבת התפלה....
ואם תראה שאותן בני אדם המתעסקים באותן הדברים ודרכי הפילוסופיא יאמרו לך שהיא
דרך סלולה ושבזה ישיגו לידיעת הבורא, לא תאבה להם, ודע כי יכזבו לך באמת. ולא תמצא
יראת חטא וענוה וקדושה אלא באותם המתעסקים במשנה ובתלמוד ובחכמה יחד, לא בדברי
חכמה בלבד'.

Guide the sheep in a peaceful pasture and rest the flock in meadows of love. It is also proper for you to admonish everyone gently to set aside the pursuit (*ha-ᶜeseq*) altogether, so that a Godfearing individual will return to diligent study of the written and oral Torah, for this is the abode of our life and through this will our standing increase. He who listens will listen, and he who refrains will refrain, for you can not admonish and compel all Israel to be saints. In such fashion were the fathers of the world accustomed to reprove even great scholars to refrain from this, and all the more to prevent beginning students from pursuing philosophy (*higgayon*), as I have found in a responsum of R. Hai Gaon of blessed memory to the Nagid, may his rest be honored, in which he wrote him as follows: "The perfection of the body and proper human behavior is [the result of] the pursuit of Mishnah and Talmud; this is what is good for Israel.... Anyone who removes his heart from this and pursues those matters *alone* will remove from himself Torah and the fear of heaven; he will ruin himself with those matters written in external books and will entirely remove from himself all the words of the Torah. And this removal will result in the confusion of a person's mind to the point where he will not be concerned about abandoning prayer.... If you will see that those people who pursue those matters and the ways of philosophy tell you that this is a paved road which enables them to attain knowledge of God, do not heed them, and know that they are in fact lying to you. You will not find fear of sin, humility and sanctity except in those who study Mishnah, Talmud, *and wisdom together, not matters of wisdom alone*."[15]

The authenticity of R. Hai's letter is in question, but this difficult

---

[15]   *Kitvei Ramban*, pp. 349-350. Whatever the meaning of *higgayon* may be in its original Talmudic context (*Bav. Berakhot* 28b), in this letter it appears to refer to philosophy.

problem need not detain us here.[16] There is no persuasive reason to
believe that it was interpolated into Nahmanides' letter, and our concern
here is with Nahmanides, not with R. Hai.[17] In the text printed by Chavel,
which is distinguished by the words I have italicized, the Gaon opposes
the exclusive study of philosophy but explicitly approves the study of
"wisdom" along with Torah. Jawitz, Chavel, and Perano endorse this
version as consistent with what they believe to be the overall tenor of
the letter. This reading, however, must overcome nearly insuperable
obstacles.

First of all, it is difficult to sustain even in its original setting. Did R.
Hai really have to polemicize against the position that one should study
no Torah at all? Moreover, Nahmanides introduces the Gaon's letter by
saying that one should gently admonish people "to set aside the pursuit
(*ha-ʿeseq*) altogether." This has to mean that philosophy should not be
studied at all. Jawitz apparently took the "pursuit" here to mean study
of the *Guide* in groups, while Chavel and Perano take it as "excessive
study of the *Guide*";[18] given their version of the quotation from R. Hai,
such desperate efforts are understandable, but they are implausible in
the extreme.

The Saraval manuscript as well as other citations of R. Hai's letter
omit the crucial words בלבד (alone) [in the phrase "those matters alone"]
and ובחכמה יחד, לא בדברי חכמה בלבד (and wisdom together, not matters
of wisdom alone).[19] Thus, R. Hai criticizes one who removes his heart

---

16 I have discussed this question in my essay in *Judaism's Encounter* (see n. 2), pp.
    68-69. The most careful recent analysis is in Amos Goldreich's dissertation, *Sefer
    Meʾirat ʿEinayim le-Rav Yitzhak de-min ʿAkko* (Jerusalem, 1981; Pirsumei ha-Makhon
    le-Limmudim Mitqaddemim, 1984), pp. 405-407. Goldreich is inclined to accept the
    authenticity of the letter; I am more inclined to be skeptical.

17 Graetz, who first challenged the authenticity of R. Hai's letter, also expressed suspicion
    that it was interpolated into our text. Once the first position is affirmed, the second
    has the advantage of avoiding the conclusion that Nahmanides was misled by a forgery.
    See H. Graetz, "Ein pseudoepigraphischen Sendschreiben, angeblich von Hai Gaon an
    Samuel Nagid," *MGWJ* 11 (1862): 37-40.

18 Chavel may equate excessive study with study in groups. See *Kitvei Ramban*, p. 349,
    n. 62: 'העסק, השקידה היתירה על ספר המורה. מבואר שכל עצמה של הצעת רבינו היתה 'להזהיר בנחת.
    אבל לא לגזור שום גזרת איסור, רק תקנה וגדר לבלתי עסוק בתלמוד זה בחבורה. Perano ("Mistica e
    Filosofia," p. 251), clearly influenced by Chavel's formulation, speaks of "un tempo
    eccessivo dedicato allo studio del *Moreh*," while Chavel's English translation of "lehaniah
    ha-ʿeseq mi-kol ve-khol" reads (p. 411), "To completely desist from engaging abundantly
    [in the study of the Moreh Nebuchim]" (bracketed phrase in the original).

19 Perles' ed., p. 194. The quotation from R. Hai in the Saraval manuscript differs in

from Torah and studies those matters—not those matters alone—and he asserts that you will find fear of sin, humility, and sanctity only in those who study Mishnah and Talmud—not in those who study Mishnah and Talmud along with philosophy. The point is that someone who turns his attention from the exclusive study of Torah will eventually reach the point of removing himself from Torah entirely. In this version, both R. Hai and Nahmanides present a coherent argument. The study of philosophy should be discouraged, period.

What, then, did Nahmanides propose to resolve the Maimonidean controversy? First, the ban on the *Sefer ha-Madda*ᶜ, which is a wonderful book, must be lifted. Second, the ban on the *Guide*, a ban which currently applies to private as well as public study, must be lifted as well. Third, a ban on group study of the *Guide* should be instituted. Fourth and finally, the study of philosophy should be entirely discouraged, but gently and without a ban.

Read in this fashion, the letter is smooth and clear—but the fourth point remains troubling. Nahmanides had studied Maimonidean philosophy, and he continued to do so. The letter of R. Hai is explicitly directed to a great scholar, and so we cannot easily appeal to special dispensation for exceptional people. I am inclined to think that this provision results in part from the exigencies of the moment and in part from a genuine element in the complex psyche of the author. Nahmanides was of two minds as he struggled with the question of philosophical study. In his own very capable hands, it could be a useful handmaiden of the Torah; for most others, it was fraught with peril. The gentle discouragement of this pursuit—even if applied to scholars—was by no means bad public policy, particularly if it could persuade the Northern Rabbis to withdraw their damaging ban.[20]

Faced with a major communal crisis, Nahmanides crafted a delicately balanced resolution. Even though the proposal was never implemented in all its details, it may well have been instrumental in helping to defuse a

other, minor ways from the passage I have reproduced from Chavel's edition, but these changes are not sufficiently significant to detain us here. On other citations of R. Hai's letter, see *Ozar ha-Geonim* to *Hagigah*, pp. 65-66, and the literature noted by Goldreich, *Sefer Me'irat 'Einayim* (above, n. 16).

[20] Note that despite his observation that even great scholars were admonished against philosophical study, Nahmanides makes a point of indicating the special importance of discouraging beginning students.

situation which jeopardized cordial intellectual and communal interaction among the three great centers of European Jewry in the formative period of their relationship. I suspect that the rabbis of Northern France regarded Nahmanides' suggestion as so nuanced that pursuing it would only lead them deeper into the morass. After reading it they decided that they should leave this matter in the hands of the local authorities, and they simply withdrew from the fray, perhaps after a formal revocation of their ban.[21] In the final analysis, it is more than likely that this was precisely what Nahmanides preferred and precisely what the Jews of Europe needed as they shaped their distinctive cultural and religious profiles aware of one another but driven by diverse instincts and aspirations to produce the rich and varied tapestry of a united and divided people.

---

[21]   For evidence that Nahmanides' letter had a significant impact on the Northern French Rabbis, see Shohet, "Berurim," p. 44.

MIRACLES AND THE NATURAL ORDER IN NAHMANIDES*

From: *Rabbi Moses Nahmanides (Ramban): Explorations in his Religious and Literary Virtuosity*, ed. by Isadore Twersky (Harvard University Press: Cambridge, Mass., 1983), pp. 107-128.

The centrality of miracles in Nahmanides' theology cannot escape the attention of even the most casual observer, and his doctrine of the hidden miracle exercised a particularly profound and abiding influence on subsequent Jewish thought. Nevertheless, his repeated emphasis on the miraculous—and particularly the unrestrained rhetoric of a few key passages—has served to obscure and distort his true position, which was far more moderate, nuanced and complex than both medieval and modern scholars have been led to believe.

I

To Nahmanides, miracles serve as the ultimate validation of all three central dogmas of Judaism: creation *ex nihilo*, divine knowledge, and providence (*hiddush, yedi'ah, hashgahah*).[1] In establishing the relationship between miracles and his first dogma, Nahmanides applies a philosophical argument in a particularly striking way. "According to the believer in the eternity of the world," he writes, "if God wished to shorten the wing of

---

*   Some of the issues analyzed in this article were discussed in a more rudimentary form in chapters one, three, and four of my master's essay, "Nahmanides' Attitude Toward Secular Learning and its Bearing upon his Stance in the Maimonidean Controversy" (Columbia University, 1965), which was directed by Prof. Gerson D. Cohen.

1   *Torat HaShem Temimah* (henceforth *THT*), in *Kitvei Ramban*, ed. by Ch. Chavel I (Jerusalem, 1963), p. 150. On Nahmanides' dogmas and their connection with miracles, see S. Schechter, "Nachmanides," in *Studies in Judaism* I (Philadelphia, 1878), pp. 118-122, and Ch. Henoch, *Ha-Ramban ke-Hoqer ve-ki-Mequbbal* (Jerusalem, 1978), pp. 159-179.

a fly or lengthen the leg of an ant he would be unable to do so."[2] Hence, miracles demonstrate creation.

The reverse contention that creation demonstrates the possibility of miracles is an assertion which goes back to Philo.[3] In this case, however, Nahmanides is applying to miracles an argument that Saadya had used about the fundamental hypothesis of creation from primeval matter. Such creation, the Gaon had contended, would have been impossible, since "God would not have [had] the power to create things out of" pre-existent matter; "it would not have accepted his command nor allowed itself to be affected according to his wish and shaped according to his design."[4] The direct source of Nahmanides' imagery, however, is not Saadya but Maimonides. In discussing the Aristotelian version of the eternity of the universe, Maimonides remarked that if the world operates through necessity and not through will, "very disgraceful conclusions will follow... Namely, it would follow that the deity, whom everyone intelligent recognizes to be perfect in every kind of perfection, could, as far as all the beings are concerned, produce nothing new in any of them; if He wished to lengthen a fly's wing or shorten a worm's foot, He would not be able to do it."[5]

The glaring anomaly in Nahmanides' borrowing of this vivid image is that Maimonides applied the argument not to any denial of *ex nihilo* creation but only to an Aristotelian universe governed by necessity;

[2]   *THT*, p. 146. All translations from Nahmanides' works are mine.

[3]   H. A. Wolfson, *Philo* (Cambridge, Massachusetts, 1948) I, pp. 298-299, 354; II, pp. 199-200. Cf. also the references in Wolfson's *Religious Philosophy* (Cambridge, Massachusetts, 1961), p. 223.

[4]   Translation from A. Altmann's selections in *Three Jewish Philosophers* (Cleveland, New York, and Philadelphia, 1960), p. 61 = *The Book of Beliefs and Opinions*, translated by S. Rosenblatt (New Haven, 1948), p. 48. Halevi (*Kuzari* I.91, and cf. V.14) also spoke of a connection between miracles and creation; he was, however, less dogmatic about the indispensability of the belief in creation *ex nihilo* since "a believer in the Torah" who accepted the reality of eternal hylic matter could nevertheless retain the conviction that "this world was renewed at a certain time and the beginning of humanity is Adam and Eve" (I.67; contrast, however, II.50). Apparently Halevi's characteristic skepticism about the decisive force of philosophical arguments—in this case the demonstration of a link between miracles and *ex nihilo* creation—ironically enables him to tolerate a radical philosophical position more readily than Saadya or Nahmanides. (On the other hand, he may have been thinking of a specific refutation of this link, perhaps along the lines of the argument that we shall be examining shortly.)

[5]   *Guide* II. 22 (Pines' translation).

according to the "Platonic" version of eternity, miracles are possible.[6] Maimonides, in fact, practically begins his discussion of the question of creation by describing how the Platonic approach can maintain both the eternity of matter and divine control over it by appealing to an analogy with the potter's relationship to his clay. Here is a case in which control is manifestly not dependent upon creation or even chronological priority.[7]

Since Nahmanides uses only the word *hiddush* (not creation *me-'ayin*) in connection with this argument in his *Torat Ha-Shem Temimah* and since Maimonides at one point uses the word *hiddush* about the Platonic view of eternity,[8] there is a fleeting temptation to suggest that Nahmanides was not pressing this particular argument, at least to the discerning reader, beyond the point where Maimonides had taken it. This temptation, however, must almost certainly be resisted, for we find Nahmanides using the same argument (though without the Maimonidean language) in his *Commentary to Exodus* explicitly about creation *ex nihilo*; miracles demonstrate *hiddush* by showing that everything is God's since he created it from nothing.[9] Nahmanides nowhere addresses the "Platonic" analogy with the potter, and it must be said that, in the very same chapter of the Guide where he presents the analogy, Maimonides himself suggests that the Aristotelian and Platonic versions of creation do not differ significantly in the eyes of one who follows the Torah.[10] Hence, it may well be that Nahmanides was disarmed by Maimonides' ambiguities and was not fully cognizant of the disparity between his use of the "fly's wing" image and the use to which it was put in his source.

In any event, we are left to speculate about Nahmanides' response to the potter analogy. He may have felt that the potter's control over his clay is far too restricted to serve as a paradigm for God's power over the world. Perhaps more significantly, he might have argued that this analogy begs the question since the control of a potter over his clay is

---

6   *Guide* II. 25.

7   *Guide* II. 13.

8   *Guide* II. 25. The word appears in Al-Harizi's translation (II. 26), which was the one Nahmanides used, as well as in Ibn Tibbon's.

9   To Exodus 13:16.

10   *Guide* II. 13. Cf. also the end of n. 14 below. For some of the peculiarities in Maimonides' treatment of Platonic eternity, see H. Davidson, "Maimonides' Secret Position on Creation," in *Studies in Medieval Jewish History and Literature*, ed. by I. Twersky (Cambridge, Massachusetts and London, England, 1979), pp. 16-40.

ultimately derived from God (Genesis 1:28; Psalms 8:7), but God's own power must be called into question if matter is primeval. Miracles are possible only, to use Shem Tov's play on a talmudic phrase, because "the mouth which prohibited is the one which permitted."[11]

However Nahmanides may have dealt with this question, the most telling aspect of his presentation involves the sharpening of another, related point made by Saadya. To the Gaon, the denial of creation *ex nihilo* is motivated by the excessive empiricism of people who believe only what their eyes see and what their senses perceive,[12] and Nahmanides twice refers to Aristotle as a man who believed only what he could sense.[13] In light of this perception, the argument from miracles can be sharpened into a remarkably effective polemical weapon: since miracles are an empirical datum, and they establish creation *ex nihilo* through a straightforward philosophical demonstration, the affirmation of eternity is a rejection of empiricism. "Hence you see the stubbornness of the leader of the philosophers, may his name be erased, for he denies a number of things that many have seen, whose truth we ourselves have witnessed, and which have become famous in the world."[14] The arch-empiricist is revealed as a pseudo-empiricist.

In an important way, this argument exemplifies Nahmanides' fundamental philosophical stance. Because revelation—and hence the content of the revelation—is an empirical datum, there is hardly much point in wasting energy and ingenuity in demonstrating such

---

[11]   Commentary to *Guide* II. 25.

[12]   For example, *Beliefs and Opinions* I, Rosenblatt's translation, pp. 38-39, 61-62, 71, 76.

[13]   *THT*, p. 147; *Comm. to Lev.* 16:18.

[14]   *THT*, p. 147. Saadya's attack against the empiricism of believers in eternity usually took the form of arguing that they too end by believing in things that they have never experienced (cf. the references in n. 12). He does appeal to miracles as well (e.g. Rosenblatt's translation, pp. 40, 58, 73), but on at least one of those occasions (and probably the others too) he seems to have in mind the less direct argument that miracles validate Scripture, which in turn teaches the doctrine of creation *ex nihilo*. In any case, he never formulates the argument found in Nahmanides as clearly, sharply, or effectively.

In Maimonides' "fly's wing" passage, the argument was based not on the fact that God had demonstrated his control of the world but on the assertion that lack of such control would be a philosophically inadmissible imperfection in the deity. In the *Treatise on the Resurrection*, however (ed. by J. Finkel [New York, 1939], p. 32, #46), which was directed to a more popular audience, Maimonides did argue that miracles demonstrate *hiddush* "as we have explained in the *Guide*." Most readers were not likely to realize that this *hiddush* can include Platonic eternity.

things as God's existence or unity, and Nahmanides never bothers with such philosophical exercises. At the same time, the use of reason to understand God, creation, and other key theological issues is essential. Those who spurn an investigation into theodicy on the grounds that it will inevitably remain a mystery are "fools who despise wisdom. For we shall benefit ourselves in the above-mentioned study by becoming wise men who know God in the manner in which he acts and in his deeds; furthermore, we shall become believers endowed with a stronger faith in him than others."[15]

In our case, the reality of miracles is taken for granted, and the connection with creation *ex nihilo* is made by a philosophical argument. Without denigrating the use of reason, Nahmanides has eliminated the boundary between revelation and reason by incorporating revealed information, openly and unselfconsciously, into what might be described as the data base for philosophical analysis. It is this approach which accounts for his discussing theological issues primarily in the context of a commentary to the revelation,[16] and it is this, I think, which attracted him to kabbalah. Nahmanides' mysticism, after all, is essentially a revealed philosophical system, and the function of kabbalah as a harmonizing force subsuming both reason and revelation may well precede and transcend Nahmanides to account for the attractiveness of medieval Jewish mysticism in precisely the time and place where it first became a major force. It is no accident that late twelfth-century Provençal Jewry was the locus of both the rise of kabbalah and a confrontation with philosophy by a Jewish community without a philosophical tradition. Jewish mysticism provided an ideal solution for a mind captivated by the philosophic quest but committed only to authentic, revealed sources. The Talmud, it is true, spoke of the danger that esoteric investigation could lead to heresy; nonetheless, the perils posed by the study of

---

15   *Sha'ar ha-Gemul*, in *Kitvei Ramban* II, p. 281. The phrase "fools who despise wisdom" (הכסילים מואסי החכמה), though based, as Chavel remarks, on Proverbs 1:22 (וכסילים ישנאו דעת), is borrowed from a similar discussion in Saadya: "Many people have erred and despised wisdom (מאסו בחכמה), some because they did not know the way to it, while some knew and entered the path but did not complete it... Therefore, let not the contemptuous fool (הכסיל הקץ) blame God for his sin." My translation from Ibn Tibbon's Hebrew. See *Sefer ha-Emunot ve-ha-De'ot* (Józewów, 1878) I, p. 41 = Rosenblatt's translation, p. 13. On the reading הכסיל הקץ (not הכסיל או הקץ), see M. Ventura, *La Philosophie de Saadia Gaon* (Paris, 1934), p. 311.

16   Cf. Chavel, *Ramban: His Life and Teachings* (New York, 1960), pp. 67-68.

esoteric doctrines revealed by God pale in comparison with the heresies awaiting a student of ultimate questions whose only guides are reason and Aristotle.[17] Within the kabbalistic system, the boundary between revelation and philosophy was completely erased, so that Nahmanides and like-minded contemporaries could satisfy their yearning for what might best be termed not a religious philosophy but a philosophical religion.

This commitment to kabbalah raises a crucial final question concerning the sincerity of the argument that we have been examining. Nahmanides demonstrates creation *ex nihilo* through an appeal to miracles—but did he really believe in creation *ex nihilo*? Scholem has shown that the mystical school in Gerona, of which Nahmanides was the most prominent representative, turned the naive understanding of the term on its head and understood *'ayin* (= *nihil*) as a word for the hidden recesses of the Godhead itself; creation is a process of emanation from the divine Nothing, not the sudden appearance of matter from ordinary nothingness.[18] Although there may be a certain disingenuousness in the kabbalist's use of this term to an uninitiated audience, Nahmanides' argument remains relatively unaffected and must almost certainly be regarded as sincere. The kabbalistic doctrine continues to assert—indeed, to insist—that the process of creation precludes the primeval existence of matter independent of God; even from a mystical perspective, then, the argument from miracles can be mobilized to deny the existence of such independent matter, and that is essentially what Nahmanides has done. Whether the alternative is creation from nothing or from Nothing depends on the reader's kabbalistic sophistication, but Nahmanides' appeal to miracles in support of his first dogma remains both ingenious and ingenuous.[19]

---

17   Though he is referring to a later period, A. S. Halkin's remarks can be applied to the twelfth century as well: "Its [kabbalah's] concern with fundamental problems and its incorporation of philosophical concepts into a system which vaunted a purely Jewish ancestry and claimed that it represented the deepest understanding of the revealed books, qualified it both to satisfy the curiosity of those who sought answers to theological and cosmological questions and to challenge Aristotelianism and its Jewish exponents as alien plants within Jewry." "Yedaiah Bedersi's Apology," in *Jewish Medieval and Renaissance Studies*, ed. by A. Altmann (Cambridge, Massachusetts, 1967), p. 183.

18   Scholem's most elaborate discussion is in *Ha-Qabbalah be-Gerona*, pp. 212-240.

19   For the possibility that Nahmanides may have attempted somehow to salvage the

II

Nahmanides goes on to assert that miracles—or more precisely, manifest miracles—validate the remaining two dogmas of divine knowledge and providence.[20] The connection here is so obvious as to be scarcely interesting, but it is in this discussion of the nature of providence that Nahmanides cites his central, seminal doctrine of the hidden miracle— and that doctrine is exceptionally interesting. Although similar views had been expressed earlier by Bahya, Halevi, and even Maimonides,[21]

straightforward understanding of creation *ex nihilo* within a mystical framework, see *Ha-Qabbalah be-Gerona*, pp. 255-265, esp. 261-265. On the subject of straightforward versus esoteric biblical exegesis (*peshat* vs. *sod*), A. Funkenstein has recently written that "*peshat* and *sod* correspond [or 'overlap'—*hofefim*] in only one place [in Nahmanides' exegesis]: kabbalah is the central dimension in understanding the reason for sacrifices (*Comm. to Lev.* 1:9). Everywhere else *peshat* and *sod* are different, and in Genesis 1:1 this reaches the point of syntactical contradiction: according to 'the way of genuine truth,' the word 'God' is not the subject of the verse but rather its object" ("Parshanuto ha-Tippologit shel ha-Ramban," *Zion* 45 [1980]:46-47). Cf. also H. H. Ben Sasson, "Rabbi Moshe ben Nahman: Ish be-Sivkhei Tequfato," *Molad*, n.s. 1 (1967):360, 362-363.

In fact, however, Nahmanides displays a pronounced tendency to equate *peshat* and *sod* by finding that the plain meaning of Scripture can be explained satisfactorily—or most satisfactorily—only by resorting to kabbalistic doctrine. Thus, only the esoteric interpretation pointing to metempsychosis really "fits the verses" of Elihu's critical speech in Job (*Comm. to Job* 32:3), only according to the kabbalistic interpretation is the sin of Moses and Aaron "mentioned explicitly in the biblical text" (*Comm. to Numbers* 20:1), only a midrash requiring kabbalistic elaboration 'fits the language of the verse best" in Genesis 6:4, only after understanding a mystical secret in connection with the second commandment will "the entire verse become clear in accordance with its simple, straightforward meaning" (*Comm. to Exodus* 20:3), and Exodus 6:2-3 will reveal its "simple, straightforward meaning" (*Comm.* ad loc.) "with nothing missing or superfluous" (*Sermon on Qohelet, Kitvei Ramban* I, p. 192) only through kabbalistic exegesis. Cf. also Scholem's remark about the *Commentary to Job, Ha-Qabbalah be-Gerona*, p. 75, specifically with respect to Job 28 (cf. too p. 230). It is particularly significant that although Nahmanides endorses the content of the kabbalistic doctrine read into that chapter by his source (R. Ezra's commentary to the Song of Songs), he expresses reservations (not noted by Scholem) about the validity of the exegesis (*Kitvei Ramban* I, p. 90). In a sense, this underlines the point; if Nahmanides were prepared to find *sod* through forced interpretation, he would have accepted such exegesis without resistance. On the importance of *peshat* to Nahmanides, see also J. Perles, "Über den Geist des Commentars des R. Moses ben Nachman zum Pentateuch und über sein Verhältniss zum Pentateuch-Commentar Raschi's," *MGWJ* 7 (1858):119-120, esp. n. 2.

20 *THT*, pp. 150, 155.

21 See *Ha-Qabbalah be-Gerona*, pp. 305, 309. Nahmanides himself (*THT*, p. 154) noted that Maimonides' *Treatise on the Resurrection* contains a passage supporting his view; the passage he had in mind, which certainly influenced him, was without question the one

no previous Jewish thinker had laid equivalent emphasis on such a conception, applied it as widely, or made it as central to his world view. The hidden miracle, then, justly came to be regarded as a Nahmanidean doctrine *par excellence*, and the intellectual image of Nahmanides has often been drawn in significant measure with this doctrine in mind. Thus, to the extent that we have misunderstood the hidden miracle, we have misunderstood Nahmanides.

In at least two formulations of his position, Nahmanides permitted himself some rhetorical excesses that have inevitably fostered such misunderstanding. "A person has no portion in the Torah of Moses," he writes, "without believing that all things that happen to us are miracles; they have nothing to do with 'nature' or 'the customary order of the world'."[22] More succinctly, "One who believes in the Torah may not believe in the existence of nature at all."[23] The analysis underlying these remarks appears almost as a refrain throughout Nahmanides' works: since the Torah promises rewards and punishments ranging from famine to plague to constant good health, and since there is nothing "natural" about the link between human behavior and such phenomena, providence must be realized through a series of hidden miracles disguised as part of an apparent natural order.[24]

It is hardly surprising, then, that students of Nahmanides have perceived him as a thinker who denied, or virtually denied, the existence of natural law. Solomon Schechter, for example, argues that "We may... maintain that in Nachmanides' system there is hardly room left for such a thing as nature or 'the order of the world'... Miracles are raised to a place in the regular scheme of things, and the difficulty regarding the possibility of God's interference with nature disappears by their very multiplication. [There is] an unbroken chain of miracles."[25]

To Gershom Scholem, Nahmanides tends

> to turn what we call the laws of nature into a sort of optical illusion, since we regard what is really a continuum of miracles as a manifestation of

---

pointed out by Scholem (Finkel's ed., pp: 33-36, #48-50), not the ones noted by Chavel in his edition of *THT* ad loc.

22   *Comm. to Exodus* 13:16; *THT*, p. 153.
23   *Sermon on Qohelet, Kitvei Ramban* I, p. 192.
24   See *Comm. to Gen.* 17:1, 46:15; *Exod.* 6:2; *Lev.* 18:29, 26:11.
25   "Nachmanides," pp. 119-120.

natural law... These hidden miracles, which are the foundation of the entire Torah, are miracles which do not appear miraculous to us... The world and the behavior of nature and their relationship to man are not at all in the category of what we call nature; they are, rather, a constant and constantly renewed miracle, a continuous chain of miracles...[26]

Nahmanides' position, Scholem says, is very close to occasionalism, a later philosophical school which denied natural law entirely, though there is one very significant exception: Nahmanides was a virtual occasionalist only with respect to Israel; other nations live in a world of nature.[27]

In his recent book on Nahmanides, Chayim Henoch makes the same comparison between the "constant miraculous renewal" in Nahmanides' thought and both occasionalists and *mutakallimun*, while pointing out, like Scholem, that this applies only to Israel.[28] Yitzhak Baer's classic *History* presents Nahmanides as an anti-rationalist who denied the natural order, Haim Hillel Ben Sasson's characterization is even more extreme and explicit, and a recent study by Amos Funkenstein refers somewhat more cautiously to "Nahmanides' tendency to blur the boundaries between the natural and the miraculous."[29]

There can be no question that Nahmanides perceives the operation of providence as a phenomenon consisting of repeated miracles. Indeed, he has forced himself into a position where he denies that God enters the causal chain in any but the most direct way.

[26]   *Ha-Qabbalah be-Gerona*, pp. 306-307.

[27]   Ibid., pp. 309-310.

[28]   *Ha-Ramban ke-Hoqer ve-ki-Mequbbal*, p. 178. Henoch goes on to emphasize the kabbalistic character of Nahmanides' position, which we shall touch on briefly a bit later. In a much earlier footnote (p. 54, n. 162), he had proposed, as we shall see, a crucial additional qualification, but there is no echo of that note in his later discussion.

[29]   See Baer's *History of the Jews in Christian Spain* I (Philadelphia, 1971), p. 245; *Toledot ha-Yehudim bi-Sefarad ha-Nozrit* (Tel Aviv, 1959), p. 145; Ben Sasson in *Molad*, n.s. 1 (1967):360-61; Funkenstein in *Zion* 45 (1980):45. Ben Sasson's discussion clearly implies that Nahmanides did not recognize a natural realm even in areas that do not impinge on human affairs; thus, it is not only "all things that happen to us" that are miracles. According to Nahmanides, we are prohibited from mixing species because this would constitute unwarranted interference with creation, a sort of hubris reflecting the conviction that we can improve on the divine handiwork. To Ben Sasson, the motivation for this interpretation stems from Nahmanides' conviction that even such a "natural" phenomenon as the maintenance of species in their present form is an ongoing miraculous process; hence, human intervention would involve an unseemly attempt to compete not merely with God's creative acts in the distant past but with miracles that He is performing at this very moment.

If we will stubbornly insist that the [non-priest] who eats of the heave-offering will not die through a change in nature, but that God will cause him to eat food that causes sickness or that he will go to war and die, the fact would remain that the astrological configuration of his constellation would have changed for ill through his sin or for good through his merit so that nature would in any event not prevail. Thus, if the alternative is that God would change this person's mind as a result of his sin so that he would eat harmful foods that he would not have eaten otherwise, it is easier to change the nature of the good food so that it will do him harm.[30]

Since there is no conceptual difference to Nahmanides between indirect, "natural" providence and miraculous divine intervention, the workings of providence are best understood as direct hidden miracles unmediated by natural forces. There is therefore hardly any point in asking why Nahmanides does not formally list the hidden miracle as one of his dogmas. He does list it—under the name "providence."[31]

Nevertheless, Nahmanides was forced by the Bible, the halakhah, and intuitions influenced by philosophy or common sense or both, to recognize that natural law often does operate—even for Jews and probably even for the Jewish collective. Consequently, a careful examination of the totality of Nahmanides' comments on this issue reveals nature in operation ninety-nine percent of the time, and it is perforce nature without

---

30 Introduction to Job, *Kitvei Ramban* I, p. 19.

31 In *THT*, p. 155, Nahmanides comes very close to saying this explicitly:

כבר נתברר כי הנסים המפורסמים מורים על החידוש ועל הידיעה שיש לו להקב"ה בפרטי העולם
ועל ההשגחה והנסים הנסתרים לדעת כל מאמין בעונש העבירות ובשכר המצות ולדעת כל מתפלל
וכל נושא עיניו לשמים, כלם מודים על החידוש ועל הידיעה וההשגחה הודאה אמיתית אלא שהיא
נסתרת והם שלש מוסדות התורה

Henoch (p. 171) cites this passage, but I don't think he takes it (as I do) as a virtual equation of hidden miracles and providence in particular. The references to *hashgahah* and *nissim nistarim* really merge into one another, and, despite the syntactical awkwardness which I must ascribe to Nahmanides, the phrase *ella shehi nisteret* seems to me to modify *hashgahah* (not *hoda'ah*) and to mean that providence takes the form of hidden miracles. (Henoch's subsequent citation of the phrase "all the fundamentals of the Torah come through hidden miracles" from *Comm. to Gen.* 46:15 as another assertion of the connection between miracles and dogmas is probably not germane; in that context, "fundamentals of the Torah" does not mean creation, knowledge and providence but reiterates Nahmanides' standard assertion that all the Torah's promises of reward and punishment [="the fundamentals of the Torah"] come through hidden miracles.) Manifest miracles are not listed among the dogmas for the reason Henoch suggests: they are not a dogma in themselves but an expression of divine power and a means by which the fundamental dogmas are validated.

providence, since "natural," indirect providence is a contradiction in terms.[32] Nahmanides' world is therefore exceptionally—extraordinarily—naturalistic precisely because of his insistence on the miraculous nature of providence.

This is, to say the least, an unexpected conclusion, and we must now take a careful look at the texts which make it inescapable.

> God's knowledge, which is his providence in the lower world, is to guard species, and even individual human beings are left to accidents until their time of reckoning comes. With respect to people of special piety (*hasidav*), however, God turns his attention to such a person to know him as an individual and to see to it that divine protection cleaves to him always; knowledge and remembrance are never separated from him at all. This is the meaning of "He withdraws not his eyes from the righteous" (Job 36:4); indeed, many verses refer to this principle, as it is written, "Behold, the eye of the Lord is on those who fear him" (Psalms 33:18), and others besides.[33]

Since he is commenting on a verse which says that God "knew" Abraham, Nahmanides here understands the term knowledge in a strong sense as the equivalent of providence, but there is no reason to think that this passage limits divine knowledge in the ordinary sense of the word.[34] The limitation on providence itself, however, is significant enough; not many people are designated *hasidim* in Nahmanides' terminology, and the attribution of constant providence to precious few individuals is made even clearer by the phrase he uses in a later passage.

> Know that miracles are performed for good or ill only for the absolutely righteous (*zaddiqim gemurim*) or the absolutely wicked. Those in the middle have good or ill occur to them according to the customary order of the world "in accordance with their way and their actions" (Ezekiel 36:17).[35]

---

32   Contrast Maimonides, *Guide* II. 48.
33   *Comm. to Gen.* 18:19.
34   Cf. the passage from Bahya cited by Chavel ad loc., and contrast L. Stein's assertion cited in n. 37 below. Note too that, if we would not assume constant divine knowledge in the weak sense, we would need to resort to complex and obscure triggering mechanisms to account for the "time of reckoning" and perhaps even for God's recognition that so-and-so has become the sort of pious man deserving of constant divine protection. See the related discussion at nn. 38-42 below.
35   *Comm. to Deut.* 11:13.

The assertion that miracles are performed only for the absolutely righteous or wicked is couched in general terms and appears to include every variety of miracles. Hence, ordinary people are excluded from the regular operation of hidden miracles and are left, as in the *Commentary to Genesis*, to the customary, natural order. The last phrase from Ezekiel, however, remains troublesome. It could mean that such people are left to some sort of indirect providence weaker than the one which works by hidden miracles, but this would directly contradict the introduction to the *Commentary to Job*, which virtually denies the existence of such providence, it would contradict the assertion in the *Commentary to Genesis* that non-*hasidim* are left to "accidents," and it would introduce a category or providence found nowhere else in Nahmanides. The most likely meaning, then, is that people left to accidents will be subjected to good or evil according to "their way and their actions" in a purely naturalistic sense; those who are careful will be safer than those who are not. Just such a position, in fact, emerges from a passage in the *Commentary to Job* that we shall examine in a moment where Nahmanides maintains that people left to accidents are likely to stumble unless they are particularly cautious.

Reinforcing this conception that God may well decide to leave people to accidents is Nahmanides' celebrated discussion of medicine, where he maintains that in an ideal Jewish society even individuals would be dealt with miraculously so that medical treatment would be either unnecessary or futile. Regrettably, people began to consult doctors, and so God left them "to natural accidents."[36] In this case, the halakhic permissibility of consulting physicians, which Nahmanides goes on to cite, undoubtedly played a role in moderating his skepticism about his own profession; the Torah, he says, does not rest its laws on miracles. This halakhic principle is not especially congenial to an occasionalist, and, as we shall see, this is not the only instance in which it worked to mitigate Nahmanides' emphasis on the miraculous.

These passages leave no alternative to a thorough rethinking of the standard image of Nahmanides. Chayim Henoch, who studied Nahmanides' *oeuvre* with painstaking care, does confront them in a footnote, and he suggests that the passages about miraculous providence may refer to the Jewish collective and not to all Jewish individuals. Nevertheless, since

36   *Comm. to Lev.* 26:11.

we have seen that he later describes Nahmanides as maintaining a view close to that of the occasionalists and the *mutakallimun*, the enormity of this concession has apparently failed to make a sufficient impression.[37] Finally, even the sharply shrunken position which applies Nahmanides' denial of the natural order only to the Jewish collective (in addition to a handful of extraordinarily righteous and wicked individuals) must be shaken by a particularly striking passage in the *Commentary to Job*.

> *He withdraws not his eyes from the righteous* (Job 36:7): This verse explains a great principle with respect to providence concerning which there are in fact many verses. For people of Torah and perfect faith believe in providence, i.e., that God watches over and protects the members of the human species… It is not said in the Torah or prophets that God watches over and protects the individuals of other groups of creatures that do not speak; rather, he guards only the species… The reason for this is clearly known, for since man recognizes his God, God in turn watches over him and protects him; this is not true of the other creatures, which do not speak and do not know their creator.

> This, then, is why he protects the righteous, for just as their heart and eyes are always with him, so are the eyes of God on them from the beginning of the year until the end, to the point where the absolutely pious man (*hasid*) who cleaves to his God always and who never separates himself from him in his thoughts by paying attention to mundane matters will be guarded always from all accidents, even those that take place in the natural course of events; such a person will be protected from these accidents through a miracle occurring to him constantly, as if he were considered one of the supernal beings who are not subject to generation and corruption by accidents. To the extent that this individual comes close to God by cleaving to him, he will be guarded especially well, while one who is far from God in his thought and deeds, even if he does not deserve death because of his sin, will be forsaken and left to accidents.

> Many verses make this point. David [*sic*] said, "He will guard the feet of his holy ones, but the wicked shall be put to silence in darkness" (I Samuel 2:9). He means by this that those who are close to God are under

---

37 See above, n. 28. One nineteenth-century scholar noticed the passage in *Comm. to Gen.* 18:19 and allowed it to make too great an impression, asserting in a brief passage that Nahmanides' view of both divine knowledge and providence is virtually identical with that of Gersonides. See L. Stein, *Die Willensfreiheit und ihr Verhältniss zur göttlichen Präscienz und Providenz bei den Jüdischen Philosophen des Mittelalters* (Berlin, 1882), pp. 126-127. See above, n. 34.

absolute protection, while those who are far from him are subject to accidents and have no one to protect them from harm, just as one who walks in the darkness is likely to fall unless he is cautious and walks slowly. David also said that "it is not with sword and spear that the Lord saves" (I Samuel 17:47), and it is written, "Behold, the eye of the Lord is on those who fear him, on those who wait for his mercy" (Psalms 33:18); i.e., God's eyes are on them when they wait for him constantly and their souls cleave to him.

Since most of the world belongs to this intermediate group, the Torah commanded that warriors be mobilized, and that the priest anointed for war send back the fearful so that they will not sap the courage of the others. It is for this reason too that we find the preparation of the order of battle in the Torah and the prophets, for example, "And David inquired of the Lord, and the Lord said, 'Do not go up; circle around behind them...' (II Samuel 5:23), and 'Go and draw toward Mount Tabor, and take with you ten thousand men" (Judges 4:6). Had they been meritorious, they would have gone out with a few people and achieved victory without arms, and had they deserved defeat, no multitude would have helped them. In this case, however, they deserved to be treated in the manner of nature and accident. This is a matter which was explained well by Maimonides in the *Guide of the Perplexed.*

As Nahmanides hints in his last sentence, much of this passage (until the final paragraph) is a paraphrase of Maimonides' discussion in *Guide* III. 18, and it is so striking in its naturalism and limitation of providence that we shall first have to devote some time to demonstrating that Nahmanides has not changed into a Maimonides in disguise. The truth is that he has introduced some subtle but crucial—and characteristic— changes into his paraphrase of the *Guide*, so that his final sentence, implying an identity of views with Maimonides, is profoundly misleading. First, despite Maimonides' use of the term pious (*hasidim* in both Ibn Tibbon and Al-Harizi) to describe people who attain the benefits of providence, the *Guide* repeatedly emphasizes the intellectual dimension as well; to put it moderately, providence is connected not only with righteousness but also with intellectual achievement. In Nahmanides, this central point of the *Guide* vanishes entirely; though even he could hardly have perceived his *hasid* as a pious fool, the emphasis on intellect is completely absent.

A second and for our purposes even more important divergence comes through Nahmanides' introduction of an apparently innocuous phrase into the final sentence of the second paragraph. Maimonides had asserted that pious intellectuals are close to God and hence attain providence while those who are far from him are likely to stumble because they remain unprotected. The absolutely wicked, who constitute an extreme example of the second category, are thus likely to fall because of an absence of protection; consequently, the citation of the verse "The wicked shall be put to silence in darkness" interpreted as blind, unguided groping in the dark is especially appropriate. Nahmanides, however, as we have seen in his commentary to Deuteronomy 11:13, believed that the absolutely wicked are punished by miraculous divine intervention, and so he slipped his crucial phrase into the Maimonidean discussion: "One who is far from God in his thoughts and deeds, *even if he does not deserve death for his sins*, will be forsaken and left to accidents." When Nahmanides then continues to paraphrase the *Guide* by citing "the wicked shall be put to silence in darkness" understood merely as absence of protection, the reference becomes forced and inappropriate. All of a sudden, "wicked" excludes the truly wicked and refers only to an intermediate category that plays no role in the Maimonidean passage. It is only because of this tampering with the analysis in the *Guide* that Nahmanides' final paragraph, which is not derived from Maimonides, can begin with a reference to "this intermediate group."

The introduction of the person who deserves death for his sins also undermines the essentially naturalistic character of Maimonides' analysis. To Maimonides, a person who reached the requisite level attained providence "by necessity" through his link with the divine overflow, and Nahmanides' discussion of his *hasid*'s achieving providence through cleaving to God (*devequt*) could also be read in a relatively naturalistic, though mystical sense.[38] Later kabbalists, in fact, were uncomfortable with the entire concept of the hidden miracle because of their conviction that the process by which human actions affect both nature and the individual's fate is one of clearcut cause and effect involving the esoteric relationship between upper and lower worlds.[39]

---

[38] On the process of *devequt*, in which the *sefirah* of *ti'feret* plays a special role, cf. Henoch, pp. 248-251. On the *hasid* who cleaves to God, cf. also *Comm. to Deut.* 5:23, 11:22; *Comm. to Lev.* 18:4; *Sermon on Qohelet, Kitvei Ramban* I, p. 192.

[39] Meir ibn Gabbai, *'Avodat HaQodesh* (Warsaw, 1894), II. 17, p. 36b (brought to my attention by Prof. Bernard Septimus); Isaiah Horowitz, *Shnei Luhot HaBerit* (Józewów, 1878), pp. 9b-10a, discussed by Chavel, *Ramban*, pp. 85-86, and Henoch, p. 56,

Nevertheless, it would almost certainly be a mistake to understand Nahmanides' miracles as entirely "naturalistic" mystical events. It is, first of all, overwhelmingly likely that Nahmanides understood sefirotic action as involving specific divine volition,[40] and so the providence attained by the *hasid* who cleaves to God does not have to be understood as coming "by necessity."[41] Moreover, the miraculous punishment of the person deserving to die for his sins certainly does not come through any cleaving to God (just as it could not come through linkage to a Maimonidean overflow), and, while an alternative kabbalistic mechanism of a naturalistic sort is theoretically feasible, Nahmanides does not provide one. In particular, the search for a "naturalistic" mystical triggering mechanism to account for the "time of reckoning" of intermediate individuals who are normally ignored would be especially difficult.[42] In short, for all its limitation of providence, this passage in the *Commentary to Job* does not lead to naturalism of a Maimonidean or even mystical variety.

The fact remains, however, that it not only provides a vigorous reassertion of the largely accidental life of ordinary individuals, it calls into question the exclusively miraculous fate of even the Jewish collective. The final paragraph of this passage, which is Nahmanides' own, asserts unambiguously that miraculous providence did not always protect the Jewish people in its biblical wars. Ironically, Nahmanides is once again forced into a naturalistic posture precisely by his miraculous conception of providence. The verses that he cites include direct advice given to the Jewish army by God himself; for someone who believed that providence normally operates through nature, these battles would constitute classic examples of divine protection of Israel. Instead, Nahmanides explicitly cites them to show that when Jews are in the intermediate category, they

---

n. 171. Prof. Septimus's *Hispano-Jewish Culture in Transition: The Career and Controversies of Ramah* (Cambridge, Mass. and London, England, 1982), which appeared after the completion of this article, contains a discussion of the argument in *'Avodat Ha-Qodesh* (pp. 110-111); the book also called my attention to a two-sentence passage in E. Gottlieb's *Mehqarim be-Sifrut ha-Qabbalah* (Tel Aviv, 1976), p. 266, which comments on the central theme of this essay with real insight (Septimus, pp. 110, 170 n. 54).

40 See Henoch, p. 18, n. 21.

41 Note that Nahmanides' remark that the *hasid* "will be protected from accidents through a miracle occurring to him constantly" is another elaboration on his Maimonidean source.

42 The systems of the later kabbalists did not generally assume the existence of a group of Jews usually left to accidents.

are abandoned to accidents, with a clear analogy to the individual who is allowed to stumble in the darkness. We are apparently left to assume that in an age without prophecy, when no divine advice is proffered, such an army would have been left to accidents pure and simple. But if a Jewish army fighting under the judges of Israel is not the Jewish collective, it is hard to imagine what is. Hence, although Nahmanides could never consider the possibility that God would allow the Jewish people to be utterly destroyed through the accidents of nature, it seems clear that even the Jewish collective is not always governed by an unbroken chain of hidden miracles.[43]

Finally, a responsum by Nahmanides on astrology raises questions about the constancy of miraculous providence even for the remaining handful of extraordinarily righteous individuals. From a talmudic discussion, he says,

> it follows that it is permissible to listen to [astrologers] and to believe them. This is clear from Abraham, who said, "I looked at astrological calculations," and from R. Akiba, who worried deeply about his daughter [who had been the subject of a dire astrological prediction] and concluded after she was saved that charity had rescued her literally from death... However, God *sometimes* [my emphasis] performs a miracle for those who fear him by nullifying the decree of the stars for them, and these are among the hidden miracles which occur in the ordinary manner of the world and upon which the entire Torah depends. Consequently, one should not consult astrologers but should rather go forth in simple faith, as it is written, "You shall be wholehearted with the Lord your God" (Deut. 18-13). If someone does see

---

43 Needless to say, miraculous providence often does govern the wars of Israel; see the references in Henoch, pp. 60-61. On the suspension of such providence from the Jewish collective, cf. Rashba's responsum (1.19) cited by Henoch, p. 57, n. 171, which asserts that, although Jews are generally excluded from astrological control, their sins can lower them to a position where this is no longer the case. Though Henoch apparently considers this inconsistent with Nahmanides' view, the passage from the *Comm. to Job* may suggest otherwise, since nature and the astrological order are pretty much synonymous. For Nahmanides' frequent denials that the Jewish people or the land of Israel are subject to the constellations, see *Sermon on Qohelet, Kitvei Ramban* I, pp. 200-201; *Sermon on Rosh HaShanah, Kitvei Ramban* I, p. 250; *Comm. to Gen.* 15:18; *Comm. to Lev.* 18:25; *Comm. to Deut.* 29:25; *THT*, p. 150. It was presumably the repeated assertions in these passages that Gentiles are subject to the constellations which persuaded Scholem and Henoch that Nahmanides' supposed denial of a natural order applied only to Jews. The belief that nature prevails in the absence of special merit was used by Solomon ibn Verga as a clever transition from religious to naturalistic explanation of Jewish exile and suffering (*Shevet Yehudah*, ed. by A. Schochet [Jerusalem, 1947], p. 127).

something undesirable through astrology, he should perform good deeds and pray a great deal; at the same time, if he saw through astrology that a particular day is not auspicious for his work, he should avoid it and not depend on a miracle. It is my view that it is prohibited to go counter to the constellations while depending on a miracle.[44]

A legal responsum requires a particularly strong measure of caution and responsibility, and it may therefore be dangerous to draw conclusions about Nahmanides' more general theological inclinations from this sort of source; even occasionalists do not walk off cliffs, and occasionalist halakhists do not advise others to do so. Nevertheless, the plain meaning of the passage appears to be that even "those who fear" God are not favored with continuous miracles, and methodological reservations cannot entirely neutralize the impact of such a remark. Thus, Nahmanides' denial of nature may not apply in undiluted form even to that final category of the absolutely righteous.[45]

Moreover, even though Nahmanides complains that Maimonides "limits miracles and increases nature,"[46] his own exegesis is by no means free of such a tendency. The plain meaning of the biblical text indicates that the rainbow was first created after the flood, but Nahmanides is prepared to resort to reinterpretation under the pressure of scientific evidence. "Against our will, we must believe the words of the Greeks that the rainbow comes about as a result of the sun's burning in the moist air, for the rainbow appears in a vessel of water placed in the sun."[47] Thus, the Bible means only that the rainbow, which had appeared from the beginning of creation, would henceforth be invested with symbolic significance. Similarly, he reinterprets a Rabbinic statement that the land of Israel was not inundated by the waters of the flood, arguing that there was no fence around it to prevent the water from entering; all the Rabbis meant was that the rain did not actually fall in Israel nor were its

---

[44]   *Kitvei Ramban* I, p. 379. The talmudic discussion that Nahmanides cites is in *B. Shabbat* 156a-b.

[45]   It may be relevant to note Maimonides' sudden insight in *Guide* III. 51, where he explains that even the pious intellectual is likely to stop concentrating on the divine for a while, and during that time he remains unprotected. Even within a less naturalistic framework than that of Maimonides, a parallel analysis is not impossible. Cf. also the somewhat enigmatic passage in *Sermon on Qohelet, Kitvei Ramban* I, p. 192, which apparently speaks of occasional accident with respect to the righteous.

[46]   *THT*, p. 154.

[47]   *Comm. to Gen.* 9:12, and cf. *THT*, p. 174.

subterranean waters let loose, but the water that originated elsewhere covered Israel as well.[48]

With respect to the age of the antediluvians, there is a well-known dispute in which Nahmanides takes Maimonides to task for ascribing extreme longevity only to the figures explicitly mentioned in the Bible. There is an almost instinctive tendency to ascribe Maimonides' position to his desire to restrict miracles[49] and Nahmanides' to his tendency to multiply them. In fact, however, Nahmanides attacks Maimonides for precisely the opposite offense. The argument in the *Guide*, he reports, is that a few people lived such long lives either because of the way they took care of themselves or as a result of a miracle. But it is hardly plausible that people could quadruple their life span by following a particular regimen; as for miracles, "why should such a miracle be performed for them when they are neither prophets nor especially righteous men?" The real reason for this longevity was the superior air before the time of the flood combined with the excellent constitution with which their recent ancestor Adam had been created, and these reasons, of course, apply to all antediluvians equally.[50]

It is a matter of special interest that Ritba's defense of Maimonides on this point already reflects what was to become the standard misreading of Nahmanides' position on hidden miracles. Maimonides, Ritba argues, believed in the constancy of natural phenomena over the generations, and so Nahmanides' naturalistic explanation about superior air could not appeal to him. As for the objection that miracles would not be performed for ordinary people, this is a peculiar argument coming from Nahmanides. He himself, after all, "has taught us that there is a great difference between a miracle like longevity that comes to a certain extent in a natural way and a miracle that comes entirely outside the natural order."[51] In other words, manifest miracles would happen only to the specially righteous, but hidden miracles happen to everyone.

---

48 *Comm. to Gen.* 8:11. As M. D. Eisenstadt pointed out in his comment ad loc. (*Perush ha-Ramban 'al HaTorah* [New York, 1958]), Nahmanides' exegesis ignores a Rabbinic statement that the inhabitants of the land of Israel died only from the vapors.

49 Maimonides wanted to leave the natural order intact, said Judah Alfakar at the height of the Maimonidean controversy, but what does it matter if someone tells you that he saw one camel or three flying in the air? See *Qovez Teshuvot ha-Rambam* (Leipzig, 1859), III, p. 2a.

50 *Comm. to Gen.* 5:4.

51 *Sefer ha-Zikkaron*, ed. by K. Kahana (Jerusalem, 1956), pp. 37-39.

Whether Nahmanides would have considered the Maimonidean version of antediluvian longevity a hidden or manifest miracle is debatable,[52] but the main point is that Ritba has misread his view of the ubiquity of the hidden miracle: such miracles too happen regularly only to "prophets or especially righteous men."

One place where Nahmanides introduces a miracle which is not in any of his sources is in the account of the flood, where he suggests that the ark miraculously contained more than its dimensions would normally allow. The problem here, however, is so acute, and the alternative solutions so implausible, that it is difficult to regard this as evidence of eagerness to multiply miracles, particularly since he makes a point of saying that the ark was made relatively large "for the purpose of minimizing the miracle."[53]

Nahmanides, then, was no occasionalist or near occasionalist. Except in the rarest of instances, the natural order governs the lives of non-Jews, both individually and collectively, as well as the overwhelming majority of Jews. The Jewish collective is often (usually?) guided by miraculous providence, but it too can find itself forsaken and left to accidents; and though the absolutely righteous and absolutely wicked also enjoy (or suffer) a chain of hidden miracles, the chain is apparently not unbroken. Moreover, Nahmanides' uncompromising insistence that providence is exclusively miraculous means that, although God is constantly aware of everyone, he does not exercise providence when nature prevails; since nature almost always prevails, the routine functioning of Nahmanides' world is, as we have already noted, extraordinarily naturalistic.

---

[52] As Kahana notes, Ritba was probably thinking of Nahmanides' assertion (*Comm. to Gen.* 46:15) that Jochebed's giving birth at the age of 130 is a hidden miracle. It is worth noting, however, that even though hidden and manifest miracles are performed through different divine names (e.g., *Comm. to Exodus* 6:2), the boundary line between them is not always hard and fast, if only because the constant repetition of certain hidden miracles can make them manifest (*Comm. to Lev.* 26:11).

[53] *Comm. to Gen.* 6:19. Nevertheless, it is noteworthy that unless Nahmanides had in mind the miniaturization of the animals in the ark (and he does not say this), the miracle he is suggesting appears to involve the sort of logical contradiction that Jewish rationalists refrained from accepting even in miracles and which they ascribed only to their Christian adversaries. See D. Lasker, *Jewish Philosophical Polemics Against Christianity in the Middle Ages* (New York, 1977), passim, and esp. pp. 25-43, and cf. my *The Jewish-Christian Debate in the High Middle Ages* (Philadelphia, 1979), pp. 351-352, esp. n. 11, for a possible affirmation of this rationalist position by Nahmanides himself.

What, then, is the meaning of Nahmanides' assertions that "a person has no portion in the Torah of Moses without believing that all things that happen to us are miracles; they have nothing to do with 'nature' or 'the customary order of the world' " and that "one who believes in the Torah may not believe in the existence of nature at all"?[54]

To resolve this question, we must look again at his standard argument for hidden miracles and the terms in which it is usually couched. As we have already seen, the essence of this argument is invariably the fact that the Torah promises rewards and punishments which cannot come naturally; hence, they are all miracles. This is true, he says, "of all the promises (ye'udim) in the Torah."[55] "The promises of the Torah (ye'udei ha-Torah) are all miracles."[56] Hidden miracles were performed for the patriarchs in the manner of "all the promises (ye'udim) of the Torah, for no good comes to a person as the reward of a good deed and no evil befalls him as a result of sin except through a miraculous act... The reward and punishment for the entire Torah in this world comes through miracles that are hidden."[57] "All the promises (ye'udim) in the Torah, favorable or unfavorable, are all miraculous and take the form of hidden miracles."[58] "All the blessings [in the Torah] are miracles."[59]

In all of these passages, Nahmanides' affirmation of miracles refers specifically to the realm of reward and punishment promised by the Torah. Similarly, when he makes the extreme assertion in his commentary that "all things that happen to us are miracles," he immediately continues, "If a person observes the commandments his reward will make him successful, and if he violates them his punishment will destroy him."[60] In his sermon *Torat HaShem Temimah*, where be repeats his strong statement about miracles, the evidence again comes from the "promises of the Torah" (ye'udei haTorah).[61] Nahmanides' intention is that "all things that happen to us" *in the context of reward and punishment* "are miracles."

The passage in his sermon does appear to be arguing for a somewhat broader conclusion, but that conclusion is not the non-existence of

54   See notes 22-23.
55   *Comm. to Gen.* 17:1.
56   *Comm. to Gen.* 46:15.
57   *Comm. to Exod.* 6:2.
58   *Comm. to Lev.* 18:29.
59   *Comm. to Lev.* 26:11.
60   *Comm. to Exod.* 13:16.
61   *THT*, p. 153.

nature. Nahmanides is concerned by Maimonides' tendency to limit miracles wherever possible, a tendency exemplified most disturbingly in his allegorical interpretation of Isaiah's prophecy that the nature of wild animals will be transformed at the end of days. Since Maimonides himself once demonstrated an understanding of ongoing miraculous providence, his apparent inclination to resist every extra miracle through the mobilization of all his considerable ingenuity appears pointless, inexplicable, and unwarranted.[62] The religiously unavoidable belief in such providence must logically lead to a relaxation of inhibitions against the recognition of miracles. There is nothing achieved by the tendency of Maimonides and Ibn Ezra to approach every miracle stated or implied in Scripture with the hope that it can be made to disappear through some naturalistic explanation; we will still be left with a world punctuated by the regular appearance of miraculous providential acts. No denial of the natural order is either explicit or implicit in this argument. Aside from the fact that such a denial would contradict a number of Nahmanides' explicit statements, it would be an extravagant inference from the evidence of *ye'udei haTorah*. The Torah's promises of reward and punishment do not demonstrate the non-existence of nature, and Nahmanides never meant to say that they do.[63]

The Nahmanides that emerges from this discussion is a complex, multi-dimensional figure whose world view is shaped by an almost bewildering variety of intellectual forces. He must grapple with the pressures of profound religious faith, philosophical argument, halakhic doctrine, mystical belief, astrological science, and Scriptural teaching to forge a concept of the miraculous that will do justice to them all. On the one hand, his God retains the unrestricted right of intervention in the

---

[62] *THT*, p. 154 (cf. n. 21). The argument in *Comm. to Gen.* 46:15 is virtually the same, except that here the target is Ibn Ezra's refusal to recognize Jochebed's advanced age when she gave birth. Here too this unreasonable resistance stems from a failure to appreciate the fact that the Torah is replete with hidden miracles. Nahmanides' statement that the punishment of a woman suspected of infidelity is the only permanent miracle established by the Torah (*Comm. to Numbers* 5:20) refers, of course, only to manifest miracles (cf. Henoch, p. 55, n. 169).

[63] The remark in the *Sermon on Qohelet* that "one who believes in the Torah may not believe in the existence of nature at all" (*Kitvei Ramban* I, p. 192) appears in an elliptical context with many of the same features as the other discussions of hidden miracles, and I am confident that it too refers to the realm of reward and punishment. See also the end of n. 45 above.

natural order; even ordinary individuals have their time of reckoning, not only the absolutely righteous or the absolutely wicked die from eating the heave-offering, non-Jewish collectives can surely be punished for sin[64]— and Nahmanides' logic requires that all these divine acts be understood as miraculous. At the same time, such interventions remain very much the exception in a world which otherwise functions in an entirely naturalistic way. Nahmanides' position allows for untrammeled miracles within a fundamentally natural order and is a striking example of his effort to integrate an uncompromising religious position into a world view that recognizes the validity of much of the philosophical achievement of the medieval world.

---

[64]   *Comm. to Gen.* 1:1.

POLEMIC, EXEGESIS, PHILOSOPHY, AND SCIENCE: REFLECTIONS ON THE TENACITY OF ASHKENAZIC MODES OF THOUGHT

From: *Jahrbuch des Simon-Dubnow-Instituts* 8 (2009): 27-39.

RATIONALIST PHILOSOPHY

The presumed absence or near-absence of what we usually call rationalism in medieval Ashkenaz raises a series of questions large and small: If rationalism is in fact absent or largely absent, what accounts for this, especially in light of recent scholarship demonstrating that Ashkenazic Jews were exposed to the works and culture of Sephardic Jewry to a greater degree than we had thought? Should the evidence of such exposure lead us to conclude that philosophical rationalism was in fact present among Northern European Jews, an approach that would greatly diminish the cultural contrast between Ashkenaz and Sepharad? Indeed, the assertion that new evidence diminishes that contrast served as the basis for one of Elisheva Carlebach's arguments against Gerson Cohen's thesis that differences between Sephardic and Ashkenazic messianism are linked to different approaches to rationalism.[1] If we insist that the contrast is real, should we assume in light of the new scholarship that Ashkenazim were in fact fully aware of rationalist ideas but refrained from utilizing or even addressing them out of motives that they had articulated clearly and consciously, at least in their own minds? Thus, as we shall see, several outstanding scholars have accounted for the absence of philosophical arguments or interpretations in specific Ashkenazic texts or intellectual endeavors such as anti-Christian polemic and biblical exegesis by positing local explanations relevant to those discrete areas or

---

[1] Elisheva Carlebach, *Between History and Hope: Jewish Messianism in Ashkenaz and Sepharad: Third Annual Lecture of the Victor J. Selmanowitz Chair of Jewish History* (New York 1998), pp. 3-4. See note 16 there for references to studies that have pointed to the interaction between the cultures.

even to particular figures. Is this the appropriate approach to account for what appears to be a large, more or less consistent cultural phenomenon? Finally, should science and rationalist philosophy be treated separately or as two aspects of the same discipline or mode of thought?

Let me begin with a working definition of rationalism (or rationalist) that I formulated a decade ago in a footnote apologizing for the use of this "admittedly imperfect term": "By rationalist I mean someone who values the philosophical works of non-Jews or of Jews influenced by them, who is relatively open to the prospect of modifying the straightforward understanding (and in rare cases rejecting the authority) of accepted Jewish texts and doctrines in light of such works, and who gravitates toward naturalistic rather than miraculous explanation." I hastened to add that "I do not regard this as a rigid, impermeable classification."[2]

If we work with this understanding of rationalism, we will find it very difficult to endorse a fundamental reassessment affirming Ashkenazic openness to the philosophical culture characteristic of medieval Sephardic thinkers. Yes, a paraphrase of Saadya's philosophical work influenced a certain sector of Ashkenazic Jews. Yes, as Ephraim Kanarfogel notes in this volume, opposition to anthropomorphism characterized this and arguably other sectors of Ashkenazic Jewry, and one might be inclined to describe such opposition as a reassessment of the straightforward understanding of accepted texts. Yes, one can find references or figures here and there that evince familiarity with philosophical works and may even allude to characteristically rationalist positions. But the instinct that tells us that the rationalist inclinations delineated in this definition are for the most part alien to Ashkenaz is not an antiquated scholarly prejudice. Exceptions remain exceptions; allusions remain allusions; rejection of anthropomorphism is not in itself rationalism; and the reading of a few books does not necessarily alter deeply entrenched modes of thought.

Ashkenazic culture was initially formed in a Northern European Christian environment largely innocent of a philosophical tradition, at least of the sort that fits the model that we have been utilizing. As Christian Europe became exposed to that tradition, it began to change,

---

[2]   "Judaism and General Culture in Medieval and Early Modern Times," in Gerald J. Blidstein, David Berger, Sid Z. Leiman, and Aharon Lichtenstein, *Judaism's Encounter with Other Cultures: Rejection or Integration?*, edited by Jacob J. Schacter (Northvale, N.J. and Jerusalem, 1997), pp. 62-63.

although even then the dominant expression of scholastic thought remained considerably more conservative than the strongly rationalist strain of Arabic and Jewish philosophy. The major figures of Ashkenazic Jewry are very unlikely to have read Latin, and so the inner workings of nascent and even mature scholasticism were largely closed to them. More to the point, whatever exposure Ashkenazic Jews may have had to the philosophical works of Sephardic Jews in Hebrew translation came after their cultural profile had been largely formed.

At this point, it is worth turning to the controversy surrounding a book to whose fundamental insight I subscribe even as I remain uncertain about its concrete theses. In 1985, Charles Radding published a study entitled *A World Made by Men* that aroused a brief but vigorous tempest. His essential argument was that Europeans in the early Middle Ages thought and acted on a moral level that corresponds not to that of modern adults but to one or another of the levels that Jean Piaget ascribes to children. Inter alia, he noted that they disregarded intent in evaluating the seriousness of a crime. Some of his critics argued that it is simply impossible for early medieval Christian legislators to have dismissed the significance of intent since they read and revered the Bible, where intent is an important element in determining the gravity of a crime and its appropriate punishment. Moreover, as Radding himself pointed out, Augustine and other patristic figures whom the medieval legislators considered authorities also ascribed significance to intent.

It seems to me, however, that this argument, which affirms that people who believe in certain books will necessarily internalize the values in those books, does not accord with psychological reality. Peoples that developed certain modes of thinking during a lengthy formative period do not quickly undergo a fundamental transformation because they embraced a belief in a text that reflects a different perspective. It is much easier to adopt a new doctrine than a new conception of reality, of the world order, and of modes of thinking and arguing. To the degree that Radding succeeded in pointing to data demonstrating that the *mentalité* of pre-twelfth-century Europeans really exemplified the moral perception that he attributes to them, the fact that this perception is not consistent with that of the Bible or of Augustine does not undermine his thesis.

If this point is correct with respect to Christian works that were seen as transcendentally authoritative —and I realize that I have essentially asserted the point rather than proven it—it follows that we should not resist the possibility that Ashkenazic Jews could have been exposed to Sephardic philosophical texts, nodded in agreement with some though surely not all of their arguments, and continued to think along lines that remained entirely alien to the spirit of those texts. I note in passing the even more far-reaching argument by Haym Soloveitchik that at least in their pietistic mode, *hasidei Ashkenaz* somehow managed to remain unaffected by the most basic concepts of the midrashic worldview that permeated the liturgy and the essential construction of collective Jewish identity.[3] To return to our concerns, a highly instructive case in point emerges in two articles by the pre-eminent scholar of the medieval philosophical debate between Jews and Christians on the nearly complete absence of philosophical polemic in Ashkenazic works preceding the end of the thirteenth century.

PHILOSOPHICAL POLEMIC

In the first of these articles, Daniel Lasker sets forth the evidence for the absence of such polemic while simultaneously demonstrating that some anti-Christian philosophical arguments were known to Ashkenazic authors even in the early period. Thus, the paraphrase of R. Saadya's work was available, but its philosophical arguments against Christianity leave no trace at all.[4] *Nestor ha-Komer* was mined, but its philosophical material, to which we shall return, usually was not. In his first article, Lasker explained the phenomenon with a formulation that I endorse:

---

[3] Soloveitchik, "The Midrash, *Sefer Hasidim* and the Changing Face of God," in *Creation and Re-Creation in Jewish Thought: Festschrift in Honor of Joseph Dan on the Occasion of His Seventieth Birthday*, ed. by Rachel Elior and Peter Schaefer (Tuebingen, ca. 2005).

[4] Upon reading the typescript of this article, Yehuda Galinsky remarked in an email message, "A trace there is, even if barely," pointing to R. Moses of Coucy's *Sefer Mitzvot Gadol*, positive commandment #2, where we find a citation from Saadya of a philosophical argument against multiplicity in God. When I brought this to Daniel Lasker's attention, he was grateful for the reference but noted that the passage cited is not among Saadya's more sophisticated arguments. I would add that R. Moses of Coucy, unlike the vast majority of Ashkenazic rabbis, spent significant time among Sephardic Jews. In any event, the passage is surely of interest, but, as Galinsky's careful formulation indicates, it does not change the larger picture.

Most Ashkenazic Jews were not familiar with 'Greek wisdom'; even the intellectuals among them were generally not fluent in philosophy. There is no reason to believe that a polemicist, who addressed his book to a Jewish audience which itself was not philosophically sophisticated, would use arguments which even he would regard as foreign.[5]

At the end of the article, he succinctly captures what I see as the key point, although I am uncomfortable with the level of familiarity with philosophical arguments that he ascribes to Ashkenazic Jews. "The lack of a Sephardi style full-scale philosophical critique of Christianity in Ashkenaz was not a function, then, of Ashkenazi ignorance. It was a result of a totally different intellectual outlook."[6] I do not think that Ashkenazim had the knowledge needed to launch a full scale philosophical critique, but I do think that their distinct intellectual outlook accounts for the almost total absence of philosophical arguments.[7]

Several years later, however, Lasker extended a greater level of generosity to Ashkenazic polemicists, and here the tendency to assume that familiarity with texts must penetrate an individual's psyche leads to a position that grants the authors of these works a greater philosophical orientation than I think they had. In the second article, he reiterated some of the evidence surveyed in the first, but this time he argued that it was primarily the Ashkenazic *audience* that had "a totally different intellectual outlook from that of Sephardic Jews." Because of this different outlook, "the Jewish polemicists felt that their audiences would not have responded well to the same type of philosophical argumentation that appealed to the Sephardic Jews....The classics of Ashkenazic polemic... all play down any possible philosophical critique of Christianity. To a great extent, it was the audience, and not so much the author, which determined that fact."[8]

5   Daniel J. Lasker, "Jewish Philosophical Polemics in Ashkenaz," in *Contra Iudaeos: Ancient and Medieval Polemics between Christians and Jews*, ed. by Ora Limor and Guy Stroumsa (Tuebingen 1996), pp. 197-198.

6   ibid, p. 212.

7   I made a briefer version of the argument in the preceding paragraphs (beginning with the discussion of Radding) in "Ha-Meshihiyyut ha-Sefaradit ve-ha-Meshihiyyut ha-Ashkenazit bi-Yemei ha-Beinayim: Behinat ha-Mahloqet ha-Historiografit," in the Avraham Grossman Festschrift, which should have appeared before the publication of this volume. [English translation in this collection]

8   Lasker, "Popular Polemics and Philosophical Truth in the Medieval Jewish Critique of Christianity, "*The Journal of Jewish Thought and Philosophy* 8 (1999): 254-255.

In light of my view that deep structures of thought are not readily undermined by exposure to a few books, I do not see convincing evidence for this distinction. The Ashkenazic polemicists and their audience inhabited the same cultural world, and very little in it resonated with Sephardic style philosophical argument. It is far from clear that an intellectual chasm separated the composers of polemical works, who stood a cut or more below the intellectual elite of Ashkenaz, from their literate readers, and some members of that audience stood above them. Moreover, numerous passages in Ashkenazic polemical works make it clear that the authors were not writing solely to bolster the morale of their Jewish readers. To a significant degree, they were providing manuals to be used by Jews in real confrontations. A Jewish polemicist would have to think twice or thrice before depriving the most capable segment of his audience of arguments that would have the greatest effect in an actual exchange with Christians. Our first assumption should be that the philosophical arguments in question did not resonate with the authors any more than with their audience.

An examination of one of the few examples of Ashkenazic philosophical polemic before the fourteenth century will, I think, reinforce this assumption. The author of *Sefer Nizzahon Yashan*, working with an argument reflecting the direct or indirect influence of *Nestor ha-Komer*, addressed the question of whether Jesus was the incarnation of just one person of the trinity or of all three. Nestor and other Jewish polemicists objected to the possibility that all three persons were incarnated by insisting either that this would constitute an impermissible separation in God—assuming the *partial* incarnation of each of the three—or, in the event of the complete incarnation of all three, that it would mean that God is limited.[9] For the last argument from the infinitude of God, the *Nizzahon Yashan* substitutes the almost amusing question, "Who was in heaven all that time?" supplemented by "Who ran the world during the three days when they were buried and none of them was either in heaven or on earth?"[10] I suppose that one could argue that the author

---

[9] For an excellent survey and analysis of these arguments, see Lasker, *Jewish Philosophical Polemics Against Christianity in the Middle Ages*, 2nd ed. (Oxford and Portland, Oregon, 2007), pp. 121-125.

[10] David Berger, *The Jewish-Christian Debate in the High Middle Ages: A Critical Edition of the* Nizzahon Vetus *with an Introduction, Translation, and Commentary* (Philadelphia, 1979), English section, p. 137. See too my discussion in Appendix 5 ("Who Was

intentionally changed the argument because he did not believe his readers would understand the point that the incarnation of all three persons would limit God. This is not, however, such an intellectually challenging argument; a *Tosafot* passage of average difficulty is considerably more daunting. I am much more inclined to assume that the author himself, who shows no signs anywhere in his lengthy work of thinking in philosophical terms, naturally shifted into language that was more congenial to his instinctive pattern of thought.

WISDOM, TORAH, AND *RATIO*

We turn now to a very recent article regarding biblical exegesis by one of the towering scholars of medieval Ashkenazic Jewry where I think we encounter an unwarranted reluctance to adopt a straightforward explanation of a phenomenon rooted in the traditionalist rabbinic mentality of that culture. Avraham Grossman has argued that Rashi's commentaries to Proverbs, Ecclesiastes, and Job 28 evince a striking, tendentious commitment to understand "wisdom" (*hokhmah*) as Torah.[11] This is the case, he says, even though the plain meaning generally points to straightforward human wisdom. Since Rashi's approach presumably requires explanation, Grossman suggests two possibilities. The first begins with the contention that Rashi's familiarity with the works of Sephardic grammarians makes it difficult to assume that he was not also familiar with the ideas of Sephardic thinkers and those Babylonian geonim who engaged in speculative pursuits, even though such familiarity is not attested in France until the works of Rashbam and especially of Bekhor Shor. Thus, Rashi may have been attempting to guide his readers away from such philosophical rationalism. The second explanation, which Grossman considers more plausible, is that Christians, at a time when polemic had reached one of its peaks, were beginning to use arguments from reason in their exchanges with Jews, and Rashi wanted to keep his readers away from an enterprise that could lead them to religious doubts.

Incarnated?"), pp. 366-369.

[11] "Ha-Metah bein Torah le-'Hokhmah' be-Perush Rashi le-Sifrut ha-Hokhmah she-ba-Miqra," in *Teshurah le-Amos: Asufat Mehqarim be-Parshanut ha-Miqra Muggeshet le-Amos Hakham*, ed. by Moshe bar Asher et al. (Alon Shevut, 2007), pp. 13-27.

For Grossman, the reason for preferring the second explanation is not because of any deficiency in the first. Rather, it follows from the emphasis in the uncensored version of Rashi's commentary on Proverbs on the dangers of Christianity, which he identifies as the seductive woman who appears so frequently in that work. Since the commentary focuses so often on this danger, and since wisdom understood as Torah is presented as the antidote to the blandishments of the seductress, it is reasonable to assume that concern with the Christian appeal to *ratio* is what motivated Rashi's insistence, in the face of the plain meaning of the text, that wisdom in fact refers to Torah with absolute consistency.

Grossman of course points to Anselm as the prime example of a contemporary of Rashi who utilized dialectic in a theological context, but the example that he supplies illustrating the polemical appeal to reason by Christians is the assertion that the exile demonstrates that the Jews have been rejected in favor of the True Israel. There is really nothing particularly new about this, and if I were to argue for the late-eleventh and early twelfth-century utilization of *ratio* in a specifically anti-Jewish polemical context, I would be more inclined to cite Odo of Tournai's (or Cambrai's) *Disputatio contra Judaeum Leonem nomine de adventu Christi filii Dei*, which reports what is likely to be a real exchange in which Odo argued for the logical necessity of Jesus' sacrifice for the forgiveness of sin.[12] This work, virtually alone, provides a serious evidentiary base for the self-conscious, explicit appeal to *ratio* by a Christian polemicist in France who engaged in actual exchanges with Jews more or less contemporary with Rashi.

Before proceeding, let me note that the issue before us, as I hope we shall see, has considerable methodological significance beyond its specific context. Moreover, historians in the last several decades have ascribed many cultural practices and literary phenomena in late antique and medieval Jewry to the influence of the Jewish-Christian confrontation. These range from midrashic passages to significant elements of the Passover *Haggadah* to the evolution of life-cycle rituals to the motivation of *peshat* exegesis as a whole to specific exegetical observations, and the assessment of these assertions has in some cases

---

12 See *On Original Sin; and, A Disputation with the Jew, Leo, concerning the Advent of Christ, the Son of God : two theological treatises / Odo of Tournai*, translated with an introduction and notes by Irven M. Resnick. (Philadelphia, ca. 1994).

produced a mini-literature.[13] Avraham Grossman's *oeuvre* is generally a paradigm of caution and sober judgment, and his essay on the influence of the Christian context on Joseph Kara's commentaries is one of the most convincing and insightful studies in this scholarly genre.[14] To the degree that my reservations about his position in our case are persuasive, they may serve as a salutary reminder of the occasional need to resist inappropriate utilization of an often valuable and persuasive scholarly approach whose seductive attractions can sometimes penetrate the defenses of even the greatest and most responsible historians.

It seems to me that in evaluating a thesis proposing an extraneous motive for a particular exegetical position, we need to begin with two fundamental questions. First, how compelling is the argument for seeking such a motive? Put differently, can the exegetical position be accounted for without undue strain by straightforward considerations emerging out of the exegete's culture and approach to text? Second, how persuasive is the extraneous motive? These considerations work in tandem. If the proposed motive is highly plausible, we may entertain it seriously even if there is little reason to seek it. If it is not particularly persuasive, we may decide that internal considerations suffice even if we began with a sense of dissatisfaction that sent us searching for external motivations.

In our case, I am not inclined to go far afield. With respect to the first question, Rashi's position can be explained to my satisfaction on the basis of traditional Ashkenazic *mentalité* without recourse to other considerations. With respect to the second question, I am not persuaded that Rashi was likely to have been motivated by concern about Sephardic *hokhmah* or Christian *ratio*.

Is Rashi's emphasis on *hokhmah* as Torah really problematic? It indeed stands in some tension with what moderns and even some Jewish medievals considered *peshat*. Rashbam (or the commentary to Job that incorporates material from Rashbam) pointedly comments that according to the *peshat*, the term *hokhmah* in Job 28:12 refers to *hokhmah mammash* (literal wisdom) and not to Torah. [15] For Rashi, however, whose

---

13   I have commented on some of that literature in "A Generation of Scholarship on Jewish-Christian Interaction in the Medieval World," *Tradition* 38:2 (Summer, 2004): 4-14.

14   "Ha-Pulmus ha-Yehudi-Nozri ve-ha-Parshanut ha-Yehudit la-Miqra be-Zarfat ba-Me'ah ha-Yod-Bet (le-Parashat Zikato shel Ri Qara el ha-Pulmus)," *Zion* 51 (1985/86): 29-60.

15   Sarah Yafet, *Perush Rabbi Shmuel ben Meir (Rashbam) le-Sefer Iyyov* (Jerusalem, ca. 2000), ad loc.

immersion in the world of midrash was deeper and in large measure taken for granted, we need to ask whether there were powerful enough reasons in the text itself to impel him toward other interpretations.

First we need to consider the weight of the midrashic tradition. Prof. Grossman refers to midrashim that understand *hokhmah* as Torah in Proverbs and elsewhere, but he argues that Rashi could have chosen other midrashim. This is a familiar and often valid argument, but in this case, even a casual look through the midrashic and other rabbinic materials reveals that the equation of Torah and *hokhmah* is simply overwhelming. It made its way into the liturgy and is treated as virtually self-evident.

Moreover, key passages in Proverbs discuss Torah, commandments (*mitzvot*), and wisdom (*hokhmah*)—as well as the righteous and the wise—in closely linked contexts. "The mouth of the righteous produces wisdom (*hokhmah*)" (Proverbs 10:31). One especially instructive example is 7:1-5:

> My son, heed my words, and store up my *mitzvot* with you. Keep my *mitzvot* and live, my Torah, as the apple of your eye. Bind them on your fingers; write them on the tablet of your mind. Say to Wisdom (*hokhmah*), "You are my sister," and call Understanding a kinswoman. She will guard you from a foreign woman whose talk is smooth.

Modern biblical scholars will say that Torah here and elsewhere in the Wisdom Literature refers to the teaching of the sage and the *mitzvot* to his directives. But to medieval Jews—including rationalists—Torah is Torah and *mitzvot* are *mitzvot*. Ralbag on this passage writes as follows:

> "My son, heed my words" in your heart. These are the stories of the Torah and the commandments of the Torah. Put them away with you to observe them. "Keep my *mitzvot* and live": The *mitzvot* of the Torah, so that you will attain eternal life. And keep my Torah as you keep the apple of your eye. It is, moreover, not sufficient that you keep the *mitzvot* in your heart; you must bind them on your fingers to do them...

Now it is true that when Ralbag comments on the next verse about wisdom he does not continue to speak of Torah, but the connection between the two in this passage is so intimate that we can hardly expect Rashi to have felt a *peshat*-driven impulse to seek a different interpretation. Thus, when the passage proceeds to speak of how wisdom protects against a foreign woman, it is more than natural for Rashi to identify this wisdom as Torah.

And so we come to two revealing passages that Grossman cites. Proverbs 2: 10-16 asserts that wisdom can save its bearer from an alien woman. Rashi affirms that the foreign woman is

> A gathering of idolatry, i.e. heresy. It is not plausible that the verse speaks of an adulteress literally understood, for how is it the praise of Torah... that it protects you from a foreign woman and not from a different transgression? Rather, this refers to heresy and idolatry, which constitutes throwing off the yoke of all the commandments.

Similarly, on Proverbs 6:24, which says, "It will keep you from an evil woman, from the smooth tongue of a foreign woman," Rashi remarks,

> The Torah will keep you from an evil woman...We must conclude that Solomon was not speaking of an evil woman but rather of heresy, which is as weighty as everything. For if you will say that this refers to a prostitute in the literal sense, is this the entire praise and reward of Torah that it protects against a prostitute and nothing else?

There is, however, a key distinction between the passages. In the first case, the verses speak of wisdom, but in the second they speak of Torah. The verse preceding 6:24 reads, "For the mitzvah is a candle, and Torah is a light," which of course even ibn Ezra and Ralbag understand in accordance with what any medieval Jew would have considered the *peshat*. It is also noteworthy that Ibn Ezra, though he understands Torah here as Torah, inserts a reference to wisdom without any textual basis. The Torah, he says, gives light, while the fool walks in the dark; thus, the way of life refers to wisdom. In this passage, at least, Torah and *hokhmah* are intertwined, virtually identified with one another, even for ibn Ezra. Even more striking is a passage in Ralbag's commentary where, as Prof. Richard Steiner noted to me, the rationalist exegete tells us that wisdom in a series of verses (Proverbs 3: 15-18) that the Rabbis had famously utilized in their encomia to the Torah very likely means precisely what the Rabbis assumed.[16]

---

16   Prof. Steiner also notes that the identification of wisdom and Torah is already present in Ben Sira 24.

Two highly relevant points emerge from this discussion. First, the parallels between passages on wisdom and on Torah are so close that an exegete with a strong predisposition to follow rabbinic precedent would have little reason to seek an understanding of wisdom different from that of the Rabbis. Second, it is extremely revealing that in his comment on the passage in chapter 2 where the biblical text speaks of *hokhmah*, Rashi demonstrates that the foreign woman is idolatry or heresy using the same argument that he does when the text speaks of Torah: "Is this the praise of Torah," he asks, that it saves you from a harlot? But you do not prove something on the basis of an interpretation that itself requires proof unless you have so internalized that interpretation that you simply take it for granted. It appears that Rashi did not even consider the possibility that the reader might say, "Wait a moment. How do you know that the verse here is referring to Torah?" Rashi's assumption could result in part from the similarity between chapters 2 and 7; as we have seen, 7:2 refers to "my Torah," which Rashi would have taken in the traditional sense. Still, for Rashi, the equation of wisdom with Torah appears to have been foundational, not just ideologically but psychologically. If this is true, as I think it is, we need to be very hesitant about assuming that he rejected the non-Torah explanation in an exegetical campaign inspired by external concerns.[17]

Let us now turn very briefly to the proposed external concerns. There is little or no evidence that Rashi was sufficiently aware of Sephardic rationalism for him to have provided a tendentious interpretation of *hokhmah* in order to protect his readers, who probably needed no such protection, from its baneful influence. What then of the dangers of the Christian use of *ratio*? Despite Odo of Tournai, the evidence that the recent introduction of this category into the lexicon of Christian polemicists had come to Rashi's attention is tenuous at best. Even the later Ashkenazic polemics do not address *ratio* as a category. When the author of the *Nizzahon Yashan*, writing two centuries after Anselm, addresses the Christian explanation for the incarnation, he deals only with the antiquated ransom theory in apparent blissful ignorance of the

---

17 None of this means that Rashi was unaware of the fact that the plain meaning of the word *hokhmah* is wisdom and that it sometimes signifies nothing more than that. Thus, he is unprepared to rely on an overarching introductory observation and instead points out to his readers on repeated occasions that their untutored instincts embracing this understanding are incorrect.

satisfaction theory in *Cur Deus Homo?*[18] Moreover, when Jews in Spain and Provence did confront arguments from *ratio*, they usually took the offensive, maintaining that it was precisely Christian dogmas that were unreasonable; it is not clear why a Jew who was the product of an often assertive Ashkenazic culture would choose to react to the challenge not by utilizing the category but by fleeing from it.

This Ashkenazic assertiveness and self-confidence— akin to the self-image noted in the title of Haym Soloveitchik's study of the laws governing the taking of interest[19]—may well play a role in the larger phenomenon that we are examining. Limited exposure, perhaps even substantial exposure, to books representing alternative ways of thinking would not easily transform the psychic world of people confident about their mode of understanding God and the world. Indeed, it is by no means clear why we should take for granted that they *should* have adopted the new approach. Are the workings of the Active Intellect really so intrinsically plausible that anyone who hears about them should nod in automatic assent? Setting this last point aside, I suspect that the self-confidence that characterized Ashkenazic Jewry played a role in its resistance to the absorption of non-Ashkenazic works and influences in the realm of Torah as well. The Jews of Southern France were more receptive—perhaps one should say more vulnerable— than Northern European Jewry to Sephardic rationalism for various reasons. First, their self-image in the area of halakhic observance studied by Soloveitchik was less secure, and this may mean something for their overall self-confidence as well. Second, the culture of Provencal Christian society during the formative period of the region's Jewry was itself marked by greater sophistication than that of the North, so that the Jews of the South may have developed a somewhat more open cultural orientation, at least *in potentia*. Most important, with the immigration of Sephardic Jews into Languedoc in the second half of the twelfth century, Provencal Jewry was exposed not just to books but to people. Sustained interaction with human beings is far more powerful than reading alone. You cannot set aside people the way you can set aside books.

---

18   *The Jewish-Christian Debate*, English section, pp. 195-196, and cf. my remarks in Appendix 2, p. 353.

19   *Halakhah, Kalkalah ve-Dimmuy Azmi: ha-Mashkona'ut bi-Yemei ha-Beinayim* (Jerusalem, ca. 1985).

IV

Finally, a word about science that will return us to the subject of *hokhmah* in medieval Ashkenazic exegesis. A decade ago, I wrote a piece on the understanding of Solomon's wisdom by Jewish exegetes.[20] In their comments on the passage in Kings describing that wisdom, both Rashi and R. Joseph Kara gave pride of place to Solomon's command of the sciences and only then went on to mention a "midrash aggadah" that understands the king's discourses on trees, birds, and fish as halakhic discussions. I noted that in Proverbs and Ecclesiastes, traditionalist commentators routinely identified wisdom with Torah, but in this instance there were powerful textual reasons to marginalize this understanding. Let me add here that if Rashi really had a driving ideological motive for avoiding an understanding of wisdom as human understanding, he should have avoided it in Kings as well as in Proverbs, Job, and Ecclesiastes despite the fact that the local context of the passage about Solomon militated against the identification of wisdom with Torah. Indeed, the very fact that Rashi does regard the identification of Solomonic wisdom with mastery of halakhah as a viable possibility makes his primary interpretation all the more difficult to explain if he had an overriding concern with preventing his readers from understanding *hokhmah* as human wisdom.

But my primary reason for citing this article is the following argument for distinguishing the attitude of Ashkenazic Jews toward science from their attitude toward philosophy:

> We should not wonder about the positive assessment of practical scientific knowledge expressed in [the] commentaries of the [Northern] French exegetes. As I have argued elsewhere,[21] the pursuit of natural science could become the subject of controversy precisely in the Sephardic orbit, where it was caught up in the web of philosophy. If the natural sciences were part of the "propaedeutic studies" leading to the queen of the sciences, they could be tainted by the unsavory reputation of the queen herself. Where they stood on their own, it is hard to imagine any grounds of principle for dismissing them or for failure to admire one who had mastered their

---

20   "'The Wisest of All Men': Solomon's Wisdom in Medieval Jewish Commentaries on the Book of Kings." In *Hazon Nahum: Studies in Jewish Law, Thought and History presented to Dr. Norman Lamm on the Occasion of his Seventieth Birthday*, ed. by Yaakov Elman and Jeffrey S. Gurock (New York, 1997), pp. 93-114.
21   "Judaism and General Culture," p. 118 and p. 134, n.131.

secrets. The very indifference of Ashkenazic Jews to philosophical study liberated them to examine the natural world with keen, unselfconscious interest.[22]

In sum, I see no reason in principle for Ashkenazic Jews to have resisted an interest in science. But the rationalist spirit of Sephardic philosophy, with its questioning of the plain meaning of biblical texts and rabbinic aggadah, its valuing of philosophical inquiry as an enterprise at least on a par with traditional study of Torah, its suspicion of miracles, and its pursuit of the works of non-Jewish thinkers, was decidedly alien to the most deeply embedded instincts of Ashkenazic Jews. When we find an approach in an Ashkenazic work or series of works that accords with the traditionalist instincts of that culture, we need not look any further in an attempt to explain it.

[22]   "The Wisest of All Men," p. 95.

MALBIM'S SECULAR KNOWLEDGE AND HIS RELATIONSHIP TO THE SPIRIT OF THE HASKALAH

From: *The Yavneh Review* 5 (Spring, 1966): 24-46.

Rabbi Meir Loeb ben Yehiel Michel (1809-1879), who became known by his initials as Malbim, was a fascinating and significant figure on the Orthodox Jewish scene in the nineteenth century. Born in Volochisk, Volhynia and troubled by a stormy Rabbinical career in a half-dozen Jewish communities, Malbim wrote a large number of books, many of which had a powerful influence upon the intellectual life of those Jews who remained opposed to the Haskalah movement, even rejuvenating the much neglected study of the Bible to a considerable extent.[1] The degree of his influence may be partially gauged by two quite divergent sources which yield the same impression — that the admiration for Malbim was almost boundless. Tzvi Hirschfeld, in an article in *Zion* 1841, which will be discussed more fully below, wrote of Malbim, "I know very well that the Jews who live in Eastern lands, upon whom the light of wisdom has not yet shone, have decided to raise him up and exalt him." Many years later, the famous Rabbi Yitzchak Isaac of Slonim said, "He is matchless in our generation and is as one of the great scholars of medieval times (*rishonim*), and one page of his books is as beloved to me as any treasure and is dearer than pearls."[2]

Yet Malbim, the champion of Orthodoxy, was imbued with a very wide range of secular knowledge; indeed, as we shall see, he could never have exercised such influence without it. It is the purpose of this paper to

---

[1] S. Glicksburg (*Ha-Derashah be-Yisrael* [Tel Aviv, 1940], p. 406) writes, "In the circles of the extremely orthodox it was permitted with difficulty to study Bible with the commentary of the 'Kempener' (= Malbim)."

[2] Quoted by Isaac Danzig in his *Alon Bakhut, Evel Kaved 'al ha-Rav ha-Gaon... Malbim* (St. Petersberg, 1879), p. 14.

examine Malbim's secular learning and to determine how he related it to his faith and to the religious, intellectual, and social developments of his time. We shall thus gain insight into the worldview of a very influential rabbi who, while remaining within the orbit of the strictest Orthodoxy, grappled with the manifold problems of the age of Haskalah.

Let us turn first to a central issue, Malbim's attitude toward the Jewish Enlightenment and toward religious reform, problems which were closely intertwined in his mind. This subject is best approached through an analysis of perhaps the most painful experience of Malbim's life, his tenure as chief rabbi of Bucharest from 1860 to 1865. Here he suffered intensely from people sympathetic to religious reform who accused him of obscurantism and who eventually had him thrown into jail, from which he was released only through the intervention of Moses Montefiore. His reaction to these events, detailed in a long article he wrote in *Ha-Levanon* 2,[3] is of great value in giving us an understanding of his feelings on these questions. We must constantly keep in mind, however, the circumstances under which this article was written. Malbim was very angry and bitter; his negative feelings will thus be exaggerated and the picture of his enemies will approach caricature. Yet exaggeration is often valuable, for it clarifies beliefs and emotions that might otherwise have remained vague.

Malbim's article, important for social and economic as well as intellectual history, divides the Jewish population of Bucharest into three groups: 1) artisans, 2) peddlers and storekeepers, and 3) the upper class. His attitude toward the first two groups is friendly, for despite their ignorance they were responsive to his preaching and careful in religious observance.[4] This friendliness toward the ignorant masses is found elsewhere in Malbim's works as well; he says, for example, that "the masses can reach the (religious) level of a scholar by supporting him."[5] These Jews apparently returned his affection, for he relates that many made valiant physical efforts to prevent his arrest,[6]

---

3   "Shenat HaYovel," *Ha-Levanon* 2 (1865): 68-71, 85-87, 101-103, 116-118, 134-136, 199-201, 230-233, 261-263, 294-297.
4   Pp. 231-233.
5   Manuscript notes published in *Eretz Hemdah* (Warsaw, 1881; henceforth *E.H.*) on Deut., p. 170.
6   "Shenat HaYovel," p. 86.

and at his funeral the crowds were so large that the city administration of Kiev had to supply a special guard.[7]

The upper class, however, was viewed by their rabbi with dislike and contempt. Malbim, as we shall see presently, felt that genuine enlightenment and religious belief are inseparable; the rich lacked the latter and, Malbim maintains, did not, despite their pretenses, possess the former. When asked by his fictitious questioner about the philosophical position of his opponents, Malbim answers that previous philosophers based their systems upon knowledge obtained through the mind, the eye, and the ear, while these "philosophers" depend upon taste, touch, and smell. "Their taste gains wisdom (ישכיל) in understanding the nature of all sorts of animals about which no Jew has ever gained wisdom; it investigates 'all animals that go on all fours and that have many feet' and all 'that have no fins or scales in the waters.' The sense of touch looks into the nature of the generative faculty... and investigates prohibited women for three [cf. Mishnah *Hagigah* 2:1] of these philosophers. And the sense of smell, because it is a spiritual faculty, was not privileged to reign on weekdays but only on the Sabbath, for those who do not smoke all week 'have their smoke rise' on the Sabbath in all streets."[8]

Now Malbim, we know, did not care much for rich people generally. This dislike goes back to his unpleasant experiences with his first wife, of a very rich family, whom he divorced largely because she wanted him to give up his studies and enter the world of business.[9] Thus, Malbim may well have antagonized these people by not treating them respectfully. But there can be little doubt that their religious observance was minimal and that this was a major factor in the development of antagonism. Malbim, as we shall see, was exaggerating when he said that their opposition was based solely on his preaching, which emphasized religious observance, but there is surely some basis for his assertion.[10]

---

[7] Danzig, *Alon Bakhut*, p. 11.

[8] "Shenat HaYovel," p. 263.

[9] David Macht, *Malbim, The Man and his Work* (1912?, reprinted from *Jewish Comment* [Baltimore, February 9-16, 1912]), p. 7.

[10] The assertion comes in the following sarcastic passage of "Shenat HaYovel" (p. 117):
ויאמר עוד (החוזה): "כי עבור שהוכיח אותם לשמור את השבת מחללו ולהנזר מבשר החזיר מלאכלו,
לכן חיתו למומתים נתנו" – פג לבי מלהאמין שהיו הדברים כפשוטן, אמרתי גם אם לא ידעו היהודים
האלה כי הזהירה התורה על חלול שבת ועל מאכלות אסורות וחשבו כי מלבי בדיתי המצוות החדשות

The militant non-observance of some of Malbim's detractors is illustrated by the well-known story that on Purim one of them sent him a sugar pig as *mishloah manot* [items of food traditionally sent to a neighbor], whereupon he paid the messenger and sent back his own picture "saying that Malbim thanks the sender for his image which the respectable gentleman was kind enough to send the rabbi, and that in return he sends his own likeness."[11] It is also told of Malbim that a non-observant Jew asked him whether smoking was permitted on the Sabbath; the answer: yes, if it is done with some change (על ידי שינוי), that is, by putting the burning side into one's mouth.[12] The fact that such incidents are related about Malbim indicates that there was strong antagonism which at least manifested itself in the form of militant opposition to religious observance and which, as we shall see, was justified on the basis of enlightenment.

Malbim's preaching, then, was a major factor in the developing animosity. Still, it is clear from his writings that he felt that a preacher must not admonish people with unmitigated harshness and severity. "One who admonishes the people... must be one of the sons of Aaron... to love peace and pursue peace, to love people and bring them closer to Torah."[13] Elsewhere, he emphasizes the fact that the reprover must see to it that he does not embarrass the person being admonished.[14] In his commentary on Genesis,[15] Malbim attributes to God an approach which he is likely to have followed himself: "This was God's custom in most of the prohibitions: to first mention what was permitted, e.g., "Six days thou shalt work"... "Six years thou shalt sow thy land"... intending to show that the prohibitions of the Sabbath and of the Sabbatical year are not impossible to observe. Here too he

---

האלה ונבאתי להם בשם ה' ונביא שקר חייב מיתה: בכ"ז הלא לא אמרתי להם "כה אמר ה' אלי אמור אל בני ישראל... כל טמא לא תאכלו", כה אמרתי להם, "כה אמר ה' אל משה נביאו זכור את יום השבת לקדשו... " וגם לפי מחשבתם כי הוספתי דברים אלה מלבי על תורת משה, הנה עברתי על לאו דלא תוסיף וחייבתי מלקות, לא מיתה! אמרתי עוד: הלא המוסיף הוא רק המוסיף דבר על דבר, ואחשבה לדעת איזה דבר שמרו מתורת משה וקיימוהו, עד שיאמרו שאני הוספתי על הדבר הזה עוד דבר זולתו? ואיך יאמרו שעברתי עמ"ש בתורה: "לא תוסיפו על הדבר", על איזה דבר?

11   Macht, op. cit., p. 13. For a different version, see A. Ettinger, *Da'at Zeqenim* (Warsaw, 1898), p. 54.
12   E. Davidson, *Sehoq Pinu* (Tel Aviv, 1951), p. 239. Cf. also p. 238, no. 874b.
13   *Torah Or* (supplementary notes to the commentary on the Pentateuch, henceforth *T.O.*) to Numbers 10:8.
14   *Com. to Lev.*, *Qedoshim* no. 43.
15   2:16-17.

meant to say (to Adam), 'After all, I have prohibited only one tree; I have prohibited only luxuries and the pleasure which causes evil, and I have not commanded that you refrain from enjoying food.'" Such a man is unlikely, despite the frequent difference between theory and practice, to have been unrestrained in the violence of his attack against the practices of the people of Bucharest. Still, the troubles he experienced in other cities as well tends to indicate that he was perhaps short-tempered and somewhat intolerant of those with whom he differed, although it should be recalled that these incidents were all after his bitter experience in Bucharest. Earlier, he had had a long and successful rabbinical career without such friction. In any event, he tells us that ten days before his arrest he came to an agreement with his opponents permitting him, as he puts it, to preach about the Sabbath and prohibited foods only to those who would willingly listen.[16] Malbim probably agreed to this compromise or at least rationalized his agreement on the basis of a realization that admonitions to his opponents would go unheeded, and one of the necessary components of the commandment "Thou shalt rebuke thy neighbor" is that he be a person who might accept reproof.[17] In any case, the agreement was broken by Malbim's enemies, and his unhappy years in Bucharest were brought to an end.[18]

At this point, we must examine the charges made against Malbim by his opponents. S. Sachs, in an article defending Malbim in *Ha-Levanon*,[19] says that he was blamed for three reasons: 1) preaching in Hebrew, 2) inability to represent the Jewish community to the government because of inability to speak languages (German, French, or Rumanian) well, 3) lack of supervision of the schools to see to it that secular subjects and languages (ספרים ולשונות) be taught. There is unquestionably much truth in all these allegations. It should, however, be pointed out that even if Malbim did not speak these languages fluently, he could read at least German quite well. This is clear from his treatise on logic (*Yesodei Hokhmat ha-Higgayon*) where he refers, in

---

[16] "Shenat HaYovel," p. 117.

[17] *Com. to Lev.*, loc. cit.

[18] Malbim probably saw his own fate reflected in Amos 5:13: "והמשכיל בעת ההיא ידום", where he comments, "עת רעה" משכילי עם היודעים רעתכם והיה דרכם להוכיח ועתה ידמו וישימו יד לפה באשר היא" ושונאים את המוכיח והורגים אותו.

[19] 2 (1865): 92-94, 106-110.

frequent parentheses, to many difficult German philosophical terms which he has translated into Hebrew.[20]

The third charge is more serious and more significant. On December 7, 1864, the Rumanian government passed a law requiring elementary education of all children between eight and twelve years of age.[21] That there was strong Jewish opposition to this law is clear from a letter from the Minister of Public Instruction sent to Jewish communities in 1865. "I have been receiving requests," writes the minister, "from several Israelite communities to continue to tolerate the old, unsystematic schools." This he refused to do and proposed instead a sort of "released time" program for Jews. He ends: "The separation of schools will perpetuate the Jews' separation from the nation, for they will not become accustomed to the life of Rumanians and will accustom themselves, from infancy, to the idea of a separation between Jews and Christians."[22] Thus, some degree of Jewish assimilation was the avowed aim of this program. Malbim probably felt that national and cultural assimilation of this sort was but the first step toward religious assimilation, and he was surely familiar and probably in sympathy with the cry of many Russian Jews, "No secular schools!"[23] It is true that he himself had broad secular knowledge, but he had not obtained it in an assimilation-oriented, government-sponsored program. Furthermore, there was long-standing Jewish precedent for permitting such studies to people of more advanced age and knowledge while prohibiting it to youngsters.[24]

Malbim's experience in Bucharest aroused within him powerful feelings of distaste for what he regarded as pseudo-enlightenment.

---

[20] Cf. also *E.H.* on Gen., p. 18. Sachs writes of Malbim, (ן"הרמבמ ל"צ) ן"הרמב ימיב יח היה אלו ובצקנ רשא ,והומכ לודג בר םרודב בוט אצמל בר לכש אצומכ םיחמש ויה זא יכ ל"ז םיפסאמה ילעבו הנרו לארשיב וברי ותומכ ,תולעמהו תומלשה לכ ללכמ דחי ול ואב (p. 109). He also makes the point that Malbim knew German, though he could not speak it fluently.

[21] E. Sincerus, *Les Juifs en Roumanie* (London and New York, 1901), p. 119.

[22] "La séparation des écoles perpetuera leur séparation de la nation; car ils ne s'habitueront pas à la vie des Roumains, et se feront, des leur enfance, a l'idée d'une séparation entre Juifs et Chrétiens." V.A. Urecke, *Oeuvres Complètes*, I, pp. 393-4. Cited in Sincerus, pp. 119-120.

[23] Cf. Gideon Katznelson, *Ha-Milhamah ha-Sifrutit bein ha-Haredim ve-ha-Maskilim* (Tel Aviv, 1954), ch. 1, esp. p. 14.

[24] Cf. the famous ban of R. Solomon ben Adret as well as a similar reaction of Italian rabbis to Azariah de' Rossi's *Me'or Einayim*. Cf. also Malbim's *Com. to Lev., Aharei Mot* no. 41, where he explains the limited value of secular learning.

He expressed these feelings in poetic form in "Shenat HaYovel": "The darkness is dispelled, you say, the light has come; you say, 'Ethics and justice were born in my time; religion and faith are slaves of my light.' You say, 'I have grown wise though my fathers were fools...' O pure and enlightened generation! When the light descended, darkness ascended from beneath it... So has darkness turned to light!... What is to be done to the shepherds of Israel who say that there are still Torah and commandments for Israel?... What is to be done to obscurantists who say that 'a commandment is a candle and Torah light' and whose ear is deaf to the voice of the times that cries, 'There is no Torah, for liberty has come'?"[25]

In truth, Malbim believed in *haskalah* — in his own way. In the introduction to his commentary on Leviticus and *Sifra*, he says that his book is intended for wise or enlightened people (משכילי עם), and he is fearful lest it be seen by obscurantists (מורדי אור). The candelabrum in the sanctuary is a symbol of the light of wisdom and knowledge (אור ההשכלה והדעת).[26] To Malbim, however, *haskalah* means either knowledge and understanding of God and Torah or the use of linguistic, logical, and even scientific tools to buttress faith or to explain it.

Malbim felt that the non-belief or "heresy" of his time was a result of a perversion of the intellectual process. He discusses the person "who sins because of disbelief and comes 'with a high hand' to deny the Sinaitic revelation as did Menasseh ben Hezekiah... who equated the words of the Torah with those of men." There is no doubt that he has in mind the reformers of the nineteenth century, for in the introduction to his commentary on Leviticus, he accuses those who gathered at Brunswick of comparing the Torah to other ancient stories and its poetry to that of Homer and the Greeks. The passage about Menasseh

---

25   סר החושך – אמרת – בא האור / אמרת: המוסר והיושר ילידי דורי / אמרת הדת והאמונה עבדי אורי / אמרת: אני השכלתי ואבותי סכלו / אני קמתי ואבותי נפלו... הדור הטהור! / הדור הנאור! / כי ברדת האור עלה החשך מתחתיה... הדור הטהור והנאור! / כך היה החשך לאור!... מה לעשות לרועי ישראל / האומרים יש עוד תורה ומצוות לישראל / האומרים תורה אחת לנו ולאבותינו / תורה צוה משה מורשה היא גם לקהילותינו / מה לעשות למורדי אור ! / האומרים דודי לי צרור המור / בין שדי ילין, דבר צוה לאלף דור, / אל תמיר כבודו בתבנית שור. / מה לעשות למורדי אור ! / האומרים אל תבכר בן כזבי בת צור / על פני בן הישראלית השנואה הבכור / אל תצמד ישראל לבעל פעור. / מה לעשות למורדי אור? האומרים נר מצוה ותורה אור, / אזנם חרשה לקול העת והתור / הקורא: אין תורה כי בא דרור "Shenat HaYovel," pp. 134-136.

26   *Rimzei ha-Mishkan* on Exodus, ch. 25. Cf. also *T.O.* on Numbers, beginning of *Beha'alotekha* and *Com. to Song of Songs* 2:5.

continues: "There is a difference between one who sins through passion — for he will later repent — and one who sins through disbelief, for he will never repent. The first act is called sin (חטא); the second — an act of perversity (עוון) because it is a perversion of intellect (עוות השכל)."[27] Malbim's pessimism about repentance is qualified somewhat in his eschatological speculations, but it is clear here that he considers the non-believer hopelessly lost. In any case, the idea that certain manifestations of the *haskalah*, viz. the anti-orthodox developments, are perversions not only of faith but also of intellect is a central one in Malbim's thought. Examples of this conviction can be easily multiplied;[28] we shall see later that he considered certain aspects of disbelief in Orthodoxy to be absolutely untenable philosophically.

Malbim, in fact, wrote a long poem called *Mashal u-Melitzah* to emphasize the interdependence of wisdom and faith. It has been suggested that this poem was written as a response to *Emet ve-Emunah* of Adam ha-Kohen. Klausner points out that the two books appeared in the same year but adds that Malbim may have seen the other work in manuscript form.[29] This seems far-fetched. It is much more likely that this poem, which was first given to the editor of *Ha-Levanon*, is the result of Bucharest; it is a poetic expression of the ideas of the unfinished "Shenat HaYovel." The latter appeared in 1865 and the former in 1867; the essential idea of both is that enlightenment without faith is folly. The fact that the chief protagonist, a man in love with Wisdom (חכמה) but repelled by her sister Fear of God (יראה), is named Rich (עשיר) lends further plausibility to this conjecture. The central point, that Wisdom and Fear of God are "twin sisters," is made over and over again.[30] It is significant that Malbim used the poetic

---

27   *Com. to Numbers* 15:30 (*Shelah* no. 48).

28   Following are a number of examples: *Com. to Gen.* 2:7: וכן בכחות הנפש המשכלת. לפעמים ישכיל *Com. to* .לדעת ה' ודרכיו ותורתו, ולפעמים ישמש בשכלו להתנכל ולהתחבל בתחבולות רשע ודרך רע וכדומה *Gen. 3:6:* כשתקדם התאוה אל השכל ואז תקרא התאוה את השכל לעזר לה, והשכל ימשך אחר התאוה ויעזר לה מותר שהדבר לאמר חרש על סיגים כסף ויחפה ואמתלאות למעשיו ובהמציא היתרים ,בתחבולות רשע בשכלו. .וחטא זה, (בחירת ע"ז בשכל) היה גדול יותר כי יד השכל והבחירה היה במעל הזה *Com. to Isaiah* 1: 29:

29   Joseph Klausner, *Historiah shel ha-Sifrut ha-Ivrit ha-Hadashah*, vol. 3 (Jerusalem, 1952/53), p. 224.

30   *Mashal u-Melitzah*, p. 22: אור חכמה אל הולך בנתיבתה / אשת חן, אם לא יגרע עונתה: / אשה רעה אל ממיר את דתה. / הישכב איש את להבת שלהבת / ולא יהיה לשרפת אש צרבת ? / — כך שוכב חיק חכמה ועוזב אם אין יראה אין / P. 110 (note): אחיות תאומות דומות יראה וחכמה מלידה מבטן ומהריון:" P. 34: תורתה! חכמה, ואם אין אמונה אין תבונה. Cf. note on p. 95. Also *Artzot ha-Shalom* (Munkacs, 1895; henceforth *Ar. Sh.*). p. 2b: .מבורכת ה' ארצי, ממגד האמונה מעל, ומתהום המחקר רובצת תחת

form to express this idea; he was interested in proving that technical skill in language can and does go hand in hand with strict fidelity to religious tradition. This too, as we shall discover, was a basic approach in all Malbim's literary endeavors.

One of the clearest examples to Malbim of the use of intellect for perverse purposes was the discovery of rationalizations to justify the abandonment of certain biblical injunctions. These rationalizations usually took the form of discovering a reason for the commandment and showing how that reason is no longer relevant. In discussing Eve's encounter with the serpent, Malbim writes, "Here we learn the serpent's method of seduction and leading astray which exists to this very day. For if people investigate the reasons for the commandments as do those of our nation who are breaking away, they ask why God prohibited five impure animals and try to discover as the reason the fact that they do damage to the body of the one who eats them. Then, when they discover that the foods are not harmful to the body, they throw away the commandment."[31] In his homiletical work, *Artzot ha-Shalom*, Malbim blames Maimonides for laying a trap into which many have fallen by saying that the reason for prohibited foods is medical.[32] Finally, he says that people who indulge in such speculation should at least be uncertain as to the reasons they advance and therefore not abandon religious observance.[33]

Thus far, we have sketched Malbim's attitude toward the Enlightenment, particularly as it affected religious reform. Later, we shall discuss other aspects of his approach and the scope and application of his secular knowledge. First, however, we must examine his attitude as reflected in his life work: biblical exegesis.

In 1839, a book of sermons by Malbim called *Artzot ha-Shalom* appeared. Tzvi Hirschfeld, in *Zion* 1841,[34] reviewed the book and asked Malbim to abandon far-fetched, homiletical interpretations of Scripture and to write a commentary based on the simple, true interpretation (*peshat*). Hirschfeld notes the fact that Malbim is greatly admired by the Jews of Eastern Europe and can thus influence them profoundly; he points, furthermore, to *Ha-Ketav ve-ha-Kabbalah* of Rabbi Jacob

---

31   *Com. to Gen.* 3:3-4.
32   *Ar. Sh.* Sermon III, p. 18a.
33   *Com. to Gen.* 2:16-17.
34   Pp. 59-62, 73-75.

Meklenburg as a work worthy of emulation by Malbim. In turning to Malbim's commentaries, we see an attempt to fulfill Hirschfeld's request by explaining the Bible according to the plain meaning, though Malbim's idea of *peshat* and that of Hirschfeld were undoubtedly quite different. But there was much more to motivate Malbim than a single review of *Artzot ha-Shalom*. There was one of the overriding ambitions of his life: to prove that modern attacks on the divine authorship of the Bible and the oral law are not based on genuine scholarship and that, on the contrary, a more profound understanding of grammar and logic can demonstrate the validity of tradition. Thus, Malbim decided to use the tools of the Enlightenment to oppose its anti-Orthodox tendencies. It should be stated at the outset that his command of the tools and the spirit of modern scholarship was far more restricted than that of a man like David Hoffmann, for example, whose goals were quite similar. Yet Malbim's influence was much wider, and his approach, both in its successes and failures, merits careful study.

Malbim tells us in his introduction to Leviticus that what really motivated him to write his commentary was the conference of reform-minded rabbis at Brunswick in 1844, although it is quite clear from the same introduction that he himself was deeply concerned with the basic problems involved and did not want to neglect the plain meaning of either the written or oral Torah. Thus, the commentary is avowedly a reaction to the times, a phenomenon which we see in the case of *Artzot ha-Shalom*[35] and *Artzot ha-Hayyim,* [a commentary on *Orah Hayyim*] which, says Y.L. Maimon,[36] was to be a commentary on the entire *Shulhan Aruch* as well. The reaction, in the case of the commentary to Leviticus, was to unite the oral and written law. It is interesting that Malbim uses the phrase *ha-ketav ve-ha-kabbalah* in this context, yet does not refer explicitly to Meklenburg at all, perhaps because his own methods were to be novel.

Malbim based his commentary on a very thorough study of Hebrew grammar,[37] a pursuit very popular among the *maskilim*. His central purpose in this pursuit was to demonstrate that "none of the

---

35   Introduction to *Ar. Sh.*, pp. 3a-b: אך בחלום חזיון ...אך אנכי תולעת עצלה!... לא עשיתי כל מאומה... תרדמה ראה לבבי את כל המעשים אשר נעשו תחת השמש ואת כל המהפכה אשר הפכו ילדי יום... ואשכב וארדם".

36   *Sarei ha-Meah* (Jerusalem, 1965), vol. 6, pp. 109-110.

37   Introduction to Isaiah.

grammarians have reached even the ankles of the first generation," a demonstration which will give "ammunition... against any heretic... denier, or critic."[38] The method Malbim employs to effect this demonstration is the bringing of proof that previous attempts to explain grammatical phenomena have been inadequate and that only the rabbinic *midrash* provides a full explanation. To do this, he conveniently assumes that fixed rules for all phenomena must be preserved at all costs, ignoring the fact that languages develop through use.[39] He would justify this assumption, of course, on the basis of the special sanctity of Hebrew. When Malbim cannot establish the accuracy of a rabbinic statement, he tries to show its probability and the impossibility of contrary demonstration. When dealing, for example, with certain rabbinic comments on the compound nature of some Hebrew words (e.g. רך אל = רכיל ;יחניף = יחן אף ;תתן אף = תנאף), Malbim shows that many words probably are compounded, "and we do not know how. The Rabbis, however, who were near the source and knew the language and its origin knew how the development took place."[40] This exaggerated agnosticism as to liguistic development ignores the role of comparative Semitic philology of which Malbim may or may not have been aware, but it aids him in making his point in an area where proof of rabbinic accuracy would be well-nigh impossible.

Malbim, in using grammatical and logical principles, is allegedly seeking the simple meaning of the text. In his introduction to Joshua, Isaiah, and the Song of Songs, he explicitly differentiates between *peshat* and *derash* and says that he seeks only the former. In his commentary to Genesis[41] he begins in one place by quoting his homiletical *Artzot ha-Shalom* and then says, "But according to our present method..." and gives another explanation. Despite the fact that Malbim ordinarily insists that the simple meaning and the rabbinic interpretation are identical, there are passages where he distinguishes the two and feels impelled to explain the simple meaning separately. "This," he writes, "is in accordance with the simple meaning (פשט). And now let us explain the verses according to the interpretation of the *Sifrei* and Talmud."[42]

---

38   Introduction to Lev.

39   *Com. to Lev.*, *Tazriaʿ* no. 17: וזה רחוק שתהיה לשוננו הקדושה כעיר פרוצה אין חומה וגדר.

40   *Com. to Lev.*, *Va-Yiqra*, no. 152; *Qedoshim* no. 40.

41   12:22-23.

42   *Com. to Deut.* 24:1.

"Till here," he writes elsewhere, "we have interpreted according to the *Mishnah* (ch. 5 of *Ma'aser Sheni*) and the *Sifrei*, and now let us explain according to the *peshat*."[43] He feels it necessary to explain the *lex talionis* according to its biblical formulation and therefore says that "in the hands of heaven" there is theoretically such punishment and payment is to be regarded as ransom money (כפר).[44] In *Eretz Hemdah*,[45] he mentions a rabbinic explanation of a non-halakhic matter together with one from the *Kuzari* as if they had equal weight. Malbim's theoretical recognition of the primacy of the simple interpretation is present in his *Artzot ha-Hayyim* as well,[46] although we shall later see that Malbim often lost sight of the simple meaning completely and indulged in the most fanciful homilies in his commentary.

We must now examine a vitally important question with regard to Malbim's biblical exegesis, and that is the extent of his familiarity with biblical criticism, both historical and textual. Probably the most significant passage in Malbim's writings which deals with higher criticism is in his introduction to Psalms. Here, he confesses that certain psalms were written under divine inspiration as late as the time of Cyrus and tries to adduce Talmudic authority for a similar opinion. He adds that he admits this "to remove from us the arguments of scoffers who ask how it is possible that in the time of David, when the monarchy was still powerful, Israel was on its land, and the decree was not yet made, that the priests should have sung about the end of the monarchy and the exile in the time of Zedekiah." Malbim, in other words, is willing to grant a small concession in order to strengthen the foundations of the faith; he is attempting to show that the divine inspiration of Psalms can be defended without farfetched reasoning that insists upon Davidic authorship.

Malbim, however, always had a double audience in mind, and to his Orthodox readers he supplied the necessary far-fetched reasoning. The Bible, he explains, traditionally has four levels of meaning (*peshat*,

---

43 *Com. to Deut.* 26:15.

44 *Com. to Lev., Emor* no. 249.

45 Gen., p. 55.

46 *Ar. H.* on *Orah Hayyim* 1.6, *Ha-Me'ir la-Aretz* no. 73: ועיין בארץ יהודה כתבתי בדרך אחר, והוא" רק בדרך החידוד. Cf. also the introductory comment of Rabbi Moses Sofer: הדברים בנויים על אדני השכל, וקרובים לאמיתתה של תורה, לא כדרך הפלפול הנהוג.

remez, derash, sod [or *kabbalah*, as he puts it] known as *PaRDeS*) and as many as seventy different valid interpretations (ע׳ פנים לתורה). Malbim is interpreting according to the simple meaning, but the traditional view may be correct on some other level. Here he is in serious logical difficulty. The principle of *PaRDeS* makes sense in some areas of exegesis; an author, especially if that author is God, can intend to convey various nuances and even levels of meaning. But it makes little sense in this case. Even if "the Torah has seventy faces," how can both David and a priest of Cyrus' time have written the same psalm? Malbim was quite aware of this difficulty and suggests that the psalm may have been written early, transmitted secretly by a few select individuals, and finally made public in the time of Cyrus. While this is hardly *derash*, *remez* or *sod*, it is an interesting attempt to solve a problem which obviously perplexed Malbim and troubled him considerably.[47]

A striking parallel to this reasoning, one, in fact, which may have influenced Malbim, is found in an article by S. D. Luzatto on Isaiah published much before Malbim wrote his introduction to Psalms.[48] Luzzatto, in defending the unity of Isaiah, wrote, "Those prophecies which refer to the distant future Isaiah did not proclaim publicly... but he wrote them down to be preserved for future generations."

It is significant that Malbim scarcely mentions the critical dissection of Isaiah and certainly does not enter into a careful polemic against it. That he knew about it is clear from his introduction to Ezekiel where he says, "This well (of Ezekiel's words) ... has been left undisturbed by the commentators and critics of the last generation, unlike the books of Isaiah and Job and other wells of holy water which come from the sanctuary which they have disturbed; and some of them have come to Marah and thrown in their trees and made the water bitter, while others closed up the wells and filled them with dust." He was well aware of the critical approach to the Song of Songs as well, and writes in his commentary, "You see that God... has closed the eyes of some of the commentators and translators of the German Bibles... who have

---

47 Following are selections from this passage: "וכתבתי לגול מעלינו טענת חמלעיגים... אולם אצלנו, אמונה אומן כי שבעים פנים לתורה וכפי דרך הדרוש והרמז והקבלה, כל המזמורים האלה כבר צפו במחזה הנביאים והמשוררים... והיו גנוזים וצפונים ביד אנשי הרוח דור דור עד עת שיצא הדבר אל הפועל ואז נאמרו בקול רם.

48 *Kerem Hemed* 7. Reprinted in *Mehqerei ha-Yahadut* (Warsaw, 1913), Vol. 1, part 2. The relevant passage [in *Mehqerei ha-Yahadut*] is on p. 38.

profaned the sanctity of this song, for they have explained it according to its outer form, according to its husk, and have considered it like the song of a harlot... They have therefore cut it in pieces and torn it to shreds... and considered it a combination of many songs — a wine song, a song of friendship, a song of spring, a song for the dance, etc."[49] In the case of Job, it is fairly clear that Malbim believed it was written by Moses, for he says in his introduction, "Its value, order, character, and wisdom are evidence that there is divine wisdom in it and that it was composed through divine inspiration by a man unique in the history of Israel (איש לא קם בישראל כמוהו)."

In the case of Isaiah and the Song of Songs, it was religiously crucial to reject higher criticism. In Job, Malbim thought the objective evidence to be clearly in favor of traditional views. His general feeling was, as he relates at the end of his introduction to Joshua, that recent commentators had either repeated what had already been done before or had gone dangerously astray. In the one case where the core of the significant religious assertion could be preserved even after the acceptance of certain critical conclusions and where the objective evidence favored such conclusions — the case of Psalms — we see Malbim torn by a number of opposing forces: his desire to show that one did not require far-fetched reasoning to affirm divine inspiration, his adherence to tradition, his Orthodox audience, his common sense. He finally arrived at an unoriginal but instructive compromise trying to preserve all elements and satisfy all his readers.

Malbim's position on textual criticism is wholly negative. It may even be probable that his opposition to lower criticism caused him to adopt a position which profoundly affected his most basic exegetical method. In his introduction to Jeremiah, he carries on a polemic against Abravanel who had dared criticize the stylistic skill of the prophet. Malbim maintains that God dictated the specific language of each prophet word for word, for if we do not affirm this and assume instead the fallibility of the prophet in transmitting the content of his prophecy then we are opening the door to an unusual sort of lower criticism (stylistic improvement rather than restoration of a corrupt text). "Then," writes Malbim, "a person would dare to add

---

49   "He-Harash ve-ha-Masger," an epilogue to the commentary on Song of Songs, vol. 2 (Jerusalem, 1956 ed. of Malbim), p. 1730.

and subtract from Holy Writ according to his stylistic preference, and the holy books will be like an open, unwalled city which 'little foxes that destroy vineyards' would enter to damage and destroy... And we are commanded not to change even one letter." In his introduction to Leviticus, Malbim refers to those who gathered at Brunswick as "little foxes" bent on destruction, a parallel which indicates that he is not merely referring to a theoretical danger here but was quite well aware of the growing tendency toward conjectural emendation even, to a limited extent, in a man as religious as Luzzatto. He may have felt that by raising the sanctity of each prophetic word to that of the Pentateuch itself he would prevent this tendency. Luzzatto, for example, did not emend Pentateuchal passages. In light of this conviction, the principles he laid down in his commentary to Isaiah that prophetic writings can contain no redundancy or superfluity in style takes on new meaning, for the style too is not the prophet's but God's. Thus, in an indirect and perhaps subsidiary way his reaction against lower criticism is responsible for the principles underlying a major part of his exegetical works.

Malbim, as we have seen, maintained that his sole quest was for the simple meaning. Yet, despite Hirschfeld's request and despite his own resolution, he very often lapses into a homiletical excursus. *Torah Or* is replete with them, but there they are at least labeled. In *Ha-Torah ve-ha-Mitzvah* (the commentary proper) as well, we find him explaining that land cannot be sold forever because the human soul is merely sojourning on earth.[50] This sort of lapse is excusable and even welcome because of its brevity and beauty, and it justifies Glicksburg's comment that Malbim introduced some very appealing homiletical ideas into his commentary which do not stray too far from the plain meaning.[51]

There are instances, however, where the homiletical passage is longer and flagrantly violates the plain meaning of the text. In *Artzot ha-Shalom*, Malbim explained that the true test of Abraham was not in the command to sacrifice his son but rather in the second command — to spare him! The test was to discover whether Abraham would feel the joy that a father naturally experiences when his son is saved or whether his only joy would be that of fulfilling "a positive commandment" (מצות עשה). The

---

50   *Com. on Lev., Behar* no. 39.
51   *Ha-Derashah be-Yisrael*, p. 406.

latter was true, and Abraham thus passed the test. This explanation is repeated at length in the commentary to Genesis and in *Eretz Hemdah*.[52] The dehumanization of Abraham had its precedents — in Abravanel, for example, upon whom Malbim often relies heavily, Abraham begs God for permission to sacrifice Isaac — but Malbim completes his interpretation with the following far-fetched exegesis of Gen. 22:12 ("And thou hast not witheld thy son, thine only son, from Me"): "Thou hast witheld" him "not" because he is "thy son, thine only son" but only because you heard a command "from Me." This type of interpretation is, unfortunately, not rare in Malbim's commentaries.[53]

We have seen, then, that Malbim's entire commentary was a reaction to the developing world of Haskalah and reform. It was the work of a man who wanted to fight these tendencies with their own tools and to prove that a proper understanding of the texts refutes almost all the major conclusions of both historical and textual criticism. But the task of trying to completely satisfy his extremely orthodox audience and to employ fully the tools of modern linguistics and research was a task too great even for a man with as fine a mind as Malbim. Hence the numerous shortcomings of a work which is, nevertheless, a valiant and valuable effort to accomplish a monumental task.

After this discussion of Malbim's attitude toward the Haskalah, biblical criticism, and reform in his great works of scholarship, we can now turn to his position on some more practical matters.

The two most important political developments among Jews during Malbim's lifetime were emancipation and the rise of proto-Zionist activity. His practical attitude toward emancipation is not quite clear, although we know of his opposition to government-sponsored schools. One fact, however, is clear and instructive. Malbim succeeded in placing emancipation within the framework of a religious philosophy of history. "In this exile," he writes, "and especially in the last generation, many states have given Jews the rights of citizens (*Buergerrecht*), and their fortune and honor have risen to the extent that there is no difference between the period of exile and the time of redemption except observance of the commandments connected with the land of Israel and the Temple. Why has God done that in this last

---

52 *Ar. Sh.*, Sermon II, p. 14a; *Com. to Gen.* 22:12; *E.H.* on Gen., p. 69.
53 Cf., for example, his almost incredible explanation of Numbers 11:5.

generation?" The answer: it is a test to determine whether the desire to return to the land of Israel and to repent is based only upon suffering. If the Jews are wise, they will not be satisfied with the temporal good to be obtained in exile; if they are foolish and remain content, God may leave them in exile indefinitely.[54] Thus, emancipation is the final, crucial test for the Jewish people, and it is a test Malbim expected them to pass. For in his commentary on Daniel he calculates that the complete redemption will take place in 1927-28; thus, according to the *Zohar* in *Shemot*, "an awakening for redemption" should begin in 1867-68. Malbim expected just such an awakening.

The awakening that did take place was proto-Zionist agitation for a return to Palestine. Chaim Heshel Braverman, in *Knesset Yisrael* of 1888,[55] writes as follows of Malbim's attitude toward this movement: "Malbim was a true lover of Zion… who approved of the intention of the 'Lovers of Zion' (חובבי ציון)… to transport a number of Jews who find it extremely difficult to make a living… to the desolate land of our fathers, to develop and till its soil and take bread out of our fatherland that has remained as a living widow for two thousand years." It is particularly interesting that Malbim, in a number of passages, emphasizes his belief that the redemption will take place in stages, the first stage expressing itself in a state with only a small amount of power.[56] Malbim's nationalistic feelings left little room for universalism, and even the book of Jonah and a verse like Amos 9:7 are interpreted—in the latter case with total disregard for the plain meaning[57]—in a manner not at all complimentary toward Gentiles.

In other practical matters of less significance we find Malbim defending old customs which had been ridiculed by *maskilim*. He defends, for example, the method of arranging marriages in which bride and groom do not see each other till the wedding. His defense is based first on biblical precedent (Isaac and Rebecca), but he then adds

---

54 Notes published in *E.H.* to Deut., p. 173. It should, however, be noted that the implication concerning indefinite exile is questionable, because in many passages Malbim says that the final date cannot be delayed.

55 *Sefer* 3, p. 212.

56 *Com. to Micah* 4:8, and see Malbim's own references there. Pointed out by Ephraim Wites, *Evel Yahid* (1887), pp. 44-45.

57 Com. to *Amos* 9.7: ...עי"י שחרות עורם "אתם" מיוחדים לי "כבני כושיים" שהם מצויינים ונכרים תמיד
והעליתי המצריים עם התערבתם ולא ..."הלא את ישראל העליתי מארץ מצרים" לזה ראיה ומביא ...אתם כן
בתמיה? "מקיר וארם מכפתור" (העליתי) "פלשתים" הכי אבל...ישראל את

the following psychological observation: "According to the modern custom, children learn to show each other love which does not exist in real life but only in parables and stage performances; therefore, when they later discover that they deceived each other, their love cools off until it might dissolve into nothingness."[58] Thus, Malbim defends a much-attacked custom not only on the basis of the Bible, but on grounds that no *maskil* could challenge: the perpetuation of love. The conservatism in dress which characterizes nineteenth century Orthodoxy is reflected in Malbim,[59] yet in his commentary to *Orah Hayyim* he defends the opinion of R. Solomon Luria that covering the head is a sign of special piety and not a legal requirement.[60]

At this point, it should be mentioned at least in passing that Malbim studied kabbalah from his youth, but he was opposed to the Hasidic movement, an opposition which caused him serious trouble in at least two towns where he was Rabbi.[61] Maimon maintains that Malbim eventually became more sympathetic to Hasidism,[62] but this never became very apparent.

Finally, we must examine Malbim's secular knowledge—in philosophy, science, and history—and discover how he used this knowledge in his works.

Malbim's early education, under R. Moshe Halevi Hurwitz, included the classics of medieval Jewish philosophy.[63] Later he was to write a commentary on *Behinat Olam* and a treatise of more than one hundred pages on the principles of logic. Malbim insisted on the validity of logical and philosophical reasoning and argued against the contrary claims of skeptics. He writes in his treatise on logic that the first step in philosophy is "to clarify the fact that it is in our power to attain knowledge through syllogistic reasoning... for the Skeptics denied this, and decided that a man cannot deduce matters through scientific reasoning but only through sense-perception and common sense. And

---

58 *Com. to Deut.* 24:1.

59 *Com. to Gen.* 48:8-9.

60 *Ar. H.* on *Orah Hayyim* Vol. 2, *Eretz Yehudah* no. 4; on 2:6, *Ha-Me'ir la-Aretz* no. 43.

61 H.N. Maggid -Steinschneider, *Ir Vilna* [Jerusalem, 1968], p. 234 note. Also Macht, *op. cit.*, p. 12.

62 *Sarei HaMeah*, vol. 4, p. 177. Malbim even wrote a treatise on *kabbalah* called מגלת סתרים (not סגולת סתרים as Macht quotes it).

63 Macht, *op. cit.*, p. 5.

for this a special study is needed called a critique of pure reason."[64] Malbim, then, maintained the possibility of reaching fairly certain conclusions in philosophical discourse.

This certainty is reflected in metaphysical questions taken up by Malbim in his other works. Knowing of Kant, Malbim nevertheless considers the belief in God to be philosophically demonstrable through the argument from design. He says, in fact, that it is almost impossible to conceive of "a fool who could think that the world came about by chance."[65] Occasionally Malbim displays an exaggerated feeling of certainty even when his argument is not particularly convincing. He writes, for example, in his discussion of God's reply to Job, that it is a "foolish question" (שאלה סכלה) to ask why God created predatory animals, because it would not be in accordance with God's glory to create "only worms and ants. His glory is shown by the fact that there are powerful animals... which He subdues with His might."[66] Sometimes, on the other hand, Malbim argues against non-believers by insisting upon the limitations of human knowledge: "Do you know God, and do you weigh your knowledge on the same scales as His?"[67]

Malbim, though he read modern philosophers, was completely immersed in the problems of medieval philosophy in general and medieval Jewish philosophy in particular. He discusses hylic matter and the question of man's soul— whether it is one with three functions or whether there are distinct souls;[68] he constantly operates with the Nahmanidean concept of the hidden miracle;[69] he deals with the opinion that angels "are made up of matter and form, their matter sometimes being of fire and sometimes of air, as is the opinion of Ibn Ezra, the *Kuzari*, and Ibn Gabirol";[70] he accepts the idea that Jews are uniquely receptive to divine inspiration (הענין האלקי) straight out of the *Kuzari*;[71]

---

64   *Yesodei Hokhmat ha-Higgayon* (Warsaw, 1900), p. 95. Occasionally, Malbim uses technical principles of this treatise in his commentaries. Cf. Deut. 4:32.
65   *Com. to Gen.* 1:1. Cf. also *Ar. Sh.* pp. 43b-44a for a more elaborate philosophical discussion. Also *E. H.* on Gen., p. 15.
66   *Com. to Job* 40:7.
67   *Ar. Sh.*, Sermon 5, p. 25a.
68   *Com. to Gen.* 2:7.
69   *Com. to Gen.* 17:3; *Exod.* 3:13, 6: 2; *Deut.* 3:24 and passim.
70   *Com. to Gen.* 18:3.
71   *Com. to Exod.* 19:1.

he frequently discusses man as a microcosm (עולם קטן) and the world as a large man;[72] he accepts the opinion that elemental fire is dark.[73]

Malbim often opposes Maimonides in philosophical matters, though he occasionally comes to his defense.[74] Malbim maintains, against Maimonides, that man is the purpose of all creation;[75] he opposes Maimonides on prophecy in two major areas;[76] most important, he maintains that modern logic has re-established the philosophic probability of *creatio ex nihilo*.[77] This assertion is repeated in his commentary on Exodus[78] with an argument that is most interesting in the age of the controversy over Darwin: "I think that the principal testimony for *ex nihilo* is the fact that we see that for thousands of years no new species has been added to the world, while according to those who believe in the eternity of the world, it would be necessary that new creatures appear from time to time as they did in the past." Here is another example of Malbim's philosophical certainty in complicated matters.

The philosophical knowledge that Malbim possessed was put to use for ethical and exegetical purposes as well as for philosophical ones. He explains, for example, that success or suffering in this world is not very important and scarcely even exists, for it is predicated upon things which are merely contingent and haven't any necessary, intrinsic existence, "as has been explained in philosophy."[79] Malbim explains the Talmudic statement that the Septuagint began, "God created in the beginning" by saying that since the Greeks believed in the eternity of the world, the biblical order could have been misunderstood as implying hylic matter co-existent with God.[80] This is a remarkably perceptive comment by a person who did not even know the philosophical uses of the Greek *arche*.

Malbim's knowledge of the sciences, particularly astronomy, was extensive if not systematic. His major use of science, as we have by

---

72   *Com. to Lev.*, Qedoshim no. 2; *Com. to Psalms* 104:1 and passim.
73   *Com. to Deut.* 4:11. Cf. Nahmanides at the beginning of Genesis.
74   Cf. *Com. to Exodus* 20:2 for a defense of Maimonides against an important criticism by Crescas.
75   *E.H.* on Gen., p. 12.
76   *E.H.* on Exod., pp. 10-11.
77   *E.H.* on Gen., p. 17.
78   20:8.
79   *Com. to Psalms* 73:20
80   *E.H.* on Gen., p.5.

now learned to expect, is in the service of religion. He shows, for example, that it is implied in Genesis that the sun, already created as a sphere, was invested with light by God on the fourth day. He continues: "Scientists have all been confused as to the light which comes from the sun and why its source is not depleted. Actually, its source can never be depleted, for it comes from the hidden light that has no end."[81] Malbim refutes an interpretation of Abravanel with a refutation based on the modern sciences,[82] yet he seems to have believed in celestial intelligences.[83] He expresses belief in astrology in many passages, though in others the belief is qualified or denied,[84] and in one place implies that he might believe in alchemy.[85] He uses his scientific knowledge extensively for biblical exegesis;[86] occasionally, however, his information is very dubious, and he relies on as old a source as *Shevilei Emunah* for medical information.[87]

This knowledge of science impelled Malbim to engage in naturalistic interpretations of some miracles. The fact that the rainbow was not seen before the flood, a problem that disturbed R. Saadyah Gaon and Nahmanides, is given a scientific explanation by Malbim.[88] So, too, he gives a scientific analogy to Abraham's seeing of stars during the day.[89]

Despite his extensive scientific knowledge, and despite his assertion that it is not the purpose of the Torah to teach science,[90] Malbim insists that the Rabbis had literally superhuman knowledge of scientific facts. "Although the power of inquiry is insufficient to clearly ascertain the nature of that thin air (of the upper atmosphere), still the Rabbis, who viewed, through the holy spirit (ברוח הקדש), places that investigation

---

[81]   *Com. to Gen.* 1:14.

[82]   *Com. to Gen.* 1:1 and 6.

[83]   *Com. to Psalms* 89:3.

[84]   Belief: *Com to Gen.* 12:1, 15:5 and elsewhere. Qualification, doubt or denial: *Com. to Deut.* 4:19 and especially *Com. to Job*, introd. to chs. 4 and 6.

[85]   *E.H.* to Gen., p. 25.

[86]   Cf. *Com. to Gen.* 1:6 (on electricity and the atmosphere), 1:25, 3:1; *E.H.* on Gen., p. 15 (on gravity) and elsewhere.

[87]   *'Aleh li-Terufah*, a commentary on ch. 4 of *Hilkhot De'ot*, pub. in *E.H.* on Numbers, p. 62. Cf. *Com. to Gen.* 6:1 and 30:1 for dubious information.

[88]   *Com. to Gen.* 9:13.

[89]   *Com. to Gen.* 15:17.

[90]   *T.O.*, note 2 to Gen. 1:1.

cannot teach, told us…"[91] When Malbim was younger, he was criticized in a letter by R. Ephraim Horowitz of Volochisk for implying that in a rabbinic dispute one opinion was that what we now call the Western Hemisphere is unpopulated. R. Ephraim exclaims, "Even if the Gentile scholars erred, is the Jewish people like all nations?!" Malbim answers by pointing out that in every dispute one opinion is erroneous; however, in deference to the principle that there must be an element of truth in both views (אלו ואלו דברי אלקים חיים), he constructs a defense for the other opinion as well.[92] Thus, we see that there were powerful social as well as intellectual pressures upon Malbim to defend the scientific infallibility of the Rabbis.

Malbim read historical works as well, particularly on ancient history. He knows that early civilizations sprung up near rivers[93] and indicates a familiarity with mythology and ancient idolatory.[94] Occasionally, he is somewhat credulous in historical matters, but he certainly read a great deal in the field.

It is clear, then, that Malbim's secular knowledge was quite extensive, and he put it to use for his central goal, the defense of his tradition.

We have seen that Malbim did not reject the pursuit of philosophy, the sciences, and other intellectual endeavors, although he was wary of including them in elementary education. He believed in *haskalah* in his own way. What he did oppose, however, was what he considered the perversion of intellect that led to the antireligious manifestations of the enlightenment. This feeling was strengthened by his position on the ability of the intellect to attain philosophical certainty.

Malbim could never have exercised the influence he did without his secular learning, for his life's work expressed itself in the use of science, logic, philosophy, grammar, and poetry to further and defend religion. This use, however, is often uncritical, because Malbim is caught in the dilemma of trying to satisfy completely his own orthodoxy and his orthodox readers and yet remain within the framework of secular scholarship. Given the approach of many of

---

91   *Com. to Gen.* 1:6.
92   Letter published as epilogue to *Ar. H.*
93   *Com. to Gen.* 2:10.
94   *Com. to Gen.* 4:22, where he makes a statement that anticipates the methodology of Cassutto and Kaufmann; Gen. 6:2, 4; Exod. 2:23; Isaiah 9:7; *E.H.* on Gen., p. 59.

his readers on the infallibility of the Rabbis in all areas, this was an impossible task. Malbim himself often gets carried away by homilies and loses sight of his resolution to approach texts in a straightforward manner.

Still, Malbim is a fascinating example of a brilliant individual who could not close his eyes to the Haskalah and to secular learning and who was yet unwilling to compromise his orthodoxy by one jot or tittle. His solution was to use his learning to defend religion, a solution which gained him enormous influence and which, whatever its failings, was a courageous effort to turn two worlds into one.

THE USES OF MAIMONIDES
BY TWENTIETH-CENTURY JEWRY

From: *Moses Maimonides: Communal Impact, Historic Legacy,*
ed. by Benny Kraut (Center for Jewish Studies, Queens College,
CUNY: New York, 2005), pp. 62-72.

The influence of iconic figures and texts can be complex to the point of inscrutability. We all know, for example, that the Devil can quote Scripture; what, then, does this tell us about the influence of Scripture? On the one hand, believers feel bound by Scriptural teachings; on the other, this very loyalty can lead them to force Scripture to say what they badly want to do or believe on other grounds. To cite a sharp pre-modern observation of this point in an area of great relevance to Maimonidean studies, R. Isaac Arama, a distinguished fifteenth-century Spanish thinker, asked why certain philosophers need the Bible at all. After all, their *modus operandi* appears to be as follows: If the Bible agrees with their philosophical views, they interpret it literally; if it does not, they interpret it allegorically or symbolically so that it is made to agree with those views. In what sense, then, are they bound or even influenced by the Bible?[1]

Maimonides is not the Bible, but he has achieved such stature in the minds of Jews that citing his authority is always useful and sometimes compelling, while dismissing him out of hand is difficult or at least undesirable. In assessing his impact or how he is used, we consequently need to ask ourselves a series of questions: Was the position in question actually formed under the impact of Maimonides? If it was formed out of other considerations, was it genuinely honed or reinforced by his authority? Is his view simply a useful aid in arguing for that position? Is the position really in tension with his but forced into compatibility

---

[1]   *Hazut Qashah*, appended to *Sefer Aqedat Yitzhak*, vol. 5 (Pressburg, 1849), chapter 8, p. 16b. Cf. Yitzhak Baer, *A History of the Jews in Christian Spain*, vol. 2 (Philadelphia and Jerusalem, 1992), p. 257.

by questionable reasoning? Has a position acknowledged to be different from his nonetheless been modified and moderated under the impact of his opposing view? What makes this complex enterprise even more daunting is the fact that Maimonidean positions themselves can be divided into those that more or less reflect straightforward recording of earlier rabbinic texts, those that endorse one strand of rabbinic opinion over another, and those that are more or less the independent views of Maimonides. The more quintessentially Maimonidean the position, the more its impact reflects that of Maimonides himself.

Maimonides' iconic status in the twentieth century was greater than that of any other Jew in post-biblical history. Now this may be true of earlier periods as well, but there was a time when Rashi might have given him a run for his money. Unlike Maimonides, whose positions as codifier and philosopher produced assertions clearly seen as his own, Rashi's originality was somewhat obscured by the fact that he was primarily an elucidator of other texts. Still, serious students of those texts understood the nature of Rashi's contribution and realized that his understanding contrasted with that of other authorities in innumerable cases. But in modern times, and especially in the twentieth century, the bulk of Jewry saw itself as very different from Rashi, while Maimonides remained a model for serious Jews in all religious denominations and even for some who saw themselves as secular. He was, after all, a physician and philosopher, perhaps a radical philosopher, as well as a Talmudist, and even his great rabbinic code was suffused with a broad, philosophical spirit.

On the other hand, the percentage of Jews who studied Maimonides seriously - or even not so seriously - was much lower in the twentieth century than in any previous period. Thus, a discussion of his impact and how he was used is primarily a discussion of elites - and largely, though far from exclusively, of Orthodox elites, who regarded his work as in some sense authoritative.

Maimonides' extraordinary standing was illustrated in an academic environment when the late Isadore Twersky of Harvard—admittedly a not-altogether typical academician—was invited to deliver the keynote address in the amphitheater of the Hebrew University's Mt. Scopus campus at the quadrennial conference of the World Congress of Jewish Studies. What he chose to do for nearly an hour was to read excerpts of Jewish testimonials through the ages to the greatness of Maimonides.

My father was a folklorist who wrote articles about legends concerning both Rashi and Maimonides. Folk legends about Rashi, he wrote, are largely depictions of the personality of a beloved father, underscoring his devotion to Torah and his outstanding character. The legends about Maimonides, on the other hand, reflect the awestruck admiration of "a village-dweller for an international personality, the attitude of an ordinary person to his relative occupying a position in the highest circles," so that the popular imagination did not even shrink from attributing to him an effort to create an immortal human being.[2]

It is not surprising, then, that few controversies in twentieth-century Jewish life bearing a religious dimension were carried on without reference to Maimonides, and often his presence loomed very large indeed, sometimes bestriding the discussion like a colossus. The reasons for this extend beyond his exceptional stature and reflect several special characteristics of his great legal code. First, despite the importance of R. Isaac Alfasi's earlier compendium, Maimonides' *Mishneh Torah* was the first comprehensive code, so that the trajectory of later decision-making was in many cases set by his judgment as to the Talmudic opinion that should prevail. Second, he included assertions that we would normally describe as theological rather than legal in that code. For some readers, this transformed an expression of opinion into a position that bore legal force. Related to this point is his formulation of a creed, some of whose elements are also incorporated in his code, in which he asserted principles that could not, he said, be rejected without crossing the line into heresy. Thus, the deviant believer would forfeit his or her portion in the world-to-come. How many people could screw up the courage to defy a figure of Maimonides' stature once the stakes had been ratcheted up to so high a level?[3] Finally, his code, unlike the later *Shulhan Arukh*, incorporated laws that applied only to a sovereign Jewish state, whether in the past or in the future. Thus, for several issues that arose in the twentieth century, Maimonides was the prime, sometimes virtually the only, classical source with something relevant and authoritative to say.

---

2   Isaiah Berger, "Ha-Rambam be-Aggadat ha-Am," in *Massad*, vol. 2, ed. by Hillel Bavli (Tel Aviv, 1936), p. 216; "Rashi be-Aggadat ha-Am" in *Rashi: Torato ve-Ishiyyuto* (New York, 1958), ed. by Simon Federbush, p. 148.

3   This is not to say that his dogmas went entirely unchallenged. See Marc B. Shapiro, *The Limits of Orthodox Theology: Maimonides' Thirteen Principles Reappraised* (London & Portland, OR, 2004).

Let us, then, take a fleeting glimpse at the role Maimonides played and continues to play in a series of issues dividing twentieth and early-twenty-first-century Jewry.

For Orthodox Jews, the issue of the permissibility and desirability of advanced secular education remains, perhaps remarkably, a major point of contention. For obvious reasons, Maimonides appears to lend support to the position affirming the desirability of such education, not only because of what he said but because of what he so patently did. Indeed, Norman Lamm once remarked that if Maimonides returned to this world, he would surely choose to teach at Yeshiva University. But, as we shall see, nothing about the uses of Maimonides is straightforward. In this instance, a genuine characteristic of Maimonides that we shall encounter again, to wit, his elitism, affords the opportunity to challenge this assessment. Thus, representatives of Traditionalist Orthodoxy have argued that Maimonides' own pursuit of philosophy was to be restricted to a small coterie of the elite. Did he not say that his great philosophical work was intended for a tiny number of readers? Did he not also say that one may not turn to philosophical pursuits without first mastering the corpus of rabbinic law? Now, these arguments do not accomplish all that their advocates wish, since they leave in place Maimonides' value judgment as to the superiority of philosophically accomplished individuals to philosophically naïve rabbinic scholars, but at least the traditionalists' educational and curricular priorities can be salvaged without an overt rejection of Maimonides.

Moreover, Maimonides did not always formulate his legal rulings in a manner conducive to the interests of Orthodox modernists. Thus, he forbade the reading of idolatrous books and apparently extended this prohibition to anything that could engender religious doubts. This passage became the basis for an article by Rabbi Yehudah Parnes, then at Yeshiva University, in the first issue of *The Torah U-Madda Journal*, a publication dedicated to the principle of integrating Torah and worldly knowledge, arguing that Jewish law requires severe restrictions on the reading habits and hence the curriculum of all Jews. I responded to this argument in an article co-authored with Lawrence Kaplan, invoking other Maimonidean texts as well as the evident behavior of Maimonides himself, but there is no better illustration of the ability to appeal to Maimonidean authority on both sides of almost any issue than an exchange in which advocates of a broad curriculum need to defend themselves against the assertion that they are defying the precedent set by a man who took all of human learning as his province.[4]

A delicate issue with a long history that became particularly acute in the late-nineteenth and twentieth centuries was the Jewish attitude toward non-Jews. Beginning in the thirteenth century, Christians pointed to Talmudic passages discriminating against Gentiles. Without diminishing the acute threat that these arguments posed to medieval Jews, one can still point out that the matter became all the more sensitive (though slightly less dangerous) in an age that began to advocate an egalitarian ethic granting Jews citizenship, genuine religious freedom, and legal equality. Here again Maimonides plays a major role on both sides of the discussion. Antisemites cited Maimonides' codification of discriminatory laws such as the exemption from returning lost objects to non-Jews, even a prohibition against doing so, while defenders of the Jews, both Jewish and Gentile, pointed to his citation in similar contexts of the biblical verse that God's mercy is upon all his creatures, as well as specific rulings such as those prohibiting theft from non-Jews as well as Jews.[5] More than one Orthodox rabbi in the late twentieth century maintained that Maimonides' formulation of the reason why one may not return lost objects to non-Jews, namely, that one would be "strengthening the hand of the world's wicked," limits the prohibition only to wicked Gentiles. For reasons rooted in the values of the commentator, an apparently general statement that non-Jews are wicked becomes an explicit distinction between those who are wicked and those who are righteous.[6]

Now, Maimonides did famously affirm that pious non-Jews have a portion in the world to come; at the same time, he conditioned this on their belief in revelation. This condition has troubled some Jews since the days of Mendelssohn, when its source was unknown. We now know the source, and one recent scholar - the late Marvin Fox - noted Maimonides' requirement, apparently approved of it, and enthusiastically endorsed a

4   Yehuda Parnes, "Torah U-Madda and Freedom of Inquiry," *The Torah U-Madda Journal* 1 (1989): 68-71; Lawrence Kaplan and David Berger, "On Freedom of Inquiry in the Rambam - and Today," *The Torah U-Madda Journal* 2 (1990): 37-50.

5   See, for example, Joseph S. Bloch, *Israel and the Nations* (Berlin and Vienna, 1927).

6   For a discussion of this and related matters, see my "Jews, Gentiles, and the Modern Egalitarian Ethos: Some Tentative Thoughts" in the forthcoming proceedings of the 2001 Orthodox Forum; on returning lost property, see the discussion at note 15 there and the references provided in that note. [The article was published in *Formulating Responses in an Egalitarian Age*, ed. by Marc Stern (Lanham, 2005), pp. 83-108.]

version of the Mishneh Torah text denying that those who observe moral laws on the basis of reason alone are even to be considered wise.[7] What motivated Fox was his own philosophical argument against the existence of a morality independent of the divine will. Most moderns, who have different instincts about morality and fairness, remain troubled, and so they eagerly point to a letter attributed to Maimonides that appeals to contradict the condition he set forth in his code.[8] It is perfectly evident that larger moral instincts are at work in the choice of which Maimonides you embrace.

This issue applies to non-Jews in general, but Maimonides has also been invoked in very different ways with specific reference to Christianity. In a famous censored passage near the end of his code (*Hilkhot Melakhim* 11:4), he explains why he thinks the divine plan arranged for the spread of Christianity and Islam. It has not been uncommon for twentieth-century Jews motivated by ecumenical sentiments to cite this explanation as evidence of Maimonides' positive stance toward those religions, to the point of asserting that he saw them as a way of preparing the world for the messianic age by disseminating monotheism. In fact, as rabbinic authorities know very well, this is not what he says at all. Christianity and Islam, he maintains, prepare the world for the messianic age by familiarizing many people with the Torah, so that the Messiah will be able to speak to them within a familiar universe of discourse. But Christianity, unlike Islam, is in Maimonides' view full-fledged *avodah zarah*, usually translated loosely but not quite accurately as idolatry.

The central philosophical and religious beliefs of Maimonides have been the subject of fierce debate in academic circles with little impact on more than a few Jews. Still, the subject deserves some attention even in this forum. Under the influence of Leo Strauss, Shlomo Pines, and others, the perception of Maimonides as a theological radical who disguised many of his real views has attained pride of place among many historians of philosophy. In this perception, Maimonides considered matter eternal, denied that God actively intervenes in human affairs, rejected physical resurrection, considered philosophical contemplation superior to prayer, and did not believe that anyone other than the most sophisticated philosopher has a portion in the world to come. For these

---

[7]   Marvin Fox, *Interpreting Maimonides* (Chicago and London, 1990), pp. 130-132.
[8]   See my "Jews, Gentiles and the Modern Egalitarian Ethos," n. 49.

scholars, his legal works and more popular philosophical teachings were intended for the political purpose of establishing a stable social order. One deep irony of this position is that the author of the standard list of Jewish dogmas would be revealed as one whose adherence to some of those dogmas is very much in question. The irony is deepened in light of the contention in Menachem Kellner's *Must a Jew Believe Anything?* that Maimonides virtually invented the notion of Jewish dogmas, a contention that I consider overstated but nonetheless reflective of an important reality.[9]

Other scholars, such as Arthur Hyman, Isadore Twersky, and Marvin Fox, resisted the extreme radicalization of Maimonides. It is, I think, very difficult to reconcile the portrait of a radical Maimonides who denied immortality to any non-philosopher with the Maimonides who fought to teach even women and children that God has no body so that they would be eligible for a portion in the world to come. Maimonides battled to establish a conception of God that in its pristine form was indeed inaccessible to the philosophically uninitiated, but I believe that he meant his dogmas sincerely as a realistic vehicle for enabling all Jews to achieve immortality. In recent years, several efforts have been made to render Maimonides the philosopher accessible and relevant to a larger audience. Kenneth Seeskin has made this an explicit objective,[10] Yeshayahu Leibowitz's depiction of an austere, distant Maimonidean God for whom halakhah is the be-all and end-all of Judaism was broadcast on Israeli radio,[11] and David Hartman's *Maimonides: Torah and the Philosophic Quest* was clearly aimed at an audience beyond the academy. But the Maimonides presented in these works and others is not always the same Maimonides.

A few moments ago, I allowed myself the expression "even women and children." The role of women is an issue that came to occupy center stage in much twentieth-century discourse, and Maimonides played no small part in Jewish debates about this matter. His dismissal of the intellectual capacity of women is well known, but his heroic image and immense influence have led committed Jewish thinkers and scholars with twentieth-century sensibilities to see if some more positive assessment can be elicited from his works. Thus, Warren Harvey argued in an article

---

9   See my review essay in *Tradition* 33:4 (1999): 81-89.
10   *Searching for a Distant God: The Legacy of Maimonides* (Oxford University Press, 2000).
11   *The Faith of Maimonides*, trans. by John Glucker (New York, 1987).

published more than twenty years ago that although Maimonides excluded women from the study of the Oral Law, and preferably even from that of the written Torah, he regarded the commandments to know God and love him, which certainly obligate women, as inextricably bound up with the study of Torah, indeed of Talmud or *gemara*. Thus, we have a powerful deduction to set against Maimonides' explicit assertion, and we ought at least to take it into account.[12]

An even stronger example of this approach is Menachem Kellner's recent article[13] contrasting Gersonides, who allegedly regards women as intellectually inferior by their very nature, with Maimonides, who allegedly sees their deficiencies as environmentally induced. Among other things, Kellner points to a passage in which Maimonides lists Moses, Aaron, and Miriam as the three individuals who died in a state reflecting the highest level of human achievement. Thus, says Kellner, one-third of those who reached the highest level ever achieved were women. (One could quarrel with his use of the plural here.) I am inclined to think that Kellner is too hard on Gersonides and too easy on Maimonides. No rationalist philosopher in the Middle Ages—including Gersonides—could really exclude all women from the capacity of attaining a high level of intellectual achievement, since these philosophers regarded such achievement as necessary for prophecy, and there were indisputably women prophets. As to Maimonides, Kellner's arguments for his higher estimation of women strike me as very weak, to the point where I understand them primarily as a result of the admirable desire to interpret the stance of the greatest of Jewish thinkers in as favorable a light as possible.

And so we come to two issues where a Maimonidean ruling placed significant restrictions on women. As Harvey pointed out in that article, it is very far from clear that the usual guidelines for deciding among conflicting talmudic opinions required the ruling that women should not be taught Torah. But that is how Maimonides ruled in his pioneering code, with lasting impact on Jewish law and practice. The twentieth century has seen major changes, but Beis Yaakov schools had to be justified as an emergency measure, and Orthodox institutions teaching Talmud to

---

12   "The Obligation of Talmud on Women according to Maimonides," *Tradition* 19:2 (Summer, 1981): 122-130.
13   "Sin'at Nashim Pilosofit bi-Yemei ha-Beinayim: ha-Ralbag le-'ummat ha-Rambam," in *Me-Romi li-Yerushalayim: Sefer Zikkaron le-Y. B. Sermonetta* (*Mehqerei Yerushalayim be-Mahashevet Yisrael* 14 [5758]), pp. 113-128.

women, though they rely on the position of Rabbi Joseph B. Soloveitchik and other distinguished authorities, are subject to ongoing criticism that requires incessant justification.

The second of these issues reflects the fact that only Maimonides' code ruled on matters relating to Jewish kingship and authority. A rabbinic text had affirmed that a Jewish king must be male, and Maimonides extended this, without a clear source, to all positions of authority (*Hilkhot Melakhim* 1:5). In pre-State Palestine, this ruling was mobilized to argue even against women's suffrage, but it was particularly relevant to the holding of political office. A discussion of this issue by Rabbi Ben Zion Uzziel illustrates strikingly some of the motifs that we have already encountered.[14] First, he berates his correspondent for suggesting that Maimonides may have misunderstood the rabbinic text under the influence of the custom of his own time. We are permitted to disagree with Maimonides, but we may not say such things about him. Second, Rabbi Uzziel stresses that Maimonides' position is not articulated in any other classical source. (Note that Maimonides' addressing of issues not dealt with by other authorities usually endows him with special authority; in this instance, it was used against him.) Finally, Rabbi Uzziel deduces from a discussion of the Tosafists that they disagree with Maimonides even though they do not say so explicitly. In the presence of a strong desire to rule against Maimonides, both inference and the silence of other sources can count against an explicit ruling. It is worth noting that the Maimonidean prohibition of positions of authority for women played a role in Saul Lieberman's opposition to the ordination of women, a stand that had a significant impact on the decision of some Conservative traditionalists to leave the Jewish Theological Seminary or break with organized Conservative Judaism when women were admitted into the rabbinical program.

The role of women in the Israeli polity leads us to the question of the State itself. Maimonides has been a central figure for both religious Zionists and religious anti-Zionists. His position that the messianic process will develop naturalistically was seized upon by religious Zionists to demonstrate that Jewish sovereignty must be reestablished by human effort, this despite his explicit admonition that we are simply to wait. His assertion that the final Temple would be built by human hands and

---

14   *Pisqei Uzziel bi-She'elot ha-Zeman* (Jerusalem, c. 1977), #24.

not, as Rashi thought, by the hand of God, reinforced this perception.[15] On the other hand, the vehemently anti- Zionist Satmar Rov pointed to Maimonides' omission in his *Book of the Commandments* of the commandment to live in Israel. The Lubavitcher Rebbe, sympathetic to the State and hawkish on territorial concessions but opposed to Zionist ideology, "proved" that the State has no messianic significance whatever by citing the fact that Maimonides did not list the return of the dispersed of Israel until a late stage of the Messianic process - this despite the fact that Maimonides wrote that the order of events in the unfolding messianic scenario is not a fundamental religious principle. The Rebbe was well aware of the rabbinic texts about gradual redemption cited by religious Zionists, but he maintained that Maimonides knew them too and had effectively ruled against them in a binding, authoritative code.

Beyond the State there is the Messiah. Here Maimonides looms enormously large. In the last two chapters of his code, he set forth criteria for identifying first a presumptive Messiah and then one who had attained his status with certainty. While many Jews had written about the Messiah, only Maimonides expressed his views in a code, which once again led some readers to grant them the force of law. A king from the House of David becomes presumptive Messiah by studying the Torah, strengthening it, compelling all Israel to obey it, and fighting the wars of the Lord. He attains the status of certain Messiah by gathering the dispersed of Israel and building the Temple in its place.

The waning years of the twentieth century produced a major messianic movement that apparently violated these Maimonidean guidelines, and it was precisely the movement whose leader had described the last two chapters of the *Mishneh Torah* as legally binding. Here we are witness to the most creative efforts to establish that a position that Maimonides explicitly rejected is in fact compatible with his guidelines. Thus, Lubavitch hasidim during the Rebbe's lifetime argued that he had achieved the criteria of presumptive Messiah. He was a king because rabbis are called kings in the Talmud; he "compelled" by persuasion; several thousand Jews qualify as "all Israel"; and mitzvah tanks qualify as instruments of the wars of the Lord. Some even argued that he had

---

15   See my discussion in "Some Ironic Consequences of Maimonides' Rationalistic Messianism" (in Hebrew), *Maimonidean Studies* 2 (1991): 1-8 (Hebrew section) [English translation in this volume].

at least begun the activities associated with the certain Messiah; he was, after all, instrumental in preserving the Jewish identity of Soviet Jews so that they could be gathered into the land of Israel, and 770 Eastern Parkway is at least the interim Temple and the spot where the final, heavenly Temple will descend before both buildings are transported to Jerusalem. As to Maimonides' assertion that if the figure in question "does not succeed to this extent or is killed, then it is known that he is not the [Messiah]," this refers only to one who was killed, not one who died of natural causes, or it refers only to a scenario in which the Messiah would arrive naturalistically, or it is irrelevant because the Rebbe did not die at all.[16] Remarkably, almost incredibly, a learned Lubavitch rabbi arguing that a supremely righteous man can annul himself to the point where he is nothing but divinity found a Maimonidean passage that allegedly reflected this conception.[17]

These are instances where people who know Maimonides' statements very well and even consider them binding nonetheless disregard or refashion them through creative exegesis. But many people who revere him reject his positions or even consider them heretical without knowing that he held them at all. Orthodox Jewish education, even in Modern circles and all the more so in Traditionalist ones, pays little attention to what we call theology. Thus, it is easy to compile a list of *explicit* positions of Maimonides - not those of the putative esoteric radical - that would be labeled heresy or near-heresy in many contemporary yeshivas. Examples include his assertion that rabbinic statements about the details of the messianic process may be unreliable, that the Rabbis could have made scientific errors, that God does not intervene in the lives of individual animals, and more. Maimonides' iconic status was achieved at the price of consigning many of his views to a black hole of forgetfulness.

In these circles, however, Maimonides' great rabbinic works are alive and well. In the course of the twentieth century, the *Mishneh Torah* moved to center stage in traditionalist bastions of Torah study. Here too there is a certain degree of irony, but it predates the twentieth century. Maimonides envisioned his code as a work that would serve as a standard handbook for scholars, summarizing the results of Talmudic

---

16   For these arguments and much more on Lubavitch messianism, see my *The Rebbe, the Messiah, and the Scandal of Orthodox Indifference* (London and Portland, Oregon, 2001).
17   Avraham Baruch Pevzner, *'Al ha-Zaddikim* (Kfar Chabad, 1991), pp. 8-10.

discussions and freeing people already familiar with those discussions from the need to revisit them in painstaking detail. He did not realize that it would become an adjunct to Talmudic study, complicating and enriching it even further.

At the dawn of the twentieth century, R. Meir Simchah of Dvinsk wrote his classic *Or Sameah* centered on Maimonides' code. The immensely influential, pathbreaking methodology of R. Chaim Soloveitchik of Brisk took Maimonides as its point of departure even as it revolutionized the study of the Talmud itself. Two generations later, R. Joseph B. Soloveitchik made Maimonides' "Laws of Repentance" the centerpiece of annual discourses during the High Holiday season that drew thousands and influenced thousands more, discourses captured in part in *On Repentance*, one of the great Jewish religious works of the century. In an effort at popularization that engendered criticism but also enjoyed modest success, the Lubavitcher Rebbe urged daily study of sections of the *Mishneh Torah* modeled after similar initiatives in the study of Mishnah and Talmud. And in the far narrower world of the academic study of Talmud in a university setting, scholars specializing in the field sought to find in Maimonides evidence of sensitivity to their own central contention, to wit, that the anonymous sections of the Babylonian Talmud are later than the rest and should be treated accordingly.

When Prof. Kraut sent the participants in this conference an e-mail message indicating that many hundreds of people had registered, I replied, "Did you tell them that Maimonides himself was speaking?" The attendance here is ample testimony to the magic of Maimonides' name. This wide appeal leads me to a final observation about the abiding power of Maimonides the communal leader and gifted writer to inspire audiences to this day.

In early 1989, I spent seven extraordinary weeks teaching at the inaugural mini-semester of the Steinsaltz yeshiva in Moscow, the first such institution to be granted government recognition since the Communist revolution. The students consisted largely of refuseniks who had risked careers and livelihoods to commit themselves to Jewish learning and observance. In addition to the study of Talmud, Bible and more, there was a slot twice a week for Jewish Thought. I decided that the text I would teach would be Maimonides' *Epistle to Yemen*, a work directed to a beleaguered Jewish community pressured to abandon its faith. It was as if Maimonides had composed the work for the students in that yeshiva. The greatest challenge in teaching the *Epistle to Yemen* in that environment was to read the words without shedding tears.

I conclude then with one small selection from the many relevant passages in which Maimonides speaks to Soviet Jews during the transitional moments between implacable persecution and the beginnings of hope.

> Persecutions are of short duration. Indeed, God assured our father Jacob that although his children would be humbled and overcome by the nations, they and not the nations would survive and endure. He declares, "Your descendants shall be as the dust of the earth," that is to say, although they will be abased like the dust that is trodden under foot, they will ultimately emerge triumphant and victorious. And as the simile implies, just as the dust settles finally upon him who tramples upon it and remains after him, so will Israel outlive its oppressors. The prophet Isaiah predicted that during its exile various peoples will succeed in their endeavor to vanquish Israel and lord over them, but that ultimately God would come to Israel's assistance and put an end to their woes and afflictions... The Lord has given us assurance through His prophets that we are indestructible and imperishable, and we will always continue to be a preeminent community. As it is impossible for God to cease to exist, so is our destruction and disappearance from the world unthinkable.[18]

18   Abraham Halkin and David Hattman, *Epistles of Maimonides: Crisis and Leadership* (Philadelphia and Jerusalem, 1993), p. 102.

THE INSTITUTE FOR JEWISH STUDIES
ON ITS EIGHTIETH BIRTHDAY

One of four talks to commemorate the anniversary of the Hebrew University's Institute delivered at the closing session of the Fourteenth World Congress for Jewish Studies

From: *Jewish Studies (Madda'ei ha-Yahadut)* 43 (2005-6): 29-36 (Hebrew). Translated by the author.

———————

A lecture on the Institute for Jewish Studies and its place in the constellation of the academic study of the Jewish people and its faith in the past, present and future no doubt deserves to be listed among those matters that have no measure (Mishnah *Pe'ah* 1:1), though it is by no means clear that it also deserves to be counted in accordance with the continuation of the mishnah among those matters whose fruits one consumes in this world and whose core remains in the world to come. Nonetheless, even if that promise is not applicable in our case, I find my reward in the very fact that I was invited to address this esteemed body in such an impressive venue.

It is customary to speak of a Jerusalem school at the time of the formation of the *yishuv* and the State that saw Jewish history through a Zionist-nationalist perspective. There is clearly much truth in this assertion. The majority of scholars in the field of Jewish Studies who arrived in the Land of Israel during the major migrations saw themselves through the prism of a monumental historical revolution that they simultaneously perceived as a continuation of the central motif in the nation's history. Nonetheless, in his book on the first decades of the Institute, David Myers pointed persuasively to the complex reality that forbids us to ignore the ideological disagreements among the greatest Judaica scholars in that period and all the more so the opposing influences, images, and aspirations that animated each of them individually.[1]

---

[1]   D.N. Myers, *Reinventing the Jewish Past: European Jewish Intellectuals and the Zionist Return to History* (New York and Oxford, 1995).

On this occasion, I would like to focus on several of the motifs that emerged in the early days of the Institute and to examine—even if superficially—how they developed and to what degree they are relevant to the world of Jewish Studies today. I refer to the abandonment of apologetics, the search for a presumably objective scholarly truth, the place of the national vision in that objective scholarly matrix, the revival of the Hebrew language, and the attitude toward scholars of Jewish history and culture who lived in the diaspora. The establishment of a center for Jewish Studies in the *yishuv* and later in the State served as the basis for the assertion that scholars in the Land of Israel would succeed in freeing themselves from the bonds of self-abnegation and the fear of what gentiles will say, so that they would be capable of dealing with the behavior and beliefs of Jews through the generations "with all their lights and shadows," as Gershom Scholem put it in his classic and penetrating article on Jewish scholarship.[2] Despite the reservations that I will express in the course of my remarks, I must emphasize that anyone familiar with the apologetic Jewish literature of the late-nineteenth and early-twentieth centuries will understand that there is indeed a deep divide between that literature and the scholarly literature that appeared under the aegis of the institution established in Jerusalem.

A striking example from the fourth decade of the Institute illustrating both the rejection of apologetics and its stubborn survival is Jacob Katz's *Bein Yehudim le-Goyim* that also appeared in an English translation entitled *Exclusiveness and Tolerance*, which enjoyed an impressively wide readership. In an essay on Rabbi Menahem ha-Meiri that preceded the book, Katz had set for himself the explicit objective of studying the attitudes of Jews toward Christianity and Christians without an apologetic orientation. And in fact, unlike his predecessors, Katz emphasized in his book that ha-Meiri's liberal approach was not at all typical. Nonetheless, as I noted some years ago, even this book contains a passage that demonstrates clearly that residence in the Land of Israel did not provide protection against older concerns. In that passage we find a fascinating difference between the English and Hebrew versions of the book. In the Hebrew text, Katz affirms that "the vision of the end of days signifies the overturning of the current order, when the dispersed and humiliated people will see

---

[2]   G. Scholem, "Mi-Tokh Hirhurim ʿal Hokhmat Yisrael," *Devarim be-Go: Pirqei Morashah u-Tehiyyah*, ed. by A. Shapira (Tel Aviv, 1976) II, p. 398.

its revenge from its tormentors. The hope for a day of revenge and the prayer for the arrival of that day may be considered as conflicting with a profession of loyalty to the government ..." Here now is the English: "A reversal of the existing order was envisaged in the messianic age, when the dispersed and humiliated Jewish people was to come into its own. The entertaining of such hopes, and the prayer for their fulfillment, might well be considered as conflicting with a profession of loyalty...." Thus, we discover that the proper equivalent of "see its revenge from its tormentors" is "was to come into its own."[3]

Katz wrote his book in 1960, when it was plausible to assume that a Hebrew book would remain, in the well-known midrashic formulation referring to the oral law, the "mystery" of the Jewish people. In the age of the internet, globalization, and the increasing role of excellent non-Jewish Judaica scholars, one cannot rely on this assumption, and we shall have occasion to return to this point presently.

The motivations for an apologetic presentation do not always stem from concern about critical reaction from the outside. The environment in which academics develop and work causes them to internalize to a large degree the values of the larger society with regard to interaction among faiths and respect for the culture of the Other. Consequently, even a Jewish scholar in the Land of Israel, who is relatively free of external pressures, will feel impelled to describe the Jewish heritage in colors that appear attractive to him, and this is after all a quintessentially apologetic approach. Moreover, it was precisely the national pride essential to Zionism that engendered a powerful desire to point to the special qualities that characterize the nation.

This inclination even affected the choice of topics for research. Thus, Yitzhak Baer abandoned the study of medieval Spanish Jewry to concentrate on the period of the Second Temple and the Mishnaic rabbis in order to uncover what he saw as the glorious foundational principles of the Jewish people. Even his unusual introduction to his great work on Spain clearly exemplifies this approach. It seems to me that Yehezkel Kaufmann abandoned the broad expanse of Jewish history analyzed in his book *Golah ve-Nekhar* and moved to the study of the biblical period

---

3   I noted this passage in my article, "Jacob Katz on Jews and Christians in the Middle Ages," in *The Pride of Jacob: Essays on Jacob Katz and his Work*, ed. by Jay M. Harris, (Cambridge, Mass., 2002), pp. 41-63.

because in his understanding that is where the historic contribution of the Jewish people was to be found. The concept of divine unity spread throughout the world, but for reasons that were clarified in *Golah ve-Nekhar*, that expansion took place not through the direct action of the nation that first produced that concept, but through messengers called Christianity and Islam. This development was simultaneously a monumental Jewish achievement and a profound Jewish tragedy. Kaufman chose to focus on the achievement without the admixture of the tragedy.[4]

The most blatant nationalist apologetics—to the point where it is almost superfluous to underscore the matter—can be found in the studies of Joseph Klausner. What is interesting is precisely his rhetorical sensitivity to concerns about subjectivity. In the introduction to his work *Jesus of Nazareth* he emphasized what he saw as the care that he takes to avoid subjectivity and apologetics, and almost forty years later he devoted the introduction to his *History of the Second Temple* to "the problem of subjectivity and relativism," affirming unequivocally that one can achieve absolute objectivity, that is, a quest for truth unaffected by any personal or political predilections whatsoever.

To a significant degree we now inhabit a different scholarly universe, one in which the very ideal of objectivity is in question. It is not just that no scholar would dare allow Ranke's famous sentence about history as it actually was to emerge from his lips or his pen; rather, the recognition that one cannot avoid subjectivity entirely has led in certain circles to an utterly unrestrained erasure of all boundaries, so that one may not express criticism even of complete fabrications. Several years ago, it became evident that Nobel Prize winner Rigoberta Menchu had invented entire chapters of her autobiography *ex nihilo*. Many historians, especially those with leftist ideologies, argued that one should nonetheless refrain from even the slightest criticism of the book since the overall reality described there is in the final analysis essentially correct, and we are dealing with a justified effort to denounce evildoers. When I expressed disapproval of this position to a distinguished Jewish historian, he replied with equanimity that every autobiography is written from a

---

4   See my observations in "Religion, Nationalism, and Historiography: Yehezkel Kaufmann's Account of Jesus and Early Christianity," *Scholars and Scholarship: The Interaction between Judaism and Other Cultures*, ed. by Leo Landman (New York, 1990), pp. 149-168.

subjective perspective that apparently differs from fiction only with respect to literary genre. Similarly, many observers reacted with utter disdain to criticisms leveled at Edward Said after it became known that he knowingly created a misleading impression that his permanent residence was in Jerusalem until he was expelled at the age of twelve in the midst of the "naqba." Needless to say, here too ideological considerations played a role, but in both cases, the widespread emphasis on the subjective element in all the social sciences and humanities facilitated reactions that in my view exceed appropriate bounds.

Subjectivity is itself a complex phenomenon with varied consequences that can be exemplified in the history of the Institute. Occasionally, the desire to reach a particular conclusion motivates a scholar to discover reliable information or achieve a plausible insight that would have eluded him or her in the absence of an internal impulse that was conceived outside the realm of academically objective purity. Thus, I argued in an article written in the eighties that Moshe David (Umberto) Cassutto succeeded in finding subtle criticisms of the actions of the patriarchs in the Book of Genesis precisely because he wanted to defend the Torah against the assertion that it lacks sensitivity to moral offenses.[5] On the other hand, the very effort to flee from apologetics can sometimes lead to an excessively pejorative characterization of the views and behavior of Jews in earlier generations. I have great respect for all the participants in the controversy surrounding the famous and important article by Israel Yuval in which he argued that the blood libel, which is assuredly a total lie, was nonetheless nurtured by Jewish behavior and Jewish beliefs. I do not wanted to enter into the actual content of the dispute that swirled around the article, but the debate itself demonstrated that both the apologetic impulse and the anti-apologetic impulse are alive and well and have the capacity to produce new approaches as well as affirmations that are open to challenge.[6]

---

5   "On the Morality of the Patriarchs in Jewish Polemic and Exegesis," in *Understanding Scripture: Explorations of Jewish and Christian Traditions of Interpretation*, ed. by Clemens Thoma and Michael Wyschogrod (New York, 1987), pp. 49-62. Reprinted with minor changes in *Modern Scholarship in the Study of Torah: Contributions and Limitations*, ed. by Shalom Carmy (Northvale and London, 1996), pp. 131-146 [reprinted in this volume].

6   Y. Yuval, "Ha-Naqam ve-ha-Qelalah, ha-Dam ve-ha-Alilah," *Zion* 58 (1992-93): 33-90, and the polemical exchange in *Zion* 59 (1994). I expressed my views regarding the issues in question in my lecture, *From Crusades to Blood Libels to Expulsions: Some New Approaches to Medieval Antisemitism*, The Second Victor J. Selmanowitz Memorial Lecture, Touro

I doubt very much that there remains in our generation a material difference between Israel and the diaspora with respect to the willingness of scholars to express opinions or present information dangerous to the image of Jews. Geographic location and even the use of a particular language can no longer protect scholars against the diffusion of their works, and it is any event evident that even those who are concerned about the consequences do not recoil entirely from the prospect that their scholarship will exert wide influence. Even scholars of Jewish studies in the diaspora have succeeded in persuading themselves that despite the revival of anti-Semitism, open and honest engagement with elements of Jewish tradition that arouse unease at the beginning of the twenty-first century will not at this point create existential danger, and even if they do—as the recent initiative among Russian anti-Semites to ban the standard code of Jewish law (*Shulhan Arukh*) suggests—any effort to conceal crucial data will be ineffectual.

However, the problem of apologetics and national pride arises now in a different context, which surely involves existential danger. The history of Zionism, relations between Jews and Arabs in the days of the *yishuv*, expulsion versus voluntary flight or emigration during the War of Independence, the behavior of the IDF or intelligence agencies in times of war and intifada—all these are not a matter for political or public relations figures alone. They are quintessentially academic topics that decidedly belong within the sphere of Jewish Studies. This assertion itself points to the transformations that have taken place in the definition of the field since the days the Institute was founded. On the one hand, scholars who identify with the State confront the challenge of objectivity since their ideological predilections are liable to lead to a presentation that obscures problematic Israeli behavior. On the other hand, scholars who identify with Palestinian aspirations are liable to endorse interpretations or even make factual assertions that violate proper standards of judgment in order to lay blame on the State and reveal its perversity. Regrettably, the atmosphere in the field of Middle Eastern Studies in European and

College Graduate School of Jewish Studies (New York, 1997) as well as in my article, "On the Image and Destiny of Gentiles in Ashkenazic Polemical Literature" (in Hebrew), *Facing the Cross: The Persecutions of 1096 in History and Historiography*, ed. by Yom Tov Assis et al. (Jerusalem, 2000), pp. 74-91 [English translation including an addendum in David Berger, *Persecution, Polemic and Dialogue: Essays in Jewish-Christian Relations* (Boston, 2010), pp. 109-138].

American universities exercises severe pressures on anyone who wishes to refrain from untrammeled attacks against the State and even against the Zionist vision itself. Here, devotion to Zionist ideology leads not to apologetics but to the capacity to maintain loyalty to balanced analysis.

When the Institute was established, the national renaissance that stood at its core was intimately connected to the revival of the Hebrew language. In a famous essay, Bialik sharply criticized scholars of Jewish Studies for writing their works in German,[7] and this original sin was to be rectified in Jerusalem. And indeed the great miracle of the revival of the language left its mark not only on scholarly academic literature in Hebrew but also on the study of the language in the Institute itself, an enterprise that continues to be pursued on the highest level. It is true that the teaching of Jewish Studies in Hebrew and even the writing of scholarly studies in Hebrew are by no means endangered species, but it is nonetheless necessary to point to the well-known academic joke that embodies too large an element of truth, to wit, that God would not receive tenure in an Israeli university because he wrote only one book—and he wrote it in Hebrew. Fifteen years ago, I spent a sabbatical in the Annenberg Research Institute in Philadelphia, and an Israeli professor specializing in the sociology of Israel saw that I was writing an article about Maimonides in Hebrew. With genuine puzzlement, he asked me, "Why are you writing in Hebrew? After all, you know how to write English." It is indeed important that knowledge of scholarly works in Jewish Studies not be restricted to readers of Hebrew, but the Institute and the departments of Jewish Studies throughout Israel have a sacred obligation to assign equal standing to Hebrew and non-Hebrew publications.

I must add that eight years ago I received a copy of a page of the schedule of the Twelfth Congress of Jewish Studies before its final publication, and I was astonished to see that in the Hebrew section my first name appeared with the spelling דייוויד, i.e., a phonetic transliteration of the name David as it is pronounced in English. I was able to correct this to the standard Hebrew spelling of what is after all a biblical name, but this phenomenon continues; an American scholar who moved to Israel informs me that he faces bureaucratic difficulties in both governmental

---

[7]   H.N. Bialik, "Al 'Hokhmat Yisrael'," *Kol Kitvei H.N. Bialik* (Tel Aviv, 1956), pp. 221-224, as well as at http://benyehuda.org/bialik/artcle22.html#_ftn1.

and academic administrative contexts that compel him to use his English name in his publications as well as on other occasions. The State that once pressured its representatives to Hebraize their names—a practice that was also improper in my view—now pressures its new citizens to set aside the Hebrew name given to them at birth. It is not difficult to imagine Bialik's reaction to this phenomenon.

Speaking of names, an examination of the names of the members of the Institute in its early days yielded only those of males. This reality clearly reflected the place of women in the academic world at large, but in the field of Jewish Studies, the exclusion of women from the study of classical Jewish texts in the religious educational tradition exacerbated this deficiency all the more. Without deep knowledge of Talmud and rabbinic literature, serious work in central areas of research in Jewish Studies was virtually impossible. This problem has not achieved full resolution to this day, but it is evident that the situation has changed. This transformation not only reflects progress in society as a whole; it also engenders substantive scholarly advances by providing a different perspective that enriches the overall field, and particularly the burgeoning studies of the history and creativity of women throughout the course of Jewish history.

Another motif that served as the subject of discussion in the early days of the Institute was the role of the Jewish religion. Several members of the Committee wanted to establish a rabbinical seminary on the European model as part of the new enterprise in Jerusalem. This proposal was not realized for understandable reasons, but the question of the relationship between the academic study of Judaism and the religion itself remains intact. On the one hand, there is a fundamental tension between faith and the untrammeled intellectual freedom that is the hallmark of academic research. At the same time, believing Jews who are familiar with the academic study of Judaism and even participate in it cannot escape—and do not wish to escape—from its interaction with their religious commitment. It is consequently no surprise that a disproportionately large percentage of students in departments of Jewish Studies in Israel come from the religious sector. As a result of unfortunate sociological forces, many secular Israelis are indeed interested in modern Hebrew literature and other areas that they do not associate with religion, but they are not interested in classical texts or pre-modern history. With respect to the study of the Bible, the picture appears more complicated, but I do not regard myself as qualified to assess the situation. In any event, we are dealing with an educational challenge that Israeli society must confront.

It is clear from everything that I have noted to this point that the quest for scholarly objectivity does not free academics from responsibility to society and its problems. On the contrary, by the very nature of things political leaders turn to universities and avail themselves of expert advice, and in the State of Israel, issues embedded in Jewish Studies are always on the agenda. Even without external consultation, the impulse toward engaged scholarship emerges out of one's social, political or religious conscience. The challenge facing responsible scholars is to mobilize the knowledge that they have accumulated in the academic environment to advance objectives important to them without distorting the results of their research and to continue to pursue that research without dictating predetermined conclusions that will provide them with ideological satisfaction. In matters of this sort, it is easy to set forth the ideal; it is far more difficult to realize it.

Finally, since I stand here as a citizen of the United States, I need to conclude with some remarks about the complex relationship between the Institute and the Israeli establishment in the field of Jewish Studies and scholars in the diaspora. From a certain perspective, Israeli scholars can feel isolated. They are careful to travel outside the country for intellectual stimulation provided by contact with academics, not necessarily in Jewish Studies, who carry out their research with the aid of novel, up-to-date methodologies. On the other hand, they speak with disdain about the overall level of diaspora Jewish Studies out of the conviction that the knowledge of Hebrew and the deep understanding of classical Jewish texts are highly deficient outside the State of Israel.

As to the perspective of Judaica scholars in the diaspora, one sometimes hears the assertion that certain areas of Jewish Studies in Israel are marked by narrow philological and textual concerns that do not interest more than a dozen or so insiders. With respect to the last point, it seems to me that linguistic and textual discipline must not be compromised even when this means that topics of narrow interest will be pursued, and the members of the Institute along with their colleagues in Israel bear maximal responsibility to protect such areas of inquiry and not to be embarrassed by those who would subject them to mockery.

I must also note the Institute's initiatives to encourage the pursuit of Jewish Studies in the diaspora both by providing educational opportunities for young scholars who come to Israel and through programs in a variety of diaspora locales. Despite all the difficulties and obstacles noted here, we are dealing in this session not simply with the founding of a single institute but with the establishment of an Israeli Center of Jewish Studies unparalleled in the world. The traditional blessing "until a hundred and twenty" is inappropriate for an organization, and so I mobilize the blessing (Genesis 24:60) that the spiritual descendants of the Institute, which has reached the point described by the Mishnah as the age of strength, "will grow into thousands of myriads."

INTERPRETING THE BIBLE

"THE WISEST OF ALL MEN": SOLOMON'S WISDOM IN MEDIEVAL JEWISH COMMENTARIES ON THE BOOK OF KINGS

From: *Hazon Nahum: Studies in Jewish Law, Thought and History presented to Dr. Norman Lamm on the Occasion of his Seventieth Birthday*, ed. by Yaakov Elman and Jeffrey S. Gurock (Yeshiva University Press: New York, 1997), pp. 93-114.

The Book of Kings informs us that Solomon was granted incomparable wisdom, but it presents a narrative of his reign which stands in considerable tension with this assertion. Both religious transgressions and troubling policy decisions engender serious doubts about Solomon's judgment, and these in turn raised a series of intriguing challenges for Jewish biblical commentators in the Middle Ages.

What is the meaning of wisdom in general and of Solomon's wisdom in particular? Was Solomon granted miraculous discernment *ex machina,* or did this divine gift build upon impressive preexisting intellectual strengths? What is the relationship between wisdom and piety? To the extent that these are intertwined, we need to understand Solomon's real or apparent transgressions. How many sins are to be imputed to him, at what points in his life did he commit them, and how serious were they? Was his marriage to Pharaoh's daughter permissible, moderately objectionable, or profoundly sinful? Did he act knowingly or inadvertently? How should we view the multiplicity of horses, the accumulation of wealth, the many wives? Is it possible that he really worshipped idols in the straightforward sense of the term? Finally, on a more mundane but no less critical level, was he guilty of policy errors, including unconscionable levels of taxation and forced labor, that led to the political catastrophes, both foreign and domestic, which followed in the wake of his reign?

Not every commentator appears sensitive to each of these questions, and occasionally the proposed solution is less interesting than the deeper issue of whether the problem is raised at all. As we shall see, both the threshold level of sensitivity and the modes of resolution can rest upon the overall worldview and cultural environment of an exegete and provide insights into the relationship between the reading of a biblical passage and attitudes toward fundamental issues of philosophy, politics, and faith.

THE CONTOURS OF SOLOMONIC WISDOM

What, then, was the nature of the extraordinary wisdom with which Solomon was blessed? Let us begin, as any exegete must, with the biblical data themselves. Strikingly, Solomon made the wisest decision of his life before he received his special blessing: he chose to request wisdom. In his crucial dream, he responds to the divine offer by asking God for "an understanding mind to judge Your people, to distinguish between good and bad; for who can judge this vast people of Yours?" (I Kings 3:9). God responds by praising Solomon for requesting "discernment in dispensing justice. ... I grant you a wise and discerning mind; there has never been anyone like you before, nor will anyone like you arise again" (I Kings 3:12).

Two chapters later, we are provided a more extensive definition:

> The Lord endowed Solomon with wisdom and discernment in great measure, with understanding as vast as the sands on the seashore. Solomon's wisdom was greater than the wisdom of all the Kedemites and than all the wisdom of the Egyptians. He was the wisest of all men... He composed three thousand proverbs, and his songs numbered one thousand and five. He discoursed about trees, from the cedar in Lebanon to the hyssop that grows out of the wall; and he discoursed about beasts, birds, creeping things, and fishes (I Kings 5:9-13).

As to concrete, explicit applications of Solomon's wisdom, we are afforded two examples: the famous judgment determining the true mother of a child, and the ability to solve the unspecified riddles posed by the Queen of Sheba (I Kings 3:16-28, 10:1-9).

Aside from judicial discernment, which can itself be understood in many ways, the biblical material leaves us extensive leeway in interpreting the character of Solomon's wisdom. Despite the apparent numbers, Rashi restricts the proverbs and songs to the biblical books ascribed to Solomon, and he makes reference to a "midrash aggadah" which understands the discourses about trees, birds, and fish as halakhic discussions. Before citing this midrash, however, he presents a straightforward reading which interprets Solomon's wisdom as medical knowledge concerning trees and animals, the usefulness of particular trees as building materials, the diet of various animals, and the like.[1] R. Joseph Kara, who hailed from the same cultural sphere as Rashi, exhibits similar inclinations, though he provides a lengthier, more detailed list of the scientific fields and specific questions which Solomon mastered, so that we are informed that the wisest of men knew the precise measure of a given animal's strength, whether or not it could be domesticated, whether it inhabited deserts or settled areas, and more. Almost as an afterthought, he too notes the midrashic comment explaining the passage in halakhic terms.[2]

Not surprisingly, we find no reference to metaphysical insights in the comments of these French exegetes. At the same time, we should not wonder about the positive assessment of practical scientific knowledge expressed in their commentaries. As I have argued elsewhere, the pursuit of natural science could become the subject of controversy precisely in the Sephardic orbit, where it was caught up in the web of philosophy. If the natural sciences were part of the "propaedeutic studies" leading to the queen of the sciences, they could be tainted by the unsavory reputation of the queen herself. Where they stood on their own, it is hard to imagine any grounds of principle for dismissing them or for failure to admire one who had mastered their secrets. The very indifference of Ashkenazic Jews to philosophical study liberated them to examine the natural world with keen, unselfconscious interest.[3]

---

[1] Commentary to I Kings 5: 12-13. The midrash is in *Pesiqta Rabbati*, chap. 14. In commenting on the earlier verses of this passage, Rashi also alludes to astronomy, or astrology (*hokhmat ha-mazzalot*), and music.

[2] *Perush R. Yosef Kara 'al Nevi'im Rishonim*, ed. by S. Eppenstein (Jerusalem, 1972), commentary to I Kings 5:13.

[3] I made the basic point in Gerald Blidstein, David Berger, Sid Z. Leiman, and Aharon Lichtenstein, *Judaism's Encounter with Other Cultures: Rejection or Integration?*, ed. by Jacob J. Schacter (Northvale, N.J., and London, 1997), p. 118, and cf. p. 134, n. 131. The intensive study of natural science might remain problematic because it takes time from the study of Torah, but this concern is far less acute or fundamental than the issues raised by pursuit of scientific knowledge as part of the philosophic quest.

Despite the citation of the midrash equating Solomon's wisdom with mastery of the Torah, the secondary role of this interpretation is striking. In Proverbs and Ecclesiastes, the Rabbis and traditionalist commentators routinely identified wisdom with Torah. Here, perhaps because of the plain meaning of the references to trees and beasts, perhaps because Solomon's wisdom appears to refer to the same disciplines pursued by the Kedemites and Egyptians, perhaps because of the apparent relevance of his wisdom to the riddles of the Queen of Sheba, this understanding is thoroughly marginalized.

At the other end of the ideological spectrum, Joseph ibn Kaspi provided an explanation tenuously rooted in the text and driven almost entirely by his thoroughgoing rationalism. Here is the meaning of Solomon's discoursing about trees and animals:

> It is evident (*mevo'ar*) that this is the science of nature, which is included in the interpretation of the account of creation and the account of the chariot, held in contempt by our masses in their sinfulness. Indeed, in our sinfulness we lost the works of Solomon and other of our sages, so that matters pertaining to the intellectual disciplines are attributed to Plato and Aristotle.[4]

Anyone with elementary discernment, then, will see an "evident" reference in this verse to Aristotelian metaphysics, which is unquestionably how ibn Kaspi understood "the account of the chariot." Here, the connection between natural science and philosophy taken for granted by certain Provençal and Spanish thinkers enabled ibn Kaspi to expand the reference to trees and beasts to the point where Solomon's self-evident command of philosophy serves as an admonition to the obscurantist objects of the exegete's acerbic critique. In fairness, the grandiose biblical rhetoric describing Solomon's wisdom opens the door to a legitimate expansion beyond trees, beasts, and fish, but the distance between this rhetoric and a confident reference to Plato and Aristotle rests upon a series of rationalist assumptions far removed from the biblical text.[5]

---

4   *Adnei Kesef*, ed. by Isaac Last (London, 1911), commentary to 5:13, p. 47.
5   These include most notably the Maimonidean identification of the accounts of creation and the chariot with physics and metaphysics and the belief that Jewish wisdom was lost to its original masters, appropriated by the Greeks, and hence available to medieval Jews primarily through the study of alien texts. On the first point, see *Hilkhot Yesodei ha-Torah*

Ralbag, whose intellectual profile was close to that of ibn Kaspi, provided an interpretation which stands somewhere between the readings of the Northern European exegetes and of his Provençal contemporary. Solomon knew the causes, composition, and essential traits of trees, beasts, and fish by investigating their nature, and he probably also knew the uses to which they could be put. Ralbag describes this knowledge with the technical language of philosophically oriented scientific discourse, and in a comment on Solomon's prayer several chapters later, he takes for granted the king's familiarity with the celestial intelligences and the acquired intellect. At the same time, he does not indicate in any way that the Solomonic wisdom singled out by Scripture is to be understood as the mastery of metaphysics.[6]

The reason for this may emerge from an examination of the position of his philosophically oriented but more conservative predecessor Radak. That position is at first a bit surprising but ultimately highly revealing. Despite his vigorous affirmation of the importance of philosophical study, Radak's understanding of these verses also attributes no special metaphysical knowledge to the wise king. Here, however, we are provided enough information to discern the explanation, which could have motivated Ralbag as well as Radak. The moment a commentator provides a definition of wisdom in our context, he is committed to the position that Solomon attained the apex of achievement in that field, surpassing all others, including Moses. Thus, it is precisely because Radak valued philosophy so highly that he refrained from identifying it with Solomon's wisdom; such an identification would have forced him to affirm that the greatest of prophets was not the greatest of philosophers. Solomon, says Radak, achieved ultimate superiority in the science of nature *(hokhmat ha-teva')*, but in the divine science *(ba-hokhmah ha-elohit)*, Moses was greater than he.[7]

Abravanel, the final commentator that I will examine in this study, was, like Radak, a philosophically oriented exegete with a conservative

---

2:11-12; 4:10, 13; *Hilkhot Talmud Torah* 1:11-12. Cf. Isadore Twersky, *Introduction to the Code of Maimonides (Mishneh Torah)* (New Haven, 1980), pp. 488-507. On the second, see the material collected in Norman Roth, "The 'Theft of Philosophy' by the Greeks from the Jews," *Classical Folia* 22 (1978): 53-67.

6   Commentary to 5:13, and cf. Commentary to 8:23.

7   Commentary to 3:12, and cf. to 5:12. See *Maimonides, Guide* 3:54, and Sara Klein-Braslavy, *Shlomo ka-Melekh ve-ha-Esoterizm ha-Pilosofi be-Mishnat ha-Rambam* (Jerusalem, 1996), pp. 121-123.

bent. In his case, however, this orientation led to more complicated conclusions. Like ibn Kaspi, Abravanel was unwilling to limit the wisdom described with such sublime rhetoric to a single field of endeavor. Solomon's intellectual perfection embraced the totality of wisdom. Indeed, Abravanel exploited this opportunity to write a lengthy excursus on the nature of wisdom itself, the categories of which it is comprised, and its limitations.[8]

This approach, however, forced him to confront the apparently unavoidable conclusion that Solomon was superior to Moses and all the other prophets in every form of wisdom despite the inextricable connection for medieval philosophers between prophecy and intellectual perfection. It is almost painful to observe Abravanel's acute discomfort with this dilemma and his difficult struggles to extricate himself from its grasp. Perhaps there is, after all, no intrinsic connection between wisdom and prophecy. Perhaps there is, but the former is not necessarily proportional to the latter. Perhaps it is proportional, but this is the case only for the highest forms of knowledge, not for the lower forms (management of household and state) in which Solomon excelled but Moses needed the advice of Jethro. (And so we watch incredulously as Solomon's perfection in the totality of wisdom, underscored in page after page of Abravanel's excursus, fades into anticlimax.)[9] Finally, perhaps the unqualified Scriptural assertion that Solomon was wiser than all who came before or after him refers only to those who failed to attain prophecy.[10]

To a certain degree, Abravanel deflects the full force of the question by arguing that Solomon obtained his wisdom miraculously, so that it may not be governed by the usual rules of nature. The immediate impetus to this position was Ralbag's hypernaturalistic assertion that the assurance of unique wisdom is incomprehensible, since nothing, not even a miracle, can provide a person with intellectual gifts that could not be attained to an equal degree by a later individual.[11] Abravanel's sharp retort is that

8   *Perush 'al Nevi'im Rishonim* (Jerusalem, 1955), pp. 466-480.

9   The suggestion is especially striking in light of the fact that in one of his preliminary questions (p. 451), Abravanel explicitly rejected Radak's assertion that Solomon's blessing was confined to natural science and did not extend to metaphysics.

10   Pp. 479-480.

11   Ralbag to 3:12. On another occasion, I hope to address the tension between Ralbag's denial of this possibility with respect to wisdom and his affirmation of precisely this reality regarding Mosaic prophecy.

Ralbag's belief in miracles and divine power is sorely wanting if he thinks that God could not miraculously grant Solomon the ability to be wiser than he.[12]

This position leads Abravanel to an extremely strong formulation of the miraculous nature of Solomonic wisdom. On the evening of Solomon's dream, he went to sleep as "a brutish man who does not know, and he awoke wise as an angel of God."[13] The first part of this sentence is, of course, hyperbole, and it would be unfair to Abravanel to hold him to it in its literal sense. On the one hand, the perception that Solomon's wisdom was miraculous guides Abravanel's understanding of both Scriptural examples of the practical application of this wisdom; on the other, his deviation from the assertion that Solomon was without prior intelligence is sometimes so sharp that it appears inconsistent even with a discounted version of that assertion.

Let us begin with the examples. The Queen of Sheba, says Abravanel, was interested precisely in the supernatural quality of Solomon's discernment. The solutions to the riddles she proposed were based on her subjective understanding; no one could have perceived her intentions naturalistically. The fact that Solomon provided precisely the interpretations which she had in mind demonstrated conclusively that his knowledge was of divine origin.[14] At first glance, it is truly remarkable that this interpretation, whose emphasis on the miraculous apparently results from Abravanel's rejection of Gersonidean naturalism, is derived from Gersonides himself. To Ralbag, Solomon's experience exemplifies the fundamental truth that knowledge can be obtained in a dream without the usual intellectual effort;[15] precisely because such knowledge was obtained in atypical fashion, it appears that its beneficiary might achieve insight that goes beyond the information available through logical reasoning.[16] Despite their very different views of the scope and nature of miracles, both Ralbag and his most distinguished critic agree that it was a form of nonrational perception which provided Solomon

---

12 P. 471.
13 Ibid.
14 Commentary to 10:2, pp. 540-541.
15 Commentary to I Kings 11, to'elet 3.
16 Commentary to I Kings 10:1: The queen wanted to see "if [Solomon] would determine the secrets that she had in mind in these riddles, for in this manner one can test if this wisdom is a gift of God. If it is, he would be able to discern her intention even though [the riddles themselves] are susceptible of other interpretations."

with his success in deciphering the riddles of the queen.[17]

With respect to the second practical application of Solomon's wisdom, Abravanel and Ralbag present contrasting approaches. The latter expresses the straightforward understanding that Solomon determined the true mother by a clever, rational ruse. To Abravanel, on the other hand, the famous stratagem appears insufficiently impressive; no "great wisdom" was needed to think of it. What really happened was that Solomon identified the true mother from an examination of the litigants' facial expressions alone, and he communicated his conclusion to his aides; only then did he pursue his stratagem to demonstrate that he had been correct.[18] Needless to say, there is not a sliver of textual evidence for this interpretation, which results either from Abravanel's commitment to his portrait of supernal wisdom or from personal experience with intrigues in royal courts that made Solomon's creative trickery seem entirely routine.

Despite Ralbag's affirmation that wisdom can sometimes be attained through dreams and prophecy without the usual effort, medieval philosophers did not believe that divine inspiration rests on individuals bereft of any preparation. In light of this conviction, Abravanel's assertion of Solomon's thorough ignorance before the dream was highly problematic. Near the beginning of the Commentary to Kings, he writes that David was concerned that Solomon, in the typical manner of youths, would be unduly influenced by Shimi son of Gera's flattering behavior toward him;[19] in fact, however, Solomon's decision to send Shimi away should be seen not as a mechanical act of obedience to his father's final wishes but as a display of intelligent initiative.[20] Much more strikingly, Abravanel's summary of Solomon's reign asserts that David's references to his son's wisdom at the beginning of Kings demonstrate "that Solomon had natural preparation for wisdom before the dream, and that knowledge was added to him through a divine overflow in a

---

[17]   On Abravanel's critical stance toward Ralbag, see Menachem Kellner, "Gersonides and his Cultured Despisers: Arama and Abravanel," *Journal of Medieval and Renaissance Studies* 6 (1976): 269-296.

[18]   Commentary to 3:24, p. 482.

[19]   Commentary to 2:8, p. 448.

[20]   Commentary to 2:36, p. 457. Note too his assertion that Solomon had to be no less than twenty years old when he became king in light of his understanding of the policies necessary to sustain his rule; see Commentary to 3:7-8, p. 466.

prophetic manner."[21] Indeed, the gold in the Temple, which symbolizes Solomon, was affixed to the cedars, which represent David, to indicate the intimate connection through which Solomon, who was similar to his father, inherited wisdom from him along with kingship.[22] Hardly "a brutish man who does not know."

WISDOM AND RELIGIOUS TRANSGRESSION

The varying perceptions of Solomon's wisdom inevitably affect the approaches to his real or apparent sins. In principle, it seems reasonable to assume that a commentator who understands this wisdom as primarily scientific and who does not see the natural sciences as a step toward the knowledge of God will face only minor obstacles in accepting the reality and, within limits, even the gravity of Solomon's transgressions. On the other hand, a broad understanding of Solomonic wisdom makes it more difficult to understand how such an individual could have sinned, particularly in light of the standard philosophical approach which saw sin as an intellectual, not merely a moral failing, and which encouraged developing the faculty of reason as the most effective weapon against the evil inclination.

Solomon's marriage to Pharaoh's daughter, which appears to violate the biblical injunction against marrying an Egyptian, took place before the dream. Needless to say, the focus of this study on Solomon's wisdom should not obscure the obvious: traditionalist commentators were disturbed by the sins of biblical heroes even in the absence of a special

---

21   Commentary to chapter 11, p. 551.
22   Commentary to chapter 8, p. 521.
       Commentators outside the philosophic tradition could presumably have affirmed
       Solomon's ignorance prior to the divine gift of wisdom with equanimity. Nonetheless
       – though I would be hesitant in the extreme to draw confident conclusions from
       this evidence – it is at least worth noting an intriguing passage in the *Sifrei* cited by
       Rashi in his commentary to Deuteronomy 1:9. "Is it possible that the one of whom
       it was written, 'He was the wisest of all men' would say 'For who can judge [this
       vast people of yours]?'?" The glaring difficulty in Rashi's – or the *Sifrei*'s – question
       is that Solomon became the world's wisest man *as a result* of his comment about
       the difficulty of judging. There appears to be an instinct at work here which cannot
       imagine that unparalleled wisdom would be granted to one who was not already
       exceptionally wise. (So *Siftei Hakhamim* ad loc., though cf. Maharal's *Gur Aryeh* ad
       loc.)

bestowal of discernment.[23] In our case, the problem was sharpened by the assumption of several exegetes that Solomon was exceedingly wise even before the dream and by the persistence of the marriage even after it.

Rashi, who is not likely to see a special connection between piety and Solomonic wisdom, understands this union as a straightforward transgression. Following Rabbinic precedent, he remarks that as long as Solomon's teacher Shimi was present, he did not establish a marital relationship with Pharaoh's family; we see, then, the critical importance of residing near one's teacher. Moreover, Rashi endorses *Seder Olam*'s rearrangement of the chronological order of I Kings 3 in order to blunt the appearance of the verse "And Solomon loved the Lord" (3:3) immediately after this forbidden marriage.[24]

R. Joseph Kara goes even further by taking the apparently neutral phrase "And he brought her to the city of David" (3:2) as evidence of compounded transgression. "Know that this point is mentioned by Scripture to indicate improper behavior. This place was designated for holiness, since the city of David, which is Zion, is where the ark of the divine covenant was brought; and this man brings Pharaoh's daughter there."[25] The comment was no doubt triggered by the Chronicler's report (II Chron. 8:11) that Solomon eventually removed Pharaoh's daughter from the city of David for this very reason, but the critical reference here clearly goes beyond what the verses require and reflects a relatively low threshold of resistance to intensifying the sin of a biblical figure.

Ralbag too extends and heightens Solomon's sinfulness with respect to his marriages, but he does not do so until chapter 11, where the biblical text itself sharply criticizes the king's behavior. The tone of Ralbag's

---

[23] See my "On the Morality of the Patriarchs in Jewish Polemic and Exegesis," in *Understanding Scripture: Explorations of Jewish and Christian Traditions of Interpretation*, ed. by Clemens Thoma and Michael Wyschogrod (New York, 1987), pp. 49-62; reprinted in *Modern Scholarship in the Study of Torah*, ed. by Shalom Carmy (Northvale, N.J., and London, 1996), pp. 131-146. Also see Avraham Grossman, *Hakhmei Zarfat ha-Rishonim* (Jerusalem, 1995), pp. 488-492.

[24] Commentary to 3:1. Rashi (to 11:39) also cites *Seder Olam*'s assertion that a thirty-six-year punishment was initially set for the Davidic kingdom to correspond to the thirty-six years that Solomon was married to Pharaoh's daughter. So too Radak to 11:39 and R. Joseph Kara to 11:41.

[25] Commentary to 3:1, where he also makes reference to the Rabbinic comment about Shimi.

comment in chapter 3, where Pharaoh's daughter is first introduced, differs markedly, and the difference reflects a crucial point which can often determine an exegete's approach. The changing local contexts of biblical data may lead to profoundly different emphases and even to outright inconsistencies in a commentator's approach. Thus, the report of the questionable marriage in chapter 3 is followed immediately by the assertion that Solomon loved the Lord though he continued to sacrifice at a variety of shrines. We have already seen how this juxtaposition disturbed Rashi and *Seder Olam*, and the reference to the shrines as the only exception to Solomon's love of God further strengthens the implication that the marriage was unobjectionable. At this point, then, Ralbag writes, "It is appropriate for you to know that Solomon married into Pharaoh's family after the latter's daughter converted; nevertheless, this was a slight deviation *(yezi'ah qezat)* from the ways of the Torah, which permitted Egyptians to enter the community only in the third generation."[26] It is difficult to envision a milder formulation.

In chapter 11, we find ourselves in a different world. Here, we no longer encounter a Solomon who loved the Lord, but one who

> loved many foreign women in addition to Pharaoh's daughter—Moabite, Ammonite, Edomite, Phoenician, and Hittite women, from the nations of which the Lord had said to the Israelites, "None of you shall join them..." Such Solomon clung to and loved... And his wives turned his heart away (vv. 1-4).

So we search Ralbag's commentary in vain for a marriage which constituted a "slight deviation" from the ways of the Torah.

> If someone will argue that it is appropriate for us to believe that [these foreign women] converted before Solomon married them, we would nonetheless be unable to avoid a conclusion of improper behavior *(genut)*. Pharaoh's daughter, after all, was prohibited from entering the community of the Lord because only the third generation is permitted to do so. Moreover, Ammonite and Moabite women also come from a nation unworthy of entering the community... , and even though the females among them were not forbidden to enter the community... , it was inappropriate for a king to marry them, since it was impossible for the offspring that he would have from them to be truly perfect.[27]

26 Commentary to 3:1.
27 Commentary to 11:1.

A genuine exegetical problem is certainly at work here, since the verses appear to imply that Solomon's marriages to women from nations other than Egypt were forbidden, while the *halakhah* actually permits marriage to converted women from all the peoples on that list. Nonetheless, the reference to necessarily deficient offspring is not forced upon Ralbag—indeed, Solomon's own descent from a Moabite convert named Ruth makes it highly problematic—and while we do not face a full-fledged contradiction, the attitude toward the truly forbidden marriage is considerably less forgiving than it was when the king who contracted it loved the Lord.[28]

The juxtaposition between Solomon's marriage and the reference to his love of the Lord led other commentators to remarkable conclusions. Radak argued that the biblical account here reveals that the Talmudic sage who limited the prohibition against marrying Egyptians to their males was correct (*nir'in devarav*) despite the fact that "the *halakhah* has not been fixed in accordance with [his] view."[29] Abravanel tells us that if he were to approach this question "according to the plain meaning of the verses," he would argue that Solomon did not sin at all, and what follows is a veritable assault upon standard Rabbinic law on this point. First, there is the rejected position cited by Radak which Solomon, who was, after all, one of the Sages, might have endorsed. Moreover, "the third generation" could begin from the Exodus, not from each act of conversion; even if the count begins with conversion, the assertion that the third generation "will enter" may mean that at this juncture such a step becomes a quasi-obligation (*be-hiyyuv u-mi-derekh mizvah*), but it is permissible even earlier; finally, "entering the community" may not mean marriage at all but admission to positions of leadership.

Only after this lengthy and vigorous presentation of the thorough rejection of Rabbinic law that a straightforward examination of the text would have impelled Abravanel to propose does he assert that the position of the Sages constitutes the transmitted truth (*ha-mequbbal ve-*

---

28   In his retrospective evaluation at the end of the biblical account of Solomon's reign, Ralbag goes so far as to say that the ultimate exile and destruction of the Temple resulted from the king's failure to heed the divine admonition that he command his children to observe the ways of the Lord (*to'elet* 33 at the end of chapter 11). This sin is nowhere in the biblical text and appears to be a deduction based on the behavior of Solomon's descendants.

29   Commentary to 3:3. See *B. Yevamot* 77b.

ha-amitti). The correct position, then, is that Solomon misinterpreted the law; he believed that after the conversion of Pharaoh's daughter he was permitted to marry her, and since this was the honest error of a young man motivated by understandable diplomatic considerations, God did not punish him for it.[30]

What Abravanel does not address is a problem which appears to follow from his all-embracing view of Solomon's wisdom after the dream. Among many other things—one is tempted to say, among all other things—Solomon was expert in "the commandments. He knew them in general and encompassed their particulars down to the most precise minutiae, just as Moses our teacher, may he rest in peace, received them from God without the slightest doubt or dispute."[31] At that point, we would imagine, Solomon should have divorced his prohibited wife. Abravanel, however, refuses to ascribe any blemish to Solomon after his dream and before the sins of his old age, so that the problem of this marriage, which had already been resolved in the Commentary to chapter 3, is not permitted to rise up again to taint the perfection of the wise king at the height of his powers.[32]

Solomon's proliferation of wives, wealth, and horses stands in stark contrast to the injunctions in Deuteronomy 17 concerning proper royal behavior. Rashi, R. Joseph Kara, Radak, and Ralbag all acknowledge this behavior as sinful, in some cases with explicit or implicit reference to the Rabbinic assertion attributing the transgressions to Solomon's self-confidence. Since the Torah makes clear that it is primarily concerned with the results that normally follow from the actions it has prohibited, Solomon concluded that an individual of his discernment could perform the acts and avoid the consequences.[33] To Ralbag, the sins resulted

---

[30] Commentary to 3:1.

[31] P. 477.

[32] The reference in I Kings 3:3 to Solomon's worship at multiple shrines raises a problem which is the mirror image of the marriage to Pharaoh's daughter. Here the Bible appears to condemn behavior which Rabbinic law considered permissible before the period of the Temple. Rashi (to 3:3) and R. Joseph Kara (to 3:2) see this as a criticism of Solomon's delay in building the Temple. Radak and Abravanel (to 3:3) regard it as a deviation from David's practice and consider it objectionable because it can lead to idolatry (Radak) or unspecified sin (Abravanel). Ralbag to 3:3 and in *to'elet* 2 at the end of chapter 11 apparently finds nothing wrong in behavior whose purpose he sees as the attainment of prophecy. In *to'elet* 1, however, he acknowledges the criticism implicit in the biblical formulation and indicates that such worship is flawed, though permissible.

[33] See Radak to 11:1 and Rashi to Ecclesiastes 1:18. Also see R. Joseph Kara to 10:28 and

not from Solomon's reliance on his wisdom but from a powerful desire which prevailed despite that wisdom.[34] None of these commentators was committed to a portrait of Solomonic perfection like that of Abravanel, and the Rabbinic affirmation of sin easily removed whatever inhibitions may nonetheless have remained. For Abravanel himself, the issue was more difficult, and we shall look at his approach when we examine the question of errors in royal policy.

For all commentators, one sin ascribed to Solomon violates the canons of both wisdom and piety so severely that it could not be suffered with equanimity.

> In his old age, his wives turned away Solomon's heart after other gods... Solomon followed Ashtoreth the goddess of the Phoenicians, and Milcom the abomination of the Ammonites... Solomon built a shrine for Chemosh the abomination of Moab... and one for Molech the abomination of the Ammonites. And this he did for all his foreign wives who offered and sacrificed to their gods (I Kings 11:4-8).

Following Talmudic precedent, Rashi and Radak insist that Solomon was faulted for failing to prevent his wives from worshipping idols, not for doing so himself.[35] Ralbag draws an explicit connection between Solomon's wisdom and the inconceivability of attributing idolatry to him personally; such a man could not have followed "these vanities and abominations given the fact that he grasped the Lord, may He be blessed, to a greater degree than others," not to speak of the fact that he wrote works under divine inspiration and twice experienced revelation directly.[36]

Abravanel repeats Ralbag's argument,[37] but he goes further by attempting to establish an almost direct causal link between Solomon's wisdom and the idolatry of his wives. Through his unique wisdom, Solomon understood "the modes of service relating to the celestial powers assigned to the nations [of his wives] through which the overflow

---

11:1. Cf. B. *Sanhedrin* 21b.

[34] *To'elet* 36 at the end of chapter 11, where Solomon is described as *homeh el ha-nashim* and possessed of a *yezer leharbot sus*.

[35] Rashi to 11:7; Radak to 11:1.

[36] Commentary to 11:4.

[37] Commentary to 11:1, p. 546.

could be lowered upon those nations."[38] Abravanel suggests that when the Gentiles flocked to learn Solomon's wisdom, it was this wisdom that they sought. Such instruction was not sinful in light of Deuteronomy 4:19, which asserts that God assigned the heavenly hosts to the nations of the world.[39] Later, however, Solomon imparted this knowledge to his wives, who put it into practice in idolatrous rites which he tolerated. By transforming the king from a passive tolerator of idolatry into an active participant in imparting its intellectual underpinnings, Abravanel has gained the exegetical advantage of accounting for very strong biblical language, but the damage to Solomon's image is not inconsiderable.

Abravanel has also gained something else; he has constructed a bridge which can bring us from the paragon of wisdom and piety that we have known until now to the sinful—and unsuccessful—ruler of I Kings 11. What Solomon did was teach wisdom to his wives—and precisely that wisdom which he had taught other Gentiles without incurring divine wrath. Nonetheless, the effect of his action was the facilitating of idolatry, a grave offense worthy of severe punishment. At this point, the miraculous nature of Solomon's ascent to the heights of wisdom becomes his undoing. Wisdom, power, and wealth all depart from him.

> Just as these perfections had rested in his home, so they left him. They came in a divine manner and with a supernal overflow, not in a natural fashion. When he separated himself from his God so that the thread of grace which had always descended upon his head was severed, those perfections departed along with the overflow which was their cause.[40]

Abravanel's Solomon, then, moves from a youth of considerable potential but little understanding to a maturity marked by unique, miraculous wisdom, to an old age that might well be characterized in the words of the wisest of men as that of "an old and foolish king who no longer has the sense to heed warnings" (Eccles. 4:13).

Despite the gravity of Solomon's sin, even Abravanel does not

---

38 Ibid. So too in the excursus on wisdom, p. 475.

39 An even stronger, surprisingly explicit assertion that this verse frees Gentiles from the obligation of monotheism appears in Abravanel's contemporary, R. Isaac Arama; see his 'Aqedat Yitzhak, chapter 88, p. 16a, and his Hazut Qashah, chapter 12, p. 32b. I hope to discuss Arama's comments, which appear to contradict the unambiguous position of Talmudic law, in another context.

40 Commentary to chapter 11, p. 552.

maintain that he himself committed idolatry. Ironically, it was precisely a commentator of an extreme philosophical bent, a man for whom it was virtually inconceivable that a philosopher of Solomon's stature could commit such a sin, who constructed a solution so radical that anything became possible. We will recall that Joseph ibn Kaspi regarded Solomon as a metaphysician par excellence. How, then, could he have been caught up in idolatry?

Although ibn Kaspi makes no reference to Maimonides, the inspiration for his answer emerged, I believe, from a famous passage in *The Guide of the Perplexed*. Maimonides conveys to us "a most extraordinary speculation" to explain how people who have achieved a high level of apprehension of God could nonetheless find themselves unprotected by divine providence. Occasionally, he explains, even such a person allows his attention to stray so that "for a certain time" his thought "is emptied of God," and "providence withdraws from him during the time when he is occupied with something else."[41]

Moses' intellect, says ibn Kaspi, was actively engaged with God without interruption, but Solomon turned away to some degree precisely because he was capable of being distracted. His wives disrupted his concentration to a limited extent even in his youth, but at that point this spiritual detour

> did not reach the point where he would worship other gods, which is the heresy called *'avon* [iniquity] in Hebrew; it did, however, reach the point where there was some deficiency in his apprehension. At the very least, there were moments (*'ittot*) at that time in which his intellect was potentially iniquitous, and this is what is called *het* [sin] in Hebrew.[42]

Once ibn Kaspi had discovered a mechanism which neutralized Solomon's supernal wisdom, nothing was ruled out, and it is apparently his position that in the king's old age, his wives turned him away to the point where he actually worshiped foreign gods.

---

[41] *The Guide of the Perplexed*, translated by Shlomo Pines (Chicago, 1963) 3:51, pp. 624-625.

[42] Commentary to 11:3. The editor (*Adnei Kesef* p. 51) notes that V. Aptowitzer suggested that *'ittot* be emended to *'ivrut*. Once one is aware of the Maimonidean basis for ibn Kaspi's suggestion, the impropriety of this emendation becomes self-evident. (In light of our earlier discussion about Solomon and Moses, it is worth underscoring ibn Kaspi's explicit assertion that the latter, whose apprehension of God never flagged, was wiser than the former.)

THE ROYAL POLICY OF THE WISEST OF KINGS

It has become abundantly clear that for some commentators, the problem of Solomon's sins was significantly exacerbated by the reports of his exceptional wisdom. For others, who limited the sphere of his wisdom and saw no intimate relationship between such wisdom and piety, the connection was tenuous and marginal. But Solomon was arguably guilty of more than religious error. His taxes and corvées, expensive building projects, lavish palace life, and elaborate stables appear to have engendered smoldering resentment which exploded into flame after his death, destroying the Davidic empire and rending the fabric of Israel. What are we to make of fundamental policy errors by the wisest of men?

Rashi and R. Joseph Kara do not raise the question and are apparently untroubled by it. This may be because their commentaries tend to focus on the verses immediately before them, and this problem—if it is a problem—arises only when one steps back and looks at the entire picture.[43] In their immediate context, the biblical accounts of taxes and building projects are part of the description of a glorious, highly successful reign. Equally or even more important, the Northern European commentators probably saw the rebellions of subject kings and the internal resistance that culminated in secession in purely religious terms. These were divine punishments for Solomon's sins and need not be connected to his policies by natural causation.

Radak and Ralbag explicitly defend Solomon against the people's charge that he had imposed a heavy yoke upon them (I Kings 12:4). At earlier points in the commentaries, we were informed that the difficult labor was done entirely by non-Israelite peoples. Both exegetes maintained that the only corvée affecting real Jews was the one in Lebanon, and Ralbag took pains to point out that it was arranged so that the work would not be unduly burdensome.[44] To Radak, the complaints expressed to Rehoboam about Solomon's taxation were entirely unjustified.

---

43 For a related observation about Ashkenazic polemicists, see my forthcoming study, "On the Uses of History in Medieval Jewish Polemic against Christianity: The Search for the Historical Jesus," in the *Festschrift* for Yosef Hayim Yerushalmi.

44 See Radak on 5:27, Ralbag on 5:29 and 9:23, and *to'elet* 15 at the end of chapter 11. Cf. Rashi on 5:30 and R. Joseph Kara on 5:29-30 and 9:23.

They lived in great tranquility in his time, so that the entire taxation was easy for them... Rather, God saw to it that they should concoct an accusation in their discussion with Rehoboam so that they should secede and crown Jeroboam.[45]

Ralbag reiterates the same point, though his more naturalistic orientation impels him to explain the complaint not by an appeal to divine intervention but as the result of the recent wars. Still, Ralbag asserts that even now the request was for nothing more than a "slight" alleviation of the burden, an elaboration of the biblical information which underscores the reasonableness of Solomon's policies.[46] Indeed, one of the lessons to be drawn from the account of Solomon's reign is precisely that the king should impose taxes and corvées to support his household and his projects.[47] Both Radak and Ralbag may well have sought to avoid unforced criticism of Solomon, but their position also appears to result, at least in the case of Ralbag, from a genuine political conviction about the acceptability, even desirability, of substantial royal taxation.

On this issue, Abravanel's stance is particularly instructive. He himself served as a courtier for more than one king, and his complex but fundamentally critical approach to monarchy is well known.[48] It is, then, striking though not surprising that he is the only one of the six exegetes I have examined who evinces sensitivity to the dangers inherent in Solomon's life of ostentatious luxury supported by onerous taxes. As we have seen, however, it is his position that at the height of Solomon's career, the king was blessed with all-embracing wisdom which would presumably have prevented serious errors. Even when Abravanel

---

45   Commentary to 12:4.

46   Commentary to 12:4.

47   *To'elet* 10 at the end of chapter 11. It is especially striking that at the conclusion of this *to'elet* affirming the desirability of such royal actions, Ralbag writes, "And this has already been explained as well in Samuel's statement when he explicated the law of kingship." But in his comment on Samuel's oration (I Samuel 8:11), Ralbag took the position that the provisions of "the law of the king" are not in fact legal rights but reflect Samuel's desire to make the people fearful of actions the king will take in violation of the laws of the Torah.

48   Aviezer Ravitsky has recently provided an analysis of some aspects of this issue in "Kings and Laws in Late Medieval Jewish Thought: Nissim of Gerona vs. Isaac Abrabanel," in *Scholars and Scholarship: The Interaction between Judaism and Other Cultures*, ed. by Leo Landman (New York, 1990), pp. 67-90; see notes 10 and 11 of his study for some of the other secondary literature.

retreated for a moment and raised the possibility that this wisdom might, after all, have been concentrated in a particular area, that area, we will recall, was precisely "the management of household and state." How, then, could Solomon in his prime have pursued policies which sowed the seeds of disaster?

The answer is that such policies are indeed unwise, but Solomon never pursued them. Like Radak and Ralbag, Abravanel maintains that the heavy labor was done by non-Israelites,[49] but he goes further than his predecessors in several respects. First, he underscores how objectionable these policies would have been had Solomon really pursued them. Scripture, he says, informs us of the true source of the king's taxes to prevent anyone from asking the following indignant questions:

> Where did Solomon obtain all these resources which he expended upon the Temple, his own palace, and other matters? Did he impose a tax upon his nation and his righteous subjects, or did he confiscate their wealth by force in accordance with the law of the king which Samuel mentioned to Saul?[50]

Second, he maintains that even the Gibeonites, who were the ones assigned the difficult physical labor, "surely agreed to do this willingly."[51] Third, he insists that monetary taxation came entirely from non-Jewish merchants engaged in international trade, "not from those doing business inside his kingdom as the commentators thought." Solomon imposed tariffs similar to those that exist in the medieval Christian and Islamic worlds. "None of Solomon's wealth which he garnered came from his servants. He took nothing from them by authority of the law of the king; rather, it all came to him from the Gentile countries outside of his kingdom."[52] The reader comes away from this passage with the unmistakable impression that Solomon's Jewish subjects paid nothing at all before the imposition of war-related taxes in the king's old age, though in the analysis of the later complaints to Rehoboam, Abravanel does acknowledge the existence of a substantial burden of taxation, which he appears to consider entirely justified, even at the height of the reign.[53]

---

[49] Commentary to 5:29, p. 492, and to 9:20, p. 539.
[50] Commentary to 9:15, p. 539. Note the contrast to Ralbag's *to'elet* 10 cited in note 47 above.
[51] Commentary to 5:29, p. 492.
[52] Commentary to 10:15, p. 542. Cf. too the excursus on wisdom, p. 476.
[53] Commentary to 12:4, p. 554.

Finally, Abravanel repeatedly lavishes unstinting praise upon a policy as problematic as the accumulation of horses, which raises the specter of outright sin. He cites and rejects the Rabbinic assertion that Solomon violated the Deuteronomic prohibition, which applies, after all, only to an excess of horses beyond what the interests of the state require. The king's horses, he says, were a source of glory and, more to the point, a deterrent to any would-be aggressor; this was the very reason for the peace that Solomonic Israel enjoyed.[54]

Unlike the other commentators, Abravanel is also sensitive to the problem of Solomon's profligate spending.

> One might ask: Even though Solomon possessed extensive wealth, why did he spend it so freely? After all, this would inevitably cause it to dwindle so that he would become impoverished.

The answer is that enormous supplies of gold were constantly arriving as a result of foreign trade, so that there was no danger that the kingdom's wealth would be depleted.[55] Later, however, after his sin, Solomon had to impose taxes both because of wars and because—for reasons Abravanel does not specify—he stopped sending out merchant vessels while still requiring substantial income to support his lavish way of life.[56] One wonders whether this was not precisely the possibility that Solomon should have foreseen. Abravanel's implicit response, I think, is that because these problems arose only as a result of sin, Solomon did not need to consider them earlier, given his reasonable, though ultimately incorrect assumption that he would remain a righteous man.

Abravanel, then, is acutely attuned to the political dangers inherent in the policies that Solomon appears to have pursued. Although his perception of Solomonic wisdom prevents him from ascribing error to Solomon in his prime, he does not solve the problem by endorsing such policies. The solution is to deny that Solomon pursued them, to ascribe them to his old age, or to argue, as in the case of lavish spending, that special circumstances justified them in this unusual, perhaps unique situation.

---

[54] The excursus on wisdom, p. 476; Commentary to 5:8, p. 487, where he cites the Talmudic indictment; Commentary to 10:26, p. 544; the summary of Solomon's reign in chapter 11, p. 551. In his commentary to Deuteronomy 17:14-20, he notes the Talmudic passage without disagreement.

[55] Commentary to 10:22, p. 543.

[56] Commentary to 11:40, p. 550.

While Abravanel cannot entirely avoid flashes of inconsistency, he stands out in his attempt to step back from the immediate context and see the overarching pattern of the narrative. The result is a dynamic portrait of Solomon that allows for a sharply drawn characterization at any given moment. For most commentators, the king was a complex figure of some ambiguity even at the peak of his powers—glorious, brilliant, yet moderately flawed. Abravanel's Solomon, on the other hand, was almost infinitely wise and virtually perfect from the moment of his dream until the sin of his old age, but before and especially after that period his defects were considerable and even decisive. Not flawed greatness, but unrealized potential followed by perfection followed in turn by fatal sin.

The varied perceptions of Solomon's wisdom and the consequent disparities in the evaluation of his piety and policy reflect fundamental differences in the cultural environments and worldviews of the exegetes we have examined and tell us a great deal about the complex interplay between texts and their interpreters. The attitude toward metaphysics, the place of the sciences, political theory, the courtier experience, a narrow or broad exegetical focus, a naturalistic or miraculous orientation, varying degrees of resistance to ascribing sin to biblical heroes, the readiness or refusal to deviate from Rabbinic tradition and interpretation—all these play a role, sometimes peripheral, sometimes significant, sometimes decisive, in the application of medieval wisdom to an understanding of the wisest of men.

ON THE MORALITY OF THE PATRIARCHS
IN JEWISH POLEMIC AND EXEGESIS[1]

From: *Understanding Scripture: Explorations of Jewish and Christian Traditions of Interpretation*, ed. by Clemens Thoma and Michael Wyschogrod (Paulist Press: New York, 1987), pp. 49-62. Reprinted with slight revisions in *Modern Scholarship in the Study of Torah: Contributions and Limitations*, ed. by Shalom Carmy (Jason Aronson: Northvale and London, 1996), pp. 131-146.

THE POLEMICAL WORLD OF THE MIDDLE AGES

On three separate occasions, Nahmanides denounces Abraham for sinful or questionable behavior.[2] The first of these passages asserts that "our father Abraham inadvertently committed a great sin" by urging Sarah to identify herself as his sister, and goes on to maintain that the very decision to go to Egypt was sinful. Later, Nahmanides expresses perplexity at Abraham's rationalization that Sarah was truly his half-sister; this appears to be an unpersuasive excuse for omitting the crucial information that she was also his wife, and although Nahmanides proceeds to suggest an explanation, his sense of moral disapproval remains the dominant feature of the discussion. Finally, he regards the treatment of Hagar by both Sarah and Abraham as a sin for which Jews are suffering to this day at the hands of the descendants of Ishmael. The bold, almost indignant tone of these passages is both striking and significant—but it is not typical.

Most medieval Jews were understandably sensitive about ascriptions of sin to the patriarchs, and the situation was rendered even more delicate by the fact that the issue of patriarchal morality often arose in a highly charged context in which Jews were placed on the defensive in the face of

---

[1]   It is a pleasure to thank my friend Professor Sid Z. Leiman for his careful reading of the manuscript. I am particularly grateful to him for the references to *Menahot* and pseudo-Jerome in n. 13, *Sefer Hasidim* and the *midrashim* in n. 14, and Ehrlich's commentary in n. 22.

[2]   Commentary to Genesis 12:10, 20:12, and 16:6.

a Christian attack. Two thirteenth-century Ashkenazic polemics reflect a somewhat surprising Christian willingness to criticize Jacob as a means of attacking his descendants. Since the patriarch was a Christian as well as a Jewish hero, such attacks on his morality were problematical: Jacob may be the father of carnal Israel, but he is the prototype of spiritual Israel as well. While criticisms of this sort are consequently absent from major Christian works, it is perfectly evident that no Jew would have invented them. On the medieval street, then, Christians did not shrink from such attacks on Jews and their forebears. Jacob, they said, was a thief and a trickster; the implication concerning his descendants hardly needed to be spelled out.

In *Sefer Yosef ha-Meqanne* we are informed that Joseph Official met a certain Dominican friar on the road to Paris who told him, "Your father Jacob was a thief; there has been no consumer of usury to equal him, for he purchased the birthright, which was worth a thousand coins, for a single plate [of lentils] worth half a coin."[3] The technical impropriety of the reference to usury merely underscores the pointed application of this critique to medieval Jews. The next passage reports a Christian argument that Jacob was a deceiver who cheated Laban by exceeding the terms of their agreement concerning the sheep to which Jacob was entitled, and this criticism is followed by the assertion that Simeon and Levi engaged in unethical behavior when they deviously persuaded the Shechemites to accept circumcision and then proceeded to kill them.[4]

With respect to Jacob, the Jewish response was conditioned by two separate considerations acting in concert. First, religious motivations quite independent of the polemical context prevented the perception of Jacob as a sinner; second, the Christian attack itself called for refutation rather than concession. Hence, Joseph[5] responded with a remarkable suggestion found also in Rashbam's commentary that Jacob paid in full for the birthright; the bread and lentils are to be understood as a meal sealing the transaction or customarily following its consummation. As Judah Rosenthal pointed out in his edition of *Yosef ha-Meqanne*, Rabbi Joseph Bekhor Shor reacted with exasperation to the apparent implausibility of this interpretation, which was almost surely motivated by both moral

---

3   *Sefer Yosef ha-Meqanne*, ed. by Judah Rosenthal (Jerusalem, 1970), pp. 40-41.
4   Rosenthal, *Sefer Yosef ha-Meqanne*, pp. 41-42.
5   Despite the manuscript, this must refer to Joseph Official and not Joseph Bekhor Shor; cf. the editor's note, and see just below.

sensitivity and polemical need. As for Laban, the answer to the Christian critique was that Jacob was the real victim of deception, and his treatment of his father-in-law was marked by extraordinary scrupulousness.[6]

Joseph Official goes on to an uncompromising defense of Simeon and Levi which is particularly interesting because this was the one instance in which a concession to the Christian accusation was tactically possible. Jacob, after all, had denounced their behavior, and even if his initial concern dealt with the danger that could result from an adverse Canaanite reaction rather than with the moral issue (Genesis 34:30), his vigorous rebuke of his sons at the end of his life (Genesis 49:5-7) could certainly have supported the assertion that he considered their action morally reprehensible as well as pragmatically unwise. Nevertheless, there is no hint of condemnation in *Yosef ha-Meqanne*; if Christians denounced Simeon and Levi, then surely Jews were obligated to defend them, especially since a sense of moral superiority was crucial to the medieval Jewish psyche in general and to the polemicist in particular.[7] Thus, Joseph tells us that the Shechemites regretted their circumcision and were in any event planning to oppress Jacob's family and take over its property; consequently, their execution was eminently justified.[8]

There is a certain irony in the fact that the Christian question in *Yosef ha-Meqanne* which immediately follows this series of objections to patriarchal behavior begins, "After all, everyone agrees that Jacob was a thoroughly righteous man; why then was he afraid of descending to hell?"[9] Although this is a return to the Christian stance that we ought to expect, there is in fact one more incident in Jacob's life that Christian polemicists apparently utilized in their debate with Jews, and this is, of course, his deception of his own father.

6   Rosenthal, *Sefer Yosef ha-Meqanne*, loc. cit.

7   On this point, see my brief discussion in *The Jewish-Christian Debate in the High Middle Ages: A Critical Edition of the Nizzahon Vetus with an Introduction, Translation and Commentary* (Northvale, NJ, 1996), pp. 25-27. I hope to elaborate in a forthcoming study on the problem of exile in medieval polemic.

8   Rosenthal, *Sefer Yosef ha-Meqanne*, p. 42. The persistence of Jewish sensitivity to this story in modern times can perhaps best be illustrated by a contemporary example of Jewish black humor. Simeon and Levi—so the explanation goes—were just as concerned as Jacob about adverse public opinion, and this is precisely why they arranged to have the Shechemites undergo the judaizing ceremony of circumcision. Once it would be perceived that it was a Jew who had been killed, no one would be concerned. Cf. *Kli Yakar* to Genesis 35:25.

9   Rosenthal, *Sefer Yosef ha-Meqanne*, p. 42.

The anonymous *Nizzahon Vetus* presents the following argument:

"I am Esau your firstborn" [Genesis 27:19]. One can say that Jacob did not lie. In fact, this can be said without distorting the simple meaning of the verse, but by explaining it as follows: I am Esau your firstborn, for Esau sold him the birthright in a manner as clear as day. It is, indeed, clear that Jacob was careful not to state an outright lie from the fact that when Isaac asked him, "Are you my son Esau?" he responded, "I am" [Genesis 27:24), and not, "I am Esau."

They go on to say that because Jacob obtained the blessings through trickery, they were fulfilled for the Gentiles and not the Jews. The answer is that even the prophet Amos [*sic*] prayed for Jacob, for he is in possession of the truth, as it is written, "You will grant truth to Jacob and mercy to Abraham, which you have sworn unto our fathers" [Micah 7:20], that is, had not the truth been with Jacob, then you would not have sworn to our fathers. [10]

The pattern holds. Once again Christians attack the patriarch's morality; this time the consequences for his descendants are spelled out with explicit clarity, and once again Jewish ingenuity is mobilized for an unflinching, unqualified defense.[11]

Nevertheless, the pattern does not always hold. Polemicists will do what is necessary to win whatever point appears crucial in a particular context, and on one occasion at least we find two Jewish writers displaying very little zeal in defending the questionable action of a biblical hero. Their motivation is hardly mysterious: Jesus had cited this action approvingly.

Jacob ben Reuben and the *Nizzahon Vetus* both comment on the story in Matthew 12 in which Jesus defends the plucking of corn by his

---

10   Berger, *The Jewish-Christian Debate*, p. 56.

11   For Rashi's rather different defense of Jacob's veracity as well as the persuasiveness of the version in the *Nizzahon Vetus* for later Jews, see my commentary in *The Jewish-Christian Debate*, pp. 246-247. It is worth noting that the *Nizzahon Vetus* also reports a Christian argument that Moses' delay in coming down from Mount Sinai (Exodus 32:1) renders him "a sinner and a liar" (p. 67). Mordechai Breuer has suggested (*Sefer Nizzahon Yashan* [Jerusalem, 1978], p. 21, n. 57) that this argument *may* have originated among Christian heretics. On the other hand, since it ends with the question "Why did he delay?" it may have been leading to a Christian answer that Moses, who was not really a sinner, was testing the Jews and found them wanting. The ancient rabbis, of course, were generally not faced with the polemical concerns of the Middle Ages, and on rare occasions the Talmud ascribes sin to the patriarchs even where the biblical evidence does not require such a conclusion; see, for example, the accusations against Abraham in *Nedarim* 32a.

hungry disciples on the Sabbath with reference to David's eating of the shewbread when he was hungry. In his late-twelfth-century *Milhamot ha-Shem*,[12] Jacob responds as follows:

> How could he cite evidence from David's eating of the shewbread when he was fleeing and in a great hurry? If David behaved unlawfully by violating the commandment on that one occasion when he was forced by the compulsion of hunger and never repeated this behavior again, how could your Messiah utilize this argument to permit the gathering of corn without qualification?

More briefly, the author of the *Nizzahon Vetus* remarks, "If David behaved improperly, this does not give them the right to pluck those ears of corn on the Sabbath."[13] Although Jacob provided mitigation for David's behavior and the *Nizzahon Vetus*'s comments might be understood as a counterfactual concession for the sake of argument ("even if I were to agree that David behaved improperly"), the impression of sin is not only allowed to stand but is actually introduced by the Jewish writers. Even more striking, Jacob continued his argument by saying that once Jesus was permitting every act of King David, "why did he not permit sexual relations with married women since David had such relations with the wife of Uriah?" Now, the Talmud had made the most vigorous efforts to deny that Bathsheba was still married to Uriah and, indeed, that David had sinned at all, and the insertion of this question—which was not essential to the argument and is in fact missing from the parallel passage in the *Nizzahon Vetus*—is a telling illustration of the impact of the search for effective polemical rhetoric.[14]

Thus far we have seen Jewish defenses of biblical heroes for reasons both religious and polemical, and criticisms of their behavior which arose from

---

[12] Edited by Judah Rosenthal (Jerusalem, 1963), p. 148.

[13] P. 182. It is important to note that the Talmud (*Menahot* 95b-96a) had suggested a legal justification for what David had done. Note too the anomalous report in pseudo-Jerome cited by L. Ginzberg, *Legends of the Jews*, vol. 6 (Philadelphia, 1928), p. 243.

[14] It is, of course, difficult to say what Jacob's view of David's relationship with Bathsheba was in dispassionate, non-polemical moments. For Abravanel's rejection of the rabbinic exculpation of David (*Shabbat* 56a), see his commentary to 2 Samuel 11-12. See also the very interesting remarks in *Sefer Hasidim*, ed. by J. Wistinetzki (Frankfurt am Main, 1924), sec. 46 (p. 43)=R. Margulies' edition (Jerusalem, 1957), sec. 174 (p. 181). Cf. also the less striking references in *Midrash Shmuel*, ed. by S. Buber (Krakau, 1893), pp. 122-123, and *Seder Eliyyahu Rabbah*, ed. by M. Ish-Shalom (Friedmann) (Vienna, 1902), p. 7.

a sensitive, straightforward reading of the text as well as from polemical concerns. It remains to be noted that the particular ideology of a Jewish commentator, if pursued with sufficient passion, could itself overcome the profound inhibitions against denouncing the morality of the patriarchs. I know of but one example of this phenomenon, but it is quite remarkable.

In his study of Jewish social thought in sixteenth- and seventeenth-century Poland, Haim Hillel Ben Sasson frequently pointed to the animus against the wealthy displayed by the prominent preacher and exegete Rabbi Ephraim Lunshitz. Among many examples of this animus, Ben Sasson draws our attention to Lunshitz's remarks about the rabbinic comment that when Jacob remained alone prior to wrestling with the angel, his purpose was to collect small vessels that he had left behind. Before Lunshitz, Jews had universally understood this as an exemplification of an admirable trait. Not so the author of the *Kli Yakar*: "A majority of commentators agree that this angel is Sammael the officer of Esau... whose desire is solely to blind (*lesamme*) the eyes. . . of the intelligence." Now, as long as Jacob refrained from the slightest sin, Sammael could not approach him, but once Jacob was guilty of even a small measure of sin, his immunity was lost. And for a rich man like Jacob to remain behind in a dangerous place for a few vessels is indeed the beginning of sin. Jacob had begun to blind himself, "for who is as blind as the lovers of money about whom it is written, 'The eyes of a man are never satiated' (Proverbs 27:20)?... Who is such a fool that he would endanger himself for such a small item? Rather, it is a mocking heart which turned him away from the straight path to succumb to such love of money, which causes forgetfulness of God."[15]

What makes this passage all the more noteworthy is that the talmudic source contains an explicitly favorable evaluation: the righteous care so much for their property because they never rob others (*Hullin* 91a). Moreover, if Lunshitz was uneasy with this talmudic evaluation, nothing was forcing him to mention the passage in the first place; the point is nowhere in the biblical text, and the *Kli Yakar* is in any event a discursive, selective commentary, which could easily have skipped the verse entirely. Clearly, he made the point because it served as an outlet for one of his driving passions. Patriarchal immunity from criticism, even in a traditional society, evidently had its limits.

---

15   *Kli Yakar* to Genesis 32:35. See Ben Sasson's *Hagut ve-Hanhagah* (Jerusalem, 1959), pp. 118-119.

BIBLICAL CRITICISM AND JEWISH EXEGESIS
IN MODERN TIMES

As the Middle Ages gave way to the modern period, the content and context of this issue were radically and fundamentally altered. Inhibitions against criticizing biblical morality began to crumble, and both Enlightenment ideologues and nineteenth-century scholars gleefully pounced upon biblical passages that appeared morally problematical. In the first instance, the target was the Bible as a whole and, ultimately, Christianity itself; in the second, it was usually the Hebrew Bible in particular, whose allegedly primitive ethics served as a preparation and a foil for the superior morality of the Gospels. In effect, an argument originally directed against Christianity was refocused to attack Judaism alone.[16]

Modern biblical scholarship, then, transformed the essential terms of this discussion, and the transformation was so profound that it ultimately inspired a reaction strikingly different from the standard medieval response. The crucial point is that the attack was no longer on the morality of the biblical personalities. To many Bible critics, the very existence of the patriarchs was in question, and the historicity of specific accounts of their behavior was surely deemed unreliable in the extreme. The attack now was on the morality of the biblical author or authors—an attack that was almost impossible in the premodern period, when the author was ultimately presumed to be God Himself.[17]

Consequently, it now became possible—perhaps even polemically desirable—for traditionally inclined Jews (whether or not they were strict fundamentalists) to take a different approach by driving a wedge between hero and author. There were indeed occasional imperfections in the moral behavior of the patriarchs, but these are condemned

---

[16] Cf. the similar medieval phenomenon in which arguments by Christian heretics against the Hebrew Bible were reworked by Orthodox Christians in their polemic with Jews. See my *Jewish-Christian Debate*, p. 6.

[17] For an exception, note Luther's remarks on Esther in his *Table Talk*: "I am so hostile to this book that I wish it did not exist, for it judaizes too much, and has too much heathen naughtiness." Cited approvingly by L. B. Paton in his discussion of "the moral teaching of the book" in *The International Critical Commentary: The Book of Esther* (1908; reprint, Edinburgh, 1951), p. 96.

by the Torah and required punishment and expiation. Whatever the exegetical merits of this approach, and they are, as we shall see, considerable, it would have been extraordinarily difficult both tactically and psychologically had the attack of the critics still been directed at the patriarchs themselves.

There is, however, a deeper issue here. The assertion that the Bible disapproves of certain behavior was not based on explicit verses of condemnation; rather, it depended on a sensitive reading of long stretches of narrative in which patterns of retribution and expiation emerged. On the simplest level, this approach demonstrated that the morality of the Torah is not inferior to that of Bible critics. On a deeper level, it undercut the effort of some critics to utilize the moral "deficiencies" of certain passages to establish divergent levels of moral sensitivity in the Pentateuch as a whole and in Genesis in particular. But on the profoundest level—at least for some proponents of this approach—it went to the heart of the essential claims of the higher criticism by arguing in a new way for the unity of Genesis. Many of the newly discovered patterns cut through the documents of the critics and emerged only from a unitary perception of the entire book; since the patterns seemed genuine, the only reasonable conclusion was that the unity of Genesis was no less real than its literary subtleties. These observations were not confined to narratives bearing on the morality of the patriarchs, but it is there that some of the most striking examples were to be found.

In the first half of this century, a number of Jewish writers—Martin Buber, Benno Jacob, Umberto Cassutto—began to note such patterns. Before going further, we are immediately confronted by a challenging, almost intractable methodological problem. I have suggested that this revisionist reading of the Bible is rooted in part in traditionalist sentiments, that it presented a new way of responding to people critical of sacred Jewish texts. At the same time, I consider the essential insights justified by an objective examination of the evidence (although my own motives are surely as "suspect" as those of the figures under discussion). Decades ago, Jacob Katz argued that one may not readily assign ulterior motives to someone whose position appears valid in light of the sources that he cites,[18] and more recently Joseph Dan has criticized a work

---

[18]   Jacob Katz "Mahloqet ha-Semikhah bein Rabbi Yaaqov Beirav ve-ha-Ralbah," *Zion* 15, secs. 3-4 (1951): 41.

about Gershom Scholem for attributing his view of kabbalah to factors other than his accurate reading of the kabbalistic texts themselves.[19] Fundamentally, these methodological caveats are very much in order, and in certain instances they are decisive. At the same time, undeniable intuitions tell us that even people who are essentially correct can be partially motivated by concerns that go beyond the cited evidence, and there ought to be some way to determine when this is likely to be so. In our case, a figure like Cassutto was clearly concerned not only with the unity of Genesis but with the standing and reputation of the biblical text. Moreover, despite the fact that he was not a fundamentalist and that he was no doubt sincere in his protestation that his essential conclusions flowed solely from an objective examination of the text, the consistency of his conservative tendencies in issue after issue where the evidence could often point either way surely reveals a personality that was inclined to seek traditional solutions.[20]

In contemporary biblical scholarship, such an inclination frequently labels one a neo-fundamentalist whose conclusions are rejected almost a priori. This is a manifest error with the most serious consequences. Even people with much stronger traditionalist tendencies than Cassutto can be motivated by those tendencies to seek evidence that turns out to be real. Kepler's laws are no less valid because he sought them as a result of his religious convictions. In this instance, a change in the attack on biblical morality liberated and then impelled people with traditionalist inclinations to see things in the text that had gone virtually unnoticed before. At first, these figures were necessarily non-fundamentalists; genuine Jewish fundamentalists would not easily shed their inhibitions about criticizing the patriarchs. With the passage of time, however, even some uncompromisingly Orthodox Jews could adopt this approach,[21] while others—probably a majority—would

---

[19]   *Qiryat Sefer* 54 (1979/80): 358-362. Dan does note (p. 361) that even in Scholem's case, extratextual considerations can play some role.

[20]   While maintaining that Cassutto's work in essentially anti-traditional, Yehezkel Kaufmann nevertheless pointed to several examples of this conservatism; see "Me-Adam ad Noah," in *Mi-Kivshonah shel ha-Yetzirah ha-Miqra'it* (Tel Aviv, 1966), p. 217.

[21]   Yissakhar Jacobson, *Binah ba-Miqra* (Tel Aviv,1960), pp 33-36; Nehama Leibowitz, *Iyyunim be-Sefer Bereshit* (Jerusalem, 1966), pp. 185-188 (English trans., *Studies in Bereshit [Genesis]* [Jerusalem, 1976], pp. 264-269); Leah Frankel, *Peraqim ba-Miqra* (Jerusalem, 1981), pp. 102-104, 143-144.

retain unabated the religious inhibitions of the past;[22] fundamentalism is far from a monolithic phenomenon.

THE BIBLE'S JUDGMENT OF PATRIARCHAL BEHAVIOR: THE CASE OF JACOB'S DECEPTION

Let us turn now to a central example of an approach that we have thus far discussed only in the abstract. At Rebecca's behest, Jacob deceived Isaac by pretending to be Esau and thereby obtained a blessing intended for his brother. We have already seen a medieval Jewish defense of Jacob's behavior, and in the entire corpus of premodern Jewish exegesis there is hardly a whisper of criticism.[23] In the twentieth century, however, a number of scholars have noted a series of indications that make it

---

[22]   Professor Lawrence Kaplan has called my attention to Rabbi A. Kotler's "How To Teach Torah," *Light* 10, 12, 13, 15, 19 (1970/71), republished as a pamphlet by Beth Medrash Govoha of Lakewood. A Hebrew version appears in Rabbi Kotler's *Osef Hiddushei Torah* (Jerusalem, 1983), pp. 402-411. "If there were any fault," writes the author, "—however slight (Hebrew: *dak min ha-dak*)—in any of the *Ovos* [patriarchs], the very essence of the Jewish people would have been different" (English pamphlet, p. 6=Hebrew p. 404). Rabbi Kotler makes it clear that his work is a reaction to modern heresy (*kefirah*), which perceives the patriarchal narratives as ordinary stories. On the other hand, Professor Kaplan notes that the popular *Pentateuch* and *Haftorahs* edited by Rabbi J. H. Hertz (1936) extols Scripture precisely because it "impartially relates both the failings and the virtues of its heroes" (commentary to Genesis 20:12, citing one of the passages from Nahmanides with which we began). Similarly, Arnold B. Ehrlich asserts that Scripture does not conceal the faults of the patriarchs; see *Miqra ki-Peshuto*, vol. 1 (New York, 1898; reprint, New York, 1969), pp. 33, 73 (to Genesis 12:14, 16 and 25:27); his German *Randglossen zur Hebräischen Bibel* (Leipzig, 1908; reprint, Hildesheim, 1968) omits the first and more important passage. Ehrlich, a brilliant maverick who was neither a traditionalist nor a conventional critic, was in many respects *sui generis* and resists inclusion in any neat classificatory scheme. Finally, Rabbi Shalom Carmy has called my attention to the willingness of representatives of the nineteenth-century Musar movement to acknowledge minor imperfections in the patriarchs as part of the movement's special approach to the analysis of human failings.

[23]   David Sykes, in his *Patterns in Genesis* (Ph.D. diss., Bernard Revel Graduate School, Yeshiva University, 1984), notes *Zohar, va-Yeshev*, 185b, which indicates that Jacob was punished for this act because even though something is done properly, God judges the pious for even a hairbreadth's deviation from the ideal. He also points to the Yemenite manuscript cited in *Torah Shelemah*, vol. 6, p. 1432, no. 181 (where the editor also notes the *Zohar* passage), which indicates that Jacob was deceived by his sons with a goat (Genesis 37:31) just as he had deceived his own father with a goat (Genesis 27:16). See also below, note 25.

exceedingly difficult to deny that the Torah implicitly but vigorously condemns Jacob's action.

First, the deception was motivated by a misreading of Isaac's intentions. The blind patriarch bestowed three blessings on his children: the first to Jacob masquerading as Esau, the second to Esau, and the third to Jacob. It was only in the third blessing, when he knew for the first time that he was addressing Jacob, that he bestowed "the blessing of Abraham to you and your seed with you so that you may inherit the land in which you dwell which God gave to Abraham" (Genesis 28:4). Although other interpretations of this sequence are possible, the most straightforward reading is that Rebecca and Jacob had gravely underestimated their husband and father. Isaac had indeed intended to bless Esau with temporal supremacy, but the blessing of Abraham—the inheritance of the holy land and the crucial mission of the patriarchs—had been reserved for Jacob from the outset. The deception was pragmatically as well as morally dubious.[24]

Jacob is then subjected to a series of misfortunes and ironies whose relationship to the initial deception cannot be accidental. He must work for his "brother" Laban (Genesis 29:15) instead of having his brothers work for him (Genesis 27:37); he is deceived by the substitution of one sibling for another in the darkness and is pointedly informed that "in our place" the younger is not placed before the older (Genesis 29:26); his sons deceive him with Joseph's garment and the blood of a goat (Genesis 37:31) just as he had deceived Isaac with Esau's garments and the skin of a goat (Genesis 27:15-16); his relationship with Esau is precisely the opposite of the one that was supposed to have been achieved—Esau is the master (Genesis 32:5, 6, 19; 33:8, 13, 14, 15) to whom his servant Jacob (32:5, 19; 33:5, 14) must bow (33:3, and contrast 27:29). Moreover, Jacob's debilitating fear of his brother results from the very act that was supposed to have established his supremacy.[25]

---

24   *Binah ba-Miqra*, loc. cit. Cf. also Malbim on Genesis 27:1 and Leibowitz, *Iyyunim*, pp. 193-195.

25   For premodern references to such arguments, see note 23; *Midrash Tanhuma*, ed. by S. Buber (Vilna, 1885), *Va-Yetzei* 11, p. 152, and the parallel passage in *Aggadat Bereshit*, ed. by S. Buber (Krakau, 1902), ch. (48) [49], p. 99, where Leah tells Jacob that he has no right to complain about being deceived since he too is a deceiver (although the midrash does not explicitly endorse her criticism); Eliezer Ashkenazi (sixteenth century) *Ma'asei ha-Shem*, vol. 1 (Jerusalem, 1972), p. 115b, who comments on Laban's remark about the younger and older but apparently considers it evidence of Laban's nastiness rather than

There is, then, ample evidence that Jacob had to undergo a series of punishments to atone for his act of deception. It is almost curious, however, that no one has noted an additional—and climactic—element in this series, which can fundamentally transform our understanding of a crucial aspect of the Joseph narrative. One reason why the point may have been missed is that there are no key words calling it to our attention, and the presence of such words not only alerts the reader but serves as a methodological guide preventing undisciplined speculation. At the same time, we cannot permit ourselves to ignore grand thematic patterns, and in this instance I think that such a pattern has been overlooked.

Leah Frankel, utilizing the "key word" approach, has noted that the root meaning "to deceive" (*resh-mem-yod*) appears in Genesis three times. The first two instances, in which Isaac tells Esau that his brother deceitfully took his blessing (Genesis 27:35) and Jacob asks Laban why he deceived him (Genesis 29:25), are clearly related to our theme.[26] Perhaps, she suggests, the third instance, in which Simeon and Levi speak deceitfully to Shechem (Genesis 34:13), is intended to indicate that Jacob was "to taste deceit carried out by *sons*. He would have to stand in the place where his father stood when his son Jacob deceived him" [her emphasis].[27] While this approach is not impossible, it seems

---

Jacob's culpability. Note too *Genesis Rabbah* 67:4, which speaks of later Jews crying out in anguish because of Esau's agonized exclamation in Genesis 27:34, and the somewhat more ambiguous midrash of unknown provenance cited by Rashi on Psalms 80:6, in which Jews shed tears as a result of Esau's tears; see Leibowitz, *Iyyunim*, p. 190. Such isolated observations over a period of more than a millennium and a half do not, I think, undermine or even significantly affect the thesis of this paper. For twentieth-century references, often containing additional arguments, see Martin Buber, *Die Schrift und ihre Verdeutschung* (Berlin, 1936), pp. 224-226; Benno Jacob, *Das Erste Buch der Tora: Genesis* (Berlin, 1934), p. 591 (abridged English translation, New York, 1974), pp. 197-198; Umberto Cassutto, *La Questione della Genesi* (Florence, 1934), esp. p. 227; idem, *Torat ha-Te'udot* (Jerusalem, 1959), pp. 55-56=*The Documentary Hypothesis* (Jerusalem, 1961), pp. 63-64; idem, "Yaakov," *Entziklopediyyah Miqra'it* (EBH), vol. 3, cc. 716-722; Jacobson, Leibowitz, and Frankel (see note 21); Nahum M. Sarna, *Understanding Genesis* (New York, 1966), pp. 183-184; Jacob Milgrom in *Conservative Judaism* 20 (1966): 73-79; J. P. Fokkelman, *Narrative Art in Genesis* (Assen and Amsterdam, 1975), pp. 128-130, 200, 223, 227; Sykes, op. cit. (note 23). With the exception of Fokkelman, all these figures, whether they are fundamentalists or not, more or less fit the traditionalist typology that I have proposed. Needless to say, the evident validity of many of these exegetical suggestions must (or at least should) eventually affect biblical scholars of all varieties.

26 Cf. *Tanhuma* and *Aggadat Bereshit* in the previous note.

27 *Peraqim ba-Miqra*, p. 104.

unlikely; although Jacob suffers indirect consequences from Simeon and Levi's trickery, he is in no sense its object, and the resemblance to his own deception is exceedingly remote.

But there is another act of filial deception in Genesis whose similarity to Jacob's seems unmistakable. Jacob concealed his identity from his father by pretending to be someone else. Similarly, his own misery and anguish reach their climax when his son Joseph conceals his identity and pretends to be something other than what he truly is. The fact that the direct victims of Joseph's deception were the brothers may be the main reason why this observation has been missed, but it is perfectly clear that Jacob is as much a victim as his sons. This point alone should make us reevaluate the key element of the Joseph cycle as the culmination of the process of expiation suffered by the patriarch, and the essential argument does not depend on anything more. But there is more. Joseph deceives his father while providing him with food just as Jacob deceived his own father while bringing him the "savory food" which he liked (Genesis 27:7, 14, 17, 25). It is not just that the brothers are Jacob's messengers and will report Joseph's deceptive words to their father (although this is quite sufficient); in the final confrontation between Joseph and Judah, the latter is explicitly a surrogate for Jacob, acting to protect Benjamin *in loco parentis* (Genesis 44:32).[28] Moreover, there is only one other place in Genesis where one person speaks to another with as many protestations of servility as Judah addresses to his "master" in that climactic confrontation; that place, of course, is the description of Jacob's servile behavior toward Esau upon his return from the house of Laban (Genesis 32:4-6, 18-21; 33:1-15).[29] In short, Joseph has not

[28]   It may be worth asking (with considerable diffidence) whether Judah's status as a surrogate for Jacob may help us resolve an old, intractable crux. In Joseph's second dream, the sun, moon, and eleven stars, presumably symbolizing his father, mother, and brothers, bow down to him (Genesis 37:9-10). But his mother was already dead at the time of the dream; less seriously, Jacob does not bow to Joseph until Genesis 47:30, by which time our intuition tells us (I think) that the dreams ought to have already been fulfilled. *Perhaps* two of the brothers who bow to Joseph represent both themselves and a parent; Judah is the surrogate for Jacob, and Benjamin, who is pointedly described as his mother's only surviving child (Genesis 44:20), is the representative of Rachel. Joseph's parents bow down to him through their offspring.

[29]   For whatever this is worth, Jacob addresses Esau as "my master" seven times in these verses (32:6, 19; 33:8, 13, 14 [twice], 15 [32:5 is not addressed to Esau]) and Judah addresses Joseph as "my master" seven times in his final speech (44:18 [twice], 19, 20, 22, 24, 33). Since seven is clearly a significant number and since Jacob is explicitly

merely concealed his identity from his father; by threatening Jacob's family from a position of mastery, he has actually taken on the role of Esau.[30] The parallel to Jacob's deception is genuinely striking.[31]

LITERARY PATTERNS AND THE DOCUMENTARY HYPOTHESIS

During the last decade, J. P. Fokkelman,[32] Robert Alter,[33] and Michael Fishbane[34] have searched the narratives of Genesis for patterns out of purely literary motivations, sometimes with the implicit assumption that the conventional documentary hypothesis remains virtually unchanged no matter how many interlocking themes are discerned. In a reaction to one of Alter's early articles on this subject, I wrote that "I think he underestimates the impact of such literary analysis on the documentary hypothesis. You can allow the 'redactor' just so much freedom of action before he turns into an author using various traditions as 'raw material.' Such an approach must ultimately shake the foundations of the regnant critical theory, not merely tinker with its periphery."[35] More recently,

---

said to have bowed to Esau seven times (Genesis 33:3 ["complete subjection," says Fokkelman, in *Narrative Art in Genesis*, p. 223]), it is at least possible that this is more than coincidence.

[30] Note too that Jacob was most concerned with Esau's threat to Rachel and her child (Genesis 33:2), and it was Rachel's child Benjamin who was singled out for persecution by the Egyptian viceroy. Finally, Professor David Shatz has called my attention to the use of the rare verb *stm*, "to hate," with regard to both Esau's hatred of Jacob (Genesis 27:41) and the brothers fear that Joseph would hate them (Genesis 50:15).

[31] The fact that Joseph's actions were no doubt motivated by other factors involving his brothers does not, of course, refute the perception that we are witnessing the final step in a divine plan to purge Jacob of his sin. It is, in fact, possible that an even later incident in Genesis is related to Jacob's deception of Isaac. The successful expiation of that sin may be symbolized by Jacob's ability, despite his failing eyesight, to discern the difference in the destinies of his older and younger grandsons (Genesis 48:10-20). Cf. Benno Jacob, *Das Erste Buch*, p. 884 (called to my attention by David Sykes), and Cassutto, *La Questione della Genesi*, p. 232. (It need hardly be said that this new approach does not end with a denunciation of biblical heroes. After a process of retribution and moral development, the ethical standing of the patriarch is beyond reproach.) Finally, it must be stressed that other moral questions like the scriptural evaluation of the treatment of Hagar and the behavior of the young Joseph are also susceptible to this mode of analysis.

[32] See n. 25.

[33] *The Art of Biblical Narrative* (New York, 1981).

[34] *Text and Texture* (New York, 1979).

[35] *Commentary* 61:3 (March, 1976): 16. It may be worth asking whether Shakespeare

the point has been made with vigor and documentation in David Sykes's dissertation, *Patterns in Genesis*.[36] To Alter's credit, he does confront the question in his later book, and although his conclusions are by no means traditional, they are not wholly consonant with those of critical orthodoxy.[37]

It is becoming clearer from year to year that Genesis is replete with linguistic and thematic patterns of subtlety and power which run through the warp and woof of the entire work. Despite the overwhelming force generated by a critical theory that has held sway for generations, scholars will not be able to hide forever behind the assertion that they are studying the art of a redactor as that word is usually understood. The issue will have to be joined.

---

has ever been described as the redactor of the various Hamlet documents because he worked with earlier, related stories.

[36]   See n. 23. My affirmation of the validity of this general approach does not, of course, imply an endorsement of every pattern or set of patterns that has been suggested, and it is self-evident that some proposals will be more persuasive than others. This mode of interpretation will always be vulnerable to the charge of arbitrary and subjective eisegesis. Nevertheless, such is the fate of almost all literary analysis, and a combination of methodological guidelines and a healthy dose of common sense can minimize, though never eliminate, undisciplined speculation. In any case, I am thoroughly persuaded that the recent literature contains more than enough convincing examples to sustain the essential point.

[37]   P. 20, and especially chap. 7 (pp. 131-154). In the present climate, it requires some courage to express such views, and Alter has already been accused of involvement in (*horribile dictu*) "the new fundamentalism" (and he has already denied it); see *Commentary* 77:2 (February 1984): 14. Cf. also Fokkelman's very brief comment on the issue in *Narrative Art*, p. 4.

YEARNING FOR REDEMPTION

THREE TYPOLOGICAL THEMES
IN EARLY JEWISH MESSIANISM:
MESSIAH SON OF JOSEPH, RABBINIC
CALCULATIONS, AND THE FIGURE OF ARMILUS

From: *AJS Review: The Journal of the Association for Jewish Studies*
10 (1985): 141-164.

The messianic dream owes its roots to biblical prophecy and its rich development to generations of sensitive and creative exegetes anxiously awaiting redemption. Scripture itself is less than generous in providing detailed information about the end of days, so ungenerous, in fact, that some modern scholars have expressed skepticism about the very appearance of a messianic figure in the biblical text.[1] While this skepticism is excessive, it reflects a reality which troubled the ancients no less than the moderns and left room for the diversity and complexity that mark the messianic idea by late antiquity.

In the first centuries after the destruction of the Second Temple, many Jews were no doubt content to leave the messianic hope as an article of faith whose precise contours would be elucidated at the time of its fulfillment.[2]

For others, however, it exercised a fascination that sometimes bordered on obsession, and such Jews looked with both eagerness and frustration at the messianic material available in Scripture. The paucity of detail was simultaneously discouraging and stimulating, serving as obstacle for the fainthearted and catalyst for the daring. The intense desire to know the events, the time, the nature, the heroes, and the

---

[1] Some examples are cited in James H. Charlesworth, "The Concept of the Messiah in the Pseudepigrapha," in *Aufstieg und Niedergang der Römischen Welt* 11.19.1, ed. by Wolfgang Haase (Berlin and New York, 1979), p. 189, n. 4.

[2] Jacob Neusner's *Messiah in Context* (Philadelphia, 1984) argues at length for the relative insignificance of the Messiah in most early rabbinic works.

villains of the end of days could not be satisfied by an examination of the explicit record of biblical prophecy, and the determined messianic theorist turned perforce to more creative approaches. The most fruitful of these was the enterprise we know as typology—the utilization of the figures, events, and periods of the past to illuminate the messianic age.

The crucial "type," which left its mark on virtually every aspect of messianic speculation, was the great redemption of the past. "As in the days of your exodus from the land of Egypt will I show him marvelous things" (Mic. 7:15). On the most obvious level, this meant that the overt miracles of the period of the exodus could be expected to return. Hence, "the Holy One, blessed be He, will in the future bring upon Edom all the plagues that He inflicted on the Egyptians."[3] As in the desert, Jews will enjoy the manna and will have no need of the light of sun or moon.[4] Theudas, like Joshua, was to split the waters of the Jordan,[5] a Jewish prophet would repeat the miracle of Jericho at Jerusalem,[6] and a man would arise who would again command an obedient sun to stop in its tracks.[7]

It is not, however, only in the realm of the overtly miraculous that themes of the first redemption will recur in the future. The Midrash informs us that the final redeemer, like Moses, will make himself known to his people and then become hidden from them before revealing himself once again at the end.[8] The prophet who was going to bring down the walls of Jerusalem hailed, like Moses, from Egypt.[9] Matthew places Jesus in Egypt in a passage whose dubious historicity makes its typological scheme all the more striking.[10] Like Moses, Jesus fasts forty days and

---

3   *Tanhuma*, ed. Buber, II, p. 43 and parallels. See L. Ginzberg, *Eine Unbekannte Jüdische Sekte* (New York and Pressburg, 1922), p. 334 (hereafter cited as *Sekte*) = *Monatsschrift für Geschichte und Wissenschaft des Judentums* 58 (1914): 412 (hereafter cited as *MGWJ*) = *An Unknown Jewish Sect* (New York, 1976), p. 234 (hereafter cited as *Sect*).

4   *Sekte*, pp. 335-336 = *MGWJ*, pp. 413-414 = *Sect*, p. 235.

5   Josephus, *Antiquities* 20.5.1.

6   Ibid. 20.8.6.

7   *Sibylline Oracles* 5.256-259. See H. M. Teeple, *The Mosaic Eschatological Prophet* (Philadelphia, 1957), pp. 10-11 (and note the references on pp. 29-31 concerning the exodus as a prototype of the final redemption). Cf. also G. Vermes, *Jesus the Jew* (New York, 1973), p. 98.

8   *Be-Midbar Rabbah* 11:3; *Shir ha-Shirim Rabbah* 2:22; *Ruth Rabbah* 5:6; *Pesikta Rabbati* 15, ed. Friedmann, p. 72b (cf. esp. n. 63 there); *Pesikta de-Rav Kahana*, ed. Buber, p. 49b. See also *Sekte*, p. 335 = *MGWJ*, p. 413 = *Sect*, p. 234.

9   Or at least he said so. See *Antiquities* 20.8.6.

10   Matt. 2:14-15. The fact that the plain meaning of Hosea 11:1 refers to the exodus means that Matthew's citation of that verse strengthens rather than weakens the typological

forty nights in the desert,[11] and messianic forerunners in the first century were to fulfill the words of Hosea (2:16-17) and Ezekiel (20:35-36) by bringing the Jews into the wilderness in preparation for redemption.[12] Finally, the rabbis inform us that in light of God's promise that He will give us joy in accordance with the duration of our suffering (Ps. 90:15), the messianic age will endure as long as the forty-year sojourn in the desert or the four-hundred-year period of the Egyptian exile.[13]

While the significance of typology in Jewish messianism is beyond question, there are several areas where its role has been inadequately appreciated, and a reexamination of three controversial messianic topics through the prism of typology will, I think, yield valuable and intriguing results.

I

The messianic precursor from the tribe of Ephraim who goes by the name Messiah son of Joseph is an anomalous figure who has properly aroused intense scholarly interest. In the most common scenario, he fights the enemies of Israel with considerable success, only to fall on the field of battle shortly before the triumphant advent of Messiah son of David. No such figure makes anything resembling a clear appearance in the Hebrew Bible, and since a dying Messiah is both inherently mysterious and superficially related to Christian belief, unremitting efforts to trace his origins have produced an abundance of diverse and creative theories.

A recent article by Joseph Heinemann proposing a revolutionary reinterpretation of this redeemer begins with an excellent summary and evaluation of the major theories, and the interested reader can consult this compact and convenient analysis.[14] One of these theories, which

interpretation.
[11] Matt. 4:2. This, of course, is a miracle, but not a redemptive one.
[12] *Antiquities* 20.8.6; *War* 2.13.4. On the typology of Moses, see Teeple, *Mosaic Eschatological Prophet,* passim; S. Isser, *The Dositheans: A Samaritan Sect in Late Antiquity* (Leiden, 1976), pp. 131-142; Vermes, *Jesus the Jew,* pp. 97-98, and esp. his references in n. 61.
[13] B. *Sanhedrin* 99a; *Pesikta Rabbati* 1, p. 4a.
[14] "The Messiah of Ephraim and the Premature Exodus of the Tribe of Ephraim," *Harvard Theological Review* 68 (1975): 1-16. A Hebrew version of the article had appeared in *Tarbiz* 40 (1971): 450-461, and has been reprinted in Heinemann's *Aggadot ve-Toldoteihen* (Jerusalem, 1974), pp. 131-141. References here will be to the version in

Heinemann (along with most other scholars) rejects, is a typological one suggested long ago by Louis Ginzberg. The rabbis, Ginzberg noted, believed that the tribe of Ephraim had left Egyptian bondage for the land of Israel before the appointed hour, and the Ephraimites' efforts at military conquest had ended in death on the field of battle. Since the ultimate recapitulation of the first redemption is at the very heart of rabbinic messianism, such an event could not go unreflected at the end of days; hence, there will arise an Ephraimite Messiah whose early struggle for redemption will end in death at the hands of the enemies of Israel.[15]

The essential argument against this extremely attractive proposal was made by Viktor Aptowitzer and is endorsed by Heinemann. The Ephraimite exodus, Aptowitzer wrote, was a "sinful undertaking" because of its effort to effect a premature redemption, and messianic parallels are to miracles, "not sacrilegious undertakings, not catastrophes."[16] In Heinemann's paraphrase, "The technique of 'analogy' is applied only to miracles and the like, not to events given a negative evaluation."[17] Finally, the sources demonstrate no negative attitude toward Messiah son of Joseph, who, unlike the Ephraimites, is far from a total failure.

Let us leave this explanation for the moment and proceed to an examination of the core of Heinemann's article, which will inadvertently lead us toward a reaffirmation of Ginzberg's typological interpretation. Heinemann's striking thesis is that the story of Messiah son of Joseph did not originally envision his tragic death; on the contrary, this Messiah was a successful warrior hero whose genesis requires no special explanation in light of the proliferation of messianic figures in this period (Elijah-Phineas, Melchizedek, and the Priestly Messiah of the Dead Sea Scrolls and the *Testaments of the Twelve Patriarchs*). Even though the earliest datable discussion of Messiah son of Joseph refers to his death,[18] the

---

HTR, where the summary of earlier theories appears on pp. 1-6.

15 Ginzberg, *Sekte*, pp. 336-339 = *MGWJ*, pp. 414-417 = *Sect*, pp. 235-238. The rabbinic sources about the Ephraimites are noted by Ginzberg and discussed by Heinemann, "Messiah of Ephraim," pp. 10-13.

16 *Parteipolitik der Hasmonäerzeit im Rabbinischen und Pseudoepigraphischen Schrifttum* (Vienna and New York, 1927), p. 107.

17 "Messiah of Ephraim," p. 4. In the Hebrew, "and the like" was the stronger "and acts of salvation" (ומעשי ישועה), which reflects Aptowitzer's assertion more closely. Whether neutral acts, which are neither redemptive nor sinful, would be recapitulated is left ambiguous.

18 The second reference in B. *Sukkah* 52a. On the problems of dating the earlier reference

original form of the story is preserved in those later Midrashim which make no such reference. This follows from two considerations. First, "if the death in battle of the Messiah son of Joseph was a generally accepted doctrine, it is quite inconceivable that a good many of the sources should ignore it; this is not the sort of 'detail' which may accidentally be omitted." Second, some of those sources speak of this Messiah as a victorious redeemer. The failure of scholars to notice the absence of the death motif results from "a kind of 'optical illusion' which makes one see what is said explicitly in some of the sources also in the ones which know nothing of it."[19]

Since the death of Messiah son of Joseph could not have been ignored once it was known, it follows that although the passages oblivious of his death are embedded in later sources, they must predate the second-century source which knows that he will die. The question now becomes not where Messiah son of Joseph comes from but what it was in the second century C.E. that brought about the motif of his death. To this Heinemann replies: the Bar Kokhba experience. Disappointed Jews attempted to retain faith in some sort of messianic role for their slain leader, and so they associated him with the heroic Messiah son of Joseph, now transformed into a tragic hero who will fall in battle.

At the same time, Heinemann argues, another, unrelated legend was undergoing a radical metamorphosis. The *Mekhilta* in *Beshallah* regards the Ephraimites who left Egypt prematurely as arrogant rebels who "kept not the covenant of God and refused to walk in his law" (Ps. 78:10); other sources, however, regard them as victims of an error in calculation, not apparently as sinners, while one source, which identifies them with the dead resurrected by Ezekiel, must surely consider them "essentially righteous men."[20]

The generation of Bar Kokhba, Heinemann says, cannot have been responsible for a story that reflects "complacent, righteous condemnation" of people who attempt to hasten redemption, with all that such condemnation would imply about so many members of that generation,

on that page, see J. Klausner, *Ha-Ra'ayon ha-Meshihi be-Yisrael* (Jerusalem, 1927), pp. 318-319.

[19] Heinemann, "Messiah of Ephraim," pp. 6-8.

[20] Ibid., pp. 10-13. Heinemann attributes special significance to this last source (B. *Sanhedrin* 92b and elsewhere); I have downplayed it somewhat for a reason that will soon become evident.

including R. Akiva. Thus, the uncompromisingly negative attitude must have preceded the Bar Kokhba experience, while those who shared that experience transformed the old view of the Ephraimites and regarded them as victims of an error or even as tragic heroes. Finally, Heinemann suggests that because the Ephraimite exodus came to be associated with contemporary events, Bar Kokhba himself became connected with that tribe and was ultimately identified with the old, newly transformed figure of Messiah son of Joseph.

This is a stimulating, often brilliant article which is nonetheless only partly persuasive. The revolutionary thesis about Messiah son of Joseph stands or falls on a single assertion: sources that speak of him as a successful, redeeming warrior without mentioning his death cannot have known of that death. To sustain Heinemann's thesis, this assertion must be more than plausible; it must have the overwhelming force necessary to compel a rearrangement of the chronological order of the sources at our disposal by dating the relevant material in the later Midrashim before the tannaitic statement about this Messiah's death. To make matters worse, the tannaitic source refers to his death in a matter-of-fact fashion as something which is apparently common knowledge.[21]

Moreover, Heinemann must concede that the later rabbis who "faithfully transmit" what he considers "the older version ... must already have been aware of the new conception of the death of Messiah ben Ephraim."[22] In short, they too were presumably victimized by the same optical illusion that has afflicted modern scholars. Though the point is not decisive, it is worth noting that the later apocalyptic Midrashim explicitly describe an often victorious Messiah son of Joseph who is nevertheless killed before the final redemption and almost immediately resurrected by Messiah son of David.

Most important, the psychological process by which a messianic warrior who will be killed nevertheless comes to be described as a conquering hero seems perfectly understandable. Whatever the origins of such a figure, Messiah son of Joseph is after all a Jew fighting the forces of evil at the dawn of the messianic age. How could the Jewish messianic imagination fail to hope for his success? And, of course, it need

---

21   "When [Messiah son of David] saw that Messiah son of Joseph was killed, he said before God, 'Master of the Universe, I ask you only for life'" (B. *Sukkah* 52a). The point was made by Klausner, *Ha-Ra'ayon ha-Meshihi be-Yisrael*, p. 318.

22   "Messiah of Ephraim," p. 8, n. 31.

hardly be said that the desires of the messianic imagination do not go unfulfilled in the texts that we are examining. A Messiah son of Joseph whose *raison d'être* is to fight and die would nonetheless be transformed almost inevitably into precisely the warrior hero that confronts us in the Midrashim that Heinemann cites. If everyone knew that this Messiah would die — and the chronological order of our sources gives us every reason to think that this is so — then there is no need to mention this in each story of his exploits; the "optical illusion" of modern scholars may well have been the reality of the third-, fourth-, and fifth-century reader. Finally, I would not even rule out the possibility that someone caught up in the triumphs of Messiah son of Joseph might have come to believe that his death in battle is only one possible outcome and that sufficient merit might render it avoidable.[23] Whether or not this is so, Heinemann has allowed a brilliant but speculative reconstruction to overpower the extant progression of sources.

On the other hand, Heinemann's insightful discussion of the Ephraimite story is, with one important exception, thoroughly persuasive. The supposed wickedness of anyone who hastened the end would simply have to be rethought in the wake of the Bar Kokhba revolt;[24] even if the messianic pretender could be considered a villain, his renowned rabbinic supporter could not. Unfortunately, Heinemann's direct evidence for a positive evaluation of the Ephraimites will not do. As my former student David Strauss has pointed out, the same page of the Talmud which records the view that Ezekiel resurrected the Ephraimites also reports other identifications of these revived "dry bones": they are those who denied the resurrection, those who have no enthusiasm for the commandments, or those who covered the Temple with abominations. Nevertheless, the basic point remains; for most Jews in the mid-second century, the Ephraimites were not and could not have been sinners.

If we now step back and look at the broader picture, we suddenly discover that something very interesting has happened. Heinemann has unwittingly refuted the centerpiece of Aptowitzer's argument against Ginzberg. If the Ephraimites are not sinners, then the typological explanation of Messiah son of Joseph no longer involves the recapitulation

---

[23]   Precisely this conviction is attested in sources from a much later period; see M. Kasher, *Ha-Tekufah ha-Gedolah* (Jerusalem, 1969), pp. 428-431.

[24]   Though there are imperfections in the analogy, one cannot help but think of the Zionist reevaluation of the *ma'pilim* of Numbers 14:40-45 in Bialik's *Metei Midbar*.

of a "sinful, sacrilegious undertaking," and we have already seen abundant evidence that it is not only miracles that will be repeated at the end of days.[25] If there existed a favorable evaluation of the Ephraimites, the point would of course grow even stronger.

Because of the structure of his article, Heinemann was virtually precluded from recognizing the implications of his own argument. By the time he reached the discussion of the Ephraimites, he had already argued that Messiah son of Joseph did not originate as a dying Messiah; if this is true, then Ginzberg's thesis is automatically refuted and is no longer a live issue. Hence, Aptowitzer's argument, which Heinemann had endorsed earlier, is no longer relevant, and the destruction of its major premise can go unnoticed. However, if we reject the article's novel thesis about Messiah son of Joseph (as I think we should) and accept its observation about the Ephraimites (as we also should), the typological genesis of Messiah son of Joseph reemerges in all its considerable attractiveness.

If Ginzberg is correct, we should expect the first references to this Messiah to deal primarily with his death in battle without any heroic overtones; the Ephraimites, even to second-century Jews, were not necessarily great heroes. The glorious victories would result from a psychological process that we have already discussed and should make their appearance only as the story develops. Though we have only one certain source as early as the second century, it is at least interesting that it fulfills this expectation to perfection.[26] The typological explanation, which fits the central, established pattern of rabbinic messianic thinking, has unwittingly been rescued, and it deserves first place in any discussion of the origins of Messiah son of Joseph.[27]

---

25   See nn. 8-13 above and cf. n. 17.

26   See n. 21 above. The same can be said about the possibly tannaitic source a bit earlier in *Sukkah* 52a.

27   Let me make it clear that I consider Heinemann's point about the likely attitude toward the Ephraimites in the post-Bar Kokhba period to be extremely useful but not absolutely indispensable for a defense of Ginzberg. A weaker defense might maintain that a condemnatory and a neutral attitude toward the Ephraimites coexisted in the pre-Bar Kokhba period and that the latter (which saw them as mistaken calculators) produced the typological figure of Messiah son of Joseph. One might even regard the severe condemnation in the *Mekhilta* and elsewhere as a later development — a reaction to the Bar Kokhba revolt by one (minority) faction that was so concerned to prevent a repetition of this disaster that they were indifferent to· the implication for R. Akiva's reputation. Nevertheless, I agree with Heinemann to the extent that I cannot imagine this as a majority view. (For a new typological explanation that does not persuade me,

II

Whether or not the Ephraimites of the Aggadah are models for Messiah son of Joseph, they are surely the precursors of a long line of messianic calculators doomed to disappointment. In the rabbinic period, attitudes toward this seductive enterprise ranged from a famous curse against the calculators to a series of messianic dates, some of which appear on the same folio of the Talmud as the curse itself.[28] A careful examination of these dates will reveal once again the overwhelming impact of typology on Jewish messianic thought.

The destruction of the Second Temple inevitably inspired messianic calculation, and one obscure report tells us of three such calculations apparently referring to the period between the destruction and the Bar Kokhba revolt. The details, however, are too sketchy to facilitate a reconstruction of the precise dates except to say that the one ascribed to R. Akiva no doubt pointed to the 130s.[29]

Between the Bar Kokhba revolt and the end of the talmudic period, we have precisely five (or perhaps four) clear rabbinic statements concentrated on two pages of the Talmud indicating the year, or in one case the jubilee, in which the Messiah will come. (1) The world will last six thousand years: two thousand chaos, two thousand Torah, and two thousand the messianic age, though our sins have delayed the long-awaited hour.[30] (2) After the four hundredth year of the destruction of the Temple, if someone offers you a field worth a thousand dinars for just one, do not buy it.[31] (3) Do not buy it after the year 4231 A.M.[32] (4) After

see Raphael Patai's suggestion that Messiah son of Joseph dies because Moses died short of the promised land [*The Messiah Texts* (New York, 1979), introd., p. xxxiii].)

Shimon Toder's "Mashiah ben David u-Mashiah ben Yosef," *Mahanayim* 124 (1970): 100-112, came to my attention after this article was completed. Though it contains no reference to Ginzberg, it maintains the typological origin of Messiah son of Joseph and notes that the attitude toward the Ephraimites in the Aggadah is not uniformly negative.

28   B. *Sanhedrin* 97b. On rabbinic opposition to calculations, note the material assembled by A. H. Silver, *A History of Messianic Speculation in Israel* (Boston, 1959), pp. 195-206.

29   See the middle of B. *Sanhedrin* 97b, and note Klausner's emendation of R. Simlai to Rabbi Ishmael (*Ha-Ra'ayon ha-Meshihi*, p. 272).

30   B. *Sanhedrin* 97a-b; B. *Avodah Zarah* 9a.

31   B. *Avodah Zarah* 9b.

32   Ibid.

the year 4291 A.M. the world will enter a period of wars leading to the messianic age.[33] (5) Elijah informed a certain rabbi that the world would last no fewer than eighty-five jubilees, and in the last jubilee the Son of David would come. When asked whether the Messiah would arrive at the beginning or the end of the jubilee and whether or not the jubilee would be completed before his advent, Elijah confessed that he did not know.[34]

It has long been recognized that the first of these dates is dependent upon a typological scheme in which the six-thousand-year duration of the earth is derived from the six days of creation; since Abraham came upon the scene not far from the year 2000, another period of two thousand years until the Messiah seemed to make typological sense.[35] The typology of the second date is also blatant; the final exile will last precisely as long as the four-hundred-year Egyptian bondage (Gen. 15:13).[36]

The next date, however, is an enigma. The simplest solution was formulated most explicitly by P. Volz, who informs us matter-of-factly that 4231 is four hundred years after 3831, which is "the year of the destruction of the Temple according to the Israelite calendar."[37]

---

33   B. *Sanhedrin* 97b.

34   Ibid. Because of a misreading of three rabbinic passages dealing with the *duration* of the messianic age, Silver presents three other dates for the time of its advent; see his *Messianic Speculation*, pp. 19-20, #3 (and contrast his correct reading of analogous material on p. 14, #2), and pp. 25-26, #1 and 2. Silver's misreading was endorsed by Yehudah Even Shmuel, *Midreshei Ge'ullah* (Jerusalem and Tel Aviv, 1954), introd., p. 42; the proof-texts cited in these passages, however, rule out this interpretation. A rabbinic statement which could be considered typological describes Balaam's speeches as taking place at the midpoint of world history; though some medievals cited this as a messianic calculation (and the proof-text tends to support such a reading), it may tell us only when the world will end. See J. *Shabbat* 6:9, fol. 8d, and cf. A. Halkin's introduction to Maimonides' *Epistle to Yemen* (New York, 1952), p. xiii. For what may be another typological calculation with details unclear, see the last statement in section 21 of the introduction to *Eikhah Rabbati*.

35   Whatever Iranian influences may have affected this calculation (see the reference in E. Urbach, *Hazal: Pirkei Emunot ve-De'ot* [Jerusalem, 1969], pp. 610-611 = *The Sages: Their Concepts and Beliefs* [Jerusalem, 1975], p. 678) cannot be allowed to overshadow the straightforward relationship with the days of creation. Cf. the associated talmudic statement (B. *Sanhedrin* 97a) about a six-thousand-year period followed by a one-thousand-year "Sabbatical" destruction.

36   The discussion of this point in Neusner's *Messiah in Context*, p. 180, creates the impression that the only duration assigned to the sojourn in Egypt by Scripture is 430 years (Exod. 12:40).

37   *Die Eschatologie der jüdischen Gemeinde im neutestamentalichen Zeitalter* (Tübingen, 1934), p. 144.

The only trouble with this is that it isn't true. The rabbis dated the destruction in 3828,[38] and the Talmud explicitly notes that there is a three-year discrepancy between 4231 and the four hundredth year after the destruction.[39] Among the medievals, the tosafists maintained that 4231 was a majority of the eighty-fifth jubilee (apparently counting by decades), while Abravanel argued the same point, suggesting that the number was obtained by adding a sabbatical cycle of seven years to the midpoint of the eighty-fifth jubilee (4225 + 7 = 4232, and the Talmud, after all, speaks of the year *after* 4231).[40]

The fundamental basis of this date, however, may really be quite simple. It is, I think, a typological date identical with four hundred years after the destruction with a three-year delay resulting from a passage in the Book of Daniel. The basic period of exile is in fact the four hundred years of the very first exile; Daniel, however, specifically says that we shall have to wait 1290 or 1335 days, here taken as additional days (Dan. 12:11-12). Though most later calculators understood these days as years, there is a recurring midrash which unequivocally understands them as days which pass during the final messianic scenario.[41] Thus, Daniel 12:11,

---

38   Or 3829. See the Ba'al ha-Ma'or's comments on *Avodah Zarah* 9b (= fol. 2b of the Rif), s.v. *amar R. Huna*. In either case, the last official year of the Temple is considered 3828, and 3829 is the first year of destruction; hence, the four hundredth year remains 4228. The years 3828 and 3829 are 68 and 69 C.E. according to the current Jewish calendar; nevertheless, the common view that the rabbis misdated the destruction of 70 C.E. by one or two years is mistaken, because their calendar differed by a year or two from the one that became standard among medieval Jews. See the Ba'al ha-Ma'or, loc. cit., and E. Frank, *Talmudic and Rabbinical Chronology* (New York, 1956). This affects other rabbinic dates as well and means, for example, that the eighty-fifth jubilee is not 441-490 C.E., as scholars routinely indicate, but 442-491 or 443-492.

39   Silver, *Messianic Speculation* (p. 26), apparently oblivious of the Talmud's comment, also considers 4231 as the four hundredth year of the destruction, since in the current Jewish calendar it is "c. [this little letter deserves notice] 470 C.E." In a puzzling passage, Urbach cites the talmudic remark about a three-year discrepancy between the four hundredth year and 4231, and in the first sentence of text following this footnote says that 4231 is identical with that year (*Hazal*, p. 613 = *Sages*, p. 682). Perhaps he is tacitly suggesting a new understanding of the talmudic statement which would take it to mean that there is a three-year difference in calculating the four hundredth year; he does not, however, say this explicitly, and it is not, in my view, a tenable reading of the passage.

40   *Tosafot Avodah Zarah* 9b, s.v. *le-ahar*; Isaac Abravanel, *Yeshu'ot Meshiho*, 1812, p. 10b. Abravanel explains 4228 (= 400 years after the destruction) in a similar fashion as a majority of the eighty-fifth jubilee in sabbatical units. (A typographical error in this edition of *Yeshu'ot Meshiho* has changed רכ"ח into רנ"ח.)

41   See the references in n. 8. The discrepancy between 1290 and 1335 determines that the

which reads, "From the time that the continual burnt-offering shall be taken away [*me'et husar ha-tamid*] and the abomination of desolation is set up, there shall be a thousand two hundred and ninety days," *must* mean that from the end of the period of exile inaugurated by the removal of the burnt-offering there shall be an additional 1290 days culminating in some important event. Then, forty-five more days will pass, reaching a total of 1335. Since the period of exile is four hundred years, waiting an additional 1290 or 1335 days adds three and a half years and leads to the conclusion that the Messiah will come just after the year 4231. In sum, this date also reflects the typology of the Egyptian exile; indeed, the *'et* of Daniel 12:11 refers specifically to this period of time. The extra three years are simply an appendage forced upon us by the Book of Daniel.[42]

Our fourth date (4291) can be dealt with quickly. Since I cannot explain it, and since the Hebrew abbreviations for 4231 (רל"א) and 4291 (רצ"א) can easily be confused, I am prepared to follow the lead of the Gaon of Vilna and emend it to 4231.[43] If this is correct, then there is nothing

Messiah will be hidden forty-five days. Though Rashi on Dan. 12:12 understandably interprets this midrash as a reference to forty-five years, its plain meaning resists such an interpretation. For forty-five days, not years, in this context, see also the apocalyptic midrashim in Even Shmuel, *Midreshei Ge'ullah*, pp. 43, 81, 104, 195. Some of the apocalypses also take the reference to "time, times, and half a time" in Dan. 7:25 and 12:7 in the literal sense of three and a half years; see *Midreshei Ge'ullah*, pp. 103 and 470, and R. Bonfil's plausible suggestion in his "'Hazon Daniel' ki-Te'udah Historit ve-Sifrutit," *Sefer Zikkaron le-Yizhak Baer* (= *Zion* 44 [1979]), p. 146.

It should also be noted that had the rabbis taken these days as years, they would have been forced to delay the redemption unbearably. Indeed, their failure to use Daniel as an important basis for calculations may result precisely from the fact that they regarded the numbers there as references to events taking place within the final messianic process; such numbers cannot be useful in predicting when the process itself will begin.

42 Even Shmuel maintains, as I do, that the number 4231 is also based on the four-hundred-year period of exile, but he accounts for the three-year delay by a rather uncomfortable expedient. He argues that what begins after 4228 is the seven-year period during which the Messiah will come; and "after three years of this seven-year period have elapsed, normal life cannot continue" (*Midreshei Ge'ullah*, introd., p. 45).

43 So too Silver, *Messianic Speculation*, p. 26, and Urbach, *Hazal*, p. 613 = *Sages*, p. 682. Though I remain skeptical, it is worth recording a characteristically brilliant explanation proposed by Gerson Cohen when I was his student at Columbia; 4291, he suggested, may constitute a sabbatical unit of years for each commandment (613 × 7). An elaborate but unpersuasive effort to account for this date was made by Even Shmuel in his introduction to *Midreshei Ge'ullah*, p. 46. The setting up of the abomination of desolation in Daniel 12: 11, he says, must have been taken as the establishment of the city of Rome, and from that point we must wait 1290 days (= years). The traditional date of the founding of Rome is 753 B.C.E., and this corresponds to 3008 A.M. (Even

to explain, and our five rabbinic dates are transformed into four.

Finally, we reach the most intractable date of all. One approach to the mysterious eighty-fifth jubilee (4201-4250 A.M.) is to regard it as a period so rife with potential messianic dates that it was a convenient way to subsume them all. Even Shmuel points to a Roman tradition predicting the end of the empire twelve hundred years after the founding of the city. This brings us to a point approximately seven years after the beginning of the crucial jubilee, and by subtracting the oft-mentioned seven-year period of the messianic advent, we can reach its starting point. Since no Jewish source mentions this Roman tradition, however, we would do well to remain skeptical. More to the point, Even Shmuel notes not only that 4228 and 4231 fall within the jubilee but that a typological calculation assigning to the exile a duration equal to that of the First or Second Temple (410 and 420 years respectively according to rabbinic chronology) would also culminate in the eighty-fifth jubilee.[44] It may

Shmuel [p. 54, n. 49] regarded this Hebrew equivalent, given in a late Jewish source, as approximate. In fact, it is precise; since there was no year zero, the Hebrew year 3000 = 761 B.C.E., even though the more familiar year 4000 = 240 C.E.) 3008 + 1290 = 4298, when Rome will fall. But the rabbis often spoke of the seven-year period in which the Messiah will come, and that period will therefore begin in 4291. This is ingenious, but aside from the fact that we have no early evidence that Jews used or knew the date 3008 as the beginning of Rome (cf. the end of n. 74 below), the reference in Daniel 12:11 to the removal of the burnt-offering, which can have no association with the date of the founding of Rome, would appear to make Even Shmuel's proposal impossible.

[44] *Midreshei Ge'ullah*, introd., pp. 45-46. Baron's summary of Even Shmuel (*A Social and Religious History of the Jews*, vol. 5 [New York, London, and Philadelphia, 1957], p. 366, n. 28) can leave the impression that this typological reasoning about the Temples is actually attested in the ancient sources. For such a calculation in the Middle Ages, see Nahmanides, *Sefer ha-Ge'ullah*, in Ch. D. Chavel, *Kitvei Ramban*, vol. 1 (Jerusalem, 1963), p. 294, citing debatable evidence from section 21 of the introduction to *Eikhah Rabbati*.

Moshe Ber suggested that the messianic hopes associated with this jubilee may have been connected with the problems of Babylonian Jewry at the time; see *Sinai* 48 (1961): 299-302. On this talmudic passage, cf. also I. Levi's note in *Revue des Études Juives* 1 (1880): 110. Urbach (*Hazal*, p. 612 = *Sages*, p. 680) may have a point in stressing Elijah's uncertainty about the precise year of redemption, but that surely does not mean that there is no messianic calculation here. This explicit uncertainty, however, does have an important corollary: it prevents us from assuming that the Talmud has in mind only the last year of the jubilee, despite the fact that the Testament of Moses (1:2 and 10:12) appears to point to the year 4250 A.M. as the year of redemption. The connection of that text to our talmudic passage was already made by R. H. Charles, *The Apocrypha and Pseudepigrapha of the Old Testament* (Oxford, 1913), 2:423, and was repeated by E. S. Artom in his commentary to 10:12 (*Ha-Sefarim ha-Hizzonim: Sippurei Aggadah*, vol. 1 [Tel Aviv, 1965]) and by S. B. Hoenig, "Dor she-Ben David Ba," *Sefer Zikkaron li-Shmuel Belkin* (New York, 1981), p. 142.

well be that this approach is correct, but since the only persuasive dates (which are all typological) fall in the second half of the jubilee, and since this would then be the only calculation which in effect gives us a choice of calculations, it seems preferable to search for an explanation that would account for the number eighty-five jubilees itself.

There have been, as far as I know, only two efforts to accomplish this. In the Middle Ages, Abravanel made the striking suggestion that the number is derived from the eighty-five letters in Numbers 10:35-36; these verses constitute a separate biblical book according to the rabbis, they are enclosed by two reversed *nuns* (a letter with the numerical value of fifty in Hebrew), the Mishnah makes special reference to these eighty-five letters in a legal context (M. *Yadayim* 3:5), and, Abravanel might have added, the content of the passage deals with the dispersal of the enemies of God.[45] One can only admire the ingenuity of this proposal, but the connection with the messianic age remains tenuous at best. Much more recently, Even Shmuel advanced the conjecture that messianic calculators may have cited the verse "Hitherto *[ad po]* shall you come, but no further" (Job 38:11) in light of the fact that the numerical value of *po* is eighty-five. Nevertheless, he apparently means only that the date may have been further validated, not originated, by this numerical equivalence, which appears in a verse that has no redemptive context and no connection with jubilees.[46]

In the absence of any satisfactory explanation of this number, it may be worthwhile to introduce a new, highly speculative typological suggestion. King David, and hence the final redeemer, had only one distinguished ancestor at the time of the first conquest of the land of Israel, which was, of course, the culmination of the first redemption. The rabbis inform us that no less a figure than Caleb, who was the prince of the tribe of Judah, was a forefather of David.[47] The typologically oriented messianist would almost inevitably look at Caleb as a possible prototype of the final redeemer or at least as a source of information about the final redemption.

As the conquest of the land reaches its completion, Caleb tells Joshua,

---

[45] *Yeshu'ot Meshiho*, p. 12a.

[46] *Midreshei Ge'ullah*, introd., p. 46. Once again, Baron's summary *(History*, 5:167) can leave the impression that this is more than a conjecture.

[47] B. *Sotah* 11b; *Sifrei* Numbers 78, Friedmann's ed., p. 19b. There seems, however, no alternative to the conclusion of the Maharsha *(Sotah* ad loc.) that the Talmud is referring to descent through one of David's female ancestors.

"I was forty years old when Moses sent me to explore the land, and I brought back an honest report. ... Moses swore an oath that day and said, 'The land on which you have set foot shall be your patrimony.' ... It is now forty-five years since God made this promise to Moses, at the time when Israel was journeying in the wilderness, and today I am eighty-five years old" (Josh. 14:7-10).

Consider the following. First, the passage contains unusual, apparently unnecessary emphasis on Caleb's age, even in light of the next verse, which tells us how his strength has remained unchanged; if forty-five years have passed, of course he is now eighty-five years old. Second, the number forty is strikingly suggestive and could have drawn the attention of a numerologically oriented reader all by itself. Can it be a coincidence that Caleb was forty years old when the decree of a forty-year exile in the desert was issued, and can it be that Scripture tells us this merely to satisfy our idle curiosity? If his age at the time of the exile reflects the length of that exile, might not his age at the time of redemption, which we have been told in such a verbose and striking way, contain information about the time of redemption? Finally — and this is what removes this suggestion from the realm of sheer speculation — the Talmud informs us that the conversation between Caleb and Joshua took place close to the time when Jews began to count jubilees, and that the numbers in these verses are there to enable us to calculate precisely when the count began.[48] The rabbis, in other words, explicitly connect jubilees with this number eighty-five, and a messianic calculator may well have asked himself whether the connection is more than just exoteric.

If this is correct, then all messianic dates in rabbinic literature pointing to the post-Bar Kokhba period result from typological reasoning. The first is based on the typology of the days of creation, the next two on the typology of the first exile and its four-hundred-year duration, and the fourth on the typology of a redemptive figure, an ancestor of the final redeemer, and his age at the culmination of the initial redemption.[49]

---

[48] B. *Arakhin* 13a. I have formulated this sentence fairly strongly in light of what I think is the correct observation at the end of *Tosafot* ad loc., s.v. Caleb.

[49] Finally — a reminder that if my speculation about Caleb is rejected, the most reasonable explanation of the eighty-fifth jubilee remains the proliferation of messianic dates within that fifty-year period, and every one of those dates is typological. Needless to say, this proliferation of dates could have enhanced the suggestiveness of the passage in Joshua as well.

III

The eschatological monster with the mysterious name Armilus has long fascinated students of early medieval apocalyptic. Born of a union between Satan and a beautiful statue, this final ruler of Rome-Edom will kill the Messiah son of Joseph only to fall victim to the ultimate, Davidic redeemer. Bald and with a leprous forehead, with one small eye and one large one, his right arm grotesquely short and his left unnaturally long, his left ear open and his right ear closed, Armilus is a figure of menacing terror.[50]

Since there is general agreement that the two references in the Targumim may well be later additions,[51] Armilus makes his first datable appearance in the third and fourth decades of the seventh century. Whatever the relevance of a few enigmatic terms in *Sefer Eliyyahu* and *Perek Eliyyahu,*[52] Armilus appears as a major actor in the eschatological drama in the Hebrew apocalypse *Sefer Zerubbavel* (ca. 628)[53] and is mentioned as a matter of course in several sections of the Greek polemic *Doctrina Jacobi Nuper Baptizati* (ca. 634).[54]

While the notion of a monstrous final ruler of Rome could have arisen directly from Daniel 7:7-8, 23-25 in conjunction with Ezekiel 38-39, it is especially likely that the Jewish apocalyptic imagination was inspired by the elaborate Christian descriptions of Antichrist as an evil Roman emperor, often taking the form of Nero *redivivus.*[55] The Christianization of the Roman Empire created an ambivalence which required Christians to envision the defeat of this monstrous figure by a good Roman emperor

---

[50]   While none of the sources portrays Armilus as Prince Charming, I have reproduced one of the most elaborate descriptions from *Midrash va-Yosha', Midreshei Ge'ullah*, p. 96. See also pp. 79, 131, 136, 320. For an English translation of some of the Armilus texts, see Patai, *Messiah Texts*, pp. 156-164.

[51]   Pseudo-Jonathan to Deut. 34:3, Isa. 11:4. Cf. A. Kohut, *Arukh ha-Shalem* (Vienna, 1878), p. 292.

[52]   For הרמלת, תרמילא, and תרמלת, see Even Shmuel, *Midreshei Ge'ullah*, pp. 42 and 51, and cf. his discussion on pp. 34-35, n. 12, 18.

[53]   Ibid., pp. 74, 79-83.

[54]   Διδασκαλία Ιακώβου Νεοβαπτίστου, ed. N. Bonwetsch, *Abhandlungen der Königlichen Gesellschaft der Wissenschaften zu Göttingen*, phil.-hist. Klasse, n.f., vol. 12, no. 3 (Berlin, 1910), pp. 4-5, 66, 70-71, 86, and more.

[55]   See W. Bousset, *The antichrist Legend* (London, 1896); J. Berger, *Die griechische Daniel Exegese — Eine altkirchliche Apokalypse* (Leiden, 1976), pp. 103-150. I see no persuasive evidence that the Christian conception comes from earlier Jewish sources (other than Daniel itself).

who is the major agent of redemption.[56] Jews, however, were under no such constraints. A single, Satanic ruler was all that Rome would produce in its final days, and stories of such a figure could be assimilated, reworked, and expanded without any of the usual inhibitions about the adoption of Christian legends; indeed, the myth was even more congenial to Jews, whose hatred of Rome was unalloyed and whose hope for its destruction was untainted by ambivalence.

The name Armilus, however, is neither biblical nor talmudic nor Christian, and its origin and meaning cry out for explanation. Ideally, such an explanation should be more than an etymology; it should tell us something more about the ideas generating the concept and may help us place it in the typological framework which is the hallmark of Jewish messianism in this period. No such understanding is achieved by Hitzig's curious suggestion that the similarities between Suetonius' description of the *armillatus* Caligula and *Sefer Zerubbavel's* depiction of Armilus mean that our monster received his name from Caligula's bracelet.[57] Such a derivation concentrates on a triviality and has justly been ignored.

Another explanation, however, which has deservedly received more serious attention, suffers from a similar, though less acute problem. Several scholars have regarded Armilus as a corruption of the name of the evil Persian deity Ahriman or Angro-Mainyus.[58] This derivation reinforces a certain sense of the exotic produced by the Armilus legend, but it evokes no specific associations with the story, nor is the similarity in the names particularly satisfying. More important, a Persian god would not have produced the resonance necessary for this figure and this name to have flourished within the Jewish messianic tradition. Ahriman strikes no familiar chord, and only in the absence of an alternative explanation should we be willing to assume that so alien a villain would find a home as a standard figure in the mainstream of Jewish messianism. But we have an alternative explanation. The problem, in fact, is that we have one too many.

---

[56] For brief summaries, see M. Reeves, *The Influence of Prophecy in the Later Middle Ages* (Oxford, 1969), pp. 299-301, and N. Cohn, *The Pursuit of the Millennium,* 2d ed. (New York, 1970), pp. 31-34. Cf. also I. Levi, "L'Apocalypse de Zorobabel et le roi de Perses Siroès," *Revue des Études Juives* 71 (1920): 59-61.

[57] F. Hitzig, *Das Buch Daniel* (Leipzig, 1850), p. 125.

[58] K. Kohler in *Jewish Encyclopedia* 1:296-297, s.v. Ahriman; Kohut in *Arukh ha-Shalem,* loc. cit., and esp. in his *Über die Jüdische Angelologie und Daemonologie in Ihrer Abhängigkeit vom Parsismus* (Leipzig, 1866), p. 62. Kohler emphasized the *gimel* in the ארמלגוס of the Targumim (see n. 51 above).

The name Armilus has not inspired much recent controversy because one derivation has carried the day to the point where the question is generally considered resolved. Scholars might sometimes go through the motions of citing earlier theories, but the prevailing attitude appears to be that this problem is behind us. Armilus is Romulus.[59]

Now this really is an attractive identification, even more attractive than is generally realized. It is not merely that Romulus founded and hence symbolizes Rome,[60] which is the empire that Armilus will rule. The Romulus identification recalls the central theme of messianic typology, in which an early figure or event recurs at the end of days. If the final redeemer will be like the first redeemer, so will the final king of Rome be like its founder. The logic of messianic reasoning led inexorably to such a notion, and it may even be that historical events provided reinforcement to the seventh-century observer. The Western Roman Empire had, after all, already fallen, and it could hardly be coincidence that the name of its final ruler was Romulus.[61]

As far as linguistic similarity is concerned, we face no serious problem. Romulus and Armilus are more than close enough to sustain the identification, and Armilus' Greek name, Ermolaos, which appears in one Hebrew apocalypse as ארמילאוס and which we shall discuss in a moment, is virtually identical with a Syriac form of Romulus (ארמלאוס) that was noted long ago by Nöldeke.[62] To clinch the argument, we even have a late-seventh-century source which makes the identification explicit. The Latin translation (though not the Greek text) of pseudo-Methodius informs us matter-of-factly that Romulus is Armaleus.[63]

---

59 See, e.g., E. Schürer, *Geschichte des Jüdischen Volkes im Zeitalter Jesu Christi* (Leipzig, 1907), II, pp. 621-622; Klausner in *Ha-Ra'ayon ha-Meshihi*, p. 232, and in *Enziklopedyah Ivrit*, 5:954-957; Levi, "Apocalypse de Zorobabel," p. 59; M. Guttmann in the German *Encyclopaedia Judaica* 3:364-366; Baron, *History*, 5:145; J. Dan, *Ha-Sippur ha-'Ivri bi-Yemei ha-Beinayim: Iyyunim be-Toledotav* (Jerusalem, 1974), p. 42.

60 Cf. Klausner, *Ha-Ra'ayon ha-Meshihi*, loc. cit.

61 Since Romulus Augustulus had at least one competitor for his dubious distinction, and since a seventh-century resident of the Eastern Roman Empire may not have shared the perception that the Western Empire had "fallen," we should perhaps be cautious about pressing this point too hard.

62 *Zeitschrift der Deutschen-Morgenländischen Gesellschaft* 39 (1895): 343.

63 Ernst Sackur, *Sibyllinische Texte und Forschungen* (Halle, 1898), p. 76. The pseudo-Methodian passage was noted by Bousset (*Antichrist Legend*, p. 105), Levi (loc. cit.), and others.

The only trouble with all this is that another, widely rejected derivation is at least as attractive as this one. It has been recognized for centuries that Armilus may be the Greek Eremolaos (Ἐρημόλαος), meaning "destroyer of a people"; the possibility, in fact, is almost forced upon us by the ארמיליאוס of *Nistarot de-Rabbi Shimon bar Yohai*[64] and the Hermolaos or Ermolaos routinely used in *Doctrina Jacobi*. The definition of Armilus in Menahem de Lonzano's early-seventeenth-century dictionary reads as follows: "This means 'destroyer of a nation.' It is a Greek word compounded from *ereme,* meaning 'destroy,' and *laos,* meaning 'a nation'; it refers to an Edomite king who will win a major victory against his enemies and destroy them and who will consequently be called Eremolaos."[65] As in the case of the Romulus identification, this approach is confirmed by a very early source — in this instance by one manuscript of *Sefer Zerubbavel* itself, which tells us that Armilus means "destroyer of a nation" in Greek.[66]

Despite these early references, it was not, as far as I know, until Graetz that the real significance of this derivation was noticed. Armilus, Graetz argued, is none other than a new Balaam, the archenemy who had tried to destroy the Jews, and whose name, according to the Talmud, means "destroyer of a people" (בלע עם = בלעם).[67] Eremolaos, he says, "is a felicitous Greek reproduction of the biblical archetype of enmity toward Israel."[68] Armilus as *eremolaos* (often without reference to Balaam) has received only the most perfunctory comment by twentieth-century scholars; those who mention the derivation at all tend to reject it summarily and virtually without discussion. Klausner's comment is

---

[64]   Even Shmuel, *Midreshei Ge'ullah,* p. 195.

[65]   *Ma'arikh,* ed. by A. Jellinek (Leipzig, 1853), p. 15.

[66]   I. Levi, *Revue des Études Juives* 68 (1914): 136 = *Midreshei Ge'ullah,* p. 387. The text of the passage is slightly corrupt, but however we emend it (see Levi's note on p. 152), it clearly says that Armilus means יחריב עם. Levi notes other early scholars who proposed this translation, and cf. also the citation from David de Lara's *Keter Kehunnah* in Kohut's *Arukh ha-Shalem,* p. 292.

[67]   B. *Sanhedrin* 105a.

[68]   "Eine *glückliche* griechische Nachbildung des biblischen Urtypus der Feindseligkeit gegen Israel" (my translation). See *Jahrbuch für Israeliten* 5265 [1864/65], ed. by J. Wertheimer and L. Kompert (Vienna, 1865), p. 19. The essay has recently been translated into English by I. Schorsch in H. Graetz, *The Structure of Jewish History and Other Essays* (New York, 1975), pp. 151-171 (notes on p. 310). Cf. also J. Levy, *Chaldäisches Wörterbuch über die Targumim und einen grossen Theil des Rabbinischen Schrifttums* (Leipzig, 1881), 1:66, s.v. Armilus.

among the most extensive: "And the suggestion that Armilus comes from the Greek *eremolaos* is especially farfetched despite the fact that it is already noted in [one manuscript of *Sefer Zerubbavel*]."[69]

It hardly seems necessary to say that modern conceptions of what is or is not farfetched do not serve as trustworthy guidelines for penetrating the early medieval apocalyptic imagination. We have already seen that Eremolaos, like Romulus, is associated with Armilus in an early source and that both derivations are linguistically appropriate and attractive. Typologically, Romulus provides the return of the first king of Rome; Balaam-Eremolaos provides the return of the archenemy of the first redeemer.[70] In light of the frequent stress on the similarities between the first and last redeemers, the Balaam derivation may well be the more attractive in this respect. Finally, there are even some concrete resemblances between Balaam and Armilus. The physical asymmetry of the monstrous king of Edom reflects the talmudic description of a Balaam who was blind in one eye and lame in one foot,[71] while Armilus' construction of seven altars in *Sefer Zerubbavel* is a transparent reminiscence of the seven altars built by Balak at Balaam's behest.[72]

These considerations force a reassessment of the regnant Romulus derivation, not because of any deficiency in that explanation, but because of the persuasiveness of an alternative. Like Buridan's ass, we are apparently condemned to eternal indecision in the face of two equally attractive options.

In fact, however, a single observation dissolves the problem and presents us with a richer and more fully persuasive picture of the mysterious figure of Armilus. Balaam *is* Romulus!

There is nothing esoteric or inordinately complex in this identification. To the seventh-century Jew steeped in midrashic lore, Balaam was Romulus not by some stretch of the exegetical imagination but as a simple matter of fact. Romulus, of course, was the first king of Rome, and the

---

69   *Enziklopedyah Ivrit* 5:955. All reference to the *eremolaos* derivation was dropped from the abridged English translation of Klausner's article in the recent *Encyclopaedia Judaica*. (Why is an article on a Jewish theme that appears in a general encyclopedia abridged when it is transferred to a Jewish encyclopedia?) Cf. also the brief references to this explanation in Schürer and Guttmann, loc. cit. (see n. 59 above).

70   On the frequent midrashic contrast between Balaam and Moses, see the references in Ginzberg, *Legends*, 6:125, n. 727.

71   B. *Sanhedrin* 105a and *Sotah* 10a; for Armilus, cf. n. 50 above.

72   Num. 23:29-30. Cf. Even Shmuel's note in *Midreshei Ge'ullah*, p. 82.

identification of Rome and Edom was the most basic commonplace. But the Bible informs us that the first king of Edom was Bela the son of Beor (Gen. 36:32; I Chron. 1:43), and some Jews made the almost inevitable identification of this king with Balaam the son of Beor.[73] Hence, even without a linguistic correspondence, the Jewish apocalypticist knew that Balaam is the person whom the Gentiles call Romulus or Armaleus; the identification was confirmed beyond all question when he noticed that Armaleus (= Eremolaos) is a direct translation of Balaam's name. The name—and to some degree the figure—of Armilus was generated by an exceptionally powerful typological impetus: the first king of Edom, who was also the archenemy of the first redeemer, will return at the end of days as both the final king of Rome and the archenemy of the final redeemer.[74]

Thus far, we are on fairly firm ground, and I am tempted to end the argument at this point; nevertheless, understanding the messianic imagination virtually requires us to take the risk of more venturesome speculations. In an isolated footnote in the general introduction to *Midreshei Ge'ullah,* Even Shmuel made the following suggestion:

> Apparently, people tended to call Rome "Aram" because of Laban the Aramaean, the deceiver *(rammai),* who "sought to destroy everything," and because of the verse, "My father was a wandering Aramaean" (Deut. 26:5), which the midrash took as "An Aramaean [Laban] sought to destroy my father [Jacob]." In the time of the Palestinian Amoraim this name was grafted on to (Remus and) Romulus ..., and thus the name Armilus was born.[75]

Although I know of no evidence that Rome was called Aram, the Laban connection may be worth pursuing for reasons unmentioned by Even Shmuel. Laban the Aramaean, the *eremolaos* who attempted to destroy the patriarch whose very name was Israel, is another alias of

73 See the Targum to I Chron. 1:43 and the reference in Ginzberg, *Legends,* 5:323, n. 324.
74 In this context, I think that the argument that Romulus was the founder of the *city* of Rome, not all of Edom, and that Bela ben Beor's city was Dinhavah (Gen. and I Chron., loc. cit.) would be a quibble. There is an overwhelming likelihood that in the apocalyptic mentality, where Rome and Edom had merged into synonyms, Romulus would have been perceived as the first king—and symbol—of all of Edom. On the fluid midrashic tradition about the founding of the city, which ranged from the time of Esau's grandson Zepho to the time of Solomon, see Ginzberg, *Legends,* 5:372, n. 425, and 6:280, n. 11.
75 *Midreshei Ge'ullah,* introd., p. 51, n. 67. The midrash cited is best known for its appearance in the Passover Haggadah.

Balaam. The full text of the same Targum that identifies Balaam as the first king of Edom reads as follows: "And these are the kings who ruled in the land of Edom before any king ruled over the children of Israel: the evil Balaam son of Beor, that is, Laban the Aramaean, who united with the sons of Esau to do harm to Jacob and his sons and who sought to destroy them."[76]

We may have arrived, then, at a threefold interpretation of Armilus in which Romulus, Balaam (= Eremolaos), and Laban (the Arami) are identified with one another. Each is described as the first king of Edom, and the apocalypses may even have understood Laban's epithet "the Arami" as a term bearing the dual meaning of "Aramaean" and "destroyer."[77] The typological richness of the figure is further enhanced. History will have come full circle. The first king of Edom, who was the archenemy of both the father of the children of Israel and the first redeemer, will return at the end of days to rule over Edom once again. Once again he will seek to destroy Israel, but he will go down instead to a decisive and this time permanent defeat at the hands of the final redeemer.[78]

* * *

As the Middle Ages wore on, the significance of typology began to wane; though this mode of messianic speculation would never be entirely displaced,[79] other factors gradually removed it from center stage. Amos

---

[76] Targum to I Chron. 1:43. On the variety of relationships between Laban and Balaam posited in rabbinic literature, see Ginzberg, *Legends*, 5:303, n. 229, and 6:123, n. 722. See also the references in R. LeDéaut and J. Robert, *Targum des Chroniques*, vol. 1 (Rome, 1971), p. 42, n. 22.

[77] Midrashic literature is not devoid of Greek puns. Is it beyond the realm of possibility that the famous and problematic midrashic interpretation of ארמי אובד אבי is based in part on an understanding of ארמי as both "Aramaean" and "destroyer"?

[78] Let me finally propose two suggestions that may be improbable but should nevertheless be noted. (a) Balaam was the son of Beor. The root *b'r* refers to an animal, and associations with the story of the she-wolf that suckled Romulus could have arisen despite the fact that *b'r* usually means a beast of burden. (b) I. Levi in "Apocalypse de Zorobabel" thought that Armilus' birth from a statue was a parody of the alleged virgin birth of Jesus. (Note especially the Christianized Armilus in Even Shmuel, *Midreshei Ge'ullah*, p. 320.) Though I am skeptical, someone attracted by this theory might want to suggest a connection with the possible talmudic association between Balaam and Jesus.

[79] If Gerson Cohen's reading of Abraham ibn Daud's *Sefer ha-Kabbalah* is correct (see his edition [Philadelphia, 1967], esp. pp. 189-222), then it is a case of typological

Funkenstein's perceptive study of the marginal role of typology in medieval Jewish exegesis is not directly concerned with messianism;[80] nevertheless, some of the factors that he proposes to account for the exegetical phenomenon have application to our concerns as well. What is perhaps most relevant is the suggestion that Jews shied away from typology because they had come to see it as a classically Christian approach.[81] Such reservations would have exerted special force in the context of messianic theory, and even Jews living in the orbit of Islam would not have escaped their impact.[82]

Nevertheless, the typological heritage was extraordinarily strong in the realm of messianism, and additional explanations need to be mobilized to explain its relative decline. The first of these is the virtual elimination of a messianic enterprise for which typology was especially suited. The medieval mind was too constrained by the authority of the now plentiful ancient texts to create new messianic personalities, and as a result, figures of the past could no longer give birth to tragic heroes and diabolical monsters at the end of days. It was primarily in the area of calculations where typology could still hold sway, but here too its dominance was challenged, this time by several new sources of information whose significance in the rabbinic period was minor or nil.

The most important of these was the Book of Daniel. We have already seen that in the earliest period Daniel's 1335 days were understood as days and that this understanding precluded their use as a clue to the time of the Messiah's advent.[83] As centuries passed, it became possible

---

messianism in its most striking form. For another illustration of what remains a significant approach, see Yehudah Liebes, "Yonah ben Amittai ke-Mashiah ben Yosef," *Mehqarim be-Kabbalah Muggashim li-Yesha'yah Tishby* (= *Mehqerei Yerushalayim be-Mahashevet Yisrael* 3, pts. 1-2 [1983-84]), pp. 269-311, and cf. n. 85 below.

80 "Parshanuto ha-Tippologit shel ha-Ramban," *Zion* 45 (1980): 35-59.

81 Ibid., p. 55.

82 The effect on such Jews would, of course, have been more limited, and it may be worth noting that the contrast between the relative messianic activism of Sephardim and the quietism of Ashkenazim in the Middle Ages is in significant measure a contrast between Jews living under Islam and those living under Christianity. In a classroom discussion of Gerson Cohen's "Messianic Postures of Ashkenazim and Sephardim," in *Studies of the Leo Baeck Institute*, ed. by Max Kreutzberger (New York, 1967), pp. 117-156, my former student Avraham Pinsker made the interesting suggestion that Jews in the Christian world, who constantly saw themselves as rejecting the claims of a false Messiah, may have been instinctively more cautious about any involvement with messianic pretenders.

83 See n. 41 above.

to understand these days as years without inordinately delaying the messianic age. Once this happened, the Bible suddenly contained a messianic calculation which, for all of its obscurity, bordered on the absolutely explicit, and the primary task of the calculator was the relatively simple one of determining the terminus from which the count begins. In addition to the date latent in Daniel, the growing, almost promiscuous use of numerical equivalence in some medieval and early modern Jewish circles turned Scripture into a treasure trove of eschatological information through a process which appeared more promising than the relatively subtle approach of typological speculation. Finally, the talmudic material itself provided a more concrete basis for calculations than the rabbis themselves had possessed, and this consideration too made their successors less reliant on the uncertain techniques of typology.

These approaches, of course, were not mutually exclusive. Daniel's 1335 years had to be coordinated with its "time, times, and half a time" (Dan. 7:25; 12:7); since these times were perceived as eras of the past whose duration points to the length of the exile, they were understood, at least in a limited sense, typologically. Abravanel extended the 1335 years to 1435 by adding the numerical value of the word "days." And in a *tour de force* which strikes me as the most stunning messianic calculation in history, sixteenth century Jews combined Daniel's number, *gematria*, and a typological rabbinic calculation to produce a messianic date of 5335 A.M. (= 1575 C.E.). The rabbis had said that after the year 4000, the messianic age should have begun, but our sins have delayed its arrival. Thus, when Daniel was told to wait 1335 years, the count must have commenced at the point where anticipation began to make sense, i.e., after the year 4000.[84] This calculation could have stood on its own, and no doubt would have. But then someone noticed the incredible: the number 1335 is embedded in the last two verses of Daniel, which read, "Happy is he who waits and comes to one thousand three hundred and thirty-five days. And now go your way until the end; you shall rest, and shall stand up to your lot at the end of days." The numerical equivalence of both verses in their entirety is precisely 5335! We can only marvel at the resistance of those who remained skeptical; at the same time, we can also marvel at the creative orchestration of diverse modes of messianic

---

[84]   See David Tamar, "Ha-Zippiyyah be-Italyah li-Shenat ha-Ge'ullah Shin-Lamed-He," *Sefunot* 2 (1958): 65-68.

calculation, an orchestration in which typology lingers, but in a decidedly secondary role.[85]

Whatever position messianic typology was ultimately to assume, its significance in early Jewish messianism was even greater than has hitherto been recognized. The much-debated Messiah son of Joseph was probably produced after all by typological speculation, typology is the most plausible source of every single rabbinic calculation in the post-Bar Kokhba period, and the intriguing monster Armilus is a typological figure of extraordinary resonance, richness, and complexity.

[85] In the Sabbatian heresy, of course, typology was mobilized once again for the same reasons that it was mobilized in Christianity: the unorthodox career of a messianic personality had to be prefigured by biblical heroes whose own careers would be subjected to subtle, innovative scrutiny.

SOME IRONIC CONSEQUENCES OF MAIMONIDES' RATIONALIST APPROACH TO THE MESSIANIC AGE

From: *Maimonidean Studies* 2 (1991): 1-8 (Hebrew section). English translation by Joel Linsider in *The Legacy of Maimonides: Religion, Reason, and Community*, ed. by Yamin Levy and Shalom Carmy
(Yashar Books: New York, 2006), pp. 79-88.

Rationalism and messianic activism are conceptual strangers. The rationalist views the world as ever following its natural course. The typical messianic activist views it as teetering on the edge of fundamental change that will topple the order of the Creation, or perhaps more accurately, restore that order to its ideal form. The rationalist perspective is hostile even to the activist who anticipates a naturalistic messianic age that is "no different from the current world except with regard to our subjugation to [foreign] kingdoms" (*Talmud Bavli, Berakhot* 34b; *Sanhedrin* 99a) since even such an activist seeks to hasten the end, while the sober and skeptical view of the rationalist reminds him that Jewish history is replete with messianic disappointment. He believes in the coming of the anticipated day, but even if the deeds of the Jewish people can help speed its arrival, he understands those deeds as the ordinary performance of *mizvot*, and not classic messianic activity. Both the psychology of the rationalist and his logic dictate his fundamental opposition to messianic activism.[1]

And yet, it is not only the case that rationalism and messianic activism sometimes coexist; inevitably, and against the will of those who uphold the banner of messianic rationalism, the rationalist orientation produces views that serve as the impetus for active messianism and provide a means

---

[1]   I have used the term "rationalist" to refer, following Nahmanides' formulation, to someone who tends to maximize nature and limit miracles, and who reacts skeptically toward beliefs that lack plausible evidence. It should be understood that the term carries no fixed definition, and when referring to medieval thinkers, one must utilize standards appropriate to that period.

of defense for messianic phenomena of even the most hysterical sort. As if impelled by a demon, the skeptical thinker extends decisive support to movements that are thoroughly inimical to his mode of thought.

I

One example of this phenomenon is set forth without reference to its implicit irony in Gerson Cohen's essay on the messianic postures of Ashkenazic and Sephardic Jews. Cohen suggests that it was precisely the rationalistic worldview of the Sephardim that generated optimism regarding the possibility of penetrating the secrets of history, and thus, some Sephardic intellectuals succumbed to the temptation of eschatological calculation. Even though these thinkers themselves were not caught up in messianic movements, they created an atmosphere charged with messianic tension, which made the masses more receptive to a variety of messiahs.[2] Cohen's thesis is intriguing, but it cannot be accepted with certainty both because the messianic movements in question were not particularly significant and because it is possible to offer other tenable explanations for Sephardic messianism.[3]

Another example of this phenomenon whose sharp irony has not been previously noted derives from the most famous messianic passage in the writings of Maimonides—the description of the messianic process that appears at the end of "The Laws of Kings":

> Do not suppose that the Messianic King must produce signs and wonders, bring about new phenomena in the world, resurrect the dead, and the like. This is not so... If a king will arise from the House of David who studies the Torah and pursues the commandments like his ancestor David in accordance with the written and oral law, and compels all Israel to follow and strengthen it and fights the wars of the Lord – this man enjoys the presumption of being the Messiah.. If he proceeds successfully, builds the Temple in its place, and gathers the dispersed of Israel, then he is surely the Messiah (*Mishneh Torah*, "Laws of Kings" 11:3-4).

[2]   Gerson D. Cohen, "Messianic Postures of Ashkenazim and Sephardim," *Studies of the Leo Baeck Institute*, ed. by Max Kreutzberger (New York, 1967), pp. 56-115.
[3]   For another explanation, see my article, "Three Typological Themes in Early Jewish Messianism: Messiah Son of Joseph, Rabbinic Calculations, and the Figure of Armilus," *AJS Review* 10 (1985): 162, n. 82.

In the following chapter, Maimonides adds the following:

> As to all these matters and others like them, no one knows how they will happen until they happen, because they are impenetrable matters among the prophets. The Sages too had no tradition about these issues; rather, they weighed the Scriptural evidence, and that is why they differed about these matters. In any event, neither the sequence of these events nor their details are fundamental to the faith, so that no one should occupy himself and spend an inordinate amount of time studying the *aggadot* and *midrashim* that deal with these and similar matters, nor should he make them central, for they lead to neither love nor fear of God. Nor should one calculate the end.... Rather, one should wait and believe in the general doctrine as we have explained (*Mishneh Torah*, "Laws of Kings" 12:2).

It is evident that Maimonides' purpose, which he formulates here almost explicitly, is to moderate and dissipate messianic tension.[4] One who understands that the statements of the rabbinic sages regarding these matters can be mistaken will not direct most of his energy toward the study of the *midrashim* that describe the redemptive process and will thus not succumb to the dangerous messianic temptation. But this practical purpose is not the only consideration that motivated Maimonides' assertion. There can be no doubt that his repudiation of signs and wonders and his rejection of confident reliance upon rabbinic *aggadot* derive from a fundamental rationalist perspective. He believed, however, that the philosophical approach and the practical objective go hand-in-hand. To provide further security, he went on to propose standards necessary for establishing not only messianic certainty, but even presumptive messianic status. Not everyone who wants lay claim to the mantle can come and do so.[5]

---

[4]   Cf. Amos Funkenstein, *Teva, Historia, u-Meshihiyyut ezel ha-Rambam* (Tel-Aviv, 1983), p. 57: "The purpose of the substantial attention that Maimonides dedicated to the messianic era was to prevent the proliferation of messianic movements seeking to hasten the End, and thus, following his forerunners who advocated a realistic messianism, he refrained from painting the Messiah in overly concrete colors. To do so would give an opening to anyone who wanted to come and proclaim himself the Messiah." We shall see as we proceed that the last part of this passage requires fundamental rethinking.

[5]   The importance of the category of presumptive Messiah in preventing the spread of messianic movements is highlighted in Aviezer Ravitsky's analysis, "Ke-fi Koah ha-Adam: Yemot ha-Mashiah be-Mishnat ha-Rambam," in *Meshihiyyut ve-Eskatologiyyah*, ed. by Zvi Baras (Jerusalem, 1983), pp. 205-206, and in David

And yet, not only was this rationalist approach inadequate to stem the tide of burgeoning messianism; under certain circumstances it actually helped fan the flames of a messianic movement by depriving its opponents of their primary weapon. In the absence of an existing movement, it may be that Maimonides' approach could convince certain types of readers to refrain from plunging into messianic activity,[6] but when messianic movements already have a solid footing, this rationalist approach brings about results diametrically opposed to those that Maimonides expected.

In the presence of a real messianic pretender whose followers affirm with certainty that the process of redemption is already upon us, what evidence is available to non-believers who wish to demonstrate beyond doubt that this is not the Messiah, nor is this the beginning of the redemption? If the figure in question is neither an ignoramus nor a heretic, the only option is to demonstrate that specific conditions that should already have been met at this stage have in fact not been fulfilled. There is simply no other argument that can refute the messianic claim with certainty.

And now, along comes Maimonides to inform us that the Messiah need not perform a single sign or wonder, and that even the rabbinic descriptions of the messianic process are not authoritative. If so, the non-believer's sole method of providing an absolute refutation of the messiah has been taken away from him. In the throes of the enthusiasm and psychological upheaval marking a powerful messianic movement, the certainty of the believer will surely wield greater force than the tentative rejection expressed by the denier. Under these conditions, even the criteria required to establish the status of presumptive Messiah offer little assistance to the skeptic. First, someone who has not yet attained the status of presumptive Messiah could still conceivably turn out to be the Messiah; thus, even one who argues that these criteria have not been met cannot rule out the possibility that the figure in question is destined to be the redeemer. Moreover, it was precisely Maimonides' rationalistic approach that compelled him to choose standards that are not so difficult

---

Hartman's introduction to A.S. Halkin and D. Hartman, *Crisis and Leadership: Epistles of Maimonides* (Philadelphia, 1985), p. 191. On Maimonides' moderate approach to events in the messianic era, see Gershom Scholem, *The Messianic Idea in Judaism* (New York, 1971), pp. 24-32.

6   Though, as we will see, even this assumption needs to be substantially qualified.

to achieve – at least in the eyes of a believer. Thus, before Shabbetai Zevi's apostasy, his followers were convinced that he was a king of Davidic ancestry who studied the Torah and pursued the commandments, that he compelled all Israel to follow and strengthen it, and that he fought the wars of the Lord if only in a spiritual sense. Similarly (after due allowance for the deep differences between the movements), just such an explicit argument can be found in publications of some circles in the Habad movement, who see all the virtues enumerated by Maimonides in the personality and deeds of the Lubavitcher Rebbe.[7] It is very difficult for a rationalist to establish pre-messianic requirements that someone who is not the Messiah would find absolutely impossible to fulfill, especially since the criteria are, by their very nature, designed to characterize an individual who could ultimately turn out not to be the Messiah.

If we now turn our attention to the largest messianic movement in the history of Judaism, we will see that we are not dealing with a merely abstract possibility. One who carefully reads *Sefer Zizat Novel Zevi* by R. Jacob Sasportas, the primary opponent of Sabbateanism before the apostasy, will realize that the Maimonidean ruling from the "Laws of Kings" was the major stumbling block that he faced, preventing him from presenting his rejection of Shabbetai Zevi's messianic claim in unequivocal terms. It is true that Sasportas continually relies on the words of Maimonides as his basis for rejecting a confident affirmation of the Sabbatean faith, and this reliance is legitimate and even convincing for those who are prepared to be convinced. However, his frequent assertion that the Sabbateans deny the validity of Maimonides' position obscures the true historic impact of this Maimonidean passage on the raging controversy regarding the Messiahship of Shabbetai Zevi.

Scholem, for example, writes that while Nehemiah Cohen relied on sources such as *Sefer Zerubbavel* and *Sefer Otot ha-Mashiah*[8] to refute the claim of the messianic pretender, Sasportas relied upon Maimonides and the plain meaning of Biblical texts.[9] This is correct. Nonetheless, it is

---

7   See M. Zelikson, *Kol Mevasser Mevasser ve-Omer, Kovez Hiddushei Torah: ha-Melekh ha-Mashiah ve-ha-Ge'ullah ha-Shelemah* (1983), pp. 14-17. See also: "Mihu Yehudi: Shabbat ha-Gadol—ve-ha-Hishtammetut ha-Gedolah," *Kfar Chabad* (1984): 53, at the end of the essay.

8   These were popular works depicting an apocalyptic drama preceding the messianic age.

9   Gershom Scholem, *Shabbetai Zevi ve-ha-Tenu'ah ha-Shabbeta'it bi-Yemei Hayyav* (Tel Aviv, 1957), pp. 557-559.

absolutely clear that if Maimonides had ended his "Laws of Kings" after Chapter 10 without ever writing the last two chapters on the Messiah, Sasportas would have presented his objections to Sabbateanism on the basis of the plain meaning of Scripture and other sources such as the *Zohar* without any need for the Maimonidean position. Even more so – and this is the main point – had Maimonides not written these final two chapters, Sasportas would have presented his rejection of Shabbetai Zevi's Messiahship not tentatively but with absolute conviction. Anyone who relies upon the passage in the *Mishneh Torah* for anti-Sabbatean purposes must also accept its authority with respect to the view that we have no definitive knowledge of the messianic process. Maimonides' position proved to be a minor and almost negligible impediment to the Sabbatean movement; its primary impact was to lend the movement major and almost definitive support.

Let us examine several illustrations from *Sefer Zizat Novel Zevi*:

> And if those who rebel against the rabbis' words [i.e., the Sabbatean believers] will say that our sages have not hit upon the truth, and, as Maimonides said, all these matters cannot be known by man until they occur, then I too agree. But I will not discard the tradition of our sages, all of whose words are justice and truth, before the messianic fulfillment. And if after that fulfillment, it turns out that their statements still do not accord [with the actual course of events], then the Messiah himself will argue on their behalf... And if you have acted out of piety by believing [in Shabbetai Zevi], you have in fact placed yourselves in the straits of serious doubt... Either way, I am innocent and bear no iniquity... Have you heard me declare in public that this is all lies and falsehood? Rather, I have told all those believers who have asked me that it is possible [that he is the Messiah], although it is a distant possibility until he has performed a messianic act.[10]

And in another passage:

> None of his initial deeds accord with the words of Rabbi Simeon bar Yochai in [*Zohar*] *Parashat Shemot*, and God forbid that we should say, like the ignorant among the masses, that none of our sages hit upon the truth. And though Maimonides stated in the above mentioned passage that no one will know these matters until they occur, he nonetheless agrees that until that time, we are to remain rooted in the tradition of our sages.[11]

10   Isaiah Tishbi, *Sefer Zizat Novel Zevi le-Rabbi Ya'akov Sasportas* (Jerusalem, 1954), p. 104.
11   Ibid., p. 119. The reference to *Zohar Parashat Shemot* points to an extensive and

It is clear from these passages that were it not for the Maimonidean ruling, the followers of Shabbetai Zevi would have been at a loss to account for the lack of congruence between what they saw as reality and the depiction of the redemptive process in rabbinic texts and the *Zohar*. It is also clear that Sasportas would have taken advantage of this lack of congruence to refute the Sabbatean messianic claim categorically. Indeed, after the apostasy, we find a letter by R. Joseph Halevi denying Shabbetai Zevi's Messiahship on the basis of passages from the Talmud and the *Zohar* that are no less relevant to the period before the apostasy, and he does so without any need for additional arguments relying upon Maimonides.[12] The importance of Maimonides for the Sabbateans themselves is manifest in the words of Nathan of Gaza, who falls back upon the Maimonidean passage even after the apostasy of his master:

> And though we have found no hint of this matter in the explicit words of the Torah, we have already seen how strange the sages' words are regarding these matters, so that we cannot fully understand anything they say in their context, as the great luminary Maimonides has also testified; their words will be understood only when the events actually unfold.[13]

I would not venture so far as to say that the success of the Sabbatean movement would have been impossible if not for the Maimonidean ruling, but there can be no doubt that we are witness here to a sharp and highly significant irony.

It is particularly interesting that Maimonides himself encountered the problem that we have been examining when he composed his *Epistle to Yemen*. The *Epistle*'s assertion that the Messiah *will* be recognized by signs and wonders results from the need to reject the messianic mission of a specific individual by establishing clearcut criteria. Thus, the discrepancy between the "Laws of Kings" and the *Epistle* on this point also demonstrates the tension between rationalism and the requirements of anti-messianic polemic during a confrontation with a real messianic movement.[14]

---

detailed description of events during the course of the messianic process that should have already occurred, at least in part, by that point in the Sabbatean movement. See *Zohar*, Part II, 7b and following.

12   Ibid., pp. 190-191, and cf. 195.
13   Ibid., p. 260. See Scholem, *Shabbetai Zevi*, p. 628.
14   See: Maimonides, *Iggerot*, ed. by Yosef Kafah (Jerusalem, 1972). There is some

II

Until now we have concerned ourselves with messianic activism of an extreme sort that did not arise out of rationalism but used it effectively as a protective shield. Now we will turn to more moderate messianic manifestations that derive in no small part from the naturalistic conception of the redemption, which continues to provide them with inspiration to this day. Thus, the ironic connection between the restrained messianism of the rationalist and messianic activism is by no means restricted to the Middle Ages and the beginning of the modern period; it extends into the modern age, leaving its mark on Religious Zionism both in the nineteenth century and in our own day. This irony arises from deep within messianic rationalism and is rooted in its very essence. On the one hand, the naturalistic conception of the redemption tends to prevent messianic delusions as well as behavior that deviates from the realm of the normal. But on the other hand, the very nature of the naturalistic conception encourages activism. If the Messiah is not destined to appear with the clouds of heaven, if it is necessary to fight the wars of the Lord in the plain sense of the word, if the Temple is not destined to descend fully assembled from the heavens, if it is necessary to re-institute *semikhah* (the direct chain of rabbinic ordination between master and pupil deriving from Sinai) and the Sanhedrin before the arrival of the redeemer, then human activity is needed to help realize the messianic hope. This conclusion appears so clear and unavoidable that some scholars and thinkers view Maimonides as a guiding spirit for religious Zionism.[15]

It seems to me that despite the logic inherent in this claim, Maimonides had no such intentions. He advises his readers simply

plausibility in Kafah's attempt to harmonize the assertion in the *Epistle* with Maimonides' position in the *Mishneh Torah*. See Kafah's notes ad loc. Nonetheless, the emphasis in the *Epistle* is certainly different from the impression given by the "Laws of Kings."

15   For this general conception from different perspectives and with different degrees of emphasis, see Joel L. Kramer, "On Maimonides' Messianic Postures," *Studies in Medieval Jewish History and Literature* II, ed. by Isadore Twersky (Cambridge, Mass., and London, England, 1984), pp. 109-142; Aryeh Botwinick, "Maimonides' Messianic Age," *Judaism* 33 (1984): 425; Menachem Kellner, "Messianic Postures in Israel Today," *Modern Judaism* 6 (1986): 197-209; Shubert Spero, "Maimonides and the Sense of History," *Tradition* 24:2 (1989): 128-137.

to "wait." The Maimonidean positions that are capable of generating messianic activism derive solely from rational and halakhic considerations. For example, the determination that *semikhah* must be re-instituted by an act of the rabbis in the land of Israel before the redemption can occur is based on a verse from Isaiah in conjunction with the quintessential Maimonidean position that the *halakhah* will not change at the End of Days and that miracles are to be left out of the messianic process.[16] This approach precludes Maimonides from describing a Sanhedrin composed of rabbis without *semikhah*, or of proposing, as did certain rabbis after him, that *semikhah* would be re-instituted with the return to earth of the prophet Elijah (who certainly had *semikhah)* from his place in the heavens. There is no intention on the part of Maimonides to encourage actions expressly designed to bring the redeemer. Nevertheless, Jacob Katz's important essay showed how his position led to the famous attempt to re-institute *semikhah* in sixteenth-century Safed out of explicit messianic motivations.[17]

Similarly, Maimonides' determination that the Third Temple will be built by human hands, a determination that was so important to R. Zevi Hirsch Kalischer in his proto-Zionist polemic, certainly did not stem from a desire to encourage messianic activism. The view that the Third Temple will fall intact from the heavens appeared in marginal sources, and Rashi introduced it into the center of Jewish messianic consciousness only as a consequence of a serious difficulty in a Talmudic passage in tractates *Sukkah* and *Rosh ha-Shanah*. There, the Talmud states that the origin of a particular rabbinic prohibition lies in a concern arising out of the possibility that the Third Temple might be built at night or on a holiday. Rashi raises an objection based on another Talmudic passage that unequivocally prohibits building the Temple during these times, and he resolves the contradiction by concluding that the Third Temple will not be built by human hands.[18] Although from a purely exegetical standpoint there is no better answer than the one offered by Rashi, a

---

16   Maimonides, *Perush ha-Mishnayot, Sanhedrin* 1:3; cf. *Hilkhot Sanhedrin* 4:11. This example is cited by several of the authors in the previous footnote. See also Funkenstein, *Teva, Historia, u-Meshihiyyut*, pp. 64-68.

17   Jacob Katz, "Mahloket ha-Semikhah bein Rabbi Ya'akov Beirav ve-ha-Ralbah," *Zion* 15 (1951): 28-45.

18   Rashi, *Sukkah* 41a s.v. *i nami; Rosh ha-Shanah* 30a s.v. *la tzerikha*. Cf. Tzvi Hirsch Kalischer, *Derishat Ziyyon*, ed. by Israel Klausner (Jerusalem, 1964), pp. 144-147.

commentator who has been influenced by rationalism will be unwilling
even to consider such a possibility. For this reason, R. Menahem ha-
Meiri does not even mention Rashi's explanation, and instead he forces
himself to manufacture a suggestion that we are concerned about the
prospect of an error by the rabbinic court, which out of love for the
Temple may allow it to be constructed during times when it is forbidden
to do so.[19] That is to say, ha-Meiri is prepared to express concern
about an error by a rabbinic court presumably functioning under the
supervision of the Messiah himself so that he will not have to entertain
the notion of buildings dropping out of the sky. Despite the rationalist
motivation, which has nothing to do with messianic activism, the
position that the Third Temple would be built by human hands- – as well
as related naturalistic approaches—had a greater potential to generate
such activism than the approach that looks forward to miracles in which
human beings play no active role.

As I have noted, there are scholars who do not see the irony in this
situation because they attribute to Maimonides a conscious, though
moderate, activist intention. I see no evidence for this motivation in his
writings, and I am not willing to create such a Maimonidean position
based on logical considerations alone, when his explicit directive is simply
to wait.[20] On the other hand, scholars who have dealt with Maimonides'

---

19   Ha-Meiri, *Beit ha-Behirah, Sukkah*, ad loc.
20   For reasons that may be scholarly and may be personal, I do not assert that
     Maimonides' own posture would have necessarily compelled him to oppose the
     messianic motif in religious Zionism, especially after the development of the
     larger movement out of other considerations; my remark at the beginning of this
     essay about movements that are "thoroughly inimical to [the rationalist's] mode
     of thought" refers to Sabbateanism and other classic messianic movements. Still,
     the encouragement of messianic activism, even of the moderate type, played no
     role in Maimonides' consciousness, but emerged willy-nilly out of his rationalist
     position.
     On the other hand, the attempt to use Maimonides to prove that there is no
     messianic significance in the establishment of the State of Israel runs afoul of the
     problem we pointed out in the first half of the essay. Proponents of this position
     customarily point out that Maimonides mentions the ingathering of the exiles only
     after the appearance of the Messiah and the rebuilding of the Temple ("Laws of
     Kings" 11:4). But Maimonides himself pointed out in his "agnostic" ruling ("Laws
     of Kings" 12:2) that the order of these events is not central to the faith. When I
     mentioned this to Zalman Alpert of the Yeshiva University Library, he graciously
     directed me to the exchange between Amnon Shapira and Dov Wolpo, *Ammudim* 413,
     415, 416 (1980): 211-214, 291-295, 345-347.

influence on messianic developments before the rise of Zionism tend to view his stand as a successful attempt to thwart messianic activism. As we have seen, this position too is highly questionable. It seems to me that we stand before an ironic paradox with significant consequences. The rationalist, while striving to moderate the messianic drive, will sometimes unwillingly enhance it.

SEPHARDIC AND ASHKENAZIC MESSIANISM IN THE MIDDLE AGES: AN ASSESSMENT OF THE HISTORIOGRAPHICAL DEBATE

From: *Rishonim ve-Aharonim: Mehqarim be-Toledot Yisrael muggashim le-Avraham Grossman* (The Zalman Shazar Center for Jewish History: Jerusalem, 2009), pp. 11-28 (Hebrew). Translated by Gabriel Wasserman and the author.

This article is dedicated to my friend Professor Avraham Grossman, an outstanding Jewish historian who deserves the highest regard not only for his intellectual achievements, but also for his exceptional personal qualities. As I already noted twenty years ago, he has taught us how to express differences of opinion with humility, impelled by the quest for truth for its own sake, and with a sense of respect for others.[1] In this essay, I set out to examine the positions of two outstanding historians with a special place in my life. Gerson Cohen was my doctoral advisor and primary mentor in the field of history, and I personally heard him espouse the well-known thesis at issue here before it reached its printed form. I still remember my reaction at the time: I was taken aback by his claim, which opposed my immediate instincts regarding the relationship between rationalism and messianic movements. But I also remember my growing sense of admiration as I came to understand the ingenuity and depth of his proposal.[2] Some years ago, Elisheva Carlebach, who studied with me as she began the process that ultimately led to her

---

[1] David Berger, "Heqer Rabbanut Ashkenaz ha-Qedumah," *Tarbiz* 53 (1984): 479.

[2] Cohen's article has been published four times: Gerson D. Cohen, "Messianic Postures of Ashkenazim and Sephardim," *Leo Baeck Memorial Lecture* #9 (1967); *Studies of the Leo Baeck Institute*, ed. by Max Kreutzberger (New York, 1967), pp. 115-156; Gerson D. Cohen, *Studies in the Variety of Rabbinic Cultures* (Philadelphia, 1991); *Essential Papers on Messianic Movements and Personalities in Jewish History*, ed. by Marc Saperstein (New York, 1992), pp. 202-233.

impressive accomplishments as a historian, wrote a sharp critique of Cohen's thesis. No one can disagree that the topic in question is of great importance, and I believe that the arguments on both sides deserve careful examination. Because I have such great respect for both the originator of the thesis and its critic, the chances that I will not slip into inappropriate formulations are greater that they might normally be, but it is not superfluous to express the hope that the image of the honoree will provide all the more protection.

What is it that Cohen claims in his article? He argues that there is a striking, almost polar, opposition between medieval Sepharad and Ashkenaz with regard to the issue of messianism. In Sepharad, we find lively discussions of messianism in the writings of commentators and intellectuals, as well as popular messianic movements. In Ashkenaz, on the other hand, there is no discussion or discourse, no ferment and no messiahs. Cohen strives to prove these assertions, and then to arrive at an explanation for the phenomenon itself.

He begins his analysis with the usual scholarly assumption that Ashkenazic Jewry had a strong connection to the Palestinian tradition, whereas Sephardic Jewry's connection was to Babylonia. Thence he proceeds to examine these two centers of early medieval Jewry, Palestine and Babylonia, for the first signs of the contrast between Ashkenazic and Sephardic attitudes toward messianism. In the Persian/Byzantine era and the beginning of the Muslim era, we find apocalyptic literature in Palestine, but no active messianic movements. Cohen's understanding is that this literature owes its existence to a sublimation of messianic energy from the world of action into the world of the imagination, to the point where it can even be viewed as a contrast to active messianism. On the other hand, Babylonia in the same period produced a number of movements with messianic characteristics, even including violent and quasi-military elements.

In Cohen's opinion, this difference between the two centers persisted throughout the Middle Ages. In the realm of straightforward activism, we can identify about a dozen messianic figures between 1065 and 1492, all of them in the Sephardic cultural orbit. We do find instances of messianic ferment in Byzantium and Sicily, but these were passing phenomena in communities that had strong ties to the Middle East. In the realm of calculations and messianic discourse, we find almost nothing in Ashkenaz. There is a letter, dated 960, from an Ashkenazic community to the Geonim of the Land of Israel asking about certain messianic matters; but the curiosity about this topic seems to have been based on reading *Sefer Zerubbavel*, and the question about the End of Days is put together with an entirely different question about *kashrut*. One of the Crusade chronicles states that the Jews were hoping that the Messiah would arrive during the 256th cycle of the Jewish calendar (1085-1104 CE), based on Jeremiah 31:6: "Ronnu le-Ya'akov simhah" ("sing with gladness for Jacob") where the numerical value of the first word, *ronnu*, is 256); however, this number reflects a calculation from a late Byzantine midrash. Rashi's calculations in his commentary on the Book of Daniel actually illustrate a lack of messianic enthusiasm, since the effort to calculate the End was forced upon him by exegetical necessity and the dates that he proposes point to a redemption that is to be delayed for generations. In the last years of the fifth millennium (which ended in the Jewish year 5000, corresponding to 1240 CE), some prophecies of the imminent End begin to appear in Ashkenaz, but this is an atypical phenomenon whose character is entirely different from the rationalistic calculations produced by Sephardim. Similarly, the calculations attested in Ashkenaz tend to be based on innovative numerical equivalencies (*gimatriyyot*), which reflect a very different way of thinking from the calculations used by the Sephardic intellectuals. Finally, the migration of French rabbis to the Land of Israel in the thirteenth century emerged out of considerations that were essentially unconnected to messianic hopes.

Let us now look at Sepharad through Cohen's lens. There, we see many calculations of the End of Days, based on rationalistic interpretations of biblical verses or rabbinic statements, on historical typology, and on astrological investigation, which was considered a scientific field of study in the Middle Ages. (Maimonides' opposition to astrology was atypical even among philosophers.) Interest in the End of Days and the date when it will occur appears in the letter of Hasdai ibn Shaprut to the King of the Khazars; in the writings of Avraham bar Hiyya, Solomon ibn Gabirol, and Judah Halevi; in Abraham ibn Daud's *Book of Tradition* (*Sefer ha-Qabbalah*); in Maimonides' *Epistle to Yemen*; in Nahmanides' *Book of the Redemption* (*Sefer ha-Ge'ullah*); and in the diverse writings of Isaac Abravanel.

Cohen connects messianic calculations and even the rise of messianic movements to rationalist modes of thought. As I have noted, I initially recoiled from this assertion; after all, our instincts do not take well to a position which states that rationalism creates activism that appears contrary to common sense. However, Cohen explains the logic of this argument. The Sephardic rationalist was convinced that God governs the universe in accordance with principles that can be grasped by reason, whereas the Ashkenazic scholar did not presume to understand God's mind. Therefore, the Sephardic rationalist was able to delve into the complexities of the unfolding historical drama, and his intellectual efforts along these lines encouraged actual messianic movements among the masses. The Ashkenazic scholar was forced to wait until the time that God Himself would decide to redeem His people and His universe, and in an environment that was not suffused with concern about messianism, the masses, too, did not become caught up in messianic movements. In the best-case situation, an Ashkenazic Jew who yearned very much for the redemption might hope for a prophetic experience from God, or might attempt to interpret the secrets concealed in biblical verses.

Moreover, Cohen argues that these distinctions in attitude toward rationalism and messianism also explain the difference between Ashkenaz and Sepharad with regard to readiness to undergo martyrdom. The Jews of Sepharad avoided martyrdom for two basic reasons: first of all, rationalism weakened their faith to a degree that undermined the inner strength necessary to sacrifice one's life; second, they were convinced that the messiah would soon come, at which point they would be able to return to Judaism.

Finally, in a brief passage that appears almost as an aside, Cohen makes an important, even revolutionary, point in the historiography of messianism: persecutions in and of themselves do not produce messianic movements. Even a scholar who utterly rejects Cohen's basic positions must give him credit for the short passage in which he lists the major persecutions from the Middle Ages through the seventeenth century and notes that not one of these produced a messianic movement. One might argue with Cohen's affirmation with respect to the expulsion from Spain and the massacres of 1648, but the basic observation remains intact in all its force, and it appears to stand unchallenged.

Cohen's article became a classic in the academic discussion of Jewish messianism in the Middle Ages, but there were nonetheless scholars who rejected his position. Israel Yuval, in his long article on the hatred that Ashkenazic Jews felt towards Christianity and the implications that he attributes to this hatred, proffered two arguments against Cohen's thesis.

First of all, if Ashkenazic Jews did not produce the sort of messianic movements that we find in other centers, this should not be seen as an expression of passivity. Ashkenazic society considered words very powerful, and so we should view their bitter curses against the gentiles and their prayers for vengeance as active messianism. Activism in the form of movements would have been redundant or perhaps even harmful. Moreover, Sephardic expressions of messianism in the realm of theory and calculations appear primarily in speculative philosophical literature, a genre that barely existed at all in Ashkenaz.[3]

But a broad and systematic critique of Cohen's thesis was presented by Carlebach in a lecture that she delivered in 1998.[4] Here, then, is a summary of her argument:

1   Cohen speaks of "aggressive military activity" in the movements that arose in Persia in the first centuries of Muslim rule. In fact, as even Cohen admits in a later article, these movements were hardly organized, and they had no true military component.

2.   Messianism was hardly foreign to Ashkenaz, nor was martyrdom absent in Sepharad. Furthermore, dying for the faith was not considered an expression of passivity by medieval Jews, for the martyrs first tried to save themselves in any way possible.

3.   Cohen sees the Ashkenazic position as an expression of passivity on the part of the rabbinic elite, whereas he sees the active messianism of Sepharad as "popular." Thus, he overlooks the conservative messianism of the Sephardic rabbis from the time of the Geonim, on to Maimonides, and through R. Jacob Sasportas. Moreover, movements with messianic characteristics "often" took place in Ashkenaz under the leadership of the rabbinic elite itself, thus evincing a character that penetrated to the very core of communities that identified with its great rabbinic scholars; on the other hand, the movements in Sepharad often came from an anti-rabbinic sector.

---

[3]   Israel Yuval, "Ha-Naqam ve-ha-Qelalah, ha-Dam ve-ha-Alilah," *Zion* 58 (1993): 60. This passage also appears in Yuval's book *Shenei Goyim be-Bitnekh* (Tel-Aviv, 2000), p. 145. See also note 19, below.

[4]   Elisheva Carlebach, *Between History and Hope: Jewish Messianism in Ashkenaz and Sepharad: Third Annual Lecture of the Victor J. Selmanowitz Chair of Jewish History,* Graduate School of Jewish Studies, Touro College (New York, 1998).

4. The use of the term "Sepharad" to embrace both the movements that arose on the fringes of Persian Jewry in the seventh century and the complex calculations born in the elitist environment of rationalist courtiers in Andalusia is highly dubious.

5. In light of a number of studies made in the past few decades pointing to cultural contacts between Ashkenaz and Sepharad, it is becoming clear that the general picture of a deep cultural divide between the Jewish centers has been exaggerated, and it is doubtful that we can use it to explain the distinctions that we are discussing.

6. A central portion of Carlebach's lecture is devoted to an analysis of the historiography of two sixteenth-century messianic movements in the writings of various Ashkenazic and Sephardic authors:

I. Asher Laemmelein:

Carlebach points to three Ashkenazic sources and three Sephardic sources that address this movement.

On the Ashkenazic side, David Ganz portrays Laemmelein as the messiah's herald, not as the messiah himself. At the same time, he describes significant messianic fervor in Ashkenaz that was generated by the news of the movement. An anonymous chronicle from early seventeenth-century Prague includes a short note about a rumor in 1502 regarding the Messiah that inspired mass acts of repentance. At the end of the sixteenth century, a student of R. Solomon Luria wrote that Laemmelein's influence had extended to Ashkenaz, to Italy, and to other lands in the Christian world.

On the Sephardic side, Gedalya ibn Yahya reports that when Laemmelein died in an unredeemed world, many Jews apostatized. Yosef ha-Kohen refers to him with the biblical pronouncement, "The prophet is a fool, the man of the spirit is insane" (Hosea 9:7), and recounts that "the Jews flocked to him, and said: 'This is a prophet, whom God has sent to be a ruler over his people Israel and to gather the dispersed of Judah from the four corners of the earth'." Yosef Sambari, who repeated Yosef ha-Kohen's remarks,[5] also noted the influence of these events on "the sinners of Israel," i.e., the apostates.

---

5   Carlebach does not note this point, although it would help support her thesis.

Christian writers who mention Laemmelein's movement view it, of course, as yet further evidence of the repeated disappointments generated by erroneous Jewish imaginings regarding the identity of the Messiah. Ashkenazic writers willfully ignore the fact that Laemmelein's failure led Jews to apostasy. In conclusion, "the historiography of the movement changes greatly based on the identity of the reporter."

Beyond the historiographical question, Carlebach notes also that despite Cohen's refusal to attribute significance to Laemmelein as well as his hypothesis that he was influenced by Sephardim, Laemmelein's recently-published writings, which were not available to Cohen, show that he was committed to Ashkenazic culture.

II. *Solomon Molkho:*

Ashkenazic authors tell the story of this figure only briefly, and tend to gloss over the messianic aspect. Josel of Rosheim describes Molkho as a proselyte who caused trouble for the community but also inspired acts of mass repentance. Rabbi Yom-Tov Lipmann Heller discusses the ritual fringes (*tzitzit*) worn by Molkho and classifies him as a martyr, but not as a messianic claimant. David Ganz writes a brief description of Molkho with no mention of messianism. The Prague chronicle reports that there were messianic expectations in the year 1523, but makes no mention of Molkho.

In two Sephardic accounts, which are longer, the messianic moment in Molkho's life is mentioned explicitly. Yosef ha-Kohen introduces Molkho with the expression, "A shoot came forth out of Portugal" (cf. Isaiah 11:1), which has clear messianic implications. Yosef Sambari explicitly says that Molkho identified himself as the Messiah. Similarly, two Christian authors write that Molkho announced that he was the Messiah.

From these data, Carlebach reaches conclusions of decisive significance for our topic. Ashkenazim write succinct accounts of messianic events, limiting the messianic aspects of the relevant figures or ignoring it entirely, for precisely the reason that Christian writers emphasize it – namely, that any failed messianic movement strengthens the Christian argument against Judaism. In this context, Carlebach turns our attention to a comment that I once noted in the name of my student Avraham Pinsker, to wit, that Ashkenazim may have hesitated to embrace messianic activism precisely because they lived in a Christian environment, where they were constantly forced to be on the defensive against faith in a false messiah. His original comment was made with reference to actual messianic activity, but Carlebach uses it to explain the historiographical phenomenon. She also points to a passage in *Sefer Hasidim* that warns against openness to messianic prophecies that could bring disgrace to the Jewish community.

7. Carlebach goes on to examine the messianic movements that did arise in Ashkenaz or related regions: the messianic tension in Byzantium at the time of the First Crusade; the expectations surrounding the 256th cycle of the calendar; the messianic ferment in the decades preceding the year 5000 (1240 CE); the migrations to the Land of Israel in the thirteenth century; and messianic expectation in 1337 attributed to Jews by a Christian Bavarian chronicle in a miracle story dealing with well-poisoning and host-desecration. She rejects Cohen's position that we need not deal with events recounted only in Christian sources, for the Ashkenazic tendency to downplay such incidents raises the likelihood that reliable reports will appear only in Christian writings.

In Carlebach's opinion, all the phenomena in this list show that there was a significant level of messianic activity in Ashkenaz, to the point where we can affirm that active expressions of messianic hope were no less a part of the collective personality of Ashkenazic Jewry than that of the Sepharadim. Cohen's thesis reflects a historiographical tradition hostile to Ashkenazic Jewry. Cohen sees in this Jewry a metaphor for a rabbinic elite suffused with fundamentalism and intolerance, in contrast to the scientific spirit that animated Sephardic Jewry. "The true deficiency of Ashkenaz resided not in its messianic posture, but in its deficient alignment with the temper of the historian."

Carlebach, like Cohen, was blessed with a sharp mind, broad knowledge, stylistic precision, broad vision, and intellectual depth. This debate addresses one of the fundamental issues that faced medieval Jewry, and it requires serious assessment of the arguments on both sides. In the remainder of this article, I shall attempt to present the case for a more modest approach than Cohen's without fully endorsing Carlebach's position.

Let us begin with my reservations about Cohen's arguments. Some of these reservations are identical to Carlebach's, but most are different.

1. It is true that the Jews of Palestine, who wrote apocalypses in the first decades of the seventh century, did not form movements that pointed to any actual individuals as messianic figures; however, the word "passive" is hardly an appropriate term to characterize them. These Jews carried out military campaigns alongside the Persians against Christian Byzantium, and it is quite plausible to conclude that some of them slaughtered Christians in Mamilla.[6] The apocalyptic writings understand these wars as part of the unfolding drama of the End of Days, and it is hard to see how any Jew who saw these events could have reject this interpretation. Even if we assume that not all the Jews who fought in these wars saw the Persian-Byzantine conflict through a messianic prism, it is clear that this community was as remote from "passivity" as East is from West.

2. In light of the Italian origins of Ashkenazic Jewry, Cohen emphasizes the fact that *Josippon*, which was written in tenth-century Italy, opposes aggressive activism, but he downplays the identical position of the Sephardi Abraham ibn Daud. (Cohen writes that while Ibn Daud did agree with the author of *Josippon* on this point, his position did not succeed in curbing the Sephardic enthusiasm for messianic movements, and Ibn Daud himself did not refrain from attempting to calculate the End.)

3. Cohen attributes great significance to Hasdai ibn Shaprut's letter asking the Khazar king whether he has any information about the coming of the Messiah. However, when he discusses a contemporaneous letter from Ashkenaz that contains almost the identical question, he sees it as nothing more than a meaningless expression of curiosity.

4. Cohen regards the intensive use of *gimatriyyot* in messianic contexts as a sign of the non-rational Ashkenazic mode of thought, but when he encounters the same approach in the writings of Abraham bar Hiyya, he views it as a marginal phenomenon.

---

[6] See K. Hilkowitz, "Li-She'elat Hishtattefutam shel Yehudim be-Kibbush Yerushalayim 'al Yedei ha-Parsim bi-Shenat 614," *Zion* 4 (1939): 307-316; Elliot S. Horowitz, "'The Vengeance of the Jews was Stronger than their Avarice': Modern Historians and the Persian Conquest of Jerusalem in 614," *Jewish Social Studies* 4:2 (1998): 1-39.

5. Although Rashi's date for the End of Days lay far in the future, we find other calculations in Ashkenaz that point to a date in the near future. As to Sepharad, despite the general tendency to provide imminent dates, Nahmanides produced a calculation that postponed the final End 140 years.

6. As I have mentioned above, Cohen did not attribute significance to Laemmelein's movement, and he hypothesized that it resulted from Sephardic influence. Carlebach's criticism of this claim is fundamentally correct, even though the movement did not arise in the heartland of Ashkenaz, and dates from the early sixteenth century.

7. I agree with Carlebach that the supposed connection between Sepharad and the peripheral movements in Persia is extremely tenuous. Moreover, it is highly doubtful that rationalism played any significant role in seventh-century Persia. Thus, the messianic ferment there was certainly based on factors that had absolutely nothing to do with Cohen's thesis. If the messianic activity in Sepharad was actually connected to Persia – or "Bablyonia" – it reflected a tradition that had no connection to scientific modes of thinking. It is entirely possible that these movements developed in Persia under Shi'ite influence (as Israel Friedlaender noted many years ago), and it is not impossible that some of the medieval movements – though not all of them – were also inspired by a similar environment.[7]

8. Our list of messianic movements in the Middle Ages is partly based on the reports of Maimonides in his *Epistle to Yemen*. Needless to say, the information which Maimonides had about these movements came mainly from the Sephardic world.

9. Although a number of studies have appeared emphasizing the acts of martyrdom that occurred in the Sephardic sphere, I believe that we can say that Cohen's distinction between the two centers still retains some validity. Nevertheless, the connection between messianism and the relative reluctance in Sepharad to

---

[7] In a personal conversation, Mark Saperstein has stressed this possibility to me. I think that many of the parallels suggested by Friedlaender are forced, but some of them are entirely reasonable. See Israel Friedlaender, "Jewish-Arabic Studies," *JQR* .n. s. 1 (1910-1911):183-205; 2 (1911-1912): 481-516; 3 (1912-1913): 235-300.

die a martyr's death is exceedingly tenuous and borders on the incoherent. On the one hand, Cohen describes a belief marked by uncertainty, and on the other, he points to a belief so strong that those who held it were prepared to convert out of firm conviction that the Messiah would come in the immediate future to save them from their distressing fate. Moreover, a simple question arises: Would it really be a good idea to greet the messiah with the words: "Welcome, my master the king! I am your servant so-and-so, the apostate"? Although forced apostasy and willing conversion are hardly the same thing, it is worth mentioning the debate in Majorca, where a Jew became more-or-less convinced that Christianity was the true faith, but to be on the safe side, he decided to remain Jewish for a few more years, until the arrival of a messianic date that was current at the time.[8]

Despite all these considerations, I also have serious reservations about the criticisms of Cohen made by Yuval and Carlebach.

There is indeed more than a grain of truth in Yuval's assertion that curses and prayers for vengeance can be classified as messianic activism in a society that views speech as a magical act. However, the Jew in the well-known joke who shouts in the study hall, "Jews! Do something! Recite Psalms!" does not exactly typify "activism" in the usual sense, even if he attributes magical impact to the recitation of Psalms. In the final analysis, Ashkenazic Jews did not make a clear distinction between the "natural" process generated by the declarations of the Jewish masses and divine activity on the cosmic plane, so that their prayers and curses—even if they included a magical element—were essentially requests for divine mercy. Furthermore, routine messianic "activism" cannot be compared to messianic movements that arise at discrete moments of history. The messianic fervor that characterizes movements cannot characterize quotidian activities, certainly not when these activities involve nothing more than speech. As to Yuval's assertion that from a magical perspective, typical messianic activism would be harmful, the fact remains that even from this perspective the expected result is the arrival of the Messiah, so that it is difficult to see any harm in his appearance. A messianic figure and his followers do not see themselves as pressing for a premature End of Days. On the contrary, such a figure would assert that the long-

---

[8] Ora Limor, *Vikkuah Majorca 1286* (Jerusalem, 1985), volume I, p. 132.

awaited time has arrived, perhaps precisely because the prayers and curses have had their effect. We must also note that Yuval's criticism is directed only against Cohen's claim that the Ashkenazic attitude toward messianism was "passive." From another perspective, Yuval's position actually reinforces Cohen's analysis since it points to a basic difference between Sephardic "rationalistic" messianism and a very different sort of messianism among Ashkenazic Jews.

As to Yuval's observation that there was virtually no speculative philosophical literature in Ashkenaz, the point itself merits serious consideration, but we must remember that when Cohen cites Sephardic materials, he includes letters, commentaries, and Abraham ibn Daud's chronicle (or chronography). Moreover, the lack of speculative philosophical works is due to a considerable extent to precisely what Cohen emphasized, to wit, the absence of speculative thought of the sort that would have generated serious analysis of the nature of the messianic era as well as sustained interest in the questions associated with it, including the calculation of when that era would begin. The distinctions that Cohen drew are not neutralized by Yuval's methodological observations, as important as the latter may be.

The sharp critique in Carlebach's summary remarks is directed against a stereotypical anti-Ashkenazic attitude that she attributes to Cohen. In her view, he adopted a negative image of the Ashkenazic "fundamentalists" in contrast to the rationalistic heroes of Sepharad. This criticism of Cohen evokes a stereotype of its own—the image of the broadly educated historian who respects the Sephardim for their variegated and open culture and disdains the Ashkenazim because they did not study philosophy and were caught up in a narrow, limited belief system.

I believe that this perception is imprecise. Despite Carlebach's assertion that Cohen attributes "a heroic and active profile"[9] to the warring messianism of the Sephardic world, his article nowhere contains any expression of respect for the putative "military messianism" of the sects in late seventh-century Persia; he does not present the adherents of these movements as heroic in any way. As to his overall assessment of Ashkenaz and Sepharad, there is some basis for Carlebach's evaluation. Cohen sees the Ashkenazim as "fundamentalists" and mentions their belief in anthropomorphism and strange *aggadot*. His statement, which

---

9   Carlebach, p. 2.

Carlebach quotes in her study, that eventually even "some fine Sephardim" internalized Ashkenazic fundamentalism[10] can create the impression that he wanted to set up a dichotomy between the enlightened Sephardim, who deserve respect, and the Ashkenazim, who deserve disdain. And indeed, it is of course true that Cohen himself identified more with the culture of the medieval Sephardim than that of the medieval Ashkenazim. Nevertheless, anyone who studied with Cohen will understand that this formulation was not meant to belittle or mock the Ashkenazim; rather, all that he meant is that distinguished Sephardim absorbed Ashkenazic influence. It is true that even in the sixties the term "fundamentalism" was not a compliment, but even in academic circles, it had not yet attained the full degree of vitriol that it bears today. Cohen did not feel disdain for the simple faith of the Ashkenazim that the Messiah would come whenever God would determine, and certainly not for their avoidance of active messianic movements. When all is said and done, does it really make sense to say that messianic uprisings fit well with "the temper of the historian"? I can testify that Cohen respected the Ashkenazim for their self-sacrifice in times of crisis as a consequence of precisely the constellation of beliefs that he presents in this study, even though he did not identify with those beliefs himself.

Similarly, Carlebach's assertion that Cohen's typology has no room for the conservative messianism of the Sephardic rabbinate from the Geonim through Maimonides through R. Jacob Sasportas requires qualification. Cohen does mention this conservatism several times and even emphasizes it. As Carlebach understands very well, his basic argument is that the rabbis related to messianism only on the level of theory, but they did so in such impressive, constant fashion that the masses were inspired to embrace messianic movements, despite the reservations and opposition of the rabbis. As to Ashkenaz, even a generous evaluation of the messianic movements there will reveal a very modest number; it is difficult to agree with the claim that movements of a messianic nature were "frequently" led there by the rabbinic elite.

As I have mentioned, Carlebach points to the discovery of contacts between the Jews of medieval Ashkenaz and Sepharad, and she sees those contacts as a basis for denying the presence of sharp, clear lines distinguishing the two cultures. This argument, for all its plausibility,

---

[10]   Cohen, p. 132 (ed. Kreuzberger).

requires us to confront a broad, complex historical-methodological question with many significant implications: When a civilization, or segment of a civilization, is already beyond its formative stage, and has an established cultural character, under what conditions might we expect that its fundamental characteristics would change due to outside influences? This is not the place to deal with the full dimensions of this question, which have the broadest implications, but generally speaking, it does not appear that cultures undergo deep changes simply on the basis of books and reports brought by travelers or even on the basis of a few personal contacts.

In 1985, the historian Charles Radding published a book which spawned a furious debate. In this book, he argued that the residents of Europe in the first half of the Middle Ages evinced modes of ethical thought that correspond not to those of adults in our society, but to those of children whose age can be identified on the basis of Jean Piaget's system of classification.[11] Among other things, Radding maintained that Europeans in that period evaluated the severity of a crime based on its consequences without reference to the perpetrator's intent. One of the criticisms leveled against Radding was that it is impossible to argue that the authors of medieval laws could have ignored the importance of intent since even in the early centuries of the Middle Ages Christian intellectuals read the Bible with the belief that it represented divine revelation, and biblical law views intent as a very important component in ascertaining the severity of a sin and the degree of its punishment. Moreover, as even Radding himself notes, Augustine and other church fathers who were regarded as authorities by medieval lawmakers, also ascribed considerable importance to intent.

However, I think that this argument, which maintains that people who believe in certain books will necessarily internalize their values, does not accord with real psychological processes. Nations that developed characteristic ways of thinking over long periods of time do not undergo fundamental changes over a few generations just because they have adopted a belief in a book that represents a different mentality. It is much easier to adopt a new doctrine than a new way of conceiving reality and the manner in which the universe operates. To the extent

---

11   Charles Radding, *A World Made by Men: Cognition and Society, 400-1200* (Chapel Hill, 1985).

that Radding has succeeded in pointing to evidence that the *mentalité* of pre-twelfth-century Europeans in fact evinced the ethical conception that he attributes to them (and this remains a debatable proposition), the fact that this conception does not fit the Bible or Augustine does not undermine his conclusion.

With respect to the Jews of medieval Ashkenaz and Sepharad, this point can be illustrated through an examination of an important article on Jewish-Christian polemic.[12] Daniel Lasker demonstrated that philosophical arguments against Christianity originating among Sephardic Jews appeared in books known to Ashkenazim. He pointed to sporadic Ashkenazic use of these arguments beginning in the mid-fourteenth century and to a nugatory number of exceptional philosophical passages before that point. The reader of Lasker's comprehensive book on medieval Jewish philosophical polemic against Christianity will plainly see that Ashkenazic polemical literature plays so negligible a role in it that deletion of the few references to this literature would effect virtually no change at all in its contents.[13] The article suggests a number of explanations for the absence of philosophical argumentation, but the one that I find most convincing is that the phenomenon is rooted in a difference in worldviews. Lasker's data effectively show us that the estrangement of Ashkenazic Jews from a philosophical mode of thought was so deeply ingrained that they could not digest philosophical concepts even to the extent needed to direct them against Christian disputants – despite the fact that arguments drawing upon them were more effective than those formulated by the Ashkenazim on their own. I do not mean to suggest that the Jews of Ashkenaz, among them sages whose "little finger is thicker than my loins," were not capable of understanding philosophical discourse. However, even one who understands and even values an argument that is embedded in a cognitive system foreign to the way of thinking in which he has been raised from childhood will not easily mobilize it and transfer it from his peripheral, passive awareness to his central, active consciousness.

In the final analysis, then, the contacts between Ashkenaz and

---

12   Daniel J. Lasker, "Jewish Philosophical Polemics in Ashkenaz," in *Contra Iudaeos: Ancient and Medieval Polemics between Christians and Jews*, ed. by Ora Limor and Guy Stroumsa (Tuebingen, 1996), pp. 195-213.
13   Daniel J. Lasker, *Jewish Philosophical Polemics against Christianity in the Middle Ages* (New York, 1977).

Sepharad were meaningful, and we should not minimize their significance. But we should also not exaggerate their significance. Deep differences separated the two cultural spheres, certainly to a sufficient degree to sustain Cohen's thesis from an abstract methodological perspective.[14]

We have arrived, then, at Carlebach's analysis of the historiographical material. We recall that the key point of her analysis is the affirmation that the Christian environment is what caused Ashkenazic Jews to refrain from recounting messianic episodes, and even when they mentioned them, they downplayed or even ignored the messianic element. Consequently, it is entirely possible that there were many more messianic movements in Ashkenaz than the ones whose memory has been preserved. In other words, the perception of a deep division between a Sepharad overflowing with messianic movements and an Ashkenaz bereft of them rests on the broken reed of flimsy historical documentation.

When I noted earlier that our list of messianic movements is based in part on Maimonides' *Epistle to Yemen*, I meant to point out the possibility that a different picture might have emerged had we possessed a fuller, more balanced record. It is clear, then, that we cannot eliminate this uncertainty entirely, and from an abstract, logical perspective, Carlebach's observation indeed sharpens it. Nonetheless, the historiographical data cited in her article do not appear to prove the point.

These data focus on only two movements, those of Laemmelein and Molkho, both in the first half of the sixteenth century. In the first instance, I see no support for the thesis that Ashkenazic writers downplayed the messianic dimension of such movements whereas Sephardic writers presented it fully. Carlebach emphasizes the fact that the Ashkenazi David Ganz characterizes Laemmelein only as a harbinger of the messiah. However, as she reports further, Ganz also informs us of messianic expectations that were associated with Laemmelein's announcement of the redemption, and the Prague Chronicle also speaks in this context of a rumor regarding the Messiah. Among the Sephardim, Ibn Yahya's formulation does not contain any clear messianic content that goes beyond what we find in the Ashkenazic sources. As noted above,

---

14   I addressed this subject more fully in "Exegesis, Polemic, Philosophy, and Science: Reflections on the Tenacity of Ashkenazic Modes of Thought," scheduled to appear in the proceedings of a conference on "The Attitude to Science and Philosophy in Ashkenazic Culture through the Ages" to be edited by Gad Freudenthal [now reprinted in this volume].

Yosef ha-Kohen and Sambari report that Laemmelein was considered a prophet sent to be a ruler over the Jewish people, who would "gather the dispersed of Judah from the four corners of the earth," but even they have no explicit statement that Laemmelein declared that he was the Messiah. Moreover, the motif of the ingathering of the exiles also appears clearly in David Ganz's chronicle. ("My grandfather, Seligman Ganz of blessed memory, destroyed an oven dedicated to baking matzah for Passover, for he was absolutely certain that in the following year, he would be baking matzah in the Holy Land."[15]) The general picture here does not reflect a significant difference between Ashkenazic and Sephardic historiography, and Carlebach herself words her conclusions from the data on Laemmelein very cautiously.[16]

In the second instance, Carlebach's analysis points to a somewhat more evident difference, but even this is not convincing. A single Sephardic source (Sambari) says explicitly that Molkho claimed to be the Messiah. Ibn Yahya, who is mentioned in the article without quotation or analysis, writes that Molkho declared that he was one of the *emissaries* of the Messiah,[17] a formulation that Carlebach characterized as avoidance of an explicit messianic identification when she dealt with Ganz's report that Laemmelein saw himself as the herald of the messiah.

Yosef ha-Kohen's use of the expression "a shoot came forth out of Portugal" does appear to allude to messianism, but in a manner so brief and indirect that one might plausibly speculate that if the author had been Ashkenazic, Carlebach would have seen such a non-explicit allusion as support for her thesis. Moreover, careful examination generates doubt as to whether or not this formula alludes to messianism at all, for Molkho wrote of himself, "Give your ears to hear the words of a worm, scarcely a man, a shoot from the stem of the men of our exile, who has emerged from our enemies".[18] Aescoly points out that the word "enemies" here refers to Portugal, a country that persecuted its Jews. It is likely, then, that this passage in the letter by Molkho is the source (whether directly

---

[15]   *Zemah David*, ed. by Mordechai Breuer (Jerusalm, 1983), p. 137, cited by Carlebach, p. 6.

[16]   I believe that she is right in her claim that Ashkenazic writers intentionally avoided describing the instances of apostasy that occurred in the wake of the movement, but this point does not necessarily mean that they avoided mentioning messianic movements in and of themselves.

[17]   Aharon Ze'ev Aescoly, *Ha-Tenu'ot ha-Meshihiyyot be-Yisrael* (Jerusalem, 1967), p. 408.

[18]   Aescoly, p. 386.

or indirectly) of Yosef ha-Kohen's expression "a shoot came forth out of Portugal," and the context in that letter refers according to its straightforward meaning to humble ancestry, not to Davidic lineage.

If David Ganz really refrained from mentioning the messianic ferment associated with Molkho out of a calculated decision to ignore messianic episodes, why does he mention the messianic stirrings inspired by the accounts concerning Laemmelein? The Prague Chronicle reports messianic expectations that spread as a consequence of Reuveni's activities. Even if Josel of Rosheim intentionally avoided any reference to the messianic aspect of Molkho's activity, we must remember that because he served as a diplomat in royal and princely courts, he could have motivated by special considerations, and it is doubtful that one may extrapolate from his behavior to that of the general population. Yom Tov Lipman Heller's mention of Molkho is only a side-point in a halakhic discussion, so that his failure to identify Molkho as a messianic figure bears no significance. In general, the omission of the fact that Molkho identified himself as the messiah is not meaningful, because it is very likely that this "fact" is not correct. There is no reason to consider Sambari's confused report to be a historically authentic account, and in a matter of this sort we cannot rely on Christian testimonies, whose self-interest with respect to this assertion is blatant.[19] The failure to mention an *erroneous* fact about a messianic declaration can hardly prove an Ashkenazic tendency to avoid reporting candid and complete information about messianic figures. Thus, Carlebach's only meaningful argument from the historiography about Molkho is that Ashkenazic sources fail to mention messianic *ferment*, not that they fail to mention Molkho's supposed self-identification as messiah. Yet even from this point of view, we are speaking about one source that mentions messianic ferment in other contexts (Ganz), a second source that mentions it here (the Prague Chronicle), a third source written by an author with a delicate and atypical position (Josel of Rosheim), and a fourth dealing primarily with an entirely different topic (Heller).

To sum up, Carlebach's methodological point about the historiographical literature is of great interest as a hypothesis, but it

---

19   I am not saying that we should reject any Christian report out of hand on the assumption that Christians invented fictional messianic movements out of whole cloth. However, when a Christian provides an account of such a movement, we cannot expect him to distinguish carefully and meticulously among a prophet, a harbinger of the Messiah, an emissary of the Messiah, and the Messiah himself.

has no convincing support from the documentation available to us. What I have written above about the tendency of Jews in Christian lands to recoil from messiahs referred, as I noted, to the embrace of messianic figures, not to the avoidance of reference to messianic movements in Hebrew books. There is a certain logic in the avoidance of such references,[20] but we do not have sufficient evidence to conclude that an Ashkenazic historiographic practice has deprived us of information about messianic movements.

Now let us attempt to sum up and propose some cautious suggestions.

It is difficult to accept Cohen's argument that there was a connection between the messianic tendencies of Babylonia and Palestine, on the one hand, and the communities of Sepharad and Ashkenaz hundreds of years later, let alone that this proposed link rested on a common rationalistic component. Similarly, the suggested link between messianic calculations and activism on the one hand and acts of apostasy on the other is baseless and without any convincing logic.

What remains is Cohen's central thesis with its three components.

1. In Sepharad, we find lively messianic discussion of a rationalistic nature, including great interest in calculating the End. In Ashkenaz, on the other hand, the dimensions of messianic discourse are much smaller, and to the degree that it existed, it was entirely different in nature and focused on prophecies and numerical equivalencies.

2. In the Sephardic sector, we find about a dozen messianic figures between 1065 and 1492. In the Ashkenazic sector, we do not find a single one.

3. These differences are rooted in the influence of Sephardic rationalism, which inspired an entire messianic literature. Once this topic was on the agenda, it led to movements despite the opposition of the rabbinic/intellectual elite.

It is clear that Cohen's first assertion is correct to the degree that

---

[20] We recall that Carlebach directs our attention to an interesting and relevant passage in *Sefer Hasidim*, ed. by Wistinetzky (Frankfurt-am-Main, 1884), section 212, pp. 76–77, in which the author warns the reader to be wary of individuals who prophesy about the messiah, for the prediction "will ultimately be revealed to the whole world, and will lead to shame and disgrace."

it addresses messianic thought, but this point in itself is neither controversial nor innovative. Similarly, messianic calculations are indeed found in the works of important thinkers in Sepharad, whereas the calculations in Ashkenaz tend to occupy a much more peripheral place. Nevertheless, we do find quite a few calculations in Ashkenaz: *Ronnu le-Ya'akov simhah* (the 256th cycle of the calendar), the end of the fifth millennium, and more, though the calculations in Sepharad are more variegated as a result of the broader intellectual vision that we might label "rationalism."

With respect to messianic movements or figures, Cohen's factual claim retains considerable persuasive power even after all the criticism that has been leveled against it. Even if we use the general term "ferment," we do not find meaningful messianic activism in the heartland of Ashkenaz except in the generation immediately before the end of the fifth millennium. Yuval has recently argued on the basis of a very interesting text that the migrations of rabbis to the Land of Israel in that generation were inspired after all by messianic motives.[21] Avraham Grossman has endorsed a messianic explanation, but he emphasizes not the significance of the year 5000 but the influence of the news that the kingdom of the Crusaders had been defeated by Saladin, which, he says, inspired messianic expectation in the communities of Ashkenaz.[22] Even if we adopt the messianic understanding of these migrations, the activism in question is simply travel to the Holy Land to pray there. It is difficult to take the Christian report about the year 1337 with all of its anti-

---

21   *Shenei Goyim be-Bitnekh*, pp. 276-283. The sixth chapter of the book is devoted to a comprehensive and fascinating analysis of the influence of messianic expectation in the years before 1240, even though there are grounds for reservations regarding some of the arguments.

22   Grossman, "Nizhonot Salah a-Din ve-ha-Hit'orerut be-Eropah la-'Aliyyah le-Erez Yisrael," in *Ve-Zot li-Yehudah: Mehqarim be-Toledot Erez Yisrael ve-Yishuvah: Muggashim li-Yehoshua ben Porat*, ed. by Yehoshua Ben-Aryeh and Elchanan Reiner (Jerusalem, 2003), pp. 362-382. Grossman adduces the following in support of his thesis: the travails that Ashkenazic Jewry was suffering at the time; the argument proffered by Christians that their victory in the Crusades was further evidence that the Jews had been rejected in favor of the "True Israel"; liturgical poems describing the desecration of Jerusalem by Christian pollution; a rabbinic statement that the redemption would come at a time of war between the great world-empires; the joy of two Ashkenazic authors (only one of whom refers to Saladin) upon hearing the news of the Muslim victories; a near-messianic description of Saladin in a work by Al-Harizi; and the text which Yuval cites. These arguments establish a reasonable possibility, but it is hard to say that the evidence is genuinely convincing.

Semitic legends too seriously, although there are no decisive grounds for rejecting the possibility that it could be based in fact. Moreover, even one who sees messianic ferment in 1096 in light of *Ronnu le-Ya'akov simhah*, and believes the Christian reports about 1337, and, in the wake of Yuval's study, lays great emphasis on the excitement leading up to 1240, would nonetheless have to admit that before Asher Laemmelein—and even he was not active in the Ashkenazic heartland—*we do not have a report of a single messianic figure in Ashkenaz.*[23]

The burden of proof rests on one who wants to challenge this picture. We may therefore move on to Cohen's third point, where he attempts to explain the phenomenon. Were popular messianic movements actually born out of the influence of elite discussion of messianism, which trickled down to the masses in distorted fashion? This is by no means impossible. The educated elite certainly maintained connections with the masses, and personalities such as Avraham Abulafia even straddled the boundary between messianic thinker and semi-messianic figure.

Nevertheless, it seems that this scenario is relevant only in Spain itself. Figures such as David Al-Ro'i, and others like him, were active in an environment that was not characterized by a rationalist component strong enough to create movements among the masses. In general, it is doubtful that we would be wondering at all about the appearance of about a dozen messianic figures over a period of hundreds of years if not for the contrast with Ashkenaz. We should consequently turn our attention not to the presence of messiahs in the Sephardic communities, but to their absence in Ashkenaz.

In the wake of a reference in Carlebach's article, I have already noted a suggestion made by my student Avraham Pinsker that Ashkenazim may have recoiled from messianic activism because they lived in a Christian environment where they were forced to defend themselves constantly against a religion that believed in a false messiah. This suggestion, however, is subject to challenge. In Christian Spain, after

---

[23]   The messiah of Linon evinces clear "eastern" characteristic, and I believe that Cohen is correct is seeing him as Sephardic rather than French. It should be noted that in a later article, Cohen dismissed all medieval messianic movements as insignificant. While there is much truth in this assertion, the contrast between Ashkenaz and Sepharad in this sphere remains unaffected. See "Messianism in Jewish History: The Myth and the Reality," in Gerson D. Cohen, *Jewish History and Jewish Destiny* (New York and Jerusalem, 1997), pp. 183-212.

all, we continue to find messianic "ferment," and sometimes even figures of a messianic character. One might respond to this difficulty by arguing that the messianic orientation of Sephardic Jewry was formed under the rule of Islam, and it did not change in the face of the "logical" concerns that might have been expected to uproot it in a Christian environment. Nevertheless, the initial explanation is just a hypothesis, and the fact that we need to defend it immediately against a reasonable challenge shows that we should probably not embrace it with conviction.

Let me move then to a different suggestion, which was also first proposed in a discussion with students. Sheila Rabin, who studied with me many years ago, suggested that the small populations of the Ashkenazic communities served as an impediment to messianic movements. She did not elaborate, but I believe that the suggestion deserves serious consideration.

The number of people who follow a messianic figure at the beginning of his career – and in most cases, even at the height of his career – are normally only a small percentage of the community's population. If the community is very small, one could hardly expect the number of believers to reach the level necessary to transform the presumed messiah from a mere curiosity to an influential personality. Furthermore, people who have intimately known the messianic figure since his childhood are not usually those who are mostly likely to be convinced by his messianic claims. From this perspective, the communities in the Sephardic sector, which were usually larger than those in Ashkenaz, were more likely to generate messianic movements.

Finally – another suggestion that is also related to the nature of small communities, but focuses primarily on the relationship between the rabbinic elite and the masses. Let us remember that Carlebach has noted the sense of identification that the members of the small Ashkenazic communities felt with the rabbinic scholars in their midst to support her claim that messianic activity by rabbis influenced the community as a whole. I have already expressed my view that messianic activity among the rabbis of Ashkenaz was in reality extremely limited. For this very reason, Carlebach's observation about the relationship between the Ashkenazic rabbis and the masses provides an opening for a new understanding of the absence of messianic movements or figures in Ashkenaz. In general, as Cohen has emphasized, rabbis did not follow messiahs. The small messianic movements in the Middle Ages arose and grew in the popular stratum of society, whereas the rabbinic elite reacted to them with suspicion, even with hostility. Consequently, we should not expect messianic movements to develop in small communities in which the "masses" are very closely linked to the rabbis. Of course, this picture of the authority held by the rabbis of Ashkenaz is exaggerated and generalized, but I believe that there is enough truth in it to support the basic argument.

We have examined a truly gripping historical and historiographical issue. After the criticisms presented both in this article and in Carlebach's lecture, Cohen's famous thesis is reduced to the point where it stands on two factual claims: (1) In medieval Spain and the Middle East, we find messianic figures; but in Ashkenaz, we find none. (2) Speculative messianic thought, including variegated calculations of the End, is characteristic specifically of Sephardic communities. It is not impossible that Cohen was correct in his attempt to associate the presence or absence of messianic figures with varying approaches to faith and thought; however, the suggested connection is not straightforward, since he must assume that rationalism created movements only indirectly. Moreover, not all the messianic claimants appeared in rationalistic environments. It is consequently preferable to turn to other considerations. In Spain and the Middle East, messianic figures occasionally appeared, sometimes as a result of influences that we can identify, or at least surmise, such as the Shiite environment or the turmoil in Yemen; but even when we do not have a good explanation for a particular movement, there is no basis for perplexity regarding the rise of a few small movements over the course of many generations. The real question is why there were no messianic figures in Ashkenaz, and here we may perhaps proffer the modest suggestions that I have proposed. Even when small communities grow to some extent over the course of time, patterns of messianic thought and expectation formed over the course of generations do not change easily, especially in light of the continuing authority and influence of the rabbinic leadership, which was very wary of embracing messianic figures. In sum, it may well be that the communal profile that characterized Ashkenazic Jewry also determined its messianic profile.

MACCABEES, ZEALOTS AND JOSEPHUS:
THE IMPACT OF ZIONISM ON JOSEPH KLAUSNER'S
HISTORY OF THE SECOND TEMPLE

From: *Studies in Josephus and the Varieties of Ancient Judaism: Louis H. Feldman Jubilee Volume*, ed. by Shaye J.D. Cohen and Joshua Schwartz (Koninklijke Brill N.V.: Leiden, 2006), pp. 15-27.

It is hardly a secret that Zionist ideology had a profound impact on Joseph Klausner's historiographic enterprise. Even a superficial perusal of his works reveals a powerful Zionist commitment expressed in both rhetoric and analysis, so much so that his right to teach the period of the Second Temple in the Hebrew University was held up for years on the grounds that he was more of a publicist and ideologue—and of the Revisionist variety no less—than a historian. Nonetheless, I believe that there is much to be said for a serious examination of the nationalist element in his multi-volume work on the Second Temple.[1] However we assess the political and scholarly arguments for and against his appointment, a man who had nothing of the historian in him would not have been appointed to Klausner's position in the world's flagship institution for Jewish Studies. With all his abundant methodological flaws, he was not a publicist pure and simple.

Since readers of this article, which will sharply underscore some of those flaws, may ultimately question this judgment, let me move immediately to a second, even more important point. The ideological use of selected episodes in a nation's history is an integral part of any nationalist movement or educational system. Zionism was no exception; indeed, its unusual, even unique, character generated a particularly acute need to establish a national history that would provide models for the struggling yishuv and the early state. The pedagogic utilization of the ancient paradigms of Jewish heroism had to draw upon academic,

---

[1]   *Historia shel ha-Bayit ha-Sheni*, 2nd ed., 5 vols. (Jerusalem, 1951), henceforth *Historia*.

not merely popular, legitimation. From this perspective, the fact that Klausner stood with one foot in the world of academic research and the other in the public square, where he exercised considerable influence, lends special interest to an analysis of his scholarly-ideological approach to key developments in Second Temple history.[2] As Klausner confronted the dilemmas of military, political and religious policy in ancient Israel, his own dilemmas illuminate not only Zionist historiography but the political and moral challenges facing the nascent, beleaguered State.

It is self-evident that Klausner was sensitive to the charges leveled at him by his colleagues at the university, and so his inaugural lecture on the Second Temple, which is also the opening chapter of the book, was devoted to the question of historical objectivity. The argument in that lecture is so strange that only the extraordinary defensiveness generated by relentless criticism can serve to explain it.

The objective study of history, says Klausner, leads to 'necessary conclusions,' to 'absolute evaluations.'[3] It is true that each generation sees the past through its own experience, but as long as the historian seeks truth to the best of his ability, his conclusions are absolute for that generation. This is an idiosyncratic use of the term 'absolute,' and when Klausner proposes a concrete example, the peculiarity of the argument is thrown into even bolder relief. A Jew and a Pole, he says, *must* evaluate Chmielnicki differently, but precisely because of the ineluctable nature of this difference, 'there is no subjectivity involved at all.' Chmielnicki persecuted the Jews but strove to improve the lot of his own people. Consequently, 'the honest scholar must see both sides of the accepted historical coin.'[4] Thus, in virtually the same breath, Klausner speaks of the absolute necessity compelling a Jew to evaluate Chmielnicki in a one-sided fashion and proceeds to present him in all his mutivalent complexity. This almost incoherent argument for untrammeled, unmodulated historical objectivity was surely generated by the subjective realities of Klausner's personal situation.

---

[2] Klausner's profound impact on certain sectors of the yishuv, an impact grounded precisely in his combined personae of scholarly researcher, Zionist thinker, and public personality, is strikingly evident in the tone of the admiring intellectual biography written by two disciples during his lifetime. See Yaakov Becker and Hayim Toren, *Yosef Klausner, ha-Ish u-Po'olo* (Tel Aviv and Jerusalem, 1947).

[3] *Historia* 1:10.

[4] *Historia* 1:11.

When we turn to the period of the Second Temple, we confront a series of personalities and events central to the self-image of both yishuv and State: the return from the Babylonian exile, the revolt of Mattathias and his sons, the achievement of independence and the pursuit of territorial expansion under the Hasmoneans, the great revolt, and the heroic stand at Masada.[5] The longest lasting of these developments was the Hasmonean dynasty, rooted in the most successful and spectacular event of the entire period, a revolt emblematic of Jewish military might and remembered not only by historians but by every Jewish child who has ever seen a Hanukkah menorah.

That revolt and that dynasty were pivotal to Zionist self-consciousness. Pinsker lamented the servile state of a people that had produced the Maccabees; Herzl declared that the Maccabees would arise once again; and in one of the most wrenching passages in all of Jewish literature, Bialik portrayed with bitter sarcasm the cellars in which "the young lions of the prayer 'Father of Mercy' and the grandsons of the Maccabees" lay hidden in their miserable cowardice.[6] Jabotinsky sharply criticized the ghetto mentality that intentionally blotted out the memory of the Maccabees, and Gedaliah Alon's refutation of the thesis that the rabbinic Sages had done something similar was formulated in particularly sharp fashion: "Did the Nation and Its Rabbis Cause the Hasmoneans to be Forgotten?"[7] Who then were these Maccabees, and are they really worthy of this extraordinary veneration?[8]

Klausner examined the Hasmonean period—and not that period alone—in an analytical framework reflecting categories of thought more characteristic of a twentieth-century Zionist scholar than of Judaean

---

[5]   In the last decade or so, several important works have, in whole or in part, analyzed the use of these and similar models in Zionist education, literature, and civic life. See Yael Zerubavel, *Recovered Roots: Collective Memory and the Meaning of Israeli National Tradition* (Chicago and London, 1995) and the literature noted there; Nachman Ben-Yehudah, *The Masada Myth: Collective Memory and Mythmaking in Israel* (Madison, Wisconsin, c. 1995); Mireille Hadas-Lebel, *Masada: Histoire et Symbole* (Paris, c. 1995); Anita Shapira, *Land and Power: The Zionist Resort to Force, 1881-1948* (New York, 1992). As early as 1937, Klausner himself had contributed to the popularization of the Masada story as a heroic, paradigmatic event. See *Land and Power*, p. 311.

[6]   See the references in *Land and Power*, pp. 14, 37.

[7]   *Mehqarim be-Toledot Yisrael* I (Tel Aviv, 1957), pp. 15-25.

[8]   For a useful survey of Jewish perceptions of the Hasmoneans from antiquity through the twentieth century, see Samuel Schafler's 1973 Jewish Theological Seminary dissertation, *The Hasmoneans in Jewish Historiography*. On Klausner, see pp. 164-167, 199-204.

fighters in the second pre-Christian century. Granted, he says, Judah Maccabee fought for the religion of Israel, but he understood that his success was nourished by '"another non-material and non-measurable force—the national will to live. When a nation has no choice other than to achieve victory or pass away from the world, it is impossible for it not to be victorious. So it was then and so it has been in our time and before our eyes."[9]

And the essential element in this "understanding"—the knowing incorporation of a nationalist consciousness into a religious ideology—characterized Judah's father as well. "[Mattathias] recognized clearly that it is appropriate to desecrate one Sabbath in order to observe many Sabbaths—in order to sustain the entire nation."[10] The undeclared shift from the Talmudic formula—that the Sabbath may in certain circumstances be desecrated so that many Sabbaths may be observed in the future—to the nationalist formula that Klausner created as if the two were self-evidently interchangeable is a striking example of ideological sleight of hand.

It emerges, moreover, that this integration of the religious and the national characterized not only the Maccabees but the bulk of the Jewish population. "Most of the nation" overcame "all manner of torments" to stand against the decrees of Antiochus.

> Tens of thousands of spiritual heroes arose in Judaea who could not be coerced to betray the Torah of their God by any torment in the world or by any threat of bizarre death. . . . There was an intuitive feeling here that by betraying their God they would also be betraying their people, and if the Torah of Israel would be destroyed so too would the People of Israel.[11]

Finally, Klausner takes a remarkable further step by elevating land over spirit, and doing so through an original piece of speculative biblical exegesis so bereft of any evidentiary support that it is mildly unusual even by the anarchic standards of the Bible critics of his day. It is likely, he says, that the psalm asserting that "the heavens belong to the Lord but the earth He gave over to man" (Ps 115:16) was written during the great victory of Judah Maccabee. The warriors,

9   *Historia* 3:19.
10   *Historia* 3:17.
11   *Historia* 2:199.

suffused by a sense of the sanctity of the Homeland (*qedushat ha-moledet*) and the joy flowing from fulfilling the divine command, felt no need for the world to come. Through their conquest, they had acquired earthly life for themselves and for their nation and were prepared to leave the heavens to the Lord their God, provided that he would give them the land as an inheritance—the land of their fathers and their children.[12]

Though the verse appears to speak of a contrast between the heavens and an earth given to humanity as a whole, the true, deeper meaning refers to the land of Israel granted to its chosen people.

Although Klausner asserts that even the pietists—the "hasidim" of the sources—were nationalists, he underscores the contrast between their primarily spiritual interests and the political orientation of the Hasmoneans. In itself, such a perspective is eminently defensible.[13] Klausner, however, goes further by ascribing to his heroes from the very beginning of their appearance on the historical stage a fully formed, unambiguous ideology that is not expressed in the sources but accords perfectly with that of the historian.

"From the outset," Judah and his brothers sought "absolute freedom." They understood that "inner—religious and national-social—freedom" is impossible without "absolute political sovereignty (*qomemiyyut*)."[14] Thus, the distinctive categories of religious freedom, national-social freedom, and political sovereignty did not merely animate Judah's policies on a subconscious level; they were a key element of his conscious ideology from the first moment of the revolt. Nor was this ideology created *ex nihilo* in the Hasmonean period. The spiritual creativity that Klausner ascribes to the four centuries between the Babylonian exile and the revolt would have been impossible in his view in the absence of "a profound yearning for political freedom."[15] Once again—an argument resting not on a documented source but on a psychohistorical generalization rooted in this instance in a sense of what the author's ideologically honed instincts have declared impossible.

---

[12] *Historia* 3:29.
[13] See *Historia* 2:182-183, and cf. 3:38. For a discussion of the role of land and politics in this context, see Doron Mendels, *The Land of Israel as a Political Concept in Hasmonean Literature* (Tuebingen, 1987).
[14] *Historia* 3:41.
[15] *Historia* 2:273.

When Klausner moves to the very different contrast between early Hasmoneans and Hellenizers, he describes the former, not surprisingly, as "the national party." In this instance, however, the interplay of ideological factors was potentially more complex. While the Zionist movement was in one sense a reaction against the classical Haskalah, to a very important degree it was its offspring. Klausner, whose other, less controversial field of expertise was modern Hebrew literature, surely identified with the movement to broaden the intellectual and cultural horizons of Eastern European Jewry, and he could not dismiss the value of Greek culture even for the Jews of antiquity. Indeed, in another work, he described his central credo as follows: "To absorb the culture of the other to the point of digesting it and transforming it into our own national-human flesh and blood— this is the ideal for which I fought during the prime of my life, and I will not stray from it till my last breath."[16] Might it not be possible, then, even necessary, to say something positive about the Jewish arch-enemies of the Maccabees?

In order to avoid this undesirable consequence, Klausner mobilizes another presumably ineluctable law of history to help him conclude that the Hellenizers' objective was not the incorporation of Greek values into Jewish culture but the annihilation of the latter in favor of the former. Some scholars, he says, maintain that the Hellenizers were correct in their desire to open provincial Jewish society to the wide-ranging culture of the Hellenistic world. This, however, misperceives the Hellenizers' intentions. "If they had possessed a liberating, essentially correct ideology, it would eventually have prevailed and been realized in life, even if little by little. The truth bursts forth and makes its way, sometimes immediately, sometimes after the passage of time."[17]

Here Klausner's questionable rhetoric about the inevitable success of "truth" conceals an even more extreme and implausible position upon which his argument really rests. In light of the progressive Hellenistic influence on the Hasmonean dynasty, what he sees as the essentially correct ideology of integrating Greek ideas and Judaism was indeed realized after the passage of time. So far so good. But how does Klausner know that this correct objective, which arguably did prevail, was not the goal of the Hellenizers? The answer cannot be the circular argument

---

[16] *Bereshit Hayah ha-Ra'ayon*, p. 172, cited in Becker and Toren, p. 13.
[17] *Historia* 3:155.

that their ideology did not prevail; rather, despite the plain meaning of his language, it must be that the group failed as a political entity, a failure that proves that it could not have had a correct worldview. In other words, his argument—if it is to be granted any coherence at all— amounts to the assertion that not only proper ideas but the political group that originates them must survive and ultimately triumph. Since this was not true of the Hellenizers, it follows that their goal was not integration but Jewish cultural suicide.[18]

The Hasmoneans ultimately attained genuine political freedom; this alone, however, did not satisfy them, and here Klausner mobilizes religion to explain and justify even more far-reaching national ambitions. Because the new rulers regularly read the Torah and the Prophets, "it was impossible for them not to sense how unnatural their situation was—that of all the Land of Israel promised to Abraham and ruled by David and Solomon, Israel remained with only the little state of Judaea."[19] Once again Klausner declares something impossible, and once again the assessment leads to a conclusion identical to the ideology of the historian, this time in its Revisionist form.

This orientation appears even more clearly in Klausner's lament over the civil war in the days of Alexander Jannaeus. If not for this internal war, he suggests, the king may have taken advantage of the opportunity afforded by the weakness of the Seleucid Empire to conquer the coastal cities of the Land of Israel—and even Tyre and Sidon. And this too is not the end of it. "There are grounds to believe that Jannaeus, like his ancestors, dreamed the great dream of returning the Kingdom of David and Solomon to its original grandeur, and even more than this—of inheriting the Seleucid Empire itself."[20] It cannot be ruled out that Jannaeus dreamed such dreams, but it is difficult to avoid the impression that the historian's vision has merged with the ambition of the Hasmonean king to the point where the two can no longer be distinguished.

Dreams, however, collide with realities, and these collisions can spawn not only practical difficulties but serious moral dilemmas. In describing the Hasmonean wars in general and the expansion of the boundaries

---

18 Cf. also *Historia* 2:145.
19 *Historia* 3:31.
20 *Historia* 3:151.

of Israel in particular, Klausner must confront the leveling of pagan temples, expulsions, the destruction of cities, and forced conversions. The ethical problems posed by such behavior disturb him, and he is occasionally prepared to express disapproval. Thus, it is as if Judah Maccabee forgot what he himself suffered from religious persecution and ignored "the slightly later dictum, 'Do not do to your fellow that which is hateful to you.'"[21] Similarly, the destruction of the Samaritan temple "can only be explained but not justified."[22] Nonetheless, Klausner's basic inclination is to provide mitigation for such acts and sometimes even to justify them.

The most striking example of such justification appears in his reaction to Simon's expulsion of pagans as part of the policy of judaizing sections of the land of Israel. It is true that these actions involved considerable cruelty, he says, but had the Hasmoneans behaved differently, the tiny Judaean state would have ceased to exist under the pressure of its neighbors, "and the end would have come for the People of Israel as a whole." Under such circumstances, "the moral criterion *cannot help* but retreat, and in its place there comes another criterion: *the possibility of survival.* . . . For our 'puny intellect,' this appears to constitute the very antithesis of justice; for the 'larger intellect,' *this is the way to justice*, the footstool of absolute justice" (emphasis in the original).[23]

Elsewhere, he returns to the "biblical view of the Land of Israel,"[24] arguing that in light of this tradition, the newly formed Judaean state "had [was *mukhrahat*] to expand eastward—toward Transjordan, northward—toward Shechem, and southward—toward Idumaea."[25] The conquest of Idumaea, complete with the forcible conversion of its inhabitants, was unavoidable. Stolen land was being recovered; a Jewish majority was a necessity for the nation; Judaea could not have been left surrounded by enemies forever. What follows is very difficult to read today: If we are concerned with "the admixture of blood, almost all the neighboring peoples were Semites, and so the race remained unaffected even after the conversion of the Idumaeans."[26] The major themes repeat themselves

---

21   *Historia* 3:33, 35.
22   *Historia* 3:86.
23   *Historia* 3:65, 66.
24   *Historia* 3:78.
25   *Historia* 3:85.
26   *Historia* 3:88.

in Klausner's evaluation of the policies of Alexander Jannaeus: "Out of historical compulsion—deeply regrettable in itself—Jannaeus was forced to destroy cities . . . whose inhabitants did not agree to accept Judaism. . . . Is it plausible that in territories called by the name 'Land of Israel' that were part of Israel in the days of David, Solomon, Ahab, Jeroboam II and Josiah, aliens and enemies should reside forever?"[27]

Klausner makes a point of emphasizing that the Jewish people as a whole supported the Hasmonean rulers no less than he. First, his idyllic characterization of this people is noteworthy in and of itself. "The true Jewish democracy [consisted of] farmers owning small homesteads, day laborers, craftsmen, and workers in fields and homes." This was "a large nation, assiduous and wise, religious-moral, laboring and satisfied with limited wealth." The typical Jewish farmer was "a religious conservative and a nationalist patriot." And this nation "defended the Hasmonean family and its aspirations as one man."[28]

Klausner provides four arguments for rejecting the historicity of the story asserting that Jannaeus crucified eight hundred of his opponents in a single day. Two of these strikingly underscore his attitude to the Hasmoneans themselves as well as his emphasis on their popular support. First, a king and high priest of the Hasmonean dynasty could not have been capable of such behavior.[29] Second, if this had really happened, "the nation would not have been devoted to the Hasmoneans with all its heart and soul and would not have spilled its blood like water for anyone in whose veins there coursed even one drop of Hasmonean blood."[30] Elsewhere, Klausner is a bit more cautious, speaking of support from "the decisive majority of the activist nation,"[31] but the fundamental emphasis remains unchanged. Finally, we hear of the special qualities of Hasmonean blood on more than one further occasion. Aristobulus II, for example, refused to accept one of Pompey's demands because "the blood of the Maccabees coursing in his veins did not allow him to debase his honor excessively."[32] One wonders what sort of blood coursed in the veins of Aristobulus's brother Hyrcanus II.

---

[27]   *Historia* 3:160.
[28]   *Historia* 3:12; 5:132: 3:43, 82.
[29]   This point was noted by Schafler, p. 201.
[30]   *Historia* 3:155.
[31]   *Historia* 3:235-36.
[32]   *Historia* 3:222.

When we turn from war and politics to cultural life, the spectrum of Klausner's views becomes wider, richer, more varied, more nuanced, and more interesting. In some respects, the single-minded nationalist perspective persists. Thus, in the aftermath of political liberation following centuries of submission to foreign rule, "it was impossible" that spiritual life would remain unchanged. "This will become clear in the course of time in the young State of Israel as well even though in the early years this is not yet very evident."[33] One of the prime characteristics of the Hasmonean period was the revival of the Hebrew language. Political independence led to "an exaltation of the soul" that "greatly reinforced national consciousness and prepared the ground for any powerful national-religious aspiration. And what national-religious possession could have been more precious and sacred to the nation than the language of the Torah and prophets that had been nearly suppressed by Greek on the one hand and Aramaic-Syriac on the other?"[34] Thus, as Klausner sees it, "the national government" along with the Council of the Jews nurtured this development and helped determine its form almost along the lines of the twentieth-century Academy for the Hebrew Language.

At the same time, conflicting ideological commitments led Klausner to less predictable evaluations as he examined larger cultural developments. In his view, a central group among the Pharisees concentrated on religious and moral concerns at the expense of the political dimension, and we might have expected him to evaluate such a group pejoratively. He understood, however, that this group laid the foundations of Jewish culture for generations to come, and his own nationalist orientation was light years removed from that of the so-called "Canaanites" in the early years of the State. For all of Zionism's "negation of exile," the stream with which Klausner identified saw itself as an organic continuation of authentic Jewish culture freed to develop in new and healthy ways in the ancient homeland. Thus, a man like Hillel could not be seen through a dark lens, and we suddenly find very different rhetoric from that to which we have become accustomed.

Hillel, we are told, had to refrain from taking a political stand during the terror regime of Herod. This was the only way that he could achieve

---

[33] *Historia* 3:9.
[34] *Historia* 3:105.

his sublime objectives.[35] As to the Pharisees in general, their emphasis on religion over state "afforded the nation eternal life" even though "it stole away its political power. The Pharisees achieved the *survival* of the nation at the expense of its *liberty*" (emphasis in the original).[36] In virtually every other context, Klausner, as we have seen, perceives the liberty of the nation as a condition of its survival. Here, looking back at the founders of rabbinic Judaism through the prism of a millennial exile, he speaks with a very different voice.

We have already encountered Klausner's reaction to the Hellenizers' efforts to open Judaea to Greek culture. In other contexts as well, he mobilizes the imperative of national survival for an even more surprising defense of cultural perspectives narrower that his own. Philo, he tells us, was a proud Jew, but in the final analysis the great Alexandrian thinker maintained that Moses and Plato had said the same things. "The nation's instinct, its feeling of self-preservation, whispered to it. . . that it may not admit this compromising ideology into its home."[37] This instinct, he adds, also explains the attitude of the anti-philosophical party during the Maimonidean controversies many generations later. This understanding, almost supportive analysis of the anti-Maimonist position adumbrates Yitzhak Baer's critical approach to Jewish openness to general culture in the Middle Ages, an approach that impelled Charles Touati to formulate a particularly sharp critique.

> According to Baer, the Jewish religion belongs to the category of myth, a term never defined but clearly understood favorably. Judaism is placed in danger by philosophical culture. For Baer, all philosophers are suspect throughout Jewish history; their adversaries... always enjoy a favorable presumption. The position of the eminent historian, the product of a German university who was reared in rigorous scientific disciplines, seems odd (*cocasse*) to us. Is Judaism, then, to be devoted always, in its entirety, by its very essence, to lack of culture (*l'inculture*)?[38]

Klausner does not go as far as Baer, though he was motivated by similar instincts, and it is fascinating to see his willingness to empathize with

---

35 *Historia* 4:125, 129-130.
36 *Historia* 3:228.
37 *Historia* 5:85.
38 Charles Touati, 'La controverse de 1303-1306 autour des études philosophiques et scientifiques,' *Revue des Études Juives* 127 (1968): 37, n. 3.

Jews who banned and even burned the works of the hero of generations of maskilim who were in large measure role models for Klausner himself.

Klausner's cultural instincts lead to a particularly interesting deviation from the anticipated line with respect to an even more pivotal figure than Philo, a figure whom historians of the Second Temple period confront every hour of every day. Klausner is acutely aware that his attitude to Josephus will surprise us, and in a passage demonstrating with painful clarity how insecure he felt in the face of criticism, he points to this explicitly as evidence that he is an objective historian.[39] He understands that we would expect him to disdain the historian-traitor; instead, he sees him as a man of initial good intentions who, even after his act of genuine treason, deserves regard as an exceptional historian. Perhaps this is indeed a sign of objectivity, but it is more likely the product of a collision of two subjective impulses. Of course Klausner was repelled by Josephus' treason, but his belief that the capacity to explain history is one of the quintessential qualities of the Jewish people[40] moved him toward an almost visceral appreciation of the talents of the major Jewish historian of antiquity.

The emotional tie that Klausner felt toward his illustrious predecessor emerges from a gripping, almost amazing passage. Josephus tells us that he chose to survive in Jodephat because had he died before transmitting the message (*diangelia*), he would have betrayed the divine charge. Klausner contends that this does not refer to the message that Vespasian would become Emperor. It refers, rather, to the destiny of Josephus himself, who somehow understood that he was fated to become the historian of the Jewish people. "A supernal force impelled him to live in order to write books that would endure for thousands of years, to survive so that he could be revealed as one of the great Jewish historians of all generations."[41]

The career of Josephus transports us to the final days of the Second Temple. Despite Klausner's qualified sympathy for the spiritually oriented Pharisees, his deeper identification is with the group that he calls "activist Pharisees," to wit, the Zealots, who enjoyed the support, as he sees it, of "the nation in its masses." Here too he must confront moral questions,

---

[39] *Historia* 3: introduction.
[40] *Historia* 2:270.
[41] *Historia* 5:190-191.

which he resolves in part by recourse to a slightly altered version of a famous line in Judah Halevi's *Kuzari*. "Their intentions were desirable, but their actions were not always desirable." Nonetheless, even if they sometimes engaged in robbery, they had no alternative. "Since they were constantly guarding the national interest, it was impossible for them to pursue remunerative work."[42]

And so we arrive at the great revolt that these Zealots precipitated. In addition to the routine reasons that Klausner proposes to explain that revolt, he suggests that the Romans encouraged it through intentional, blatant provocations inspiring an uprising that they could then exploit to destroy the threat posed to them by the "metropolis of world Jewry."[43] Once again, warring tendencies in the historian's psyche produce a slightly unexpected result. Klausner is prepared to depict his heroic Jewish rebels as dupes of a successful Roman stratagem in order to magnify the importance, power, and centrality of world Jewry.

Finally, even the failure of the revolt does not demonstrate that it was mistaken. On the contrary, simple submission to Rome would have led to decline and, ultimately, to the disappearance of the nation. Instead,

> a destruction following glorious, remarkable wars of the sort fought by the "bandits" and "ruffians" against the dominant Roman Empire, wars that remained in the memory of all generations, was not an absolute destruction. It was not the Torah alone that sustained us in our exile. The memories of a monumental struggle with the great world power preserved in Talmud and Midrash, in Josippon and other of our narratives also led to long life, indeed, to eternal life. [Such a] nation will never be destroyed.[44]

It is difficult to agree that the actions of the "bandits," which were sharply criticized in most of the sources informing the consciousness of Jews in exile, played a central role in sustaining the spirit of persecuted Jews in medieval and early modern times. But in the Zionist period, refashioned in the works of Klausner and others, they surely did. Even one who reads Klausner's *History* for the purpose of analyzing its ideological *Tendenz* cannot help but feel the deep pathos that informs his work, and there can be no question that readers were inspired, educators energized,

---

42   *Historia* 5:29-30.
43   *Historia* 5:132, 140, 141.
44   *Historia* 5:136-137.

students instructed, and public opinion molded. In full awareness of Klausner's historiographic sins, some observers with Zionist sympathies may nonetheless set aside an academic lens and conclude that not only were his intentions desirable, but, under the pressing circumstances in which he wrote, even his actions may have achieved ends that partially atone for those sins.

THE FRAGILITY OF RELIGIOUS DOCTRINE: ACCOUNTING FOR ORTHODOX ACQUIESCENCE IN THE BELIEF IN A SECOND COMING*

From: *Modern Judaism* 22 (2002): 103-114.

In the last seven years, we have witnessed a watershed in the history of Judaism that cries out for explanation. With minimal resistance, in the full view of world Jewry, two propositions from which every mainstream Jew in the last millennium would have instantly recoiled have become legitimate options within Orthodox Judaism:

1. A specific descendant of King David may be identified with certainty as the Messiah even though he died in an unredeemed world. The criteria always deemed necessary for a confident identification of the Messiah—the temporal redemption of the Jewish people, a rebuilt Temple, peace and prosperity, the universal recognition of the God of Israel—are null and void.

2. The messianic faith of Judaism allows for the following scenario: God will finally send the true Messiah to embark upon his redemptive mission. The long-awaited redeemer will declare that all preparations for the redemption have been completed and announce without qualification that the fulfillment is absolutely imminent. He will begin the process of gathering the dispersed of Israel to the Holy Land. He will proclaim himself a prophet, point clearly to his messianic status, and declare that the only remaining task is to greet him as Messiah. And then he will die and be buried without redeeming the world. To put the matter more succinctly, the true Messiah's redemptive mission, publicly

---

* This article is an adaptation and elaboration of chapter 13 of my *The Rebbe, the Messiah, and the Scandal of Orthodox Indifference* (London and Portland, Oregon, 2001). The first few paragraphs are adapted from the book's Introduction.

proclaimed and vigorously pursued, will be interrupted by death and burial and then consummated through a Second Coming.

While the vast majority of Jews continue to perceive these as alien propositions, and the Rabbinical Council of America has declared that there is no place for such doctrines in Judaism, the assertion that contemporary Orthodox Jewry effectively legitimates these beliefs rests on a simple observation: A large segment—almost certainly a substantial majority—of Chabad hasidim affirm that the Lubavitcher Rebbe, Rabbi Menachem Mendel Schneerson, who was laid to rest in 1994, did everything subsumed under proposition two and will soon return to complete the redemption in his capacity as the Messiah. Adherents of this belief, including those who have ruled that it is required by Jewish law, routinely hold significant religious posts with the sanction of major Orthodox authorities unconnected to their movement.

These range from the offices of the Israeli Rabbinate to the ranks of mainstream Rabbinical organizations to the chairmanship of Rabbinic courts in both Israel and the diaspora, not to speak of service as scribes, ritual slaughterers, teachers, and administrators of schools and religious organizations receiving support from mainstream Orthodoxy. Shortly after signing a public ruling that Jewish law obligates all Jews to accept the messiahship of the deceased Rebbe, a Montreal rabbi was appointed head of the rabbinical court of the entire city. In summer, 2001, one could pick up a flyer in Jerusalem advertising a program for children run by a local Chabad house that begins with the logo of the Jerusalem Department of Torah Culture and ends with the slogan, "May our Master, Teacher and Rabbi the King Messiah live forever." For much of Orthodox Jewry, the classic boundaries of Judaism's messianic faith are no more.

I take it for granted that a typical Orthodox Jew ten years ago would have questioned the sanity of anyone asserting that adherents of such posthumous messianism would be recognized as Orthodox rabbis in perfectly good standing. If this assumption is correct, then the current status quo represents a startlingly swift, profound transformation. I refer not to the messianist belief itself but to the failure of mainstream Orthodoxy to marginalize the believers. What can account for such acquiescence in a community that prides itself on strict adherence to tradition and often denies that social factors play any significant role in shaping its beliefs and practices?

Let me begin with a broad, theoretical consideration and then move to a constellation of more specific factors that render this development not merely comprehensible but so ineluctable that efforts to roll it back face almost insuperable hurdles. I do not command sufficient expertise in the comparative sociology of religion to set up rules of general applicability governing such transformations. It seems to me, however, that Chabad is marked by a combination of characteristics critical for making this sort of religious upheaval possible. Both an in-group and an out-group, it is sufficiently self-contained, even sectarian, to generate a deviationist ideology and sufficiently integrated to make that ideology an acceptable option within the larger community.

On the one hand, Chabad hasidim see themselves as bearers of the only fully authentic expression of Judaism. It is through their leaders that the progressive revelation of the inner Torah has taken place; it is their rebbes who have been the potential messiahs of recent generations; it is their emissaries who are the agents of the redemptive process, destined to be granted front row seats near the Messiah when he comes;[1] it is to a location adjoining their headquarters in Crown Heights that the ultimate, heavenly Temple will descend before moving to Jerusalem.[2] The sense that they are different not only facilitates the creation of a theology undisciplined by mainstream consensus; it leads mainstream Jews to minimize the impact of that theology because it is perceived as marginal and hence not threatening.

On the other hand, Lubavitch hasidim engage in outreach to all Jews, emphasize the value of loving all of Israel, make highly sophisticated use of mass media, retain ties with other hasidim and Orthodox Jews even as they refrain from participating in many common endeavors, hold posts integrated into the warp and woof of Orthodox communal life, and establish deep reservoirs of sympathy through activities that almost all Orthodox Jews cannot help but admire. Thus, their beliefs can decidedly change the Jewish religion writ large.

---

1   Note the little vignette in *Kfar Chabad* 731 (Eve of *Sukkot*, 5757; Sept. 27, 1996), where the Rebbe tells the discouraged wife of an emissary, "We are on the verge of being privileged to experience the coming of the Messiah. You must decide where you want to be at that time—pushed far back among the masses or together with the emissaries who see the face of the king and sit first in the kingdom."

2   See R. Menachem Mendel Schneerson, *Kuntres be-Inyan Mikdash Me'at Zeh Beit Rabbenu she-be-Bavel* (Brooklyn, N.Y., 1992).

Within this framework, then, let us turn to specific causes, reasons, and rationales—stated and unstated—for the effective Orthodox decision to allow this process to unfold.

THE IDEAL OF UNITY AND THE AVOIDANCE OF COMMUNAL STRIFE

The point is self-evident. Every practicing Jew has heard countless sermons about the imperative to love one's neighbor, particularly one's Jewish neighbor. At the barest minimum, the annual Torah reading about Korah's rebellion against Moses (Numbers 16-17) generates discourses about the severe prohibition against fomenting disputes within the community. While rhetoric about this value cuts across all Orthodox— and Jewish—lines, it is especially compelling for Modern Orthodox Jews who maintain cordial, even formal relations with other denominations and pride themselves on embracing an ideal of tolerance.

The impact of this tolerant self-image, which borders on self-definition, can cut very deep. It is nurtured not only by a positive ideology but by disdain for the narrowness and intolerance that are seen as quintessential traits of the orthodoxies of the Right. It is reinforced by humorous putdowns whose power to mold as well as express self-perceptions should not be underestimated. Thus, a widely repeated joke explains that God serves Leviathan fish at the messianic banquet out of solicitude for those participants who will not eat the meat because they do not trust God's *shehitah* (ritual slaughter). Modern Orthodox Jews who have made a habit of poking fun at the Traditionalist Orthodox for divisive hyper-religiosity are now faced with the prospect of evaluating the status of Lubavitch *shehitah* in light of the belief of some hasidim that the Rebbe is not only the Messiah but pure divinity. Even the few who take this matter seriously can find it psychologically impossible to don the mantle of those they see as religious fanatics and engage in the very behavior they have been mocking for years.

From the perspective of the abstract principles of Orthodox Judaism, the argument from tolerance and unity is beside the point. A few weeks after the Torah reading about Korah, very different sermons are preached about the zeal of Phineas (Numbers 25). No Orthodox Jew believes that everyone committed to the Jewish community has the right to serve as an Orthodox rabbi irrespective of his religious outlook because of the value of unity. Resort to this principle is relevant only after one has concluded that Lubavitch messianism is essentially within the boundaries of Orthodoxy. Since this is precisely what is at issue, the argument begs the question, and its powerful appeal is rooted in a different instinct to which we now turn.

ORTHOPRAXY AND APPEARANCE

Though my presentation in this scholarly venue is academic in substance and largely irenic in tone, it is no secret that I have pursued a rhetorically charged campaign to change the widespread Orthodox indifference to this development. Two distinguished academic observers of contemporary Orthodoxy have chided me for incurable naivete in imagining that matters of faith play any significant role in the community. Anyone who looks and acts the way Lubavitch hasidim do will be treated as an Orthodox Jew. Period. A traditional talmudist in full agreement with my position told me, "If the messianists looked like you, people would react differently." Similarly, two other academics argued that issues of faith can be relevant, but only when the deviations come from the left, that is, from a group seen as more modernist than that of the critic.

In several conversations with fully Orthodox Jews, both Traditionalist and Modern, I have heard formulations that come close to an unalloyedly orthoprax position, to wit, that any Jew who observes the commandments remains within the fold. It is no accident that enemies of Lubavitch through the years have laid special stress on deviations from the straightforward requirements of *halakhah*. This argument rests upon Chabad justifications for not sleeping in a *sukkah*, not eating the third Sabbath meal, waiting till well into the night to recite the afternoon prayer upon the Rebbe's return from his father-in-law's gravesite, and, on one occasion in 1991, delaying the morning prayer on *Sukkot* till 3:30 P.M.[3]

The theoretical superstructure of Orthodoxy insists on the importance of doctrinal as well as behavioral criteria in defining membership in

---

[3] With respect to the first two issues, the problem was less with the practice itself than with the seemingly principled rejection of the requirement. On that *Sukkot* day in 1991, see Binyamin Lipkin, *Heshbono shel Olam* (Lod, 2000), pp. 112-113.

the group.[4] Nonetheless, my critics are certainly correct in arguing that an instinct placing almost exclusive emphasis on observance of the commandments has played a key role in discouraging a serious, effective reaction to Chabad messianism. In pre-modern times, when visible conformity to ritual standards was taken for granted, it could not overwhelm all other criteria in determining an individual's communal standing. For contemporary Jews, full observance of Orthodox law is so clearly seen as an unambiguous marker that theology can become virtually irrelevant.

This instinct extends even to areas of belief that technically impinge on *halakhah*. Observers cannot imagine that some Lubavitch hasidim really maintain beliefs about the Rebbe's divinity amounting to *avodah zarah*, which roughly means the formal recognition or worship as God of an entity that is in fact not God. Sociologically, then, a proviso needs to be appended to this definition: such recognition or worship is *avodah zarah* provided that the believer is someone other than a Sabbath-observing Jew wearing a wig or a black hat. Judaism, which was once a great faith, has become an agglomeration of dress, deportment, and rituals.

This very point about external appearance and ritual observance was made in *Yated Ne'eman*, a newspaper published in Israel by one group that does delegitimate the messianists and, indeed, all of Chabad—the followers of R. Elazar Menachem Man Schach of the Ponevezh yeshiva in Bnei Brak.[5] The challenge, said the author, is to transcend externals and recognize the illegitimacy of these superficially Orthodox Jews. This sector of Israeli Orthodoxy and its counterparts in some American yeshivas do not act on this issue because they believe they have already acted.

THE BALKANIZATION OF ORTHODOXY, OR THE ORTHODOXY OF ENCLAVES

Why do such Jews remain relatively passive at this point despite the evident ineffectiveness of their efforts in the wider community? While part of the explanation lies in despair born of frustration and another,

---

4   See my review of Menachem Kellner, *Must a Jew Believe Anything?*, *Tradition* 33/4 (Summer, 1999): 81-89.
5   See Natan Ze'ev Grossman, in the Hebrew *Yated Ne'eman*, March 13, 1998, pp. 15, 22.

conflicting part in a rose-colored belief that by now everyone sees that R. Schach was correct, there is a deeper issue that plays a very important role in other sectors of the Orthodox community as well. The challenge of modernity and the growth of religious deviationism have impelled much of Orthodoxy to turn inward. One consequence of this orientation has been the attenuation of the instinctive sense of a Jewish religious collective extending beyond one's own group. Moreover, and very much to the point, "group" does not even refer to Orthodoxy as a whole but to a much smaller entity.

The main focus of many Orthodox Jews is on their own subgroup, *anshei shlomenu* in the terminology of hasidic communities, *yeshiva layt* in non-hasidic groups, and so on. Consequently, the argument that something called Judaism, even Orthodox Judaism, has changed because of the legitimation of Lubavitch messianists, invokes categories that have lost much of their force. I do not mean to suggest that Orthodox Jews—even in Traditionalist circles—have entirely rejected their responsibilities to the larger community, but instincts have undoubtedly changed. The question posed—even in Modern circles—is, "Does anyone in my immediate environment believe that the Rebbe is the Messiah?" If the answer is no, then the rise of this movement becomes a curiosity or at most a mildly disturbing development. A blinkered, myopic question produces a blinkered, myopic response.

ORTHODOX INTERDEPENDENCE,
OR THE INTERLOCKING OF THE ENCLAVES

Paradoxically, another critically important explanation stands in stark contrast to the psychology of balkanization, namely, the reality of interdependence. Lubavitch messianists, for all their sectarianism, are so entwined in the larger Orthodox community—and even the Jewish community as a whole—that excision is extraordinarily difficult.

I have had more than one conversation in which an Orthodox Jew would argue that Lubavitch is after all a relatively small, ultimately peripheral movement and then agree under questioning that he or she would have considerable difficulty living without it. Rabbinic courts headed by messianist rabbis interact regularly with other courts. How should they be regarded? Scores of Israeli rabbis holding posts throughout the country have signed a halakhic ruling requiring belief in the messiahship of the Rebbe.[6] How easy would it be to remove them from office? Messianist rabbis play a significant role in countries throughout the world. How realistic is it to propose that they be marginalized? A respected, Lubavitch-run *kashrut* organization is the supervisor of choice for restaurants full of messianist propaganda. How does one deal with it? Rejecting Lubavitch ritual slaughter or refusing to attend a messianist synagogue would cause no little inconvenience to religiously observant travelers—Orthodox and non-Orthodox— and require significant modification of vacation plans. How realistic is the expectation that concern with a matter of abstract theology will change established behaviors? A significant number of Jews reside in places to which most Jews merely travel. How can they be expected to react to the assertion that the food, the synagogue, and the school upon which they rely have suddenly been rendered unacceptable?

The matter is complicated further by the fact that not all Lubavitch hasidim are messianists and not all messianists endorse a theology of *avodah zarah*. It is much easier to accept false assurances that a majority maintain Orthodox beliefs than it is to take the very difficult steps implied in the previous paragraph. Rather than face these consequences, Jews force themselves to conclude that second-coming messianism promoted by people whose services they need is not really second-coming messianism, that legitimation is not legitimation, that *avodah zarah* is not *avodah zarah*. Of all the causes of inaction, this is the most intractable, and it may well result in a permanent and profound transformation of Judaism.

"GOOD THINGS"

"But they do so many good things." I cannot count the number of times I have heard this sentence or its equivalent. Some of these "things" are acts of kindness that are not specific to Judaism; others involve the teaching of Torah and the successful dissemination of Jewish rituals to the proverbial four corners of the earth. Much of the loyalty to Lubavitch on the local level flows from personal relationships established with Jews of all stripes—Orthodox, Conservative, Reform, even secular—in need

---

6   *Hatzofeh*, January 17, 2000.

of an understanding heart, a sympathetic ear, a favor large (sometimes very large) or small. In an increasingly impersonal society, Lubavitch emissaries exult in the joy of others and empathize with their sadness, forging bonds that cannot be broken by mere theology. On the ritual level, they not only encourage the wearing of *tefillin* and the lighting of Sabbath candles; they provide travelers with kosher food, a Passover seder, a prayer service, and more. The beneficiaries of this largesse cannot help but feel the most profound gratitude.

Once again, looking at this consideration through a purely theoretical Orthodox prism renders it highly problematic. If the recognition of Lubavitch messianists as Orthodox rabbis really destroys the parameters of Judaism's messianic faith (as it surely does), then the issue needs to be framed in global terms. You can gain ten thousand (or one hundred thousand, or one million) additional observant Jews at the price of accepting a fundamental change in a core belief of Judaism. Are you prepared to pay that price? Posed in the abstract to an Orthodox audience, this should be a rhetorical question. But people are rarely motivated by abstractions or by concern for the course of history writ large. How, they ask, can we not be impressed with this selfless family that has established a synagogue in a spiritual wilderness and persuaded people who would have lost their Jewish identity entirely to observe the Torah? In such a struggle between heart and mind, the mind stands little chance.[7]

TRANSIENT INSANITY

I have heard the assertion that the messianists are crazy no less frequently than the argument that "they do good things." Sometimes this appears to mean that because the belief is insane it will surely not last and should therefore be treated with benign—or malign—neglect. In this version, the contention is problematic but coherent. In most cases, however, the word *meshugoyim* (crazy people) or *meshugaas* (craziness) seems to

---

7   Arguments for the delegitimation of Lubavitch messianism can, of course, also appeal to the heart, and I have attempted in other forums to evoke such emotions to the best of my ability. See, for example, *The Rebbe, the Messiah, and the Scandal of Orthodox Indifference*, where I argue that Orthodox Judaism has effectively declared that "on a matter of fundamental principle our martyred ancestors were wrong and their Christian murderers were right" (p. 75).

be intended as a self-contained argument. Because they are crazy, they cannot be taken seriously and should be ignored—or even supported for their "good things." Precisely because it is so difficult to assign a coherent meaning to this argument, it reveals once again the operation of a deep instinct that seeks any avenue to avoid the unwanted conclusion that messianists should be excluded from Orthodoxy.

Most people who proffer this argument appear to agree that the messianist belief stands in contradiction to the classical Jewish messianic faith. But if this is so, it is difficult to see how the "fact" that it is also a form of craziness qualifies the believer to be a rabbi, judge, principal, or teacher. Does the very fact that it is crazy somehow make it compatible with Judaism?[8] Imagine a colloquy in which someone objects to hiring a messianist rabbi. A supporter of the appointment responds, "It is true that he maintains a profoundly un-Jewish belief, but this drawback is neutralized by a countervailing consideration that works in his favor. He is crazy."

Moreover, the large majority of messianists are not crazy in any clinical sense; to suggest that they are is crazy. The non-messianists in Chabad face daunting obstacles in their efforts to interpret teachings of the Rebbe that appear to point to his messiahship. Against this background, for a hasid to defend the messianist position through a variety of learned and complex strategies is decidedly not a violation of the canons of reason. An outside observer is, of course, free to argue that belief in the resurrection of the dead, or in a personal Messiah, or, for that matter, in God, is itself irrational. By that criterion, however, all serious Orthodox Jews (and, for that matter, Christians) are crazy.

This is not to deny that the percentage of unbalanced individuals is probably somewhat higher in the messianist population than in the Jewish population as a whole. Extreme doctrines like the belief that the Rebbe is fully alive can easily elicit contemptuous jokes, and this too is an important factor in preventing serious responses. The assumption that only *meshugoyim* could possibly believe that the Rebbe is the Messiah also contributes to a dramatically unrealistic underestimate of the extent of messianism in Chabad. After all, say many observers, since I know that Rabbi so-and-so is a perfectly normal person; it follows that

---

8   For those concerned with the posthumous destiny of people who might be heretics, the assertion that they are crazy can serve as mitigation. This, however, does not appear to be the primary context is which the argument is used.

he could not possibly be a believer.[9]

The association of messianism with insanity also bears on the confident predictions of the inevitable, imminent disappearance of belief in the messiahship of the Rebbe. The fact that a religion called Christianity, which also believes in a dying and resurrected redeemer, has not yet disappeared ought to give at least some pause to these prognosticators. Let me reinforce this point by adducing a much more recent and hence even more apt example.

Mormonism was born in modern times as a dramatically deviant form of Christianity. It makes highly problematic historical assertions about relatively recent events. Its theology makes that of Lubavitch messianists appear like the very soul of rationality. It has a sophisticated, well-educated constituency. It sends emissaries to the ends of the earth to make converts and is, I believe, the fastest growing religion in the world. Whatever one thinks of the rationality of the first generation of believers, children brought up in such a faith can surely accept it without damage to their rational faculties. If Mormonism flourishes, why is Chabad messianism necessarily condemned to extinction?

I will not hazard a prediction as to the medium or long term survival of this belief. Menachem Friedman, the most distinguished sociologist of Orthodoxy in Israel, believes that in a leaderless movement, the group with the most fervent message is likely to prevail. If so, then all the worldwide institutions of Chabad will eventually be mobilized to spread this version of Judaism. However that may be, I certainly do not see what will destroy this faith as long as the rest of Orthodoxy legitimates messianist rabbis and the bulk of the Chabad educational system remains in messianist hands. Confident prognostications of imminent demise fly in the face of reason.[10]

---

9   It is not uncommon for ordinary Orthodox Jews to find themselves subjected to analogous misperceptions. Many years ago, a non-Jewish colleague in my department took it for granted that I did not follow a bizarre practice that she had just been told about, to wit, that Orthodox Jews will not drink wine handled by Gentiles. Somewhat more recently, two Jewish colleagues asked me about an article in the *New York Times* describing a *shatnez*-testing laboratory in Brooklyn. When I proceeded to show them the non-*shatnez* label in my jacket, they managed to remain polite but were clearly nonplussed to discover that a person who usually appeared reasonably sane actually adhered to such outlandish regulations. All this notwithstanding the fact that I wear a yarmulke at work and make my Orthodox affiliation clear in more ways than I can recount.

10   The failure to take this development seriously has led more than one person to suggest

THE WANING OF A CHRISTIAN THREAT AND THE ATROPHY OF JEWISH MESSIANIC INSTINCTS

With the decline of a pervasive Christian threat, familiarity with messianic texts and sensitivity to messianic deviationism has waned to the vanishing point even among learned Jews. Jewish polemical texts are not part of the Orthodox curriculum nor (outside Chabad) are treatises dealing with redemption. Moreover, I think that the celebrated observation that many Orthodox Jews no longer trust the traditions with which they were raised is also germane to this development.[11] In previous generations, Jews would have paid little attention to messianist sectarians who "proved" that their belief is acceptable by pointing to one line in *Sanhedrin* 98b. Now, unbound by a consensus once imbibed by every Jewish tailor and shoemaker with his mother's milk, and oblivious of a rich polemical literature, they function as *tabulae rasae* for every unfamiliar text introduced to them. While they will not go so far as to embrace the belief in the Rebbe's messiahship, they can be persuaded that there is nothing fundamentally wrong with it.

JUST ANOTHER CHANGE

Finally, several people who understand very well that Lubavitch messianism has no legitimate precedent in Judaism have nonetheless chided me for attributing so much significance to this development. After all, they say, I am a historian, and a historian of ideas no less. I should know better than most that beliefs change, that religions evolve. Hasidism itself was an innovation. Religious Zionism was an innovation.

that I stop wasting my time on it. A very distinguished scholar who is an observant Jew urged me to remain focused on the area where I do important work: the Middle Ages. In other words, I should spend all my time studying what is really significant, namely, Jewish arguments against Christianity in the Middle Ages, rather than diverting my attention to the trivial issue of whether Jews still believe those arguments. I wonder what this scholar tells his students about the uses of history.

11 See Menachem Friedman, "Life Tradition and Book Tradition in the Development of Ultraorthodox Judaism," in *Judaism from Within and from Without: Anthropological Studies*, ed. by Harvey Goldberg (Albany, 1987), pp. 235-255; Haym Soloveitchik, "Rupture and Reconstruction: The Transformation of Contemporary Orthodoxy," *Tradition* 28:4 (Summer, 1994): 64-130.

Why must I remain in a state of arrested development, embalmed in the world of the Barcelona disputation?

I am inclined to think that this argument is not a primary cause of Orthodox inaction because it appeals only to the most modernist worldview within Orthodoxy. Some Lubavitch hasidim, however, have also mobilized it for polemical purposes. Since it involves an issue of religious judgment and has been posed to me in a personal way, I take the liberty of injecting an overtly personal response into this analysis.

It should not be necessary to say that historians are permitted to have commitments to abiding principles. The decision to study history is not a decision to embrace change as one's supreme value. All religious traditions have boundaries, and any adherent of such a tradition faces the challenge of deciding whether or not a particular innovation subverts core elements of that tradition. Here is my response to one of these critics:

> I consider this issue [especially] serious for roughly the following reasons: 1- It involves a key element in the understanding of one of the *iqqarei ha-emunah* (fundamentals of the faith). 2- Comparable movements throughout Jewish history have been thoroughly, vehemently, angrily delegitimated by *klal Yisrael* [the Jewish collective]. I refer both to the movements that persisted after the candidate's death and the movements that died with his death precisely because their posthumous survival was unthinkable. 3- Denial of such a belief has been a part of the very definition of Judaism in innumerable confrontations with the Christian mission. Accepting it as a harmless enthusiasm awards victory to Christianity on a fundamental matter of principle. 4- It has led to *avodah zarah* in both past instances and shows signs of doing so again.

THE DIFFICULTIES OF "STARTING A FIGHT WITH LUBAVITCH"

Finally, there are pragmatic obstacles that beset any effort to delegitimate this belief and its adherents. Lubavitch messianists are the dominant part of an influential movement with impressive human, financial, and political resources that defends its interests vigorously. Few people have the stomach to pursue a cause that will cause them to be publicly labeled—as I can testify from personal experience—haters, dividers, liars, heretics, egotistical seekers of fame and fortune, ignoramuses, snakes, asses, and pigs. The reluctance to "start a fight with Lubavitch" is palpable, particularly on the part of those whose institutions might lose support from Chabad sympathizers or whose positions might even be jeopardized. Since a large majority of Orthodox Jews rely on a very small number of rabbinic authorities to make decisions of such moment, it is only necessary to deter a relative handful of people from taking action.

* * * * * *

A phenomenon that appears at first, uncritical glance to be inexplicable turns out upon examination to be overdetermined. Primarily social factors abetted at critical points by religious sensibilities can sweep away a central doctrine of a well established faith with a millennial history of withstanding the most severe pressure. Had this change been imposed from without, Orthodox Jews would have resisted at all costs. But it came from within, and to this point it has prevailed.

EPILOGUE

"THE COUNTENANCE OF HIS FATHER": TWENTY-FIVE YEARS SINCE THE PASSING OF *HADOAR* AUTHOR ISAIAH BERGER OF BLESSED MEMORY

Hadoar 78:4 (December 25, 1998) (Hebrew). Translated by the author.

I grew up on the front lines of an incessant war between books and clothing, and the books had the better of it. In the bookcases, they reigned supreme, while in the closets the long coats and dresses had to defend themselves against the infiltrations and attacks of the new volumes that multiplied without cease.

This lust for books may have resulted from the fact that my father had virtually no formal education in either Jewish or general studies and attained most of his knowledge not from teachers but through constant, wide-ranging reading. His father, who was a rabbi in Zinkov in Ukraine, passed away when his younger son was a baby. The elder son migrated to Canada, where he succeeded in setting up a business, and as time passed he helped his mother and younger brother come to New York via Canada when my father was sixteen years old.

The young immigrant studied for some time in Rabbi Isaac Elchanan Theological Seminary of Yeshiva University, but he carved out an independent path for himself in areas that interested him and decided to educate himself outside the framework of organized educational institutions.[1] The evidence furnished by the dates noted in his books indicates that he began to form his library in 1927 when he was twenty-one years old, and in the following year his first scholarly article appeared in *Ha-Tzofeh le-Hokhmat Yisrael* ("Le-Toledot Meqorotav ve-Hashpaʿato shel Sefer Shaʿashuʿim le-R. Yosef ben Meir Zabbara"). The article is

---

[1] Nonetheless, he wrote two enthusiastic articles about Yeshiva, one on its fiftieth anniversary (*Hadoar* 16:32), and another on the opening of Stern College ("Mikhlalah li-Benot Yisrael," *Hadoar* 33:40).

remarkable for the range of expertise that it displays in Jewish literature throughout the generations, and there is no doubt that readers would have been stunned had they known that the author is a twenty-two year old without an academic degree.

Nonetheless, my father experienced difficulty in his search for a means of livelihood, in large measure because learning was his heart's desire, but also as a result of character traits like modesty, lack of initiative in economic matters, and sometimes even an excess of decency. I remember his telling me that one of the obstacles that he faced as a teacher in a primary school for part-time Jewish study (a Talmud Torah) over a period of several months—a position that was in any event not designed to generate great wealth— was his refusal on ethical grounds to utilize the proven method suggested to him to control disruptive children, namely, to appoint them as monitors over the other pupils.

Eventually, he opened a bookstore that served primarily as a warehouse. He periodically issued a catalogue with a list of books in Hebrew and other languages that dealt mainly with Jewish themes but to a non-trivial extent also with general folklore and other areas of study that interested him. An important scholar informed me quite recently that he saves the catalogues of "Isaiah Berger, Books" as documents of importance for the history of Jewish culture in the United States.

In the thirties, articles by Isaiah Berger began to appear in *Hadoar*, including reviews of overarching studies like Joseph Klausner's *History of Modern Jewish Literature* (*Hadoar* 19:30) and Meyer Waxman's *A History of Jewish Literature* (*Hadoar* 16:31, and 21:22). These essays combined heartfelt positive evaluation and pointed, sometimes sharply formulated criticism. In 1954, shortly after the passing of Menachem Ribalow [the founder and long-time editor], he began his work on the editorial staff of *Hadoar* on a regular basis. The catalogues that he published provided him with an opportunity to continue his involvement with the books that served as the source of his spiritual sustenance, but his daily livelihood came from his position with *Hadoar*, where he remained almost until his passing in 1973.

He was of course acquainted with all the prominent figures in the Hebrew movement in the Unites States—Ribalow, Daniel Persky, Moshe Meisels, A.R. Malachi, and many more. Even though his main areas of expertise were folklore, proverbs, and literature, he wrote a major article on "Jewish Scholarship in America" surveying such scholarship from

1848 until the date of the study (1939).[2] His task at *Hadoar* included the reading and correcting of the large majority of articles, and beginning with the mid-1960's he transformed the section on "Books Received by the Editors" (which he wrote anonymously) from a simple list to a succinct analysis of studies in all fields and periods, to the point where one could characterize him as Samuel David Luzzatto once characterized himself: "Nihil judaicum alienum est mihi."[3]

He was graced with a well-developed sense of humor, and his scholarly interest in jokes did not remain restricted to research. Despite the smile that frequently played across his lips, he took very seriously the cultural aim of *Hadoar* as he understood it and vigorously opposed proposals to lower the journal's intellectual level for the sake of achieving popularity. This seriousness marked his attitude toward all matters of culture and language. We did not speak Hebrew at home, but my father insisted on the purity of language even in English. When I would intersperse words in Hebrew or Yiddish into an English conversation, he could not tolerate the admixture, and he would always stop me by asking, "How do you say that in English?" He was also not among the despisers of Yiddish, and he wrote articles on Peretz in *Yivo Bleter* and in *Die Goldene Kait* without any diminution of his engaging literary style.

In addition, he served as a translator in English, Hebrew, and Yiddish. In these instances as well his name was not mentioned, and generally

---

[2]   "Hokhmat Yisra'el ba-America," *Sefer ha-Shanah li-Yehudei America li-Shenat Tav Resh Tzadi Tet*, ed. by Menachem Ribalow (New York, 1939), pp. 345-378.

[3]   He wrote short notes or reports on events in the Hebrew movement anonymously or with an abbreviated byline (Y. B. or just B. or sometimes Y. ben Yitzhak). In addition to his position in *Hadoar*, he also did editorial work for Ktav Publishing House, where he prepared inter alia detailed indexes in the form of entire volumes to the *Hebrew College Annual* and the old series of the *Jewish Quarterly Review*, indexes that are based (as one of the reviewers of the project noted) not on the reading of the titles alone but on the study of the articles themselves.

In an earlier period, he helped Israel Davidson prepare *Otzar ha-Meshalim ve-ha-Pitgamim* (Jerusalem, 1957) to the degree that by his own testimony he almost deserved to be described as an author, and he was disappointed that his name did not appear anywhere in the book. (This may be because the work was not completed in the author's lifetime. In one place in the introduction by Shmuel Ashkenazi, who prepared the volume for publication, there is a reference to "the author and his assistants" [p. 15].) He left behind many notes containing material relevant to the study of folklore and proverbs. He was especially interested in the topic of the "evil eye," but did not live to publish the large amount of material that he assembled. [I will be happy to supply this material to any scholar in the field who can put it to good use.]

speaking I have no information regarding the articles that he translated. I must, however, note one translation of a particularly important work. At the end of the 1950's. he put great efforts into translating a lengthy lecture by Rabbi Joseph B. Soloveitchik from Yiddish into Hebrew. The lecture never appeared in Yiddish and was first published in Hebrew in the collection *Torah u-Melukhah: Al Meqom ha-Medinah ba-Yahadut* (Jerusalem, 1961), edited by S. Federbush, who turned to my father with the request to translate Rabbi Soloveitchik's work from its original language. I am referring to the famous essay, "Qol Dodi Dofeq." When the essay appeared in print, my father reacted with disappointment when he saw the extent of the changes introduced by Rabbi Soloveitchik, but he consoled himself somewhat with the observation that in the final analysis his translation still served as the foundation for the published version.

The first major article that he wrote when I was capable of appreciating his work to some degree was a study entitled "Rashi in Popular Legend" ("Rashi be-Aggadat ha-Am")[4], which appeared as a sort of companion piece to his important, much earlier article on "Maimonides in Popular Legend" ("Ha-Rambam be-Aggadat ha-Am").[5] The new article, written not only in response to the invitation of the editor of the collection but also thanks to the encouragement of my mother, appeared when I was fifteen-years-old, and I read it with the enthusiasm of a son beginning to appreciate the stature of his father. The Hebrew dedication that he wrote in the offprint that he gave me resonates in my memory to this day: "On your fifteenth birthday, I present you my dear son David with this booklet of mine on Rashi who is beloved and admired by you. May our Torah always be your delight, and may you find favor in the eyes of God and man. Your father who hugs, kisses and respects you."

The final verb, which was underlined, made a profound impression on me because my father was never impressed by elementary achievements. He derived enjoyment from my public reading of the Torah and *haftarah*—I learned the proper cantillation of the *haftarah* from him—but my general

---

4   *Rashi: Torato ve-Ishiyyuto*, ed. by Simon Federbush (New York, 1958), pp. 147-179.
5   *Massad: Me'assef le-Divrei Sifrut* 2, ed. by Hillel Bavli (Tel Aviv, 1936), pp. 216-238. In his book *Shivhei ha-Rambam* (Jerusalem, 1998), Yitzhak Avishur cites this study dozens of times. He writes among other things that the article "includes everything that was known at the time about stories concerning Maimonides" and that "from the time of Berger's study no article of importance on popular stories concerning Maimonides appeared until...1962" (pp. 15, 17).

impression when I was a child was that he did not get particularly excited over the trivial things I was capable of learning or accomplishing. I recognized that he had exalted expectations, even when they were expressed—if they were expressed at all—in a calm and relaxed fashion. He once told me with a smile that he would be happy if I would know the content of one small bookshelf, and he showed me the shelf containing the volumes printed in a small format by the publishing house "Horeb": the Babylonian Talmud in four volumes, the Palestinian Talmud in two, *Shulhan Arukh* in two, *Mishneh Torah* in two, the Mishnah, *Midrash Rabbah*, *Midrash Tanhuma*, *Yalkut Shim'oni*, *Humash* with the *Miqra'ot Gedolot* commentaries and *Nakh* with the *Miqra'ot Gedolot* commentaries.[6]

It may be that one should not draw conclusions from off-the-cuff comments accompanied by a smile, but I had no doubt whatever that this was precisely what my father wanted. The only imprecision in his remarks was that he wanted even more than that. Among the many books that surrounded me at home in my high school years, I was particularly attracted to Nahmanides' commentary to the Pentateuch and his disputation with Pablo Christiani, to *Mehqerei ha-Yahadut* of S. D. Luzzatto, and to the poems of Bialik. The ability to hold discussions with my father about matters that he considered important engendered great satisfaction for both of us, and a new stage in our relationship developed, even though neither of us could relate seriously to the subject to which the other devoted his leisure hours: I had no talent in chess, and he never succeeded in understanding a scintilla of the rules of baseball.

The list of "Horeb" publications underscores another central characteristic that was not altogether typical in the Hebrew movement: the intimate connection to Jewish tradition, to the observance of the commandments, to Torah in its full sense. If the Hebrew movement of the twentieth century was born at the knees of the Jewish Enlightenment,

---

6   My father loved those little books passionately. When I studied at the Rabbi Isaac Elchanan Theological Seminary, we were granted permission to bring a copy of the entire Babylonian Talmud to a major examination in Talmud. With considerable difficulty, I succeeded in persuading my father to allow me to bring that little four-volume Talmud to the yeshivah. When I returned home that evening, I had to stop on the way for several hours at Columbia University, and I left a full suitcase in the car with those four volumes next to it. The suitcase was stolen, but the books remained. I told my friends that I saw the hand of providence in the fact that the suitcase had been too full to fit the volumes of the Talmud in it, because if the books had been stolen—even without the suitcase—I would not have dared to come home.

or *Haskalah*, my father's worldview was born at the knees of the religious *Haskalah*. Needless to say, the term *Haskalah* does not fit the current century, and my father also felt great affection for hasidism in a fashion that was not at all typical of the original *Haskalah*, even in its religious manifestation. Although he did not live the life of a hasid, he read hasidic works, writing notes recording hasidic observations and "words of Torah" that touched him both as a scholar and as a Jew.

I was educated in the Yeshiva of Flatbush, a modern yeshivah where the discourse in Jewish studies classes was conducted in Hebrew, but the decision to send me there came primarily from my mother. My father was prepared to have me study in Yeshiva Chaim Berlin because of the emphasis on the study of Talmud.[7] As I noted, he did not know his father, but on several occasions, he referred to a conversation that made a deep impression on him. He once met a non-religious Jew who grew up in Zinkov and asked him if he knew Rabbi Yitzhak Berger. The immediate reaction was, "I must go into the other room and find a skullcap before I can discuss him." This heritage generated a religious dimension in my father that merged almost seamlessly with the cultural atmosphere of the Hebrew movement on all its levels.

Approximately twenty years after my father's passing, my first grandchild was born. He was named after my father, and at the meal marking his circumcision, I cited the Hebrew lines written on my father's monument. As a historian, I must tell my students that one can learn a great deal about the values of a society from tombstone inscriptions, but one learns very little about the deceased themselves. But as a son, I call upon Him who knows hidden things to witness that these lines describe faithfully and almost without exaggeration the rare qualities that characterized my father of blessed memory:

יקר רוח ועדין נפש
גבוה משכמו ומעלה ונחבא אל הכלים
אוהב את המקום
אוהב את הבריות
סופר חוקר וחובב ספר
בקי בכל חדרי התורה והחכמה

---

[7] Many years later, Joel Braverman, the celebrated principal of the Yeshivah of Flatbush, told me that he succeeded in expanding the time devoted to Talmud study from one hour a day to two after a lengthy debate with members of the school's Board of Education. "I explained to them," he said, "the importance of the study of Talmud, since without Talmud it is impossible to understand Bialik."

(Precious in spirit and refined in soul
Taller from his shoulders upward yet hidden among the vessels[8]
Loving God and loving mankind[9]
Author, scholar, and lover of books
Erudite in all the recesses of Torah and wisdom.)[10]

When my father passed away, my mother was inconsolable. On a number of occasions, she expressed her conviction that a person like him was simply not to be found, and she could not forget a sentence that he uttered on his deathbed. At that point, his words were not always clear, but while apparently referring to his imminent passing, he suddenly said, "Yeshayahu ve-Sarah Chanah Berger" (his name and that of my mother). My mother understood these words as an invitation to accompany him to the world to come, and she indeed passed away less than a year later. She asked me to write his words on her monument. I was unable to find a felicitous way of fulfilling this request with absolute literalness, but on the line before the date of her passing, I wrote, "Aletah la-marom lehityahed im nishmat ba'alah" ("She ascended heavenward to be united with the soul of her husband").[11]

May their souls be bound up in the bond of life.

---

8   Cf. I Samuel 10:22-23.

9   *Ethics of the Fathers* 6:1, 6.

10   I borrowed the first line from the eulogy delivered by Tovia Preschel at the funeral. See too Preschel's article, "Yeshayahu Berger z"l" (*Hadoar* 53:11) where most of my father's important articles are mentioned, and the letter to the editor in 53:14 ,"Le-Zekher R. Yeshaya Berger z"l." (If I remember correctly, the author of that letter, which is signed Qore Pashut [A Simple Reader] was A.R. Malachi.) Aside from the articles listed by Preschel and Malachi and the plethora of smaller pieces in *Hadoar*, I note a political analysis where my father expressed his views on the Dumbarton-Oakes conference, the secession of "Si'ah Bet" from Mapai, and the beginning of the activity of *Lehi* ("Bein ha-Zemannim," *Bitzaron* 5 [1944]: 379-382. The article is signed, "Ben Yitzhak.")

11   [The full inscription—once again with nary an exaggeration—reads as follows:

בת ישראל נאמנה לבוראה/ מסורה ללא שיעור להוריה בעלה ובנה/ ועמוד התווך של כל משפחתה/ חלשה בגופה ואדירה ברוחה/ בינה ואצילות ועוז והדר לבושה./ עלתה למרום להתיחד עם נשמת בעלה/ ז' חשון, תשל"ה.

(A daughter of Israel loyal to her Creator,/ Devoted without measure to her parents, husband, and son/ And the central pillar of her entire family./ Weak in body and powerful in spirit,/ Wisdom, nobility, strength and grandeur were her raiment./ She ascended heavenward to be united with the soul of her husband/ 7 Cheshvan, 5735.)]

INDEX

Unelaborated references in the notes are not listed in the index.

CPSIA information can be obtained at www.ICGtesting.com
Printed in the USA
BVOW010750190112

280882BV00001B/6/P